COMMONPLACE CULTURE
IN WESTERN EUROPE IN THE
EARLY MODERN PERIOD
I

Reformation, Counter–Reformation and Revolt

GRONINGEN STUDIES IN CULTURAL CHANGE

GENERAL EDITOR
H.W. Hoen

EDITORIAL BOARD
J.N. Bremmer, J.J.H. Dekker, G.J. Dorleijn,
A.A. MacDonald, B.H. Stolte, A.J. Vanderjagt

Volume XXXIX

COMMONPLACE CULTURE IN WESTERN EUROPE IN THE EARLY MODERN PERIOD
I

Reformation, Counter–Reformation and Revolt

EDITED BY

David Cowling and Mette B. Bruun

PEETERS

LEUVEN - PARIS - WALPOLE, MA

2011

Illustration on cover: Hans Holbein (attrib.), 'Hercules Germanicus', 1522 (Zürich, Zentralbibliothek).

A catalogue record for this book is available from the Library of Congress.

D/2011/0602/15

ISBN: 978-90-429-2474-1
© Peeters, Bondgenotenlaan 153, 3000 Leuven

CONTENTS

vi

PREFACE AND ACKNOWLEDGEMENTS

In 1999, the local Groningen Research School for the Study of the Humanities, and the Groningen members of the national Netherlands Research School for Medieval Studies succeeded in obtaining a grant for an innovative, large-scale, collective research programme entitled *Cultural Change: Dynamics and Diagnosis*. Supported by the faculties of Arts, Philosophy and Theology and financed by the Board of the University of Groningen, the *Cultural Change* programme constitutes an excellent opportunity to promote multidisciplinary approaches to phenomena characteristic of transformation processes in the fields of politics, literature and history, philosophy and theology. In order to enhance programmatic cohesion, three crucial 'moments' in European history were selected: 1) Late Antiquity to the Early Middle Ages (*c*.200–*c*.600), 2) Late Medieval to the Early Modern period (*c*.1450–*c*.1650), and 3) the 'Long Nineteenth Century' (1789–*c*.1918). In 2000 and 2002 further grants were obtained for *Cultural Change: Impact and Integration* and *Cultural Change: Perception and Representation* respectively. Several international conferences and workshops have already been organised and more are planned for the coming years.

This is the third of three volumes from the project 'Authority and Persuasion: the Role of Commonplaces in Western Europe (*c*.1450-*c*.1800)'. The project was launched by scholars from the universities of Copenhagen, Durham and Groningen and generously funded by the Danish National Research Foundation, the British Academy and the Netherlands Organisation for Scientific Research (NWO). In the project the notion of commonplace was broadened to include means of persuasion in all kinds of texts as well as the visual arts, theatre, music and other media. This volume offers the papers presented at a workshop, organized in Copenhagen, 25 and 26 November, 2006.

This first volume, subtitled 'Reformation, Counter-Reformation and Revolt', focuses on the role of argument from commonplaces, whether linguistic, textual, visual, performative, or musical, during a period of rapid and far-reaching ideological and social change characterised by theological controversies and political turmoil. Progressing from a strict to a more flexible definition of the commonplace, the thirteen contributions to this volume explore the role of the commonplace in the early modern classroom, its place in contemporary polemic and controversy as well as its relationship with (disputed) authority, and trace its presence across a variety of media in the visual, theatrical, and spatial arts.

We thank the Board of the University of Groningen for the financial support given to the *Cultural Change* programmes.

The editors are particularly grateful to Marijke Wubbolts for helping to organise the workshop which was the inspiration for this volume, and Gorus van Oordt for preparing the texts for publication.

Herman W. Hoen, General Editor

INTRODUCTION

David Cowling

Much like the art of memory, famously described by Frances A. Yates as an 'invisible' art,[1] the commonplace has left its mark on early modern culture in ways that are not always obvious to the observer, contemporary or modern. The culture of the commonplace is, of course, most readily perceptible in the printed commonplace-books that offered their readers ready-made structures for the finding and elaboration of arguments, whether in the early modern classroom, the pulpit, or the political arena. The use – and abuse – of commonplace material, typically quotations from classical or biblical sources, is evident in much early modern writing and is taken to a high level of self-reflexive sophistication by celebrated writers such as Montaigne. But what of less sophisticated texts and their authors, or the products of visual or musical culture? Is it legitimate to discern the presence of commonplace material, or of the patterns of thought and reasoning fostered by a training in commonplacing, across the full range of early modern cultural output? What role does commonplace material play in the communication and attempted legitimation of authority during a period of religious, political, and social upheaval and contestation?

The present volume inaugurates a series of three books covering the period c.1450-c.1800, based on work undertaken at workshops held at the universities of Copenhagen, Durham, and Groningen over the course of 2006-2008, which were generously funded by the Netherlands Organisation for Scientific Research (NWO), the Danish National Research Foundation, and the British Academy.[2] The initial project brief, drawn up by Martin Gosman of the Groningen Research School for the Study of the Humanities in collaboration with members of the steering group, emphasised the importance of persuasion as a means by which authorities – broadly defined as religious or political groups with or without an existing institutional base – sought to win over a target group – ranging from the learned to the illiterate – and to ensure their participation in a shared enterprise. Previous studies of early

---

[1] F. A. Yates, *The Art of Memory* (London, 1966), p. 17.
[2] The project steering group consisted of the following: Mette B. Bruun and Nils Holger Petersen (University of Copenhagen); Kathryn Banks and David Cowling (Durham University); Philiep Bossier and Joop W. Koopmans (University of Groningen).

modern techniques of persuasion had, he argued, paid disproportionate attention to elite culture while leaving more popular cultural forms largely
unexplored and, in so doing, had neglected the sociological 'legibility' of
various techniques of persuasion. The project's working hypothesis was that
it was precisely in these more popular and vernacular forms, including political and religious pamphlets and treatises, theatrical performances, ceremonial, newspapers, music, and architecture, designed to reach, convince,
and – ideally – seduce the masses, that a concentration of commonplace material was to be found.

    It is, however, clear that any attempt to explore and analyse the culture
of the commonplace in early modern Europe must be informed by a clear
understanding of the notion of the 'commonplace' itself. As Ann Moss reminds us in the first chapter of this book (which itself serves as an excellent
introduction to the underpinnings of commonplace culture in the period), a
strict definition of this term implies the practice, inherited from classical
rhetorical theory and inculcated in the Renaissance classroom, of collecting
quotations from classical and biblical sources and arranging them under a
set of headings in a 'commonplace-book', where they might serve as material for moral reflection, memory training, and rhetorical argument.[3] Far
from providing a fixed and unchanging point of reference for writers and
their readers, however, such ordered collections of quotations lent themselves, in the Reformation and Counter-Reformation period, to partisan contributions to theological debate and religious polemic, demonstrating the
ability of quoted material to be turned to a number of – at times contradictory – uses. The openness of such material to contestation and its potential
for dynamic change are evident in a number of contributions to this volume,
and point towards the somewhat broader definition of the commonplace that
has been adopted for this project. Contributors have been asked to attend
both to Moss's exposition of the role of the commonplace, understood
stricto sensu as a constituent of a commonplace-book, and to a broader conception of the commonplace as material that enjoyed both a history of use in
a given society or language community and a wide currency in that society.
Such material could be common enough to appear semantically unproblem-
atic and, indeed, self-evident; it could exist in a range of modes of representation, from the linguistic (where it might take the form of a proverb or a
common locution) to the visual or, indeed, musical; it could be used unself-
consciously to appeal to widely accepted 'facts', or, more interestingly, as a
means of reinforcing culturally sanctioned – or desired – modes of thought

---

[3] For an extensive treatment of the topic of commonplaces and commonplace-books
from Antiquity to the seventeenth century, see A. Moss, *Printed Commonplace-
Books and the Structuring of Renaissance Thought* (Oxford, 1996).

and perception. As such, far from constituting a set of simple clichés or banalities, as a modern understanding of the term might suggest, early modern commonplaces, we argue, were powerful tools of persuasion in both learned and more popular contexts.[4]

The three volumes of the *Commonplace Culture* series take their cue from key features of the three centuries around which they are organised. This first volume, subtitled 'Reformation, Counter-Reformation and Revolt', focuses on the role of argument from commonplaces, whether linguistic, textual, visual, performative, or musical, during a period of rapid and far-reaching ideological and social change characterised by theological controversies and political turmoil. The second volume, 'Consolidation of God-Given Power', addresses the use of commonplace material in the seventeenth century as part of the attempt by those in power to distance themselves from the disorders of the recent past and to shore up fragile religious and political stability by appealing to the divinely ordained nature of that stability. The final volume, 'Legitimation of Authority', tackles the eighteenth century, a period during which the attempted stabilisation of the preceding century and its God-given nature were widely contested. That commonplaces themselves were coming under increasing pressure during this later period will be obvious both from the contributions to our third volume and, indeed, from the fact that commonplace-books themselves, as Moss has noted elsewhere,[5] ceased to enjoy wide currency and became a more marginal cultural phenomenon. At the same time, however, newspapers and periodicals were starting to reach a much broader readership and were beginning to trade in commonplaces of their own, suggesting an interesting shift from a commonplace culture based on the accumulated and ordered wisdom of the past towards a new mass culture of recycled 'truths'.

The present volume mirrors, in its structure, the progression from a strict to a more flexible definition of the commonplace set out above. Ann Moss's introductory chapter, 'Power and Persuasion: Commonplace Culture in Early Modern Europe', sets out the parameters for the study of the workings of the commonplace across a range of media. Having noted that a close familiarity with *loci communes* and the means of collecting, organising, and retrieving them was a staple of early modern elementary education, Moss goes on to provide an account of the process of commonplacing, as advocated by Erasmus and others, drawing attention to its dynamic nature and

---

[4] For a wide-ranging consideration of the role of such material in western culture, see *Lieux communs, topoi, stéréotypes, clichés*, ed. C. Plantin (Paris, 1993). The relationship between commonplaces, *topoi* and clichés has been explored in detail by F. Goyet (*Le Sublime du 'lieu commun': l'invention rhétorique dans l'Antiquité et à la Renaissance* (Paris, 1996), pp. 20-25).

[5] *Printed Commonplace-Books*, pp. 279-280.

the possibility for individual compilers of commonplace-books to make idiosyncratic choices, grouping contradictory quotations and examples under the same head, or the same quotation under different heads, and thus undermining their potentially univocal nature. This inherent flexibility of commonplace material, which could both confirm and, crucially, subvert authority, was clearly of great import for Reformation and Counter-Reformation disputants and polemicists, who skilfully turned the same biblical material to radically different and confessionally loaded ends. Moss also draws attention to the use of commonplaces in preaching, which tended to favour the rhetorical figure of similitude for the opportunities it provided for homely, entertaining, or even exotic development of doctrinal and ethical points. Once commonplace material had passed into the vernacular, this tendency to base arguments on shared everyday experience rather than on book learning intensified; having lost the detailed scholarly apparatus that characterised Latin commonplace-books, enabling the reader to return to the source of a given quotation, vernacular commonplace-books tended to erode the distinction between identifiable authorities and the folk wisdom encapsulated in popular proverbs. In addition, collections of vernacular commonplaces, in asserting the equality of contemporary writers with those of Antiquity, participated, in the seventeenth century, in the movement that was to culminate in the *Querelle des anciens et des modernes*. Finally, Moss addresses the question of the presence of commonplaces beyond the realm of the purely textual, acknowledging that practitioners of the visual, spatial and decorative arts were themselves imbued with the culture of the commonplace and sought, through both sententious aphorisms and pictorial material, to reach a public similarly primed to recognise the use and reuse of such familiar material.

Other contributions to this volume explore the areas mapped out by Moss while extending the focus of her remarks, moving from a consideration of the role of the commonplace in the early modern classroom, through studies of its place in contemporary polemic and controversy and its relationship with (disputed) authority, to its presence across a variety of media in the visual, theatrical, and spatial arts.

Raphaële Fruet ('Jesuit Teaching on Topics: The First Book of the *De arte rhetorica libri tres*') studies the mechanics of the Jesuit teaching of commonplaces in Cypriano Soarez's influential textbook of rhetoric, *De arte rhetorica libri tres* of c.1560, showing how the use and typographical presentation of classical authorities and commonplaces evolved over the long publishing history of the work and considering their role in the Jesuit *praelectio*. Here, as elsewhere in this volume, the choice of classical authorities by early modern writers appears to be far from ideologically neutral, and Fruet suggests that a preference for those speeches by Cicero that denounce the enemies of the state (Verres and Catiline) betrays the Jesuits' support for the growing absolutism of the French crown at a time when they themselves were coming under fire from French Gallicans because of the Spanish origins of their order.

Arnoud Visser ('The Authority of Augustine in the Early Reformation: The Examples of Erasmus and Hoogstraeten') considers the apparently monolithic influence of Saint Augustine on the theological debates of the Reformation period, emphasising the diversity of contexts –humanist, Lutheran, and Roman Catholic – in which his work is used as an authority. Through analysis of the *Cum divo Augustino colloquia* of the Dominican Jacob van Hoogstraeten and Erasmus's *Antibarbarorum liber*, Visser demonstrates that recourse to the authority of Augustine – itself a form of commonplace in the sixteenth century – was conditioned by what he terms the 'economy of authority', an intellectual market mechanism in which the selection of authoritative quotations was determined by the agenda of the opposing group. Thus Hoogstraeten sought to correct passages from Luther (who himself made copious use of Augustine) by means of quotations from Augustine, and Erasmus, through the character of James Batt, held up Augustine as an example of classically authentic rhetoric to 'barbarians' writing debased scholastic Latin. By allowing their use of material derived from Augustine to be influenced by what their opponents would expect, the participants in debates of this kind did, however, open up a space in which communication between humanists and scholastics became possible.

Sven Rune Havsteen ('Music as a *Topos* in the Lutheran Construction of a Confessional Identity in the Sixteenth and Seventeenth Centuries') considers the importance of music within the Lutheran church in northern Germany and Scandinavia and its role in the development of a confessional identity distinct from that of both Roman Catholics and Calvinists. While music enjoyed a high status in Lutheran religious life as a gift of God and a powerful adjuvant for the proclamation of the gospel message, featuring as one of the *loci communes* in Aurifaber's edition of Luther's *Tischreden*, the Calvinist stance was critical towards both vocal and organ music, as evident in the controversy surrounding the use of music in the Christian liturgy that surfaced in the Colloquy of Montbéliard (1586) and again in Anhalt in 1596. The centrality of music as a means of communication between God and man remained firmly anchored as a commonplace of Lutheran thought into the seventeenth century.

Patrick Vandermeersch ('The Roman Catholic Doctrine on Abortion: The Curious History of a Commonplace') explores the unstable and disputed nature of apparently commonplace material within Roman Catholic theology through the example of the Church's teaching on abortion. Vandermeersch demonstrates, by means of close analysis of contradictory bulls promulgated by two sixteenth-century popes, that Catholic doctrine on abortion (namely that it is murder) is in fact a very recently constructed commonplace, and that attitudes in the early modern period were much more variable and, indeed, subject to revision, suggesting that, despite attempts by Catholic theologians such as Melchior Cano to create univocal hierarchies of theological knowledge, *loci* were not fixed places of argument, but rather sites of contestation.

Ninna Jørgensen's chapter (*'Die gelerten, die verkerten*: Commonplaces in the Reformers' Apologies for the Overturning of Ecclesiastical Authority') provides a bridge between the contributions dealing with the role of commonplaces in theological disputation and those concerned with vernacular culture. Jørgensen highlights the importance of popular locutions and proverbs for Reformation theologians, for whom they provided trustworthy and apparently self-evident commonsense knowledge in concise form. Such vernacular commonplaces, which were designed to persuade or to edify, were recognised by Reformers such as Luther and the pamphleteers of 1520-1521 for their memorable quality and their anti-scholastic nature. They also enabled both Reformist and Roman Catholic theologians to 'frame' doctrinal debates in such a way as to cast their opponents in an unfavourable light.

David Cowling ('Commonplaces and Everyday Wisdom in Henri Estienne') draws on elements of the cognitivist theory of metaphor in his discussion of the humanist Henri Estienne's use of figurative language in the service of a 'defence' of the French language against Italian influence in the 1560s and 1570s. Vernacular commonplaces are understood as a constituent of everyday language, grounded in shared knowledge of the domestic sphere, with low cognitive salience but a significant potential for persuasion via an appeal to apparently commonsense knowledge. Commonplace metaphors of purity and bastardy, balanced economic exchange, and good household management are used by Estienne to attack prominent features of contemporary Italian linguistic and cultural influence in France. Cowling suggests that, despite Estienne's own production of Latin-language commonplace-books, his vernacular commonplaces are not grounded in the learned tradition but rather in a shared culture of the everyday that is also perceptible in the vernacular works of contemporary Calvinist theologians.

Kathryn Banks ('Royal Authority and Commonplace Similitudes in French Natural-Philosophical Poetry: Duchesne's *Grand Miroir du Monde* and Du Bartas's *Sepmaine*') studies commonplace similitudes in French natural-philosophical poetry against the backdrop of the Wars of Religion. Arguing that similarity was a central epistemological category of this poetic genre, Banks demonstrates how Du Bartas and Duchesne figured the relationship between the king and his subjects in terms of the relationship between the sun and the universe. This similitude, like the extended analogy between the king and the ichneumon developed by Duchesne, drew on commonplace material but did not bear a fixed meaning. Such commonplace analogies, Banks argues, could be used (much like commonplaces themselves) in the service of competing views, and could be shaped by political events; as such, they provided questions about royal power rather than ready-made answers.

Stijn Bussels's chapter ('To Take in a Town with Gentle Words: The Use of *Loci* in the Antwerp entry of 1549') directs the focus of the volume towards the presence of commonplace material in other media by analysing the role of non-verbal communication in one of Charles V's royal entries. Drawing on Cicero's recognition in the *De oratore* that different levels of persuasive discourse need to be marshalled by the orator, Bussels asks whether all spectators could understand what they saw and distinguishes, through examples, between high-level communication between the educated burghers of Antwerp and the Habsburgs mediated through humanist inscriptions on triumphal arches and *tableaux vivants*, on the one hand, and the more inclusive use of Charles' visual device and, indeed, the foregrounding of the impressive bodily features of male and female actors on the other. Commonplace visual representations, Bussels argues, were in the final analysis more important for the onlookers, and thus more effective as agents of persuasion, than the often incomprehensible or illegible Latin textual material incorporated into the décor of the entry.

Philiep Bossier ('Italian Actors as Agents of Rebellion against Commonplaces in the Age of Counter-Reformation') studies the ways in which female actors in sixteenth-century Italy sought to overcome negative commonplaces opposing their presence on the stage, becoming, in the process, emblematic of the new professionalised theatre system. Just as commonplaces themselves could be used dynamically to adapt to new political and social realities, so the stock characters of Italian theatre resisted stereotypical interpretations based on simple binary oppositions (good vs bad, master vs servant) and occupied a new cultural space between high and low culture. Bossier also demonstrates how a female playwright such as Maddelena Campiglia, author of the pastoral drama *Flori* (1588), herself used literary commonplaces, such as the metaphor of the text as the child of its author, to assert her own literary professionalism.

Nils Holger Petersen's chapter ('Commonplaces in Religious Upbringing in Sixteenth-Century Italian Youth Confraternities: Iacopo Ansaldi and the *Compagnia dell'Arcangelo Raffaello*') examines the role of commonplaces – broadly defined to include textual material, aesthetic judgements and the arguments used to justify the place of music and singing in elementary instruction – in doctrinal teaching for boys in sixteenth-century Italy.

Petersen shows how Iacopo Ansaldi, author of a *Dottrina cristiana* (1585) and lay overseer of the Florentine confraternity of the Archangel Raphael, drew on commonplace material from the Jesuit tradition in promoting the efficacy of song as a means of catechetical instruction, which accorded well with the confraternity's sustained emphasis on *lauda* singing as part of its educative activities.

Barbara Ravelhofer's chapter ('Choreography as Commonplace') applies the notion of the commonplace to the medium of dance. Drawing on early modern manuals of choreography, Ravelhofer identifies three key commonplaces used to justify the practice of dancing and to defend it from attack, namely dance as a socialising force, warnings against the dangers of excessive speed, and dance as a silent language, which she exemplifies through the analysis of texts by Domenico da Piacenza, Fabritio Caroso, and the Jesuit Bernardino Stefonio. Ravelhofer demonstrates the important role played by dance in early modern education and the links established between the figures traced by dancers and early modern aesthetics, asking pertinent questions about the ability of dance to signify and to educate, and its legibility to its viewers across the social classes.

The final paper in this volume provides a link to the concerns of our second volume. Mette B. Bruun ('Commonplaces in *Cendrillon* and *Peau d'Ane*: Between Academic Dispute, Folklore Magic, and Moral Instruction') assesses evidence for the use of commonplace material in the religious instruction of lay people after the Counter-Reformation by focusing on two fairytales by Charles Perrault, in which the author champions a cultural ethos and religious ethos underpinned by, on the one hand, his intervention in the *Querelle des anciens et des modernes* on the side of the *modernes*, and, on the other, his knowledge of Jansenist doctrine. Having, in his contribution to the *Querelle*, denounced the texts of Antiquity as worthless for the purposes of moral edification, Perrault chose to address his contemporaries (or, rather, their children) on their own moral and historical home ground by means of narratives that rewarded honesty, patience, hard work, and obedience; his reworking of the commonplace material of the fairytale, Bruun argues, is similarly characterised by the presence of elements of contemporary debates that would have resonated with his adult readers.

Bruun's chapter ends with a reflection on the 'merger of universality and individuality' that she sees as being characteristic of the fairytale genre. The same could be said of commonplaces more generally. As Francis Goyet has remarked, the classical orator using a *locus communis* is no longer pleading just for his own client, but for the totality of human society and the whole of human knowledge ('le Tout').[6] All the chapters in this volume

---

[6] F. Goyet, *Le Sublime du 'lieu commun'*, p. 250.

grapple, to a greater or a lesser extent, with this fundamental aspect of the commonplace, which can be understood as an instantiation within a specific (historical, geographical, linguistic, political, social, religious) context of a universal truth. While the balance between the universal and the individual may vary from chapter to chapter, the volume as a whole demonstrates the mutually illuminating insights that result from the consideration of these two constituents of the commonplace.

CONTRIBUTORS

Kathryn Banks is Lecturer in French at Durham University.

Philiep Bossier is Professor of Historical Romance Literature and Culture at the University of Groningen.

Mette B. Bruun is Professor of Church History at the University of Copenhagen.

Stijn Bussels is Lecturer at the University of Groningen and Postdoctoral Research Fellow at Leiden University.

David Cowling is Professor of French and Head of the School of Modern Languages and Cultures at Durham University.

Raphaële Fruet is post-doc in the Faculty of Modern and Medieval Languages, University of Cambridge.

Sven Rune Havsteen is Associate Research Professor at the Danish National Research Foundation: Centre for the Study of the Cultural Heritage of Medieval Rituals, University of Copenhagen.

Ninna Jørgensen is Associate Research Professor in the Department of Church History, University of Copenhagen.

Ann Moss is a retired Professor of French at Durham University and a Fellow of the British Academy.

Nils Holger Petersen is Associate Professor of Church History and Centre Leader, Danish National Research Foundation: Centre for the Study of the Cultural Heritage of Medieval Rituals, University of Copenhagen.

Barbara Ravelhofer is Reader in English Literature at Durham University.

Patrick Vandermeersch is Emeritus Professor of the Psychology of Religion at the University of Groningen.

Arnoud Visser is a Postdoctoral Researcher at the Institute for Cultural Disciplines, University of Leiden.

POWER AND PERSUASION

COMMONPLACE CULTURE IN EARLY MODERN EUROPE

Ann Moss

What is a commonplace? The range of the research project that generated the present volume was calibrated against a fairly elastic understanding of what constituted a commonplace in the early modern period in Western Europe. The initial description of the project asked contributors to attend to some very general attempts at definition, doubtless equally applicable to the way commonplaces functioned in periods outside the one with which the project was primarily concerned. These definitions included the following: commonplaces are cultural material with both past and present currency within a given language community; their reference is to opinions commonly accepted as valid; they are deployed primarily as tools for argument in discourse designed to promote and reinforce culturally sanctioned modes of thought; and, furthermore, commonplace propositions have a ritualised character that makes of them recognisable modes of communication coded for universal reception, be it as familiar forms of verbal expression, hackneyed metaphors, normative rules, or recurring patterns. The papers presented at the workshop exploited the elasticity of this description of commonplaces to explore in highly imaginative ways how they were transposed as themes and clichés in different media targeted to audiences of varying degrees of intellectual sophistication.

As the present volume bears witness, all this carried the commonplace into places of innovative and exciting research. But participants in the workshop were also advised to recognise the boundaries of a clearly delineated historical period, that of the Reformation and Counter-Reformation. So, in order to localise commonplaces as instructed, it seems pertinent to narrow the focus of investigation a little and describe in some detail how commonplaces were actually defined in the early modern era. It is important to do so, because the early modern concept of commonplaces was not elastic at all. It was the solid outcome of highly self-conscious theorising and critical reflection on practice, generating definitions and instructions for use that varied little over time and place and were familiar in standardised form in countless textbooks. The world of its genesis and evolution was the elite environment of the Latin grammar class in humanist schools devoted to the

language arts: grammar, rhetoric, and dialectic. It was there, at the age of
nine or ten, at a highly formative moment in their intellectual development,
that boys would absorb the culture of commonplaces or, as they would have
known them, *loci communes*.

The modern student of *loci communes* can find no better tutor than the
master-manipulator of commonplaces, Erasmus himself, and, although I
have done this on other occasions, I make no apology for borrowing the
seminal instructions contained in his *De duplici copia verborum ac rerum*
of 1512. *De copia* is a book about finding subject matter for spoken and
written discourse and also words to develop it as abundantly as possible.
The best methodology for achieving this is to make a searchable collection
of commonplaces. First provide yourself with a notebook and inscribe headings on each page (Erasmus calls these headings 'places') so that you end
up with as full a list of topics as possible. Take these headings (or places)
partly from the main types and subdivisions of the vices and virtues, and
partly from those things that are of particular note in human affairs and that
are apt to crop up most frequently when we have to put forward a case. Prepare yourself a sufficient number of headings, arrange them in your notebook in whatever order you prefer, and subdivide them one by one into labelled sections. Then whatever you come across in any author, particularly
if it is especially striking, you will be able to note it down in its appropriate
place. It may be a story or a fable or an example or an occurrence or a pithy
remark or a witty saying or any other clever form of words or a proverb or a
metaphor or a similitude. This will ensure that what you read will stay more
firmly fixed in your mind and that you will learn to make use of the riches
you have acquired by reading. For, whenever occasion demands, you will
have ready to hand a supply of material for spoken or written composition,
because you will have, as it were, a well organised set of pigeonholes, from
which you may extract what you want.[1]

This procedure was called commonplacing, and the pupil's manuscript
notebook was a commonplace book. Publishers immediately smelled a
market opportunity, and commonplace books were printed in ever increasing numbers and ever increasing dimensions to supplement or replace the
individual's collecting efforts. But even these printed commonplace books
invited their readers to add to their content with new heads and, especially,
new excerpted items to illustrate the heads. Erasmus has introduced us to
the intellectual horizons and working practices of early modern writers,

---

[1] Paraphrased from Erasmus, *De duplici copia verborum ac rerum*, ed. B. I. Knott,
in: Erasmus, *Opera omnia*, I/6 (Amsterdam, 1988), pp. 258-261; for the history of
commonplace books, see A. Moss, *Printed Common-Place Books and the Structuring of Renaissance Thought* (Oxford, 1996).

whose mental habits were formed, as was most often the case, in the humanist schoolroom. *De copia*'s directives will map our way towards one of the main commonplaces of the current volume of essays: the heading 'authority'.

First, Erasmus stated his preferred subject matter for place-headings, or commonplaces. That matter was moral in the broadest sense: vices and virtues and their subdivisions, things of note in human affairs. Vices and virtues, and all varieties of human behaviour, individual and communal, were indeed to remain the staple substance of generalist commonplace books. In parallel with this, and in accordance with laws of demand and supply, it was writing and speaking on moral issues, in every genre, that was to be the area of discourse most heavily larded with commonplaces during the early modern period. The method of collecting material under topic-heads soon spread, however, to subjects of inquiry that intersected with the moral sphere but were not totally contained within it, to theology, natural sciences, history, politics, and so on. Discipline-specific commonplace books were produced to regulate the interrelationship of each discipline's constitutive elements. Even so, the primacy of the moral commonplace book and its early influence on the developing minds of students preoccupied with sorting material to match its headings tended to foster the assumption that all knowledge could be plotted onto a preconceived moral grid.

Erasmus next referred to the order in which commonplace heads were to be arranged. Some regarded the heads in commonplace books as a *summa* of knowledge and elaborated schemes to replicate the hierarchical order of Nature from God to things inanimate, allocating to man and his concerns a disproportionate place in the middle. Such schemes could potentially reduce the whole universe to commonplaces. There were even some, including the very influential Melanchthon, who claimed unassailable authority for commonplace heads, because, far from being invented casually or arbitrarily, they corresponded to the deep structures of Nature.[2] Other editors adopted prior models for distributing moral topics: the Ten Commandments, the Seven Virtues and the Seven Deadly Sins, the catalogue of virtues and vices in the *Summa Theologica* of Thomas Aquinas, the spec-

---

[2] Melanchthon, *De locis communibus ratio*, in: C. G. Bretschneider and H. E. Bindseil, eds, *Opera*, 28 vols. (Brunswick, etc., 1834-1860), XX (1854), cols. 695-698 (col. 698). By the early seventeenth century, commonplace books, grown enormously in size, merged with encyclopaedias, whether ordered alphabetically or by topic. All sorts of schemes for ordering knowledge, from bibliographies to libraries, adopted the model of commonplace books and the various methods they used for organising heads (see A. Moss, 'Locating Knowledge', in: K. A. E. Enenkel and W. Neuber, eds, *Cognition and the Book: Typologies of Formal Organisation of Knowledge in the Printed Book of the Early Modern Period* (Leiden, 2005), pp. 35-49).

trum of virtues and related opposites in Aristotle's *Nicomachean Ethics*, the order in which Valerius Maximus had listed his *Exempla*.[3] In such cases, authority was invested in the very framing of moral inquiry, as well as in the opinions collected in the commonplace book. Yet there could be contradiction. The moral scheme adopted could be Christian or it could be pagan, and, though they coexisted in the humanist schoolroom, there was not necessarily complete symbiosis between the two. Well before the end of the sixteenth century, however, the desire to make commonplace books searchable and the information within them easily retrievable meant that topics were invariably arranged alphabetically. Alphabetical order carries no moral authority.

Whatever the scheme for their ordering, it was what the heads contained that carried most authority. The spaces under the heads were filled with relevant quotations, ideally selected by individuals from their own reading, in practice more conveniently pre-packaged in printed commonplace books. The texts quoted were extracts from the *boni authores*, the 'good authors' of Latin and Greek antiquity, invested for the humanist schoolboy (and for his master) with the received authority of ancient wisdom. Their authoritative nature was underlined by the fact that, normally, they were ascribed to their source. Furthermore, the commonplace book was not just a collection of authoritative opinions. It was also a repository of examples of formulaic ways of expressing those opinions to maximum and memorable effect: definitions, descriptions, pithy remarks, examples from history and fiction, proverbs, apophthegms, metaphors, and similitudes. Both the observations made in the quotations and their ritualised encoding had the authority of the writers to whom they were attributed. Moreover, at least in the case of the more carefully manufactured printed commonplace books, their very look inspires a respectful attitude in those who search them. Their carefully patterned layout of heads, quotations, and text references is imposing in itself.

Yet, the commonplace book partook of the fluidity of manuscript production as well as the static quality of print. Whether he was transcribing into a private notebook or adding to a printed compendium, the individual commonplacer could make quite idiosyncratic choices. Under his place-headings, he could store quotations that had the latent capacity to explode their containers. Contradictory quotations and contrary examples could be gathered under a single head, undermining each other by their juxtaposition. The same quotation could appear under quite different heads. The universe

---

[3] Examples in Moss, *Printed Common-Place Books*; perhaps the most complex example of moral ordering is Theodor Zwinger's encyclopaedic *Theatrum vitae humanae* (Basle, 1565).

of discourse of commonplace books, both manuscript and printed, was unbounded, and thought was not constrained. Their categories could overspill as more and more quotations were added. Their collected extracts could amplify, qualify, and subvert, as well as confirm, authority.

This ambivalence was also quite capable of affecting the way the commonplace book was used. For it was not just a collection of excerpted texts, but an agent of production. Erasmus had said that the young commonplacer would have to hand a ready supply of material for written and spoken composition, particularly when 'you have to put forward a case'. This implies that the commonplace book was of particular use in persuasive and argumentative discourse. And, indeed, in the early modern period, structured discourse was generally considered to be persuasive in intent. The stratagems of persuasive argument most favoured by the humanists, and taught at the same time as the young boy was constructing his commonplace book, were known as *loci*, 'places'. These were dialectical strategies derived from attention to arguments from definition, genus and species, conjugates, similarity, difference, causes, effects, adjuncts, opposites, comparisons, and so on. The place of argument most obviously filled by the commonplace book was argument from testimony, from accredited purveyors of received wisdom. To make this move, the writer or speaker had only to look up quotations in his commonplace book, lift them out, and adduce them as proof. In addition, the headed excerpts could be used to support any of the other dialectical proof 'places' listed above. They could, moreover, be deployed to support the other side of any argument, to consolidate an established position, but also to destabilise it. The schoolboy was taught to argue opposite sides of any case, *in utramque partem*, and his commonplace book was his most effective tool. It also supplied him with weapons for the looser strategies of rhetoric, enlivening argument with realistic examples and winning assent with clever turns of phrase. His commonplace book was an abundant resource of descriptions, aphorisms, examples, apophthegms, metaphors, and similitudes that the writer could either transfer directly as quotation or use as a model to devise his own ritualised formulation of a commonplace.

So, did this culture of commonplaces, conceived with the rigour just described, promote authoritarian control? In some ways, it probably did. This methodology for reading and for producing text was dominant for well over a hundred years after Erasmus. During that time, heads and excerpts were recycled from commonplace book to commonplace book. The headings used and the texts stored beneath them constituted in effect the cultural matrix of early modern Europe. Moreover, the method of commonplacing instilled in the minds of its practitioners the sense that all new knowledge and all new experience could and should be found its proper place within a pre-selected and pre-ordered scheme. The commonplace book functioning thus was a force for conservatism in the accumulation and application of knowledge, including scientific knowledge. Even with respect to the social and political *status quo*, it has been argued that anyone with a mind furnished from a particularly well-stocked commonplace book, that is to say with a superabundance of the cultural capital in general circulation, could employ it to secure superior status within the political hegemony and the social establishment.[4] On the other hand, the individual practitioner was the owner of his own resource and master of his own production. He could flexibly exploit juxtaposed contrary excerpts collected in his commonplace book to manoeuvre authoritative argument against standard opinions. He could expand its range, and thereby the range of his own discourse, beyond received ideas and inherited categories. In such hands, the commonplace book had the potential to free thought.[5] In one major respect, however, the commonplace book was certainly an important factor for cultural cohesion, if not necessarily political agreement or ideological conservatism. The universal employment of commonplace books in the education of the ruling classes across Western Europe bonded the Latin-literate elite in a community of shared points of reference, core texts, and common practice, that resisted dissolution when Europe fractured along confessional lines. Within its secular culture, now so well established on classical foundations, the writing community continued to converse fluently, whether in Latin or in the vernaculars. And when either side of the religious divide 'had to put forward a case', it formulated it according to dialectical and rhetorical stratagems that all controversialists recognised as valid modes of argument. Our next task is to observe how Reformers and Counter Reformers exploited this common culture of the commonplace to establish authority and assert control.

It is possibly not too much to claim that commonplaces revolutionised theological argument in 1521. That was the date of the first edition of Philip

---

[4] See S. Greenblatt, *Renaissance Self-Fashioning: From More to Shakespeare* (Chicago/London, 1980).

[5] In effect, the proximity of quotations pulling in contrary directions under a single head could produce a very slippery moral discourse, in which moral qualities were redescribed as their opposites. This development is explored with reference to rhetoric in general in Q. Skinner, *Reason and Rhetoric in the Philosophy of Hobbes* (Cambridge, 1996), especially in the discussion of paradiastole (chapt. 4, pp. 138-180). For a sceptical commonplacer with political interests, see K. Sharpe, *Reading Revolutions: The Politics of Reading in Early Modern England* (New Haven/London, 2000). The thinker who employed quotations most effectively to question established positions was Michel de Montaigne; behind his *Essais* there undoubtedly lay a commonplace book, or, as he preferred to put it, the *Essais* were that book ('Du pedantisme', *Essais*, I, xxv, in *Œuvres complètes*, eds M. Rat and A. Thibaudet (Paris, 1962)).

Melanchthon's *Loci communes rerum theologicarum*, a work revised, amplified, and republished many times subsequently.[6] Luther's young disciple
had already promoted argument by commonplaces and, indeed, the keeping
of commonplace books, in his *De rhetorica* of 1519. His book on the commonplaces of theology supplies theological argument with a methodology
that differs from the formal procedure of question, response, objection, and
reply that had structured theological disputation in the late medieval period
and was still standard practice. Melanchthon dissociates himself very
clearly from this philosophical 'problem solving', and substitutes for it what
he calls elsewhere a 'didactic rhetoric' that teaches and preaches religious
doctrine by making dialectical moves involving the recognised places of
argument. This contrasted radically with the orientation and intent of the
logic of the late medieval schoolmen that had been so closely associated
with late medieval Catholic theology. Their logic aimed at apodeictic truth,
necessary conclusions irrefutable by reason, and was primarily geared to
analysis of propositions. Dialectic that proceeds by places, on the other
hand, was a methodology for constructing arguments, rather than testing
them, and a strategy for convincing one's opponent, through an array of
persuasive proofs, of what was most plausibly the case. It was closely
linked to the commonplace book, whose heads and authoritative quotations
could be used to underwrite this argumentative strategy with proof from testimony.[7]

   Melanchthon's theological *Loci communes* exhibit this methodology in
the means he employs to persuade his reader of the truth of the case he is
making. He also goes much further, shifting the very basis of theological
argument and changing its language. Melanchthon shuns any equation of
theology with rational philosophy and eschews the language of metaphysi-
cal speculation. His authority is not reason, but the word of God revealed in
Scripture. And the way to search the truth of Scripture is by employing a
method of biblical commentary that distributes the matter of Scripture under
commonplace heads directly derived from it. Melanchthon's *Loci communes* are just such heads, 'free will', 'gospel', 'grace', justification and
faith', and many others. Beneath the heads are short paragraphs of exposition and argument that can be read sequentially or lifted out and recycled.
Later editions of the *Loci communes* add more and more supporting quotations from Scripture and other sources. It is easy to detect the Lutheran bias

---

[6] For theological argument by commonplaces, see A. Moss, *Renaissance Truth and
the Latin Language Turn* (Oxford, 2003), especially chapt. 7 (pp. 157-188).
[7] For a very clear exposition of the relative status of probable and necessary conclusions in medieval philosophy, in particular in the thought of Saint Thomas Aquinas,
see E. F. Byrne, *Probability and Opinion: A Study in the Medieval Presuppositions
of Post-Medieval Theories of Probability* (The Hague, 1968).

of such heads, but Melanchthon claims to be deriving his theology from a properly systematic reading of Scripture, one that could even, supported by the plausible arguments of dialectic, challenge traditionally asserted articles of faith. That was a challenge that had to be answered. Every bit as challenging was the language change so clearly evident in the *Loci communes*. The Latin of scholastic theology and of the logic that structured its arguments was highly technical and very far from ordinary speech. The language of commonplace rhetoric and commonplace proof, though still Latin, was a much more widely intelligible Latin, the common speech of classical Rome taught in the grammar class in humanist schools and translatable without undue difficulty into the vernaculars. Melanchthon's promotion of commonplace procedures for text analysis and theological argument, couched in non-specialist language, had a possibly unintended outcome. Anyone could now think and talk theology with a natural authority, provided they understood the force of rational argument, had mastered the relatively easy moves of the dialectical places, and knew where to look for testimony to illustrate the topics of debate. And, unlike scholastic logic with its special language, there was no reason why theological argument conducted according to places should be restricted to speakers of Latin.

Catholic theologians might well read the Bible differently, but they too were now increasingly cohabiters with the Reformers in the culture of commonplaces, and were coming to understand that theological debate would have to operate within that common culture. The very first Catholic commonplace response to Melanchthon, in 1525, was by Johann Eck, a highly accomplished master of scholastic logic and traditional theological argument. But his title announces that he has decided to attack the Lutherans on Melanchthon's chosen ground: *Enchiridion locorum communium adversus Lutheranos*. And he realises that the new method, coupled with the Reformers' advance in sectors of society that could understand it and were liable to be convinced by it, forces him to relate to an entirely different audience than the company of professional theologians he is used to talking to. Eck's *loci communes* are specifically for those who are too busy or too simple-minded to pore over the recondite volumes of past heroes, but need arms to combat heretics. He sections his book by commonplace heads, representing topics about which the heretics will argue: the authority of the Church versus the authority of Scripture, the veneration of saints, and so on, and he supplies the faithful with quotations from Scripture and other texts with which to confound the opposition. Eck perhaps misjudges the intellectual level at which his readers might be called to operate by Lutheran debaters schooled in teaching-rhetoric. His language is far plainer than Melanchthon's, and his arguments here (very different from the sophistication of his scholastic logic) are both weak and strident. Nevertheless, the book ran into numerous editions. It had gone down market from Melanchthon's work, but it had constructed a readership that could manoeuvre quotations from authoritative texts to resource commonplaces of argument.

Theological argument proceeded for many years under commonplace heads, and theological commonplace books for preaching and debate were lucrative business for printers both Protestant and Catholic. By the end of the sixteenth century, they had in several instances, like their secular counterparts, become huge referenced encyclopaedias. A case in point is the *Loci communes* of the exiled Italian Reformer, Peter Martyr Vermigli, first printed, at London, in 1576. This is in fact a compilation of extracts from his many works made by Robert Masson (Le Maçon), the minister of the French church in London, arranged under commonplace heads that basically replicate the order of Calvin's *Institutes*.[8] At the other end of the commonplace-book spectrum in England, but much indebted to Vermigli, we encounter John Marbecke's *Booke of Notes and Commonplaces*.[9] This resembles many continental commonplace books supplying grounds for argument and authorities to quote in contemporary polemic, except that Marbecke inserts English authors using their own tongue among his translations, 'that being weaponed with much artillerie, we may be able to resist and overthrow whatsoever the whole Popish army shal assay to assalt us with al' (sig.a iii^v).

The primary function of theological commonplace books was to support argumentative and teaching discourse. Fuelled by polemic, they did, nevertheless, stimulate some very interesting lines of inquiry and new strategies for debate. In their desire to undermine the authority claimed by their opponents, Protestants and Catholics both turned their attention to the citations collected in theological commonplace books and recycled in argument. The focus then moved from their efficacious deployment in debate, to the status of these citations as testimony to truth, and the investigation became for the first time seriously historical. The rigorously Lutheran Matthias Flacius Illyricus gathered a team of researchers to assemble excerpts

---

[8] An English version, *The Common Places of the most famous and renowned Divine Doctor Peter Martyr*, appeared in 1583. For the context of the Vermigli compilation within the commonplace tradition, see C. Vasoli, '*Loci communes* and the Rhetorical and Dialectical Tradition', in: J. C. McLelland, ed., *Peter Martyr Vermigli and Italian Reform* (Waterloo, Ontario, 1980), pp. 17-28; and for the *Loci communes* itself, C. Strohm, 'Petrus Martyr Vermiglis *Loci communes* und Calvins *Institutio christianae religionis*', in: E. Campi, ed., *Peter Martyr Vermigli: Humanism, Republicanism, Reformation* (Geneva, 2002), pp. 77-104.

[9] *A Booke of Notes and Common Places, with their expositions, collected and gathered out of the Workes of divers singular Writers and brought Alphabetically into order* (London, 1581).

from religious writers from the patristic era to the thirteenth century for the large volumes known collectively as the *Magdeburg Centuries*. The researchers and organisers of the volumes were to 'imitate the organisation and honey-making of bees', which is a similitude employed time and again in textbooks of the time to describe the activity of commonplacing.[10] They plotted the history of the Christian church, century by century, under a series of headings that are reproduced volume by volume. These headings refer to the historical situation of the church, its governance, doctrine, practice, and so on, and are largely filled by excerpts from texts written in the century in question, particularly in the case of the many sub-headings for articles of doctrine. This is no objective history. The preface to each century-volume makes clear how each period has degenerated further and further from pristine truth. Readers can easily cross-reference between the heads to compare so-called authorities and see how they have successively corrupted doctrine and perverted practice, reaching a nadir in the thirteenth century with the simultaneous tyranny of popes and malevolent obscurantism of scholastic philosophy. Moreover, and this is one of the chief polemical strengths of the book, it becomes clear that the sources on which the Catholics rely contradict themselves and contradict the earlier, purer sources. What is new about this approach is that it has turned the commonplace book format into a tool of comparative historical criticism in order to undermine the validity of authorities on which the compilers' religious opponents will rely.

Meanwhile, those opponents were on the same track. Melchior Cano's *De locis theologicis*, published at Salamanca in 1563, despite its title, was not a theological commonplace book. It is an attempt to establish the status of proofs from authority by locating the tradition of the apostles, earlier and later theological writers, decrees of councils and popes, philosophers, and historians in a descending order of validity, but one in which they all have a place. The objective is to undermine the Protestants' exclusive recourse to the sole authority of Scripture, to confirm historical continuity, and to au-

---

[10] The full title of the *Centuries* is: *Ecclesiastica Historia, integram ecclesiae Christi ideam quantum ad locum, propagationem, tranquillitatem, doctrinam, haereses, ceremonias, gubernationem, schismata, synodos, personas, miracula, martyria, religiones extra ecclesiam, et statum Imperii politicum attinet, secundum singulas centurias complectens* (Basle, 1561-1574). See H. Scheible, *Die Entstehung der Magdeburgen Zenturien: ein Beitrag zur Geschichte der historiographischen Methode* (Gütersloh, 1966); O. K. Olson, *Matthias Flacius and the Survival of Luther's Reform* (Wiesbaden, 2002), pp. 256-279. For the various figurative ways of describing commonplace books and their making, consult the index in Moss, *Printed Commonplace-Books*.

thenticate 'novelties' at the point of their introduction.[11] On both sides of the divide there is an historicising turn which was to shift the parameters of debate.

Melanchthon's commonplace teaching-rhetoric was as influential on sermons as it was on debate. The Protestants produced countless manuals for preaching by commonplaces, and Catholics followed suit. Protestants, in particular, but also many Catholics, structured their sermons according to the place moves of dialectical argument. All preachers called on the persuasive power of the looser strategies of rhetoric. One favourite from among the figures of thought listed in the rhetorical manuals was similitude. It was recognised that argument from likeness had dialectical force, though it was perhaps the weakest of all the places of proof. But what it lacked in logical rigour, it made up for in an abundance of opportunities to diversify and intrigue. Commonplace books of similitudes quoted from the Bible and from ancient and more recent authors arranged them under moral and doctrinal heads recommended to preachers. Catholic printers recycled medieval collections of similitudes, originally designed for a very different preaching method, but supplying a vast repertoire of similes, often of an exotic and fantastic kind. Persuasion by the attraction stratagems of entertainment is in evidence here, as well as teaching.

The spectrum of reception envisaged by compilers of commonplaced similitudes was very wide. At its most sophisticated end lies the long essay called *Similitudinum methodus* with which, in 1575, Theodor Zwinger introduced a moral commonplace book of Latin similitudes originally collected by Erasmus.[12] Zwinger grounds similitude in Aristotelian logic, locating it within the argumentative paradigm of the syllogism and scrutinising propositions related by similitude in terms of essence and accident, predicables and categories, efficient and final causes. This is in effect to bind the probabilistic dialectic of places, of which similitude was one, as well as similitude's capacity for ethical instruction and displays of wit, back into strict logic, with all the potency for conviction that that implies. At the opposite end of this spectrum, in 1600, we have *A Treasurie or Store-house of Similes both pleasaunt, delightfull, and profitable, for all estates of men in generall, newly collected into Heades and Common Places* by Robert Cawdrey.[13] Cawdrey's compilation is meant for preachers looking for material

---

[11] For Cano, see P. Walter, 'Philipp Melanchthon und Melchior Cano: zur theologischen Erkenntnis- und Methodenlehre im 16. Jahrhundert', in: G. Frank and K. Meerhoff, eds, *Melanchthon und Europa* (Stuttgart, 2002), pp. 67-84.

[12] The *Similitudinum methodus* serves as an introduction, pp. 3-112, to Zwinger's edition of *Conr[adi] Lycosthenis Rubeacensis similium loci communes* (Basle, 1575).

[13] London, 1600; repr. Amsterdam/New York, 1971.

to amplify sermons, but the intended audience includes 'even the very simplest and ignorantest reader', for whom they 'decypher out', or decode, the 'grounds and principles of Christian religion' (sig. A2^v). Cawdrey very specifically relates his classification of his similitudes collected under commonplace heads to the theological revolution engineered by Philip Melanchthon's *Loci communes* and its methodology for building the exposition of dogma on the commonplaces of the Christian religion.[14] Cawdrey's alphabetically ordered heads map out the territory of Protestant doctrine and fill it with similitudes gathered for the most part from the Bible and explained in some detail. Not all of them, however, have their roots in Scripture. The Book of Nature also provides an amazing abundance of similitudes, furnishing that appetite for *copia* first stimulated in schoolboys filling up their commonplace books in the Latin school. But Cawdrey's Book of Nature appears to be written in plain English. Hypocrites are like dandelions, fleabane, celandine, wholewort, silkworms, dodders, oleander, horseflower, horned clover, ...

Our brief examination of the methodology of commonplace argument at work in theological discourse has brought us more than once to the borderlands of Latin and vernacular. These borderlands often, though not invariably, signal a passage from elite to less intellectually sophisticated culture. Many of the papers that follow in this volume amply illustrate a further item on our original agenda, which was to consider how discourse that sought to persuade by commonplaces was aimed at specific audiences, and, in particular, how it 'reached, convinced, and seduced the masses'. Some publishers of commonplace books certainly targeted the vernacular speech communities, though books, by definition, presuppose literacy, or at any rate an audience in which knowledge is conveyed orally from books. So, what happened to commonplace argument and commonplace books when they went 'down market'? In some instances, the published commonplace book clearly envisaged an eventual reception by a community of hearers, as well as its immediate reception by readers. Cawdrey's English similitudes systematised and emblematised a world of nature known by common experience and not from books. Moreover, he did this in order to amass a written resource for oral discourse, for sermons. Of all the genres of formal oral discourse, sermons were the most frequently performed and probably the most persuasive. Through sermons interlarded with Cawdrey's very novel, yet universally accessible, similitudes, preachers could instruct their flocks

---

[14] See the epistle to the reader, sigs. A3+2^v-A3+3^v: 'For so many, (or the most part of the Commonplaces) will be in effect, almost as good and profitable for instruction, as some whole Booke written of that point and matter'; Cawdrey lists, as an example, his seventeen sub-heads for the commonplace 'faith'.

to read edifying and doctrinally 'correct' messages in the familiar things of their surroundings. The environment of the uneducated masses was thereby incorporated into the signifying universe of Protestant moral authority, mediated by commonplaces.

The direct conduit for Latin commonplace culture into the vernacular speech community was translation. The most popular of all Latin prose commonplace books was a collection of excerpts from Cicero, originally compiled in 1541. A dual language version in French and Latin was published at Paris in 1574, dedicated to the son of a highly placed aristocrat, the Prince de Condé.[15] The commonplace book is thus removed from the Latin classroom and the culture it generated. It is insinuated into the grandest political and social circles as a mirror for adults accustomed to affairs of state. But these new readers pass through this mirror into exactly the same moral universe as the monolingual Latin original had constructed from quotations classified under loosely co-ordinated heads that gathered together the various species of prudent and imprudent conduct. The matter of the Latin has been absorbed, though the language into which it is transported retains none of the stylistic idiosyncrasies of the Latin authors quoted in Latin. The language of authority in French is blandly homogeneous, and when poetry is quoted it invariably comes through as mnemonic rhyming couplets.[16]

Besides stylistic sophistication, the most significant thing that tends to get lost in translation is the scholarly apparatus of Latin commonplace books. That had enabled quotations to be traced back to source. Its disappearance means that authority becomes anonymous and uniformly dispersed throughout the book, to be taken en bloc, as it were, with no means of qualifying it by informed knowledge of its provenance. Once attributions are discarded, Latin-derived commonplace books slip easily into the 'low' culture of vernacular proverb-collections. Gabriel Meurier's *Thresor de sentences dorées, proverbes et dicts communs*, first published at Antwerp in 1568 and thereafter repeatedly in France, provides a long list of authorities

---

[15] Full title: François de Belleforest, *Les Sentences illustres de M. T. Ciceron, et les Apophthegmes, avec quelques sentences de pieté, recueillies des euvres du mesme Ciceron. Aussi les plus remarquables Sentences, tant de Terence que de plusieurs autres autheurs et les Sentences de Demosthene de n'agueres tirées du grec, et mises en latin* (Paris, 1574).

[16] For an English example of commonplaces in translation, see W. Baldwin, *Treatice of Moral Philosophy* (London, 1571). This book is possibly functioning at a lower level of intellectual and social pretension than Belleforest. It begins with the lives and sayings of ancient philosophers and other worthies, and then its heads replicate the lay-out of the most familiar kind of hierarchically arranged commonplace book, going from God and the world, though the mainstays of social order, to social relationships, virtues, vices, and deadly sins.

from which its 'golden' matter is mined, but they have left no visible trace. What it contains are popular proverbs in popular French, contextualised in a social environment that certainly had no Latin speakers. It is a poor-relation commonplace book, but one with a definite agenda. In addition to guaranteeing the moral formation of his young readers and improving their letter-writing skills, Gabriel Meurier is intent on assuring their upward social mobility. He aims to dispatch them with a good supply of ready repartee wherewith to catch the benevolent attention of French-speaking 'gens de bien'.[17]

What vernacular commonplace books lost in terms of the weight of classical Latin authority, they soon won back, but in another guise. A volume like the *Parnasse des poetes françois modernes*, compiled by Gilles Corrozet and published at Paris in 1571, signals yet another cultural revolution engineered by commonplaces.[18] Extracts from all the major French-language poets since Clément Marot appear there under alphabetically ordered commonplace heads. The French headings replicate the categories of a typical Latin commonplace book devoted to moral topics. Vernacular culture is asserting equality with the elite culture of Antiquity. Its poetry has the same moral seriousness, the same moral scope, and the same claim to be taken as a model for expression and quoted for its acumen. The commonplacing of vernacular literature gives it the seal of authority, and this is as true for English as for French. *England's Parnassus* appeared in 1600, and the authors collected under its heads were Spenser, Marlowe, Sidney, Shakespeare, Jonson, et al.[19]

Authors have asserted themselves in the vernacular commonplace book and returned it to the high culture end of the market. But at the lower end, rather untidy, anonymous little vernacular compilations were promoting a development by which modern literary culture would escape forever the authority of the ancients. In the early years of the seventeenth century, a number of little books appeared, mostly printed in the French provinces, variously called *Fleurs du bien dire*, or *Marguerites*, or even *Marguerites des*

---

[17] A good English example of such a commonplace book is Nicolas Ling's *Politeuphia* or *Wits Commonwealth* of 1597. Very few of its collected *sententiae* are ascribed to an author. Its collection of prose definitions and aphorisms, similitudes, and examples are thoroughly naturalised into vernacular culture by being juxtaposed with native English proverbs. For commonplace-book types of publication as a means for constructing the self for the social stage, see M. T. Crane, *Framing Authority: Self and Society in Sixteenth-Century England* (Princeton, 1993).

[18] Full title: *Le Parnasse des poetes francois modernes, contenant leurs plus riches et graves sentences, discours, descriptions, et doctes enseignemens* (Paris, 1571).

[19] Robert Allott, *Englands Parnassus: or the choysest flowers of our moderne poets* (London, 1600).

lieux communs.[20] The commonplaced excerpts in these compilations, totally denuded of their provenance, were marketed as the most beautifully turned phrases to use in compositions to do with love or other topics. In one case, the headings are in fact indications of types of letters in which the collected phrases may be elegantly varied and conjoined.[21] Examples of such letters are also given, and, when read consecutively, an epistolary commonplace book of this kind hovers on the brink of being an epistolary novel, with 'lettres passionnées' passing between a lover and a lady 'extremement amoureuse'.[22] And so, the vernacular commonplace book attends the birth of the novel. And, in its early years, the novel will keep commonplace heads in waiting on its margins, waiting for the reader to select its choicest phrases and transcribe them into a commonplace book. Honoré D'Urfé's huge romantic novel, *Astrée*, is a treasury of commonplaces signalled in its margins, its highly imaginative fiction a powerful and persuasive authority for moral order in the public and the private sphere.

While the improbable couples of the *Astrée* conversed in commonplaces in woodland glades hung with text messages in the form of poems and enigmas, their real-life readers were also very likely to inhabit spaces visibly inscribed with commonplaces. These might be very public spaces. Houses fronting onto town streets often had short moral aphorisms or quotations from the Bible displayed in gold- or silver-painted letters on lintels or on beams running across the façade (many still exist, faithfully refurbished or copied down the centuries). The passer-by is thus contained within the public value system of the city community, solidly promoted by its prominent and successful citizens. Perhaps even more to the point, those prominent and successful citizens were advertising their adherence to the cohesive culture from which they derived power and influence. Similar inscriptions decorated the interior of houses, on walls and ceilings, domesticating the worthy sentiments by which the household was to be ruled, and displaying them for the approving gaze of visitors.

The role of text in the visual, spatial, and decorative arts was particularly important in the early modern era, and this must be attributed in no

---

[20] Probably the most frequently reprinted of these was François Desrues, *Les Marguerites françoises; ou fleurs du bien dire.*

[21] Its use is indicated on the title-page: *Les Marguerites des lieux communs et excellentes sentences. Avec plusieurs comparaisons et similitudes sur une partie d'icelles. Ausquels sont compris les plus beaux traits dont on peut user en amour et autres discours* (Lyon, 1604).

[22] For example, *Les Fleurs du bien dire: recueillies és cabinets des plus rares esprits de ce temps, pour exprimer les passions amoureuses, tant de l'un comme de l'autre sexe. Avec un nouveau recueil des traits plus signalez en forme de lieux communs, dont on se peut servir en toutes sortes de discours amoureux* (Lyon, 1604).

small measure to the fact that producers and consumers all shared in the commonplace culture of the period. From their early forays in constructing commonplace collections, they retained an appetite for sententious aphorisms, tags from classical authors, and the more morally biased verses of the Bible, all texts that carried authority. And these were just the right length for inscribing on stones, on wooden panelling and beams, on windows, and on tapestries. These short texts had, moreover, by the mid-sixteenth century acquired the ability to communicate pictorially. The initial medium for this was the emblem book, in which intriguingly enigmatic pictures were given an explicatory 'voice' by mottoes printed within the frame surrounding the engraving or alongside. The mottoes provided moral interpretations of the pictures in very succinct phrases that not infrequently resembled, or even reproduced, the headings or the adages to be found in commonplace books. The convergence of emblem pictures and commonplace book was truly inaugurated in 1548, when the most widely known emblem book, Alciato's *Emblemata*, was reorganised under commonplace heads, and its engravings grouped under virtues and vices.[23] From then on, commonplace text excerpts accompany emblems in their various permutations. In private places, they decorated tapestries and wall hangings. In the public arena, they dramatically proclaimed political messages on temporary monuments and transitory *tableaux vivants* that greeted monarchs and legates come in state to impose their authority on their loyal, or not so loyal, towns.

Some examples of monumentally inscribed quotations were not so transitory. The visitor who looks up to the interior roof of Saint Peter's in Rome will be awed by the strongly incised and everywhere visible quotations from the Bible. They can very well be read as excerpts displayed under a single head: the charge to Peter/the Petrine authority of Rome. This literal culmination of all that soaring grandeur in those texts was meant to impose an authority that brooked no demur. It aimed to impress, and it does. Yet, it is a moot point whether the quotations on that ceiling have proved more powerful in their after-effect than excerpts and aphorisms written on the ceiling of a much more private space. The beams of Michel de Montaigne's library carried Greek and Latin texts, biblical and pagan, that he had no doubt extracted from the books that lined its shelves. When he looked up from reading and writing, the commonplace book above his head was always open laterally with quotations and aphorisms that deflated the pretensions of hu-

---

[23] For the incorporation of emblems into commonplace books, see A. Moss, 'Emblems into Commonplaces: The Anthologies of Josephus Langius', in: K. A. E. Enenkel and A. S. Q. Visser, eds, *Mundus Emblematicus: Studies in Neo-Latin Emblem Books* (Turnhout, 2003), pp. 1-16; conversely, emblem books were not infrequently amplified with additional quotations filling out the commonplace headings to which emblem pictures were assigned.

man reason and cast doubt on intellectual certainty of any kind. And flying along the main cross-beam that joined them and supported the whole structure were the sceptical responses to that uncertainty, culled from Sextus Empiricus: 'I do not lay hold of any proposition', 'I suspend judgement', 'I keep examining'.[24] The commonplace book very often enshrined and imposed culturally sanctioned modes of thought and the authoritative pronouncements of the dominant belief system. That was one reason why it lasted so long. But it also nurtured the individual, questioning mind.

---

[24] For a thorough description of Montaigne's talking ceiling, see A. Legros, *Essais sur poutres: inscriptions et peintures de la tour de Montaigne, berceau des 'Essais'* (Paris, 2003).

JESUIT TEACHING ON TOPICS

THE FIRST BOOK OF THE *DE ARTE RHETORICA LIBRI TRES*

Raphaële Fruet

The *De arte rhetorica libri tres*, a textbook of rhetoric written by the Span-ish Jesuit Cypriano Soarez around 1560,[1] was an educational best-seller during the second half of the sixteenth and the whole of the seventeenth century. Reprinted more than two hundred and seven times, it spread across the whole of Europe through the network of Jesuit colleges.[2]

In this respect, the *De arte* was a powerful tool for the dissemination of defined uses of topics and, along with them, ways of thinking, writing, and, most of all, preaching. In her contribution to this volume, Ann Moss has mentioned these functions of topics or places; she has also defined their double nature as rules of inference in a dialectical system of argument, and as authorities in a rhetorical system of persuasion – the former being com-monplaces *stricto sensu*. Topics are present in the *De arte* in two capacities: first, as commonplaces, they are the subject of its first book, which deals with invention. Secondly, in the form of authorities drawn from classical culture, topics are woven together throughout the compendium – Aristotle and the ubiquitous Cicero, along with Quintilian, provide the theoretical definitions and principles, and Ciceronian speeches and classical Latin po-etry the examples.

---

[1] See A. de Backer, *Bibliothèque des écrivains de la Compagnie de Jésus: ou, noti-ces bibliographiques de tous les ouvrages publiés par les membres de la Compagnie de Jésus, depuis la fondation de l'ordre jusqu'à nos jours* (Liège, 1853-1861), VII, p. 1332.

[2] See L. J. Flynn, 'The De arte rhetorica of Cyprian Soarez, s.j.', *The Quarterly Journal of Speech* 42 (1956), pp. 367-374. The European network of Jesuit colleges grew exponentially during the first half of the sixteenth century. They were first in-tended to provide a good education for the members of the Company; yet they were also open to the lay public, and they were free because they were subsidised by the town they settled in. For financial reasons, and because of their pedagogical success, Jesuit colleges increasingly attracted the sons of the wealthy, and drew increasingly on a lay public. The Council of Trent (1545-1563) made them the pedagogical army of the Counter-Reformation. In 1773, when the Order was suppressed, there were more than eight hundred Jesuit colleges spread around the world. See J. W. O'Malley, *The First Jesuits* (Cambridge, MA, 1993), chapt. 6, pp. 201-239.

In this chapter, I will read one section of the first book of the *De arte* that deals with the topic 'from comparison', *De comparatione*,[3] against the background of, on the one hand, the Jesuits' *Ratio studiorum*, and, on the other, Soarez's prefatory letter to the reader. Three groups of editions – A, B and C – emerge from the editions I have consulted. This study focuses mainly on groups A and B. The *summae* of Group C are digests derived from Group B. These *summae* belonged to the Jesuit pedagogical apparatus for the humanities class, and had a mnemonic function, as we will see.[4] Group A is the original version of the text. Group B is the authoritative 'Roman edition', amended by the Jesuit John Perpinian, who had partici-pated in the elaboration of the 1599 *Ratio studiorum*. By reading the *De arte* alongside the *Ratio*, I intend to investigate the nature of the Jesuit pedagogy of topics: how did they teach topics? How did they conceive of places of argument? What authorities did they favour? By providing an-swers to these questions that draw on the avowed purposes of the *De arte* as described by Soarez in his prefatory letter, but also on the geographical and political contexts of publication, I hope to detect some specific features of Jesuit ideology, and to demonstrate how their pedagogy of topics reveals epistemological and political choices. Indeed, although, in terms of educa-tion, Catholic and Protestant humanistic ideologies displayed basic common features that crossed ideological borders,[5] Peter Bayley has pointed out that the two best-seller syllabuses of rhetoric in seventeenth-century France were the *De arte*, mainly used in Catholic schools, and Talon's *Rhetorica*, mainly used in Protestant ones.[6]

1. *Teaching topics: Jesuit pedagogical strategies*

Topics in the *De arte* are present both as dialectical places of argument (or commonplaces) and as authorities. These two categories seem to overlap,

---

[3] See appendices at the end of this chapter. '*De comparatione*' is chapt. XVII in Group A, and chapt. XVIII in Group B. The (implicit) rule of inference which gov-erns an argument 'from comparison' is often 'what is predicated of the first element of the comparison is predicated of the second'.

[4] See notes 12 and 20 below.

[5] The rigour and quality of Jesuit pedagogy is acknowledged by Protestants them-selves; see L. Giard, ed., *Les Jésuites à la Renaissance* (Paris, 1995), p. XIX: 'les admirateurs ne leur ont pas fait défaut, dans tous les camps, y compris du côté de la Réforme: en Angleterre, Francis Bacon a plusieurs fois loué leur savoir et leurs écoles, en Allemagne, les Luthériens lisent et citent les grands traités issus des cours de Coimbra ou du Collegio Romano'.

[6] See P. Bayley, *French Pulpit Oratory, 1598-1650: A Study in Themes and Styles* (Cambridge, 1980), p. 22: 'On balance, a Catholic was more likely to read Soarez, a Protestant, to read Talon'.

especially as the theoretical definitions are also direct quotations from ancient rhetorical treatises. Yet, the texts of Group A (that is, those published
in 1569 and 1615) emphasise the logical dimension of commonplaces by
using marginal glosses as argumentative markers, in addition to full references to authorities. By contrast, Group B texts favour the authoritative dimension of topics: marginal glosses are used only for full references to authorities.[7] Variants between one text and another in Group A, but also between Group A and Group B, reflect the students' progress from year to
year in the Jesuit curriculum, and exhibit increasing compliance with the
rules of the *Ratio studiorum*.

1.1 *Topics and the Jesuit praelectio: the texts of Group A*

Group A texts reveal an attempt to be exhaustive and systematic insofar as
they merge the two main functions of topics as authorities and dialectical
places of argument (commonplaces).

The commonplace 'from definition' determines the order of the main
text, and justifies the use of marginal glosses as argumentative markers. Indeed, the main text moves from generic definitions to more specific ones,
whilst argumentative markers in the margins highlight this theoretical order
of the text.

With regard to topics as authorities, some whole sections of the *De
arte*, from the theoretical principles to the examples, are built by piling up
authorities. These borrowings are not hidden: references are given either
directly in the main text by means of a name (*ut Cicero ait*), or in the marginal glosses, in the form of abbreviated titles ('Topic', for Cicero's *Topica*,
'Q' for Quintilian's *Institutio oratoria*, 'Part.' for Cicero's *Partitiones oratoriae*). Each specific definition is illustrated by means of a series of exam-

---

[7] There are also differences in the selection of examples within Group A: the 1615
edition is more copious than the 1569 one (see below, notes 8 and 9). On the other
hand, the authoritative Roman edition provides a fixed, set text throughout the period. Examples are woven as follows into the Roman edition: two quotations from
Cicero's *In Catilinam* and a truncated one from *In Verrem* illustrate the a *majoribus*
comparison, then comes the definition of the *a minori ad majus* comparison, illustrated by three quotations in italics from Ovid's *Remedia amoris* and Horace's *Epis-
tulae*, and finally by another quotation from *In Catilinam* which is a standard example of this type of comparison since Quintilian (who calls it similitude). The remaining type of comparison, *a pari*, is defined and illustrated by a running definition-
and-example paraphrased from Cicero's *De oratore*, and further illustrated by a
paraphrased example from *In Verrem*.

ples taken from different genres, either classical poetry[8] or Ciceronian prose oratory.[9] The examples in prose are retranslated in an explanatory paraphrase. This structure and the content it orders provide the basis for the Jesuit *praelectio*. The *Ratio studiorum* clearly defines this exercise of textual analysis, specifying that only ancient authors are to be studied. The teacher must prepare his lecture beforehand. As for the lecture itself, it should observe the following principles: first, the lecturer must read out loud the excerpt he is going to work on in one go – except if it is too long, as might happen in the classes of humanities or rhetoric. Then, he must give a brief summary of the main argument, and, when it proves necessary, its connections with what happened or was argued before. Then he reads the text in detail, and pauses after each sentence in order to clarify the vocabulary, to show the connections between each moment of the text, or to paraphrase an obscure meaning, either in Latin, or in the vernacular. If in the vernacular, the original order of the sentences must be kept as much as possible, so that the student's ear gets accustomed to the Latin rhythm. Finally, he starts reading the text again and comments upon it according to the class to which he is lecturing.[10] These comments can be more or less copious: in the grammar class, they will concentrate on the linguistic features of the text studied; in the humanities class, they will study a stylistic, generic, or argumentative feature and how this functions in different authors. In the rhetoric class, they will concentrate on the principles of eloquence and their productiveness, and make reference to different theoretical authorities.

In Group A, some variants appear between the 1569 and 1615 editions, which betray different pedagogical ideas about authorities. In the 1569 text, authorities are used only as examples, whereas, in the 1615 text, they also provide references for further readings of the classical, theoretical texts. In this respect, the 1569 edition seems to be designed for the humanities class, whereas the 1615 edition would be fit for the rhetoric class. The 1569 edition makes a clear distinction between theory and examples. Principles are highlighted by argumentative markers without full references in one mar-

---

[8] Quotations from poetry in the 1569 editions include: Virgil, Ovid and Horace to illustrate the *a minoribus ad majora* comparison. They are the same in the 1615 version, although the Virgilian quotation is shorter.

[9] Prose quotations in the 1615 edition are purely Ciceronian. The rhetorical terminology of comparisons (*comparatio minimorum, majorum, parium*) and the definition of the *parium comparatio* are borrowed from Aristotle's *Topica* and the *Partitiones oratoriae*. Out of six prose quotations, three are from the *Pro Archia*, one from the *In Verrem*, one from the *Philippicae orationes*, and one from the *De provinciis consularibus oratio*.

[10] See E. Gil, ed., *El Systema educativo de la compania de Jesus: la 'Ratio studiorum'* (Madrid, 1992), pp. 196-198, *Regula* 27.

gin; examples illustrating each specific definition are referred to authorities in the other margin. References to theoretical authorities are deemed unnecessary to the teacher, and irrelevant to the student; this is why it would seem reasonable to infer that this textbook was meant for the humanities class.[11] Marginal glosses as argumentative markers provide the theoretical skeleton of a *praelectio* for the teacher and a clear summary that can help the student in memorising it,[12] whereas references to Latin poetry and Ciceronian speeches point towards further reading, through which students can improve their linguistic and stylistic command of good Latinity.[13]

The 1615 edition, on the other hand, exhibits a more comprehensive conception of authorities: they can be either theoretical or illustrative, as the marginal glosses show. Theoretical references indicate that the teacher is meant to comment on the principles of rhetoric and to compare different rhetorical conceptions, or that the pupil can read the treatises referred to. Marginal glosses point towards further reading of not only standard paradigms of good Latinity, but also theoretical paradigms of eloquence. In this respect, this edition seems designed for the rhetoric class.

Thus the material space of the book reveals different levels of integration of topics as authorities, depending on pedagogical needs. In the humanities class, the student is meant to become familiar with the standards of classical Latin and culture by reading the great speeches of Cicero, or the works of the great poets. In the rhetoric class, he must grasp the principles of Latin eloquence by investigating the theoretical treatises. This pedagogical structure underlines the specific nature of the progress from one class to another, towards a greater theoretical complexity, that characterises the Jesuit system of education.

1.2 Group B: the 'De arte' in the Jesuit curriculum: abiding by the rules of the 'Ratio studiorum'

In Group B as in Group A, examples taken from prose are integrated typographically in the main text, whereas examples taken from poetry are isolated from the main text, and placed in italic font. Moreover; the main text and the system of references in marginal glosses remain the same in both groups.

---

[11] In Group A and B, all the editions consulted were in a handy in-8 or even in-12 format, and bound in parchment. We can assume that they were owned by students (see notes 13 and 21 below).

[12] The *summae* of Group C seem to be designed for the same mnemonic purposes.

[13] The 1573 edition confirms this hypothesis: a continuous flow of interlinear manuscript glosses appears to be the notes taken by the student during the *praelectio*.

However, Group B differs from Group A in two important regards: the selection of examples is quite different, and argumentative markers in the form of marginal glosses disappear.

Group B reflects the influence of the *Ratio studiorum* on Jesuit pedagogy: the *Ratio* 'freezes' the *De arte* in one authoritative version that is meant as a starting-point for a *praelectio* and can no longer function as a standalone textbook. All the editions consulted belong to the first half of the seventeenth century, when the regulations of the 1599 *Ratio studiorum* were deeply entrenched in Jesuit schools throughout Europe. John Perpinian, who corrected the text, had taken part in the elaboration of the *Ratio*. The amendments to the *De arte* match the regulations of the *Ratio*, while the *Ratio* does confer on the *De arte* the status of a pedagogical authority, meant to be used mainly in the humanities and rhetoric classes.[14] We will see that Group B seems particularly suitable for the rhetoric class. This interplay between abiding by the rules and granting authority justifies the immutability of the *De arte* and defines the new shape of the material space of the book in Group B.

First, the influence of the *Ratio* is demonstrated in the marginal references to authorities. Quintilian as a theoretical authority disappears, in accordance with rules one and six of the professor of rhetoric in the *Ratio*. The only authorities mentioned regarding precepts of rhetoric are Cicero and Aristotle. Aristotle can supplement Cicero if necessary; but the main source remains Cicero:

> *Praecepta, etsi undique peti et observari possunt, explicandi tamen non sunt in quotidiana praelectione, nisi rhetorici Ciceronis libri, et Aristotelis tum Rhetorica, si videbitur, tum Poetica.*[15]

> As far as the rules are concerned, even though one can point them out in every text, they must not be explained in the everyday lecture, except for the books of Cicero and either Aristotle's *Rhetoric* or, if it seems fit, his *Poetics*.

Moreover, new Ciceronian examples are added in the main text. In terms of Latinity, Cicero is the paradigm advertised by the *Ratio*. In every class, the first hour of the morning is a recitation taken from Cicero, as the second rule organising every class illustrates. The first rule of each *gradus* defines the texts to be studied and used, and calls for a strict Ciceronianism:

---

[14] The *De arte* is referred to as 'Cypriani Summa'. See Gil, *El Systema educativo*, p. 175, *Regula* 13; p.197, *Regula* 29, *praelectio praeceptorum*; p. 222, *Regula* 1, *Gradus*; p. 224, *Regula* 2, *Divisio temporis*, etc.

[15] Gil, *El Systema educativo*, p. 210, *Regula* 1, *Gradus*. My transl.

Stylus (quamquam probatissimi etiam historici et poetae delibantur) ex uno fere Cicerone sumendus est; et omnes quidem eius libri ad stylum aptissimi, orationes tamen solae praelegendae, ut artis praecepta in orationibus expressa cernantur.[16]

Regarding style, although the most excellent historians and poets are also considered, it must be selected almost exclusively from Cicero. Moreover, although his books are all perfectly fit for the learning of style, one will lecture only on his orations, so that the rules of the art will be understood as they are expressed in orations.

Yet, in the humanities class, remarkable lines from poets may be quoted for their stylistic qualities, and historians may be referred to for the purpose of erudition: this justifies the three poetry quotations in both Group A and B. It would, in any case, seem difficult to escape poetry when dealing with the highly poetic locus of comparison.[17]

Although the *De arte* is mentioned in the *Ratio* as a source to be used from the superior class of grammar to the class of humanities and rhetoric,[18] it seems that the texts of Group B are particularly suitable for the class of rhetoric. The *Ratio* mentions the Ciceronian texts to be used as examples in each class: they are to be of increasing complexity. The student will start in the grammar class by reading the letters and private correspondence.[19] In

---

[16] Gil, *El Systema educativo*, p. 210, *Regula* 1, *Gradus*.

[17] Gil, *El Systema educativo*, p. 210, *Regula* 1, *Gradus*: *Ad cognitionem linguae, quae in proprietate maxime et copia consistit, in quotidianis praelectionibus explicetur; ex oratoribus unus Cicero iis fere libris, qui philosophiam de moribus continent; ex historicis Caesar, Salustius, Livius, Curtius, et si qui sunt similes; ex poetis praecipue Virgilius, exceptis Eclogis et quarto Aeneidos; praeterea odae Horatii selectae, item elegiae, epigrammata et alia poemata illustrium poetarum antiquorum* ('For the purpose of language acquisition, which consists mainly of propriety and rhetorical abundance, the following authors shall be explained in daily lectures: among orators, only Cicero, particularly in his books dealing with ethics; among historians, Caesar, Sallust, Livy, Curtius, and others like them; among the poets, Virgil mainly, except for the *Eclogues* and the fourth book of the *Aeneid*, then selected *Odes* from Horace, also elegies, epigrams and other poems from the most brilliant (famous) ancient poets').

[18] See L. J. Flynn, 'Sources and influences of Soarez' *De arte rhetorica*', *The Quarterly Journal of Speech* 43 (1957), pp. 257-265, for a survey of the pedagogical uses of the *De arte* according to the class. Book III is a reference for the second semester of the superior class of grammar. Book I is a core reference for the class of rhetoric.

[19] Gil, *El Systema educativo*, p. 232, *Regula* 1, *Gradus*: *Quod ad lectiones pertinet, ex oratoribus quidem explicari poterunt primo semestri gravissimae quaeque Ciceronis ad Familiares, ad Atticum, ad Quintum fratrem epistolae, altero vero liber de*

the humanities class, the *Ratio* specifies the *Pro Archia*.[20] Finally, in the rhetoric class, Cicero's speeches should be studied in order to see how the precepts of eloquence are put into practice. In Group A, the Ciceronian examples are suitable for the humanities class; the *Pro Archia* is pervasive. In Group B, only political speeches (the *In Catilinam* and *In Verrem*) are chosen. Although no specific Ciceronian speech is mentioned in the *Ratio* for the rhetoric class, the examples chosen are taken from texts that do show eloquence put into action. The *Pro Archia* is a nationalistic defence of poetry; it turns out to be a defence of the liberal arts and of eloquence itself. However, this is not the case for the *In Catilinam* and *In Verrem*: rediscovering the rules of eloquence at work behind them implies a greater mastery of the system of precepts in question, and a greater capacity for abstraction.

Finally, the system of marginal glosses also changes. One can understand this feature as a sign that the *De arte* is no longer meant to be a standalone textbook; it needs to be supplemented by other pedagogical techniques as part of the Jesuit pedagogical framework. Marginal glosses as argumentative markers disappear in group B, but the system of authoritative references becomes more accurate; references to a Ciceronian text refer to the chapter or the section in question by means of numbers. These features and the disappearance of the systematic pattern in the main text (definition + quotation + explanatory paraphrase) show a greater integration of the pedagogical techniques and tools of the Jesuit system. Indeed, the *De arte* of Group B does not stand by itself, and could not be memorised as such. It does, however, still provide a good skeleton for a teacher to prepare a *praelectio*. Moreover, a conceptual, alphabetical index of the *rerum memorabilium* is found systematically at the end of the book, whereas it only appears in one edition – 1615 – in Group A. The presence of this index, the replacement of full quotations by summarised references, and the disappearance of the argumentative markers accompanying the main text imply

---

Amicitia, de Senectute, Paradoxa, et alia huiusmodi ('Regarding the content of lectures, in the first semester, the teacher will explain on the one hand some of Cicero's most important letters to his friends, to Atticus, to his brother Quintus, but also his essays *On Friendship*, *On Old Age*, *Stoic Paradoxes*, and others of the same kind').
[20] Gil, *El Systema educativo*, p. 210, *Regula 1, Gradus: Praeceptorum rheticae brevis summa ex Cypriano, secundo scilicet semestri, tradetur; quo tempore, omissa philosophia Ciceronis, faciliores aliquae eiusdem orationes, ut pro lege Manilia, pro Archia, pro Marcello, ceteraeque ad Caesarem habitae sumi poterunt* ('The short digest of Cyprian's *De Arte* concerned with the rules of rhetoric shall be dealt with during the second semester. During that time, one will put aside Cicero's philosophical texts and will be able to summarise some of his easier orations, such as the *Pro lege Manilia*, *Pro Archia*, *Pro Marcello*, and all the remaining ones addressed to Caesar'). This 'short digest' is likely to be the *summa* of Group C.

that the student must have used the *De arte* as a propaedeutic tool, as a source for references, and as a skeletal framework which he would have filled in with the notes taken during the class, and from his own readings of Cicero's works.[21]

2. Teaching authorities: epistemological and political choices

2.1 Rhetoric and dialectic: the epistemological choice of Aristotle

In this section, I will focus on the Jesuit teaching of topics as authorities: what ancient sources are selected, and why? In Groups A and B, a prologue or *proemium* explains the goal of the *De arte*, and justifies its selection and editing of ancient sources.

This prologue defines a good education as the reading of the best authors. It uses the figure of Demosthenes. The great orator was a disciple of Aristotle, the great philosopher and himself disciple of Plato. This lineage asserts the connection between philosophy and eloquence, *ratio* and *oratio*, on the one hand, and establishes Aristotle as the true heir and perfector of philosophy on the other. This rationalist praise of rhetoric culminates in a lengthy celebration of the ability of reason to traverse the treasures of Nature, whilst eloquence polishes and organises this rational harvest of marvels:

> *Nam primo terram pervagata [ratio]? non modo eius forma, situm, foecunditatem, sed eorum etiam, quae in ea gignuntur, varietatem, usum naturamque cognovit. Tum mare ingressa profundum et immensum, quot genera quamque disparia degentium in eo belluarum investigavit? Ex in siderum ornatum, et pulchritudinem admirans, cognito prius aere, et his, quae ex eo generantur, in coelum usque penetravit. In quibus rebus tam multis, tam variis, tam disjunctis, tam abditis adque obscuris investigandis si tanta fuit rationis sagacitas, et solertia; in expolienda oratione, quae eius comes, et interpres est, non minori profecto fuit culpa.*[22]

---

[21] This practice, which could already account for the manuscript gloss in the 1573 edition from Group A (mentioned in note 13 above), seems to have become a pedagogical requirement in Group B. This practice can be read diachronically, as the result of a more mature and complex conception of the relation between textbooks and teaching in the evolution of Jesuit pedagogy; it can also be read synchronically, in that a greater autonomy is expected from the pupil in the rhetoric class than in the grammar or humanities classes. For the historian, these books are a reminder that the material remnants are only traces of actual practices we know little about.

[22] C. Soarez, *De arte* (Seville, 1569), *proemium*, n. pag., 4ᵛ (my transl.).

Indeed, did not reason first traverse the world? Not only did it comprehend the world's foundation and fruitfulness from its design, but also the variety, usefulness and essence of all those which are born within this design. Once reason delved into the depths of the immense sea, how numerous and varied the species of beasts living there did it discover? Then once air – and what is born from it – was known, reason, marvelling at the fine apparel and beauty of the stars, entered as far as the heavens. Although the acuteness of reason alone, and its skilfulness, were responsible for the discovery of so many, varied, remote and secret things, nevertheless the polishing was indeed the action of oration, reason's comrade and interpreter.

One possible source and subject of eloquence in this extract is knowledge of the natural world, that is, natural philosophy.[23] In this respect, the extract conforms to the Aristotelian definition, in the *Topica*, of a dialectical use of topics as places of argument (commonplaces). Places of argument provide the premises of syllogisms that deal with probable matters, that is, the human world of praxis, but also the very premises or axioms underpinning each discipline of knowledge, which cannot be proven.[24] Not only does this *proemium* assert the strong connections between rhetoric and philosophy, it also rebuilds the architectonics of Aristotelian knowledge, and demonstrates the epistemologically conservative choices of the Company in this area. The organisation of Jesuit textbooks, especially those on Aristotle,[25] shows the influence of the strong logical framework of the *modus parisiensis* on their pedagogy, and connects them to neo-scholasticism. Topics play a major role in this process. Although Aristotle is not directly present in the main text of the *De arte*, he remains the overarching epistemological authority, mediated through Cicero's theoretical treatises on oratory. In Group A, Aristotelianism appears in the very order of the main text and the argumentative mark-

---

[23] The uses of this resource for pulpit eloquence are made clear by the Jesuit Binet's *Essay des merveilles de Nature et des plus nobles artifices* (Paris, 1620). Not only is this text a glittering miscellany designed to nourish Court eloquence; it is also an encyclopaedia. See M. Fumaroli, *L'Age de l'éloquence: rhétorique et 'res litteraria' de la Renaissance au seuil de l'âge classique* (Geneva, 2002), pp. 264-273.

[24] See Aristotle, *Topica*, transl. E. M. Forster (London, 1960), I. 11. 104b1-18 (p. 277).

[25] The main text in Greek runs alongside the Latin translation, followed by the scholastic *quaestiones* and *responsiones*. On the scholastic practice of disputation, see O'Malley, *The First Jesuits*, p. 217; L. Lukács, ed., *Monumenta paedagogica Societatis Jesu*, VII, *Collectanea de Ratio studiorum, 1586-1616* (Rome, 1992), pp. 461-462: in the letter entitled *Acta visitionis collegiorum*, points 13 to 17 deal with the practice of disputation in metaphysics, logic, and physics in the Parisian colleges.

ers that underline it. This order is deduced from the concept of definition.[26] Aristotelian logic also governs the theoretical definition of comparison, identifying it as a genre that subsumes three different species. These heavily scholastic and logical definitions of 'definition' and 'similitude' are inherited from a medieval tradition of dialectic, and mapped onto the rhetorical teaching of the Jesuits. There is no such feature in Talon's *Rhetorica*: dialectic is made distinct from rhetoric, and rhetoric deals only with *elocutio* and *pronuntiatio*. Comparison, in this respect, is not a trope, but a logical pattern whose definitions and species appear in Ramus's *Dialectique*.[27] This difference in the location of the commonplace 'from comparison' reveals other disciplinary boundaries at work in the formation of knowledge, as well as the Aristotelian orthodoxy that governs Jesuit ideology.[28] Marc Fumaroli has studied the ideological implications of such choices in respect of religious eloquence. By once more tying rhetoric to dialectic, the Jesuits justify the claim of rhetoric to deal with truth and cleanse it from the accusation of decadent sophistry. This position justifies the use of rhetorical devices in Christian eloquence, and serves to legitimate the claim that there is an historical continuity between ancient and Christian eloquence.[29]

---

[26] Definition is a major concept of the *Organon*. It is one of the fundamental categories in the logical toolkit set up prior to the theory of syllogism in the treatises of the *Categories* and *On Interpretation*. It is also made distinct from demonstration in the *Posterior Analytics*. Finally, it is a topic, or a place of argument in the *Topica*. In this case, the place 'from definition' is a label for a series of logical rules of inference in debate, all of which are means of defining: from the individual to the species and the genus (definition by specific difference of definition proper), from the name to its referent (definition of the name), from essential and inessential qualities (definition as description, the humanistic favourite). On these inferences, see Aristotle, *Topica*, I. 5. 101b37-102a31 (pp. 280-285).

[27] P. Ramus, *Dialectique, 1555: un manifeste de la Pléiade*, ed. N. Bruyère (Paris, 1996), p. 34.

[28] It is also worth noting that, on these grounds, Soarez's *proemium* concentrates on the rational dimension of rhetoric as the polished form of order, whereas Talon's initial definition of rhetoric privileges its expressive, emotive powers: the first authority that comes to his mind regarding the power of rhetoric is Plato. See O. Talon, *Audomari Talaei Rhetorica, e P. Rami (...) praelectionibus observata et libris duobus divisa* (Paris, 1572), chapt. 1 (*Quid Rhetorica?*), p. 5. Dialectic in the Ramist scheme is a discipline that deals with truth and the *res* of discourse, whereas rhetoric deals with the ability to exercise persuasion and with the *verba* of discourse: it can be sophistry.

[29] See A. Moss, chapter in this volume, pp. 1-17 (pp. 5-6): Zwinger's relocation of the place 'from simile' within dialectic seems to have had the same purpose. As a logical pattern, similitude deals with the question of truth and cannot be reduced to a rhetorical ornament.

2.2 Preaching through examples

We saw that the *Ratio studiorum* concentrated on the importance of getting
the pupil's ear accustomed to the rhythm of Latin sentences. Following this
line, the prefatory letter to the *De arte* celebrates the power of eloquence.
The intromission of representations (*species*) through the listener's ear has
an impact on his soul: it brings solace to the afflicted (*moerentes consolen-
tur*), it raises drowsy minds (*torpentes excitet*), and gives strength to the de-
pressed (*afflictos erigat*).[30] Eloquence is fit for the ear. It might be relevant
to note at this stage that, in his chapter on metaphor, a trope that bears structural features in common, though in a different domain, with the commonplace of comparison, Talon draws attention to its visual power, and asserts
the pre-eminence of the sense of sight over the sense of hearing.[31] Two different conceptions of how the effectiveness of eloquence is put into action
appear here. Indeed, references to classical poetry in the *De comparatione*
are justified by the highly poetic dimension of this very place of argument.
The rhetorical quality of these lines also derives, however, from their
rhythm: they are meant to be recited and listened to. The auditory marvel
that eloquence performs is at work in classical poetry, but also in preaching:
the theme of consolation in the extract that we have just discussed points
towards the Christian use of eloquence. The prefatory letter asserts this continuity between classical and Christian eloquence by reading the classical
heritage retrospectively in a way that justifies censorship: just as a vine
needs to be cut back in order to produce better grapes, so ancient sources
must be 'cleansed' of their heresies and lustful, immoral aspects. Indeed,
the letter ends with vibrant praise of Christian eloquence, and finally asserts
the goal of Jesuit rhetoric, that is, preaching. Christian eloquence, whose
dissemination is essential, performs a truly religious function: by celebrating God, it binds the human community to itself and to its Creator.

> (…) *continuo existet illa divina et coelestis Christianae eloquentiae pulchri-
> tudo, quae tanto erit praeclara magis, et eximia quanto diligentius ad omnium
> hominum utilitatem conferetur et ad laudes celebrandas Dei. Opt. Max qui
> sermonem homini dedit ad societatem, et conjunctionem cum hominibus tuen-
> dam.*[32]

---

[30] See C. Soarez, *De arte* (Seville, 1569), *proemium*, n. pag., 4^v.
[31] Talon, *Rhetorica*, chapt. 6 (*De metaphora*), p. 39.
[32] Soarez, *De arte* (Seville, 1569), *proemium*, n. pag., 6^r.

This divine and celestial beauty of Christian eloquence shall persist for ever, and shall be all the more splendid, and excellent, that it shall contribute more diligently to the usefulness of all men and to the celebration of God's praises, He who gave speech to man in order to protect the association and alliance between men.

The oral, rhythmical dimension of eloquence, the continuity between the ancient and the Christian tradition, as well as the long history of the use of the place 'from simile' in preaching,[33] justify the choice of two poetic extracts in the *De comparatione*. The quotation from Ovid is excerpted from the *Remedia amoris*.[34] The poet's interlocutor is advised to leave Rome, and stay away from love, however painful it might be to do so. The comparison draws attention to the question of saving one's soul rather than one's body: we are ready to endure pain to save our body, but we will not tolerate any pain to save our souls, although it is more important than our body. This would fit perfectly into a Christian exhortation on the topic of salvation. In the same way, the first poetic quotation from Virgil[35] delivers a Christian lesson: God, through death, puts an end to the most severe pain. Jesuit preaching starts at school, by directing the pupil's attention to religious topics through references to ancient sources. Indeed, the topic of preparing for one's death and salvation was at the core of the French conciliar decrees on funeral orations.[36]

2.3 *Ciceronianism in prose examples and the significance of the variants between Groups A and B*

All the prose examples in the *De comparatione* are taken from Cicero. This is no surprise in a textbook of rhetoric: the *aetas Ciceroniana* described by Fumaroli crossed every religious, geographical, and social boundary during the period. Although the interpretation of Ciceronian rhetoric in relation to philosophy, politics, and sacred eloquence is constrained by this system of boundaries, the very polemics about it bear witness to a consensus about the

---

[33] See Moss, chapter in this volume, pp. 1-17. The culture of commonplaces draws upon and rejuvenates the use of similitude in pulpit oratory: 'Commonplace books of similitudes quoted from the Bible and from ancient and more recent authors arranged them under moral and doctrinal heads recommended to preachers. Catholic printers recycled medieval collections of similitudes, originally designed for a very different preaching method, but supplying a vast repertoire of similes' (p. 11).

[34] See Ovid, *Remedia amoris* (Leipzig, 1907), p. 253, ll. 229-30.

[35] See Virgil, *Aeneis* (Leipzig, 1895), p. 228 (I. 195).

[36] See Bayley, *French Pulpit Oratory*, p. 45.

validity of the Ciceronian model of good Latinity for those embarking on
the school curriculum.

The prefatory celebration of eloquence as the common, rational shaping
of knowledge, its initial definition (*Dicere est ornate, graviter et copiose
loqui*),[37] and the habitual references to the *De oratore*, allow us to understand the Jesuit conception of Ciceronianism as a well-balanced eclecticism
relying on solid erudition on the one hand, and a sense of the power of verbal ornament on the other.

This conception accounts for the selection of examples in Group A.
Quotations from poetry are followed by references to the *Pro Archia*. In this
speech, Cicero is defending the case of a Greek immigrant threatened with
the loss of the Roman citizenship he had been endowed with several years
previously: to Cicero, Archias is a true Roman, because he is one of the best
contemporary poets in the Latin language. Cicero thereby asserts the importance of the liberal arts for the formation of a good Roman *humanitas*. In
winning this trial, Cicero achieved in politics what he had wanted to achieve
in philosophy and rhetoric, namely the assimilation of Hellenism by Roman
culture in order to define a new *Romanitas*. The *De comparatione* stages
this debate anew in the educational arena: ancient, pagan sources can be
profitably assimilated within both a Christian – we saw how the quotations
from Ovid and Virgil could be easily Christianised – and a national culture.
Indeed, adaptation to national particularisms and use of the vernacular are
part of the Jesuits' requirements.[38]

References to the *Pro Archia* disappear in Group B, where they are replaced by prominent references to the *In Verrem* and *In Catilinam*. My explanation of this phenomenon will necessarily be hypothetical in nature,
since the ideological reading of topics as authorities, even when they are
studied in context, cannot freeze them into a fixed interpretation;[39] what is
more, my identification of the editions of Group B is as yet incomplete. The
facts are as follows: all the Group B editions consulted so far are French
(Rouen, Romain de Bauvais, 1614; Paris, Cramoisy, 1630; Rouen, 1633;
Aquitaine, 1641; Lyon, *s.d.*). Their text is the Roman version of the *De arte*,
amended in 1564 by John Perpinian, whose career as a Jesuit had led him
from Rome to France (Paris and Lyon). He specialised in both secular and
religious oratory: his *Orationes duoveginti* were reprinted several times.
They include funeral orations, *encomia*, and five polemics against Protes-

---

[37] See C. Soarez, *De arte* (Seville, 1569), *proemium,* n. pag., 4ʳ.
[38] See O'Malley, *The First Jesuits*, pp. 201-239.
[39] The hermeneutic plasticity of topics is part of their very definition, as Ann Blair
has shown in the case of Jean Bodin. See A. Blair, *The Theater of Nature: Jean
Bodin and Renaissance Science* (Princeton, 1997).

tantism. He was a friend of the French humanist Marc-Antoine Muret,[40] who taught Aristotle's *Nicomachean Ethics* in Rome between 1563 and 1565. Fumaroli has emphasised the importance of Muret in what he calls the second Ciceronian Renaissance.[41] Muret underlined the Ciceronian link between philosophy and eloquence, asserting the unity of classical and secular eloquence. He defined secular eloquence in terms of written, attic Ciceronianism: an *ars scribendi* that belongs to the prince and defines the specific media of communication used by those in power. This last point is crucial: with Muret, the Ciceronian model of secular eloquence is tied to the political order of absolutism.

I would like to argue that it is this model, particularly well suited to the political situation of the Jesuits in France, that accounts for the variations in the Ciceronian examples used in Groups A and B of the *De arte*. Since 1577, the Sorbonne had denied degrees in philosophy and theology to any pupil educated in a Jesuit school. Rhetoric, and secular rhetoric designed for a lay public, therefore became the main subject in which the Jesuits could assert their pedagogical mastery. This mastery had long been challenged by the *Parlements* and the Sorbonne: when they tried to establish themselves in France in the 1560s, Jesuits faced Gallican diffidence towards a religious order of Spaniards, bound by a special vow to the Pope, and perceived as a threat to the absolute royal authority.[42] The Jesuit defence was therefore to assert their loyalty to the absolute power of the King of France, be it Henry IV, who never forgot that some Jesuits had belonged to the Catholic League, or to Louis XIII. In this respect, the quotations from the *In Verrem* and *In Catilinam* assert this loyalty and give a lesson in civic education to the Jesuits' pupils. Both speeches are fierce denunciations of betrayals of the State: Verres embodies personal greed in conflict with the interests of the State, whereas Catilina is the archetype of the conspirator. The Group B editions seem to have targeted a readership consisting of the sons of the *no-*

---

[40] See Backer, *Bibliothèque des écrivains de la Compagnie de Jésus*, VI, pp. 547-551. Here is the biographical note on Perpinian: 'Il brilla à Coimbre et à Rome par ses leçons d'éloquence, à Lyon et à Paris par ses explications de l'Ecriture Sainte. Il mourut à Paris, le 28 octobre 1566, et sa mort fut regardée comme une grande perte pour les lettres. Il se fit admirer, dit De Thou (...) par deux grandes lumières de leur temps, Marc-Antoine Muret et Paul Manuce'. In 1572, Perpinian's discourse on eloquence was printed along with Muret's works on that topic. Part of the correspondence between the two men was printed in Lyon in 1604 by Pillehotte.

[41] Fumaroli, *L'Age de l'éloquence*, pp. 162-172.

[42] On the political difficulties of the Jesuits in France and their strategy of epideictic celebration of the King as a sign of loyalty, see Fumaroli, *L'Age de l'éloquence*, pp. 232-246; A. Scaglione, *The Liberal Arts and the Jesuit College System* (Philadelphia, 1986), p. 111.

blesse de robe and the *noblesse d'épée*: Cramoisy, who produced the 1630 Paris edition, was the official printer for the Jesuits in Paris,[43] printing works of erudition from, as well as the textbooks for, the Collège de Clermont, which had been reopened by Louis XIII in 1618. This college welcomed the sons of both the *noblesse d'épée*, which followed the injunctions of the King and the Court, and the *noblesse de robe*, which was susceptible to the style of the Court on the one hand, and the rigour of Jesuit erudition on the other.[44] We can assume that Group B stems from this Parisian edition: the prefatory letter from the printer that announces a systematic edition of Cicero's works is repeated in the 1633, 1641, and the undated editions. The Rouen editions, both prior and posterior to the Cramoisy edition, targeted the students of the important Jesuit college in the city, which welcomed the children of the nobility and also of the rising bourgeoisie. The same ethic is thus taught to the children of social actors who challenged or could challenge the absolute power of the King. The variations in the quotations from Cicero found in the texts of Group A and Group B could therefore be accounted for as revealing the specificity of the Jesuit political position in France. Confined to the education of a lay public and specialising in the teaching of rhetoric, they made a political use of their educational mandate, playing their part in the establishment of an absolute monarchy that was attempting to assert its power vis-à-vis the two social categories that had already risen against it at the time of the League, and would do so again in 1649, during the *Fronde*.

In studying how the Jesuits taught topics, both as commonplaces and as authorities, in the *De arte*, we become aware that they are used as the means of articulating an epistemological position grounded in ideology: by spreading their conception of what rhetoric should be in relation to other disciplines, but also as a social practice, the Jesuits played their part in the development of an absolute monarchy, and of the cultural paradigm of balance and order generated by it.

---

[43] See Fumaroli, *L'Age de l'éloquence*, p. 250.
[44] *Idem*, pp. 246, 249.

APPENDICES

I. Group A: the 1569 and 1615 editions

I.a The 1569 edition (Gallica)

De comparatione. Capit. 27.

Ocus à cōparatione ſimplex
quidē eſt, ſed tripliciter tra-
ctatur: à comparatione nimirum maiorum, vel minorum,
vel parium. A comparatio-
ne maiorum ducitur argumē
tum, cum contendimus vt id,
quod in re maiori valet, valeat

Arg. à ma-
ioribus ad
minora.

RHET. LIB. A. 11

1. Æneid. Leat in minori. Virgilius.
O paſſi grauiora, dabit Deus his quoq̃ finem.
A minoribus ad maiora ducitur argumentum, vt, id
quod in minori re valet, valeat in maiori.

Arg. à mino
ribus ad ma
iora.

Ouidius.
Vt corpus redimas, ferrum patieris & ignes.
Arida nec ſitiens ora lauabis aqua.
Vt valeat animo, quicquam tolerare negabis?
At pretium pars hæc torpore mūus habet.

Et Horatius.
Vt iugulent homines, ſurgunt de nocte latrones.
Vt te ipſum ſerues, non expergiſceris?

In epiſt.
Li. 1. ad
Lollii.
In Top.

Parium autem comparatio nec elationem habet, nec
ſubmiſſionem, eſt enim æqualis. Multa autē ſunt, quæ
æqualitate ipſa comparantur, quæ ita ferè concludun-
tur, Si conſilio iuuare ciues & auxilio æqua in laude
ponendum eſt, pari gloria debet eſſe ij, qui conſulunt,
& ij qui defendunt. At quod primum & quod ſequi-
tur igitur.

Argu. à pa
ribus.

Cōſilio iu-
uabāt Iuriſ
conſulti) au
xilio Orato
res.

I.b *The 1615 edition*

Locus a comparatione simplex quidem est, sed triplicer tractatur, a comparatione nimirum maiorum vel minorum, vel parium. A comparatione maiorum dicitur argumentum cum contendimus, ut id, quod in re maiori valet, valeat in minori.	*Arg.a maioribus ad minora. InTop.Q.li.5.c10. In To Aenei. I. in ora pro Arch*
Virgilius: *O passi graviora, dabit Deus his quoque finem.*	
Ab hoc loco ducitur illud Cic. Est ridiculum, ad ea, quae habemus, nihil dicere: quaerere, quae habere non possumus: & de hominum memoria tacere, litterarum memoriam flagitare, & cum habeas amplissimi viri religionem, intergerrimi municipii jusjurandum, fidemque ea quae depravari nullo modo possunt, repudiare; tabulas, quas idem dicis solere corrumpi desiderare. Perinde enim est, atque hoc: certiora testimonia in causa habemus non sunt igitur a nobis tabulae postulandae. Idem pro eodem: Saxa, et solitudines voci respondent bestiae saepe immanes cantu flectuntur, atque consistunt: nos instituti rebus optimis, non poetarum voce moveamur? Ad minoribus ad maiora ducitur argumentum, ut id, quod in minori re valet, valeat in maiori. Cic in eadem oratione. Ergo ille corporis motu (loquitur autem de Roscio) tantum sibi amorem conciliarat a nobis omnibus: nos animorum incredibiles motus celeritatemque negligemus; idem enim est, ac si diceret: omnes Roscium Comoedum, cuius levius erat artificium magni faciebant, nos Archiam summum poetam negligemus? Idem in Anton. L. Brutus regem superbum non tulit: D. Brutus sceleratum, atque impium regnare patietur Antonium.	*In ora. Pro Arch.* *Arg a minoribus ad maiora. In topic.*
Ovidius: *Ut corpus redimas, ferrum patieris, & ignes. / Arida nec sitiens ora lavabis aqua: / Ut valeas animo, quidquam tolerare negabis: / At pretium pars hac corpore maius habet.*	
Et Horatius: *Ut iugulent homines, surgunt de nocte latrones. / Ut te ipsum serves non expergisceris*	*In epis. li.I ad Lollium*
Parium autem comparatio nec elationem habet, nec submissionem, est enim aequalis. Multa autem sunt quae aequalitate comparantur, quae ita facere concluduntur. Si consilio juvare civet, & auxilio aqua in laude ponendum est: pari gloria debent esse ii, qui consulunt, & ii, qui defendunt. Ad quod primum; & quod sequitur igitur. Huc pertinet illusd eiusdem. Cic; Si finem edicto praetoris afferunt cale. Ian. Cur non initium quoque edicti a cale. Ian. & in alia oratione; Cur eadem resp. quae me in amicos inflammare potuit, inimicis placare non possit?	*Arg. a paribus. InTop. Consilio iuvabant Iuris consulti auxilio. Orat.Act.3. De Proiscons.*

II. *Group B: the 1630 Cramoisy edition*

Locus a comparatione simplex quidem est, sed triplicer tractatur: a comparatione nimirum maiorum vel minorum, vel parium. A comparatione maiorum ducitur argumentum hoc modo: Si quod magis videtur convenire non convenit, ne id quidem quod minus: ut, non me fefellit Catilina, non modo res tanta, tam atrox, tam incredibilis, verum id quod multo magis est admirandum, dies etenim si summi viri, & clarissimi vires Saturni & Gracchorum, & Flacci, & superiorum complurium sanguine non modo se contaminarunt, sed etiam honestarunt, certe verendum mihi non erat ne quid hoc parricida civium interfecto, invidiae mihi in posteritatem redundaret.	Arist.2. Top.c.4 & 4 Rhetor. & 2.Rhet
A minoribus ad maiora ducitur argumentum hoc pacto, si quod minus videtur convenire, tamen convenit, & ergo & id quod videtur magis.	
Ovidius: *Ut corpus redimas, ferrum patieris, & igneis. / Arida vel sitiens ora lavabis aqua: / Ut valeas animo, quidquam tolerare negabis / At pretium pars hac corpore maius habet.*	
Et Horatius: *Ut iugulent homines, surgunt de nocte latrones. / Ut te ipsum serves non expergisceris*	*In epis. li.I ad Lollium*
Cicero, sicut apud majores, publice gratis coactis fabris, operisq; imperatis ex aedificari, atque effici potuit majore igitur ratione navis Cybea, & in Catil.I. Servi me hercule mei si me, &c.	
Parium autem comparatio nec elationem habet, nec submissionem: est enim aequalis. Multa autem sunt quae aequalitate ipsa comparantur, quae ita fere concluduntur. Eripuit contra Rempu. Pecunias ergo & largitus est: &, Si tibi non sicuit imperare navem Mamertinis foederatis, non licuit imperare Taurominitanis item foederatis, aut si illis iure est imperata navis etiam illis potuit im-	*2.de Or.lib.5.Verr*

III. *Group C: the Lyon summa of 1656.*

Quotuplex institui potest Comparatio? R. Triplex: Prima a maioribus: ut, *non peccarunt qui Saturninum interfecere, non ergo qui Catilinam.* Secunda a Minoribus. *Surgunt latrones ut furentur, quidni adolescentes ut studeant?* Tertio a Patribus: ut, *Virtute frater tuus excellit, cur tu quoque non excelleris?*	*Comparatio.*

THE AUTHORITY OF AUGUSTINE IN THE
EARLY REFORMATION

THE EXAMPLES OF ERASMUS AND HOOGSTRAETEN

Arnoud Visser

The significance of Augustine of Hippo for the European Reformation is almost a commonplace in the modern sense of the word: an historical truism, a scholarly cliché. Historians have long acknowledged Augustine's 'influence' over the evangelicals as 'pivotal', and described Luther's theological message as 'a new statement of Augustine's ideas on salvation'. The Catholic response to this message was no less informed by Augustinian thought, however, and in particular by his ideas about the sacraments and the unity of the church. For this reason the church historian B. B. Warfield could summarise the Reformation as the 'ultimate triumph of Augustine's doctrine of grace over Augustine's doctrine of the Church'.[1] The prominence of the Church father is reflected in the dissemination of his works in the sixteenth century. No fewer than sixteen monumental *opera omnia* editions were published, and, more significantly, he towers over all the other fathers in patristic anthologies. More than sixty percent of the quotations in these collections refer to him, or to what proved to be pseudo-Augustine.[2]

Augustine's overwhelming presence has thus created the image of a monolithic and impenetrable influence. This picture is reinforced by the use of the term 'Augustinianism'. Two decades ago, William Bouwsma famously argued that Augustinianism represented one of the two ideological faces of humanist thought, next to the Stoa.[3] In a recent study of Augustine

---

[1] A. E. McGrath, *The Intellectual Origins of the European Reformation* (Oxford, 1987), pp. 175-182; D. MacCulloch, *Reformation: Europe's House Divided 1490-1700* (London, 2003), pp. 107-114; quotation of Warfield on p. 114

[2] *Index Aureliensis: Catalogus librorum sedecimo saeculo impressorum*, part 1, I (Baden-Baden, 1966), pp. 397-445; see A. N. S. Lane, 'Justification in Sixteenth-Century Patristic Anthologies', in: L. Grane, A. Schindler, and M. Wriedt, eds, *Auctoritas Patrum: Contributions on the Reception of the Church Fathers in the Fifteenth and Sixteenth Centuries* (Mainz, 1993), pp. 69-95.

[3] W. Bouwsma, 'The Two Faces of Humanism: Stoicism and Augustinianism in Renaissance Thought', in: H. A. Oberman and T. Brady, eds, *Itinerarium italicum: The Profile of the Italian Renaissance in the Mirror of its European Transformations* (Leiden, 1975), pp. 3-60.

in the Italian Renaissance, Meredith Gill even concludes that 'the entire Renaissance program is consistent with the teachings of the Augustinian school, and its focus on Scripture, on patristics, and original sources'.[4] It is hardly surprising, then, that some have given up hope of coming to a more precise picture of Augustine's significance. In the *Oxford Dictionary of the Reformation*, for instance, the Luther expert Hans-Ulrich Delius considers it 'a moot question, for all the reformers owed an indirect debt to Augustinian traditions in ways that today can no longer be calculated'.[5]

Although in itself not untrue, Delius's sweeping remark is strangely paradoxical. If the Augustinian traditions are so difficult to trace, how do we know they are so influential? The root of the problem seems to be the quest for intellectual origins and the ensuing language of 'influence'. The example of Augustine's influence on Martin Luther, which seems to have prompted Delius's observation, is a case in point. In this case modern scholars have found it impossible to distinguish between a direct influence of Augustine's works and traces of Augustinian ideas that circulated within either the Augustinian Order, or the *schola Augustiniana moderna* in particular.[6] Detailed study has, however, led to more precise distinctions between various forms of Augustinianism. Therefore, the image of a monolithic and inscrutable influence should be resisted. In fact, the results have partly undermined the concept of influence itself. Leif Grane, for instance, has demonstrated how Luther used Augustine's works in a fragmented, highly selective way.[7] Luther did not 'faithfully follow' the church father's ideas, but selected and reshaped elements of his thought.

Moreover, in a way Delius even understates his case. It was not only reformers who used Augustine's texts; humanists and orthodox Catholics employed them to defend their own causes. In other words, the appeal to the Church father was partly a stock argument, based on a shared set of 'places' for finding arguments, commonplaces in a classical sense of the word, or *loci communes*. In classical and early modern usage, the term commonplace

---

[4] M. J. Gill, *Augustine in the Italian Renaissance: Art and Philosophy from Petrarch to Michelangelo* (Cambridge, 2005), p. 206.

[5] H. J. Hillerbrand, ed., *The Oxford Dictionary of the Reformation*, I (Oxford/New York, 1996), pp. 98-99.

[6] See P. D. Krey's entry 'Luther' in A. D. Fitzgerald, ed., *Augustine through the Ages* (Grand Rapids, MA/Cambridge, 1999), pp. 516-518; A. Beutel, ed., *Luther Handbuch* (Tübingen, 2005), pp. 45-49; a survey of relevant places is given by H.-U. Delius, *Augustin als Quelle Luthers: eine Materialsammlung* (Berlin, 1984); McGrath, *Intellectual Origins*, pp. 108-121.

[7] L. Grane, 'Augustins *Expositio quarundam propositionum ex epistola apostoli ad Romanos* in Luthers Römerbriefvorlesung', *Zeitschrift für Theologie und Kirche* 69 (1972), pp. 304-330.

could have a variety of rhetorical and philosophical senses, ranging from abstract categories to concrete, standard examples. Based on the metaphor of a physical 'place' (the Greek *topos*, and later in Latin *locus*), the term was generally meant to facilitate structuring and organising knowledge. In our analysis the concept is used to denote the system of creating arguments by means of lists of general categories. An orator dealing with a *person*, for example, could find arguments by looking at the categories of family, nationality, country, sex, age, upbringing, physical appearance, etc.

The use of Augustine by means of an explicit quotation also fits in a particular category: the commonplace of 'testimony', introducing a citation to support one's point.[8] According to rhetorical theory, the success of this appeal to external witnesses depended on authority, which in turn was forged by character or circumstance. For, as Cicero explains, 'the greatest authority belonging to nature lies in virtue; in the field of time there are many things which can confer authority: talent, power, age, one's fortune, skill, practice, necessity, occasionally also the fortuitous combination of event'.[9] What, then, does this tell us about the authority of Augustine? How could he be used for such wildly conflicting ideas?

Augustine's oeuvre provides a first explanation for his diverging reception. Apart from landmarks such as *Confessions* and *City of God*, his impressive bibliography can roughly be organised around the three major polemics in which he was involved during his life: against the Manicheans, the Donatists, and the Pelagians. The scope of Augustine's often polemical works and his intellectual development thus complicate the idea of a coherent body of thought. And yet the oeuvre alone cannot fully explain the versatility of Augustine's authority, and its use for opposite purposes and contrasting ideas. For this the readers are first responsible.

In this chapter, I want to assess the authority of Augustine in the early Reformation by investigating two examples from opposite camps. I will ar-

---

[8] See D. E. Mortensen, 'The *Loci* of Cicero', *Rhetorica* 26 (2008), pp. 31-56; F. Goyet, *Le Sublime du 'lieu commun': l'invention rhétorique dans l'Antiquité et à la Renaissance* (Paris, 1996); A. Moss, *Printed Commonplace-Books and the Structuring of Renaissance Thought* (Oxford, 1996), pp. 1-23; a seminal study for the use of the church fathers as *auctoritates* is P. Fraenkel, *Testimonia Patrum: The Function of the Patristic Argument in the Theology of Philip Melanchthon* (Geneva, 1961).

[9] *Testimonium autem nunc dicimus omne quod ab aliqua re externa sumitur ad faciendam fidem. Persona autem non qualiscumque est testimoni pondus habet; ad fidem enim faciendam auctoritas quaeritur, sed auctoritatem aut natura aut tempus affert. Naturae auctoritas in virtute inest maxima; in tempore autem multa sunt quae afferant auctoritatem: ingenium, opes, aetas, fortuna, ars, usus, necessitas, concursio, etiam non numquam rerum fortuitarum*, Cicero, *Topica*, 73, ed. and transl. T. Reinhardt (Oxford, 2003).

gue that the use of the church father was to a large extent determined by the economy of authority. This term is used to highlight the fact that Augustine's authority is not fixed, but defined by an intellectual market mechanism, something which Cicero holistically terms 'the circumstances' (*tempus*).[10] Since credibility depends on what other readers, often opponents, find acceptable, the agenda of the polemicists was largely dictated by their opponents. They indirectly guided the selection of authoritative quotations to be used as ammunition. Those who appealed to Augustine's *auctoritas* were thus not fully in control, but were merely trying to anticipate the support of their readership.[11] In other words, by looking at Augustine as a commonplace in the debate, we can better understand the versatility of his authority.

The two particular cases we are concerned with here were both composed as dialogues, published around 1520, and both fiercely polemical in tone. The well-known and well-studied *Antibarbarians* of Erasmus constitutes one of the most entertaining humanist defences of classical literature.[12] The other work, probably less entertaining even though largely concerned with the subject of 'sin', has received virtually no attention to date. It is *Colloquies with Saint Augustine* (*Cum divo Augustino colloquia*) by Jacob of Hoogstraeten, the Dominican theologian and inquisitor, best known for his involvement in the Reuchlin affair (see Ill. 1).[13]

---

[10] *Ibidem.*

[11] I prefer 'economy' to the term 'politics', since it better reflects the lack of control participants have over the power that *auctoritas* can exert.

[12] *Antibarbarorum liber*, in: K. Kumaniecki, ed., *Opera omnia Desiderii Erasmi Roterodami*, I.1 (Amsterdam, 1969); English transl. and introduction by M. Mann Philips in *The Antibarbarians*, ed. C. R. Thompson, *Collected Works of Erasmus*, XXIII (Toronto, 1978; hereafter cited as CWE 23); see also J. D. Tracy, '"Against the Barbarians": The Young Erasmus and his Humanist Contemporaries', *Sixteenth Century Journal* 11 (1980), pp. 3-22; I. Bejczy, 'Overcoming the Middle Ages: Historical Reasoning in Erasmus's Antibarbarian Writings', *Erasmus of Rotterdam Society Yearbook* 16 (1996), pp. 34-53.

[13] For Hoogstraeten (Hochstratus; Hoogstraten), see H. Peterse, *Jacobus Hoogstraeten gegen Johannes Reuchlin: ein Beitrag zur Geschichte des Antijudaismus im 16. Jahrhundert* (Mainz, 1995); P. Bietenholz and T. Deutscher, eds, *Contemporaries of Erasmus: A Biographical Register of the Renaissance and Reformation (Toronto, 1985)*, pp. 200-202; on his theological position, see two articles by S. S. Ickert, 'Defending and Defining the ordo salutis: Martin Luther vs. Jacob van Hoogstraten', *Archiv für Reformationsgeschichte* 78 (1987), pp. 81-97; idem, 'Catholic Controversialist Theology and Sola Scriptura: The Case of Jacob van Hoogstraten', *The Catholic Historical Review* 74 (1988), pp. 13-33.

Hoogstraeten and the 'Cum divo Augustino colloquia' (1521-1522)

Hoogstraeten's *Colloquies* are presented as a scholastic correction of 'the immense and evil errors of Martin Luther'.[14] The work was published in two books between 1521 and 1522, the first dedicated to the Pope (Adrian VI), the second to the Emperor (Charles V). The title of the book is slightly misleading, for two reasons: first, the reader will not find 'conversational dialogues'. Instead, Hoogstraeten's work presents somewhat static scholastic disputations (around 50 in total).[15] They take their cue from passages from Luther, which are addressed (or corrected) by means of Augustinian quotations. The closest feature to a dialogue is the presence of a pupil character (*discipulus*), who functions as an intermediary, summarising positions, and asking for further clarifications. This character is the only one who speaks. He does not address Luther directly, however, but readily exposes contradictions, errors, and lies in his conversation with Augustine. In his presentation, Hoogstraeten shows the scholastic style for which he was so viciously (and hilariously) satirised in the *Letters of Obscure Men* and other parodies, using distinctly un-ciceronian neologisms, technical terms and logical categories, etc.

Secondly, not all of the colloquies involve Augustine. In some Jerome features, and in one place Hoogstraeten even strikes up a conversation with Gregory the Great, but a more significant number present the fictional characters of 'Critobulus the Lutheran' and Atticus, the defender of scholastic theology.[16] These are based on Jerome's dialogue 'Against the Pelagians'. Significantly, Hoogstraeten declares that he uses these characters for a more

---

[14] *Ad sanctissimum dominum nostrum pontificem modernum, cuius nomen pontificale nondum innotuit, Reverendi patris, artium et sacrae theologiae professoris, atque hereticae pravitatis per Coloniens[em], Moguntinens[em], et Treverens[em], provincias Inquisitoris F. Iacobi Hochstratani, cum divo Augustino Colloquia, contra enormes atque perversos Martini Lutheri errores* (...) *pars prima cui Compendium quoddam generale praemittitur* (...) (Cologne, 1522); the second part: *Ad illustrissimum ac serenissimum principem Carolum cesarem Romanorum imperatorem et Hispaniarum regem catholicum, victorem quoque ac triumphatorem semper Augustum, Reverendi patris artium et sacrae theologiae professoris, atque haereticae pravitatis per Coloniensem, Maguntinensem et Treverensem provincias Inquisitoris Fratris Iacobi de Hochstraten cum divo Augustino Colloquia contra enormes atque perversos Martini Lutheri errores* (...) (Cologne, 1521).

[15] On the technique of disputations, see O. Weijers, *La 'Disputatio' dans les facultés des arts au moyen âge* (Turnhout, 2002).

[16] In part 2, Jerome is interlocutor in disp. 5 and 6 of book 1; Gregory is introduced in disp. 4 of book 3, and Atticus and Critobulus feature in the eight disputations of book 2, and in disputations 5-9 of book 4.

aggressive, rhetorically destructive approach to Luther's ideas, in contrast to the more constructive demonstration of the truth.

So much for the form of this work. What about the content? Part one offers a systematic, and rather repetitive refutation of Luther's conception of sin as developed in the wake of the reformer's disputation with the scholastic theologian Johannes Eck at Leipzig (June 1519). Whereas Luther thought man remained sinful even after baptism, Hoogstraeten argued that baptism completely freed man of sin. In his view, it was necessary to differentiate between different forms of sin. Primal sin (*concupiscentia*) remained present even after baptism, as a disease, or *affectio*, as Hoogstraeten has Augustine explain. Actual sin (*peccatum*) or crimes are avoidable and can be managed in different ways. All this is basically a defence of traditional scholastic approaches to the subject. The second part of the *Colloquia* covers partly the same ground, but also defends the authority of the Church, the use of indulgences, and the existence of purgatory.

To what form of reception, then, does all this lead? How is Augustine's work received in these dialogues? There are three characteristics, I believe, that typify Hoogstraeten's Augustine. First, he is a man of doctrinal discipline. Augustine is used to answer theological questions definitively. The *Colloquia* does not offer a free conversation between equals, but a confrontation with the truth. This is reflected in the works from which Hoogstraeten culled the quotations. Exegetical works and doctrinal theory dominate. We do not see the spiritual quest of the *Confessions*, or the revisionist approach of the *Retractations*.

Secondly, since it was Luther who started the problems, the Augustine lined up to refute him has distinctly Lutheran interests. Hoogstraeten makes most use of Augustine's anti-Pelagian works, where the vision of man's sinful nature and complete dependence on grace was most fully developed. This is the body of texts that is nowadays mostly associated with austere versions of Protestantism, such as Calvinism. This may seem a surprising orientation for a Catholic inquisitor. In fact, however, it is determined by the dynamics of the debate. Luther had legitimised his attacks on traditional theology with precisely these texts. Therefore, Hoogstraeten now confronts Luther with the real teachings of the Church father; the father, in fact, of Luther's own order, as Hoogstraeten subtly reminds us in the preface. Thus, reception, one might say, is Hoogstraeten's instrument to beat Luther with his own stick.

As a third characteristic, I would suggest, the dialogue with Augustine is used to woo readers who are critical about the scholastic approach. Since at this time the Reformation was still largely linked with the humanist project, Hoogstraeten realised that his opponents would not be convinced by means of traditional syllogisms. Therefore, he tries to anticipate his opponents by somewhat clumsy, but nonetheless clear references to the classical tradition. An intriguing example is Hoogstraeten's account that he was inspired to write the book by a vision, in which a 'heavenly lady' (*virgo caelestis*) appeared to him, together with Augustine himself, urging him to fight the Lutheran heresy.[17] This is strongly reminiscent of Petrarch's *Secretum*, where the persona of Francesco similarly enters into a dialogue with Augustine in the presence of Lady Truth. Other examples include the use of the title *Colloquia* several years after the first edition of Erasmus's book of the same name, the appearance of Jerome's characters Critobulus and Atticus, and occasional classical references.[18]

Erasmus and the 'Antibarbarians'

In Erasmus's *Antibarbarians*, we do not just see another Augustine, but a completely different construction of authority (see Ill. 2). Erasmus's use of Augustine here has been investigated in some detail by Charles Béné, but his conclusions are open to some revision.[19] The outline of the dialogue is perhaps familiar: Erasmus describes his encounter with four friends in an idyllic setting in Brabant. The main topic of their conversation is the decline of classical literature in their days. What 'huge disaster' (*vasta calamitas*), they wonder, could have created a situation in which 'those who are the top of learning today' are hardly a match for the 'toilet cleaners' of Antiquity, as Erasmus initially put it.[20] Several explanations are put forward: one sug-

---

[17] *Pars secunda*, dedicatory letter to the emperor, fols. A1^v-2^r.

[18] E.g. *Fulminant tonitrua, parturiunt montes, procul dubio mus nascetur exiguus* (...), *Colloquia*, pars prima, disputatio prima, fol. a2^r.

[19] C. Béné, *Erasme et saint Augustin, ou influence de saint Augustin sur l'humanisme d'Erasme* (Geneva, 1969), esp. pp. 59-87.

[20] *Antibarbari*, ed. Kumaniecki, p. 45: *Quaerebamus non sine vehementi admiratione, quae tam vasta calamitas tam uberem, tam florentem ac laetam optimarum artium frugem dissipasset; quod tam dirum et immane proluvium omnes prope veterum literas olim purissimas tam turpiter confudisset; qui fieret ut nos priscos scriptores tam immenso intervallo sequeremur, ut qui nunc doctrinae tenerent arcem, pauculis quibusdam exceptis, vix ideonei viderentur qui cum priscorum mulierculis aut pueris elementariis in palaestra literaria possent decertare, et qui nunc imperatores exercitum ducerent, apud illos ne inter gregarios quidem milites ascribi mererentur* ('[W]e tried to discover, and not without sharp wonder, what the disaster was that had swept away the rich, flourishing, joyful fruits of the finest culture, and why a tragic and terrible deluge had shamefully overwhelmed all the literature of the ancients which used to be so pure. How did it happen that there is such an enormous distance between ourselves and the writers of Antiquity; that men who are now at the summit of learning, a few only excepted, hardly seem worthy to enter the literary arena against women and children, mere beginners, of the ancient world; and that the present generals of our army would not deserve enrolment among their common

gests it is all in the stars, another sees Christianity as the cause (or at least the trigger) and a third blames it on the natural degeneration of the earth. The core of the book, however, is the contribution of the fourth character, James Batt. He argues that *ignorance* is responsible for the situation, frequently under the mask of religion. Urged on by the others, he then delivers a fully developed speech attacking the barbarians, often synonymous with scholastic theologians and the clergy. In doing so, Augustine is one of his main authorities, only surpassed by Jerome (sixteen explicit and one silent reference). The significance of these references varies. Half of them mention Augustine only briefly, as a general example of good practice. Often they are part of an enumeration.[21] The other references comprise quotations and discussions of concrete works. The most elaborate examples occur in the section entitled 'Authorities confuted with authorities', where Erasmus has Batt discuss large extracts from *De doctrina christiana*, Augustine's hermeneutical guide to the study of the Bible. These last extracts are all taken from the second book of this work. Augustine is here concerned with discussing knowledge as an instrument for spiritual growth. Erasmus lifts these quotations out of this spiritual context to employ them for his own more apologetic purposes. Béné has studied the transformation of Augustine's work in detail, and I will not present a new micro-analysis here.

Like Hoogstraeten, Erasmus thus finds support in Augustine, but he frames his authority in a very different way. In contrast to Hoogstraeten's dialogue, the *Antibarbarians* leaves much room for ambiguity. Erasmus's characterisation of Batt is a case in point. He is represented as lively, jocular, and, above all, intemperately passionate. His views are described with sympathy, but his *persona* has exaggerated, farcical features: he is said to vomit, for instance, when seeing a barbarian, and he pleads for the reintroduction of Roman laws of execution for bad teachers, involving savage torture. Batt is repeatedly teased by the other characters, including Erasmus's persona of himself. As a result, Batt has the traits of a scholarly jester, who can afford to speak with unusual candour, but whose larger-than-life personality also isolates him from reality. His clownish portrayal, to a certain extent, disarms his radical views. Identifying Batt with Erasmus, like Béné did and many others still do, disregards this ambiguity and may lead to a misplaced, essentialist quest for Erasmus's 'own' views.

---

soldiers?'). The earlier Gouda version still has the more offensive 'toilet cleaners' instead of 'women and children': (...) *vix idonei viderentur quibus olim latrine committi debuerint* (...).

[21] Such as on p. 78, l. 13; p. 85, l. 3; p. 86, l. 10; p. 97, l. 1; p. 126, ll. 22-24; p. 128, ll. 6-10, p. 128, l. 18; p. 129, l. 2; p. 130, l. 32; p. 133, ll. 27-29.

Apart from the Batt persona, the other element that creates ambiguity is the motif of rhetorical exercise. Batt's speech is not just a vehicle for communicating his views, it is a performance with a highly competitive slant. The whole exercise is repeatedly described as a battle, and Batt several times openly discusses his tactics. Just like the friends in the dialogue, the reader is invited to enjoy this rhetorical *tour de force*, without necessarily concurring with all that is said. This aesthetics clearly has a sceptical side to it, which did not escape the earliest readers either: the Parisian humanist Robert Gaguin, for instance, to whom Erasmus had sent an early version in 1495, commented that the text was not without 'fierce discussion of the type of Carneades'.[22] The most subversive product of this sceptical perspective was perhaps the lost second book of the *Antibarbarians*, consisting of an attack against literature. Apparently, it was so effective that it convinced Erasmus's English friend John Colet that he should abandon eloquence altogether, much to Erasmus's surprise.[23]

This self-consciously rhetorical setting also affects the authority of Augustine. Instead of representing truth, as he did in Hoogstraeten, the antibarbarian Augustine openly serves as a rhetorical example, selected from a host of other possibilities. So, rather than describing Augustine's role as a 'guide', 'teacher', or 'inspiration', as Béné did (p. 344), I would argue that Erasmus exploits Augustine primarily for rhetorical reasons. It is telling, for example, to see that Jerome is cited more favourably (and more frequently). Yet Batt knows that this scholarly church father carries less authority with the barbarians, 'who do not [even] count [him] among the theologians, but among the practitioners of eloquence'.[24]

Thus, despite the difference in presentation, we see an interesting parallel between Hoogstraeten and Erasmus. In both cases, the reception of the church father is largely dictated by their opponents. After Hoogstraeten's 'Lutheran Augustine', we have here Erasmus's scholastic Augustine, against whom the traditional theologians could hardly object: as Batt said, he is 'of strict conscience – not to say hyper-critical' (CWE 23, p. 94). Some citations, such as Augustine's systematic, technical classification of knowledge, are clearly meant to accommodate the scholastic mind-set. Moreover, even Batt himself flirts with scholastic methods when he compiles a *summa* of Augustine's argument, almost resembling Hoogstraeten's approach. Meanwhile, Batt's personal reservations are barely hidden: he

---

[22] Gaguin to Erasmus [October 7 (?), 1495], ep. 46, *Opus epistolarum Desiderii Erasmi Roterodami*, ed. P. S. Allen and H. M. Allen, I (Oxford 1906), ll. 30-31: *Apte componis, ornas venuste; nec deest tibi Carneadis vehemens disputatio.* Quoted by Kumaniecki, p. 10.

[23] Erasmus to John Sapidus, [c. June 1520], ep. 1110, ed. Allen, ll. 25-33.

[24] CWE 23, p. 98; Erasmus, *Antibarbari*, p. 118, ll. 14-18.

criticises Augustine's style, repeatedly calls him 'verbose', and, while quoting the church father, apologises several times for boring the audience.[25] All this, however, strengthens the rhetorical effect: for a 'barbarian', the reservation of a humanist 'poet' like Batt could only increase the church father's credibility.[26]

Connections

In her recent eye-opening study of the Latin language turn, Ann Moss noted a lack of communication between the parties of humanists and scholastic theologians around 1520. 'In dialogues of this period from Northern Europe', she writes, 'humanists and late-medieval Latin speakers tend to talk among themselves, separately'. She further illustrates this with examples of silencing tactics. Making a similar point about 'the question of authoritative prooftexts', Erika Rummel notes that the parties 'had difficulties in finding common ground'.[27] Although both dialogues were probably most convincing to their respective home-audiences, I would argue that Hoogstraeten and Erasmus show a strong sense of communication, which becomes particularly clear in their use of Augustine. True, there is a tendency to silence the opponent, and the differences in language often lead to complete misunderstanding. Still, both authors attempt to convince the opponent through the voice of Augustine.

---

[25] Erasmus, *Antibarbari*, p. 114, ll. 17-18: *Sed ne omnem disputationem, quae verbosissima est, repretam, verbis illius omissis, rei summam paucis amplectar* ('To avoid repeating the whole argument, which is a most prolix one, I will omit his actual words and sum up the whole thing briefly'; CWE 23, pp. 94-95); p. 115, ll. 5-6: *At ne (...) quidem pigebit (...) modo ne vos audire pigeat* ('I should even be ready to cite the opinion of Saint Augustine about each one of these, but you must also be willing to hear'; CWE 23, p. 95); *ibidem*, ll. 6-13: *porro quod ad dialecticen attinet (...) verbose et curiosiuscule suo more disputat* ('as to what pertains to dialectic, he argues lengthily and meticulously as usual'; CWE 23, p. 95); p. 116, ll. 4-6: *Omnes harum disputationum ambages (...) in eundem fere modo disputat (...) parvi refert meminisse* ('All the complications of the discussions he enters into in the same way (...) it is scarcely profitable to recall'; CWE 23, p. 96).

[26] The implicit reservations against Augustine match Erasmus's critical attitude towards Augustine elsewhere; see J. Chomarat, *Grammaire et Rhétorique chez Erasme* (Paris, 1981), p. 177; V. Mellinghoff-Bourgerie, 'Erasme éditeur et interprète de Saint Augustin', in: K. Flasch and D. de Courcelles, eds, *Augustinus in der Neuzeit* (Turnhout, 1996), pp. 53-81; A. Visser, 'Reading Augustine through Erasmus' Eyes: Humanist Scholarship and Paratextual Guidance in the Wake of the Reformation', *Erasmus of Rotterdam Society Yearbook* 28 (2008), pp. 67-90.

[27] A. Moss, *Renaissance Truth and the Latin Language Turn* (Oxford, 2003), p. 117; E. Rummel, *The Humanist-Scholastic Debate in the Renaissance and Reformation* (Cambridge, MA, 1995), pp. 7-8.

From a social perspective, one might add that communication could in fact hardly be avoided. Although humanists and scholastics belonged to different 'speech communities', they shared the same space. Hoogstraeten and Erasmus, for one, did communicate. In 1519, for instance, Hoogstraeten attacked Erasmus's views on divorce. Erasmus reacted with a wily letter, stressing the 'common bond of [their] professional studies' and giving advice 'with the best and most affectionate intentions'. He does not spare his criticism either. Hoogstraeten's attack was overblown, schoolmasterly, and unfair, he thinks, 'as though I were unaware of the opinions of the early fathers or the decrees of the church (...)'. He himself, he argues, '[asserted] nothing absolutely (...) I am all for discussion, I decide nothing'.[28] Later that year, Hoogstraeten visited Louvain, where Erasmus then stayed, to present the theologians there with the condemnation of Luther by the Cologne faculty of theology, but he also brought a compromising letter of Erasmus to Luther. At this time Erasmus's relationship with the Louvain theologians was problematic enough. These conflicts in fact sparked some of the most virulent attacks on the monks in the last revision of the *Antibarbarians*. In the end, Erasmus and Hoogstraeten managed to resolve their dispute, when they met in 1520.

These glimpses of the wider social context are significant for understanding the flexible reception of Augustine in the early Reformation. For although it was Augustine who offered the ideas, it was the world outside his text that determined the 'economy of authority'. From a purely intellectual perspective, it might be surprising to see Hoogstraeten's endorsement of Augustine's most 'Lutheran' side, or Erasmus's simultaneous appeal to and criticism of the bishop from Hippo. But these examples have shown that both authors were less concerned with appropriating the historical Augustine's thought than with depriving the opponent of their claim to tradition. Their selection of quotations from the Church father's vast oeuvre reveals a fragmented way of reading and writing, guided by rhetorical principles, and structured by shared categories of arguments. Although it represents only one aspect of the varied practice of commonplaces, the appeal to authority is particularly illuminating, since it reveals how the use of sources could be functional rather than ideological. As such it can help intellectual historians better to understand the contemporary conditions of these debates, as well as alert them, again, to the limitations of knotty notions of influence and intellectual ownership.

---

[28] Erasmus to Hoogstraeten, August 11, 1519, ep. 1006, *Opus epistolarum*. For an English transl. see *Collected Works of Erasmus*, VII, pp. 44-54.

1. Hans Holbein (attrib.), 'Hercules Germanicus', 1522 (Zürich, Zentralbibliothek). As an early opponent of Luther and a fierce critic of the humanist Johannes Reuchlin, Hoogstraeten was attacked by both evangelical and humanist parties. This anonymous print underlined Hoogstraeten's prominence as a defender of traditional theology. Luther is represented as Hercules, slaying his scholastic opponents (such as Aristotle, Ockham, Thomas Aquinas, Duns Scotus), while the pope is strangled by a cord Luther holds between his teeth. Hoogstraeten is the next to be beaten.

2. Portrait medal of Erasmus by Quinten Metsys, 1519 (London, British Museum). Depicted on the reverse is the boundary god Terminus, and the device *Cedo nulli* ('I yield to no-one'). This image caused controversy among Erasmus's adversaries, who saw it as a sign of arrogance.

MUSIC AS A *TOPOS* IN THE LUTHERAN CONSTRUCTION OF A CONFESSIONAL IDENTITY IN THE SIXTEENTH AND SEVENTEENTH CENTURIES

Sven Rune Havsteen

The prominent position of music in sixteenth- and seventeenth-century Lutheran culture in Northern Germany and Scandinavia is evident in the rich production of musical works and the widespread musical institutions related to the Lutheran churches and courts, such as the *Kantorei*, the organist office, and the *Hofkapelle*. This salient feature is probably associated with a basically positive attitude towards music, manifested in various ways in the theology of Lutherans and rooted in Martin Luther's (1483-1546) own thinking.[1] Luther's interest in music is reflected in his reform of the Mass, which attests to a significant awareness of the musical dimension of liturgy. This awareness was manifested not only in his concern for the musical form of the liturgical chant,[2] but also and in particular in Luther's engagement in the production of hymns[3] in the vernacular, an effort closely related to an

---

[1] See K. Honemeyer, *Luthers Musikanschauung: Studien zur Frage ihrer geschichtlichen Grundlagen* (inaugural dissertation, University of Münster, 1941), p. 8 (note). For a general introduction to Luther and his relationship to music, see also O. Söhngen, *Theologie der Musik* (Kassel, 1967), pp. 80-112; H. Guicharrousse, *Les Musiques de Luther* (Geneva, 1995); R. A. Leaver, *Luther's Liturgical Music: Principles and Implications* (Grand Rapids/Cambridge, 2007).

[2] In connection with the reform that resulted in the elaboration of a German Mass *Deudsche Messe und ordnung Gottis dienst*, in: *D. Martin Luthers Werke: kritische Gesamtausgabe* (Weimar, 1883-1948) [hereafter WA], XIX, pp. 72-541, the importance that Luther assigned to the musical aspects of liturgy is documented by the fact that he involved the professional musicians Johann Walter (1496-1570) and Konrad Rupsch (1475-1530) in assisting him. From Johann Walter's account of the collaboration, printed in Michael Praetorius, *Syntagma musicum*, I (Wittenberg, 1615; repr. Kassel, 1959), pp. 451-452, an insight is gained also into Luther's own involvement in the musical shaping of the Mass. See also F. Blume, *Geschichte der evangelischen Kirchenmusik* (Kassel, [2]1965), p. 36.

[3] Thirty-six hymns can with certainty be ascribed to Luther. The production began in 1523, culminated in 1524, and was continued on a smaller scale until the end of his life. They became immensely popular and were printed in numerous hymnals. The *Etlich Christlich lider Lobgesang un[n] Psalm dem rainen wort Gottes gemeß auß der heylige[n] schrifft durch mancherley hochgelerter gemacht in den Kirchen zu singen wie es dann [z]um tayl berayt zu Wittenberg in uebung ist* (Nuremberg,

understanding of congregational hymn-singing as a constituent part of liturgy.[4] Luther's ideas concerning the use of hymns are expressed, for instance, in a letter, probably from the end of 1523, to Georg Spalatin (1484-
1545), in which he presents the plan of creating psalms or spiritual songs in
the vernacular with the aim of propagating the word of God among the people.[5] In order to promote this propagation, we are further informed, the
hymns should be worked out in a comprehensible form, using simple, popular expressions.[6] In the preface to the so-called *Walter Choir Book*[7] of 1524,
where twenty-four of his hymns were printed, Luther points to the purpose
of writing hymns, stating that they contribute to the 'noising' and 'spreading abroad of the holy gospel'.[8] Luther's hymns were widely distributed and
printed in numerous hymnals throughout his life, and also became an important component of later hymnals within the Lutheran denomination.[9]
Even though it has not been entirely clarified to what extent Luther's ideas
of congregational hymn-singing were realised in practice, the role of hymns
in the first stage of the Reformation is notable, and has led scholars to describe the Reformation movement as a singing movement, an observation
based on historical records that present the singing of the Lutheran hymns

---

1523-1524; repr. Kassel, 1957), the so-called *Achtliederbuch* was the first, with four
Luther hymns, originally published as one-sheet prints, among them the well-known
Nun freut euch liben Christ gmein and *Aus tiefer Not schrei ich zu dir*. See, further,
Blume, *Geschichte*, pp. 22-27.

[4] See, further, W. Blankenburg, 'Der gottesdienstliche Liedgesang der Gemeinde',
in: K. F. Müller and W. Blankenburg, eds, *Leiturgia: Handbuch des evangelischen
Gottesdienstes*, IV: *Die Musik des evangelischen Gottesdienstes* (Kassel, 1961),
pp. 560-659; Blume, *Geschichte*, pp. 38-68.
[5] *Consilium est, exemplo prophetarum et priscorum partum ecclesiae psalmos ver-
naculos condere pro vulgo, id est spirituales cantilenas, quo verbum Dei vel cantu
inter populos maneat*, in: WA, XXXV, p. 73.
[6] *Ibidem*.
[7] The *Geystliche gesangk Buchleyn* (Worms, [2]1525; repr. Kassel, 1979) was printed
in Wittenberg, with polyphonic musical settings by Johann Walter.
[8] 'Dem nach hab ich auch, sampt ettlichen andern, zum gutten anfang und ursach
zugeben die es besser vermügen, ettliche geystliche lieder zusamen bracht, das heylige Evangelion, so itzt von Gottes gnaden wider auff gangen ist, zu treyben und
schwanck zu bringen', *Vorrhede D. Martini Luthers*, in: WA, XXXV, p. 474; transl.
in *Luther's Works*, LIII (*Liturgy and Hymns*), ed. U. S. Leupold (Philadelphia,
1965), p. 316.
[9] The so-called Klug hymnal, *Geistliche lieder auffs new gebessert* (Wittenberg,
[2]1533; repr. Kassel, 1983), authorised by Luther, and published by the printer Joseph Klug, contained a number of his hymns and became a paradigm for the Lutheran hymnal. See further Blume, *Geschichte*, pp. 27-32.

as an important way of manifesting and promoting the evangelical faith in the struggle with the Roman Catholic Church and its representatives.[10]

As music or singing was an important theological issue in the view of Luther and his followers, its liturgical use occasioned reflections that formed what could be called a theological discourse accompanying an important religious practice. The purpose of this was to communicate insights that in various respects could legitimise the performance of the art of music as an element in the Lutheran *praxis pietatis*. The role of music was discussed in relation to fundamental theological positions, thus elucidating Lutheran doctrine and *praxis pietatis*. This enterprise stemmed from a need within the Lutheran community for a theological clarification. As such it contributed to the establishment of confessional identity internally, but certainly also externally in relation to other religious denominations.

This chapter investigates the nature of the sixteenth- and seventeenth-century musico-theological discourse in the Lutheran context. More specifically attention is concentrated on the structuring of the discourse on music, and, related to this, its place and function in relation to the question of confessional identity within the discourse field of theology. An examination of the relevant source material, covering a variety of genres, will highlight a recurrent pattern that determines the considerations on music. This salient feature brings to mind the phenomenon of *commonplace*-thinking, prevalent in the culture of the epoch. It points to a form of reflection that is based on a corpus of commonly recognised approaches to a field of knowledge, or *subject*. In the following presentation, music will be interpreted as a *topos* in the context of this thinking, actualised in different historical situations.

Martin Luther's various reflections on music were not given expression in large-scale elaborations, but were put forward in prefaces to the new hymnals and to musical collections, or recorded in his *Tischreden*.[11] Even if fragmentary in nature, they contribute to a view where music enters into a close relationship with theology and the practice of faith, and is thus as-

---

[10] See J. Block, *Verstehen durch Musik: das gesungene Wort in der Theologie. Ein hermeneutischer Beitrag zur Hymnologie am Beispiel Martin Luthers* (Tübingen/Basel, 2002), pp. 13-14.

[11] On Luther's musico-theological thinking, see Honemeyer, *Luthers Musikanschauung*; W. Blankenburg, 'Luther und die Musik', in: W. Blankenburg, *Kirche und Musik: gesammelte Aufsätze zur Geschichte der gottesdienstlichen Musik*, ed. E. Hübner and R. Steiger (Göttingen, 1979), pp. 17-30; O. Söhngen, *Theologie der Musik*, pp. 80-112; C. Krummacher, *Musik als Praxis Pietatis: zum Selbstverständnis evangelischer Kirchenmusik* (Göttingen, 1994), pp. 11-40; Block, *Verstehen*.

signed a high status in religious life. The so-called *Encomion musices*[12] is a fine example of this attitude. In this text Luther establishes a range of basic elements for a positive appraisal of music; among them the idea of music as a gift of God: *vellem certe ex animo laudatum, et omnibus commendatum esse donum illud divinum et excellentissimum Musicum* ('I would like with the whole of my heart to praise and commend music to all as being the most excellent and divine gift').[13]

The idea of music as a divine gift became a recurrent theme in later Lutheran musico-theological thinking. It was supplemented by insights into the power of music on human affects, which were already manifest in antique and medieval thinking, and were to be further developed in the post-Reformation period. According to Luther, music is the *domina et gubernatrix affectuum humanorum* ('mistress and ruler of human affects').[14] In this capacity, so he indicated, music has a wide range of positive effects on human existence. For instance, music is capable of transforming negative mental states into positive ones, including the driving away of evil forces, a point corroborated with reference to 1 Samuel 16 (the story of the expulsion of Saul's evil spirit through David's playing of the harp) – a classical biblical passage in musico-theological discourse, also before Luther. Luther further underlined the value of music when joined to the word of God: word and music 'co-operate in the mind of the listener',[15] thus supporting the proclamation of the gospel.

Luther's sense and appreciation of the more elaborate forms of the art of music (polyphony), also recorded in the *Tischreden*, are expressed in a declaration towards the end of the *Encomion*, where he dwells with wonder on the phenomenon of polyphony, which to him reflects divine wisdom:

Hic tandem gustare cum stupore licet (sed non comprehendere) absolutam et perfectam sapientiam Dei in opere suo mirabili Musicae, in quo una et eadem voce canitur suo tenore pergente, pluribus interim vocibus circum circa mirabiliter ludentibus, exultantibus et iucundissimis gestibus eandem ornantibus,

---

[12] Preface to the Wittenberg printer Georg Rhau's collection of motets, *Symphoniae iucundae atque adeo breves quatuor vocum, ab optimis quibusque musicis compositae* (Wittenberg, 1538; modern edition by H. Albrecht (Kassel, 1959); WA, L, pp. 364-374). For the text and its history, see also W. Blankenburg, 'Überlieferung und Textgeschichte von Martin Luthers *Encomion musices*', *Luther-Jahrbuch* 39 (1972), pp. 80-104. Rhau's collection comprises works by composers like Ludwig Senfl, Heinrich Isaac, Pierre de la Rue, and Johann Walter.

[13] WA, L, p. 368. Unless otherwise indicated, translations are my own.

[14] WA, L, p. 371.

[15] *Inde enim tot Cantica et Psalmi, in quibus simul agunt et sermo et vox in animo auditoris*, WA, L, p. 372.

et velut iuxta eam divinam quandam choream ducentibus, ut iis, qui saltem modice afficiunter, nihil mirabilius hoc seculo extare videatur.[16]

At this point it is legitimate to taste with wonder (but not with comprehension) the absolute and perfect wisdom of God in his admirable work, music, in which one and the same voice carries on, while more voices play around it in a wondrous way, jubilant, adorning it with delightful gestures, and as if performing a divine dance, so that those who are at least moderately affected do not find anything in this world more miraculous.

When we come to examine the Lutheran tradition of the later sixteenth and seventeenth centuries, it is obvious that music was maintained as an important issue, first and foremost on the practical level. But music also became an important *topos* in theological reflection after Luther's death. An indication of this is Johannes Aurifaber's (1519-1575) edition of Luther's table talks, the *Tischreden oder Colloquia Lutheri* of 1566.[17] As mentioned in the preface, these texts were structured according to the *loci communes* principle,[18] that is, the editor collected the sayings of Luther under headings that referred to the main articles of Lutheran theology or confession.[19] In a Protestant context the method was displayed at an early stage by Philip Melanchthon (1497-1560) in his *Loci communes rerum theologicarum* (Basel, 1521, and later editions), a systematic exposition of Luther's theology with a focus on those principal concepts which, in particular, captured and summarised the concerns of Reformation theology. This way of composing texts and books became popular during the sixteenth and seventeenth centuries within both Protestant denominations, especially with regard to theological and moral issues. The *loci* method with its headings or rubrics called attention to topics of common interest, or to viewpoints shared by a religious community, or maintained by authorities. In Aurifaber's collection of

---

[16] WA, L, pp. 372-373.

[17] *Tischreden oder Colloquia Doct. Mart. Luthers, so er in vielen Jaren gegen gelarten Leuten auch frembden Gesten und seinen Tischgesellen gefüret, nach den Heubtstücken unserer christlichen Lere zusammengetragen* (repr. Leipzig/Konstanz, 1967; WA, *Tr* (Tischreden), VI). The collection went through several later editions.

[18] (...) *von mir in gewisse Locos Communes distribuiret und verfasset, Vorrede*, in: WA, *Tr*, VI, p. XV.

[19] See also E. H. Rehermann, 'Die protestantischen Exempelsammlungen des 16. und 17. Jahrhunderts: Versuch eines Überblicks und einer Charakterisierung nach Aufbau und Inhalt', in: W. Brückner, ed., *Volkserzählung und Reformation: ein Handbuch zur Tradierung und Funktion von Erzählstoffen und Erzählliteratur im Protestantismus* (Berlin, 1974), pp. 580-645.

Luther sayings we find eighty headings, or *loci communes*, covering not only the main sections of contemporary theological doctrine, such as, for instance, the sacraments (the Lord's Supper and Baptism), the ceremonies, and the Mass, but also a number of other topics, among them one with the heading 'On music' (*Von der Musica*).[20] The fact that music has its own rubric indicates that it was considered a topical field of significance in the religious forum of the Lutherans after Luther.

This phenomenon is further documented by theological discussions and publications from the later part of the sixteenth century. The position of Martin Luther appears to have been a formative factor in the establishment of music as a *topos* or *locus* in the domain of Protestant theology. The heritage of Luther was administered with different emphasis, and new aspects were added. Nonetheless, the source material attests to some co-ordinates of permanence in the sixteenth- and seventeenth-century musico-theological discourse that are in line with Luther's basic assumptions and his attitude to music. These features come across not only through the recurrent Luther quotations, but also because of the prevalent thought pattern. Against this background, it seems fruitful to consider music in the light of the concept of *commonplace*. In this context *commonplace* refers not only to a particular topic, but also to the set of reflections related to it, that is its role as a store of viewpoints or arguments, and a variety of textual (including biblical) places,[21] pertinent to the discussions of the use of the art of music. Considered as a *commonplace*, music played a part in the profiling of Lutheran doctrine and practice. It outlined, for internal reasons, the significance of an element of religious practice for the members of a confessional community. In that sense the discourse on music contributed to the demarcation of religious territory and can be considered a part of the construction of confessional identity, not only for internal, but certainly also for external reasons, in relation to rival religious communities, that is, in the historical context, Calvinists and Roman Catholics.

In what follows, some examples will be given that may highlight the nature of the sixteenth- and seventeenth-century discourse on music from a Lutheran perspective. The first is taken from the sixteenth-century Lutheran theologian Cyriacus Spangenberg's (1528-1604) voluminous work *Cithara Lutheri* from 1581.[22] The work is a collection of sermons on Luther's

---

[20] WA, *Tr*, VI, p. 348.
[21] This understanding is close to the one put forward by Ann Moss in the initial remarks of her chapter in this volume (pp. 1-17).
[22] *Cithara Lutheri: die Schönen, Christlichen Trostreichen Psalmen und Geistlichen Lieder, des Hochwirdigen Thewren Lehrers und Diener Gottes D. Martini Luthers* (Erfurt, 1581).

hymns, and, in accordance with Spangenberg's homiletic project, the introductory text unfolds as a sermon with the heading *Von Psalmen singen eine Predigte* ('On the singing of hymns').[23] This choice of theme is in itself significant. Contrary to what might have been expected, given the background of the Lutheran *sola scriptura* principle, the religious instruction has as its point of departure not the Bible but a religious practice, particularly connected with the Lutherans. The approach could be characterised as a theological self-reflection, in which the confessional profile is underlined.

This introductory sermon provides us with a number of significant statements. To give a few examples: as a first step, Spangenberg justifies the choice of Luther's hymnal – rather than the Bible – as an object for interpretation, by referring to the biblical basis of the hymnal texts. In this way the scriptural principle is maintained, and consequently the hymns are considered inspired texts, referred to as *Meistergesenge* of the Holy Ghost – with Luther as the mouthpiece of the Spirit.[24] Luther's hymn texts are thus established as modernisations of the biblical text, at the same time as the religious use of them is legitimised.

Another important reason for dealing with the hymns is the fact, pointed out in the text, that the hymnal summarises the whole Christian religion with all its articles of faith, thus constituting what Spangenberg calls the 'Der Leyen Loci Communes, Oder Heuptartickel Christlicher Lere' ('*Loci Communes* of laymen, or main articles of the Christian doctrine for laymen').[25] The importance of this approach was already signalled in the exordium of the sermon, with reference to a classical musico-theological scriptural place, Colossians 3.16.[26] From a doctrinal point of view, the hymnal is thus assigned an important pedagogical function in the propagation of the Lutheran understanding of Christianity.

A third observation relates more directly to the musical dimension. Spangenberg underlines the fact that music facilitates the process of religious learning, publicly and privately, by way of supporting memory. What is learned is better preserved by way of singing, and he states, with reference to his own experience:

> das man alle mal das jenige so in Gesangweiss gefasset ehe lernet und lenger behelt denn was man sonst redet un saget.[27]

---

[23] *Cithara Lutheri*, p. *ij et sqq. (pagination is missing).

[24] *Idem*, p. *iij.

[25] *Ibidem*.

[26] 'Lieben Brueder, leret und vermanet euch selbs mit Psalmen, Lobgesengen und Geistlichen lieblichen Liedern, un singet dem Herrn in ewren hertzen', *Idem*, p. * ij.

[27] *Idem*, p. * iij.

that you always learn and keep longer in mind that which is expressed through singing, than that which you speak and talk about.

To this statement is added, among other things, a basic theological remark on the necessary relation between faith and singing. In fact, the observation is made in the form of a hidden quotation from Luther's preface to the so-called *Babst hymnal*:

> Gott hat unser Hertz undt Muth frölich gemacht durch seinen lieben Sohn, welchen er für uns gegeben hat zur Erlösung von Sünden, Todt und Teufel. Wer solches mit ernst gleubet, der kans nicht lassen; er muß frölich und mit Lust davon singen und sagen, das es andere auch hören und herzu kommen. Wer aber nicht davon singen und sagen will, das ist ein zeichen, das ers nicht gleubt und nicht ins newe fröliche Testament, Sondern unter das alte faule unlustige Testament gehöret.[28]

> For God has cheered our hearts and minds through his dear son, whom he gave for us to redeem us from sin, death, and the devil. He who believes this earnestly cannot be quiet about it. But he must gladly and willingly sing and speak about it, so that others may also come and hear it. And whoever does not want to sing and speak of it shows that he does not believe, and that he does not belong under the new and joyful testament, but under the old, lazy, and tedious testament.

From this Lutheran perspective, faith is singled out as a phenomenon that requires an audible, sonorous expression of the joy evoked by the proclamation of the gospel. As a consequence, music represents an important dimension and an indispensable expression of faith. To strengthen the argument, Lutheran hymn singing is further presented by Spangenberg as a continuation of true Christian worship, represented by biblical as well as later historical figures.[29] Luther and Lutheranism are thus authorised, so to speak, by a large-scale historical reference.

Spangenberg's reflections on hymn singing point to a strong and conscious commitment to basic elements in the heritage of Luther. First and foremost, attention is directed to the aspect of proclamation in relation to the practice of singing, and, closely connected to this, its pedagogical value. But Spangenberg also includes the experiential view that holds music to be

---

[28] *Idem*, p. vi (cf. WA, XXXV, p. 477), transl. in *Luther's Works*, LIII, p. 333. The so-called Babst hymnal, *Geystliche Lieder mit einer newen vorrhede D. Mart. Luth.* (Leipzig, 1545; repr. Kassel, 1929) was published by the printer Valentin Babst.
[29] *Cithara Lutheri*, p. *v.

a basic medium of the expression of the affective side of faith, making, so to speak, music and faith correlative phenomena. With these lines of thought a common frame of reference is indicated that not only represents a continuation of traditional Lutheran views, but was also to be repeated by later generations of theological writers, thus contributing to the specification of the Lutheran confessional tradition.[30]

Controversy was an important feature of sixteenth-century theological debate, and, unsurprisingly, this also affected musico-theological discussions. This means that the attitude towards music, or the *uses* of music, became more explicitly a touchstone in determining confessional identity. It is obvious that the discourse in question reveals a dependence on viewpoints that belong to an already established frame of thought, but it is also notable that certain aspects of the considerations were accentuated. This comes to the fore in the last third of the sixteenth century in discussions of controversy between Lutheran and Calvinist theologians, such as the so-called *Montbéliard colloquy* of 1586 involving, first and foremost, Jacob Andreae (1528-1590), Lutheran professor of theology at the University of Tübingen, and Théodore de Bèze (1519-1609), the leading theological figure of the Calvinists. The meeting was arranged in order to pave the way for a theological rapprochement between Lutherans and the reformed, and, in the first place, because of the situation at the local level, the county of Montbéliard,[31] where the two religious denominations were confronting each other. But the initiative was also related to the religious wars in France, as well as the international political situation, where the need for a compromise that could unite the Protestant parties in Europe against the Roman Catholics was manifest.[32] The main issues dealt with at the colloquy were the key questions of dogma, such as the Lord's Supper, but other topics were taken up, such as Christology, baptism, the use of images and music in the churches, and, finally, predestination. The proceedings of the colloquy, later published,[33] clearly record the differences of opinion among the two parties, thus outlining, at the same time, their confessional identities. This may also

---

[30] It should be noted that the topic of music was further developed and deepened by Spangenberg in *Von der edlen unnd hochberuembten Kunst der Musica, unnd deren Ankunfft, Lob, Nutz, unnd Wirkung, auch wie die Meistersenger auffkhommenn vollkommener Bericht* (Strasbourg, 1598; repr. Hildesheim, 1966).

[31] The county belonged to the Lutheran duchy of Württemberg.

[32] See J. Raitt, *The Colloquy of Montbéliard: Religion and Politics in the Sixteenth Century* (New York/Oxford, 1993).

[33] See *Acta Colloquii Montis Belligartensis* (Tübingen, 1587); *Ad acta Colloquii Montisbelgardensis* (…) *Theodori Bezae responsio* (Geneva, 1588).

be observed in relation to music, although the divergence at this point was less pronounced, and some agreement after all was achieved in this matter.[34]

An important question in the discussion of music in this context was the status of instrumental music, including organ music, in liturgy. The topic, together with that of images, was taken up by the Lutheran party and involved two main issues, put forward in thesis form:[35] the question of whether organ music is prohibited by God, and thus to be eliminated from the churches (thesis IV), and the claim that instrumental music, on the basis of the word of God, is not disapproved of, but commended by the Holy Ghost (thesis VIII).[36] It should be noted, however, that vocal music was also put on the agenda during the discussion.

These theses elicited a negative response from the reformed faction. This was to be expected when viewed in the light of various negative manifestations on the part of the reformed churches, such as the occurrence of violent incidents where organs had been destroyed, as mentioned later in the discussion. The colloquy revealed, however, that Théodore de Bèze did not adhere to an altogether negative attitude towards music. Thus he recognised the power of music to move the soul of man, and he assigned a prominent role to it in connection with the praise of God.[37] While maintaining this position, he also called attention to the dangers of misuse; as when musical instruments, including the organ, were used to play immoral tunes. And he took up a critical stance – in line with Calvin – towards instrumental music. To this he added vocal polyphony, because it implied a transfer of attention from the word of God, considered to be the focal point of Protestant liturgy, to the sound itself, thus giving way to a reprehensible cultivation of the pleasures of the ear:

> *Et quod ad organa Musica attinet: Musicen minime damnamus: sed ubi can-*
> *tatur harmonice, quod mente non intelligitur, res ipsa ostendit, quid inde con-*

---

[34] The colloquy's relation to music is discussed in J. L. Irwin, *Neither Voice nor Heart Alone: German Lutheran Theology of Music in the Age of the Baroque* (New York, 1993), pp. 13-15. See also Raitt, *The Colloquy*, pp. 136-137, for a short comment on this part of the discussion.

[35] The heading of this section of the colloquy indicates that the subject of the theses to be taken up is *de Templis Papisticis, de Imaginibus, Organis Musicis in templo*, *Acta Colloquii*, pp. 389-423; *Ad acta Colloquii*, pp. 17-37.

[36] *Quorum Musica instrumentalis in templo a Spiritu sancto non reprehensa, sed commendata fuit*, *Acta Colloquii*, p. 391. The claim is based on scriptural testimony drawn from Psalm 150.3: *Laudate Dominum in chordis et organo*, as well as with reference to the example of Old Testament kings (David, etc.), who accepted instrumental music in the cult.

[37] *Acta Colloquii*, p. 410.

sequatur, nempe ut paulatim magna pars cultus Dei in cantiunculas mutetetur, et non Dei verbo mentes pascantur, sed inanis sonis aures mulceantur.[38]

As far as organ music is concerned, we do not at all condemn the music; but when you sing together with more voices something that the mind does not understand, it is obvious what follows: that gradually the greater part of the service is transformed into songs, and the mind is not nourished by the word of God, but the ears are entertained with vain sounds.

Quando autem Organo aut alii instrumentis Musicis in Ecclesia luditur, aut variis vocibus canitur, ut a populo non intelligatur; ibi sonus tantum in auribus retinetur, et de sono magis cogitatur, quam de rebus, quae canuntur.[39]

But when the organ or other musical instruments are played, or when singing with different voices takes place in the Church, so that it is not understood by the people, then the sound is retained merely in the ears, and you think more of the sound than of the things that are sung.

The reformed position was characterised by a rational mode of thinking that made intelligibility in liturgy a crucial point. For this reason de Bèze accepted only a musical practice that facilitated the access of the mind or soul to the meaning of that which was mediated through music. This claim was met, according to de Bèze, by vocal singing in unison and implied the omission of musical instruments, a practice that he considered to be a continuation of ancient Christian tradition.[40] In addition to these clarifications, and most likely in order to show a conciliatory stance, he pointed at the end to the adiaphoratic[41] status of music, implying that music could be used or omitted – without offending God.[42]

---

[38] *Idem*, p. 394.

[39] *Idem*, p. 410.

[40] *Et si igitur Musices usum rectum, et praesertim concinendis uti decet Dei laudibus accomodatum, minime damnamus. Illam tamen symphoniacum Musicen, sive voci adiungantur instrumenta, sive minus, (…) sapienter existimo fecisse, qui in Ecclesiis aboleverunt, et, sola vocis gravi, pia et et religiosa cantione contenti, illam ex caetibus publicis eliminarunt. Veteres certe Christiani in suis kryptois ante lucanos hymnos, teste Plinio secundo, cecenerunt, lingua nimirum et Musica ab omnibus intellecta* (…), *Ad acta*, p. 37. The singing of the Psalter is considered an instance of proper liturgical singing, *Acta Colloquii*, p. 410.

[41] The concept of *adiaphoron*, introduced in the Protestant context by Melanchthon, referred in Lutheran theology primarily to phenomena belonging to the liturgical sphere that were considered indifferent in relation to salvation, i.e. external ceremonial traditions that were not under divine command or prohibition, but instituted by man, and thus a matter of freedom. In article 10 of the *Formula Concordiae* (1577),

The contribution of the Lutheran theologian Jacob Andreae to the discussion manifested a somewhat different attitude towards music. He did not share the critical stance of his reformed counterpart in relation to the liturgical use of polyphonic music; on the contrary, he underlined his positive opinion with the statement that this category of music should be considered a 'unique gift of God', and was, for this reason, definitely to be used in liturgy.[43] And, in line with this, he also called attention to the capacity of polyphonic music to evoke a feeling of devotion and bring about a due veneration of God.[44] This understanding of music was elaborated further by Andreae. In the first place, he made a social distinction by observing that the intelligibility of the musicalised text was not necessarily eliminated by the music in question, but that this was dependent on the level of education enjoyed by the listener:

> *Respondeo res ipsas, quae figurali Musica canuntur, non omnibus ignotas, sed eruditis, et qui latinè, aut ipsam Musicam didicerunt, benè notas esse, quibus etiam in illa harmonia afficiuntur.*[45]

I respond that the things that the *musica figuralis* is concerned with are not unknown to all, but well known to the educated, who have learned Latin or even music, and those things will also affect them in addition to the harmony.

To this he added a note, based on his personal experience of the power or positive effects of polyphonic music and its divine origin. In this passage Andreae underlined the devotional value of music. In the context of liturgy, so he claimed, polyphonic and instrumental music, through the display of harmony, contributed to a devotional intensification, from which liturgical elements such as prayers and sermons could profit:

---

the question of the *adiaphora* was discussed, but the subject (though not the term) was taken up already in the *Confessio Augustana* (1530), for instance in article XV. See *Die Bekenntnisschriften der evangelisch-lutherischen Kirche, herausgegeben im Gedenkjahr der Augsburgischen Konfession 1930* (Göttingen, 1976), pp. 1053-1063 and 69-70.

[42] *Acta Colloquii*, pp. 410-411. At this point the reference is explicitly to instrumental music, but in the context it also applies to polyphonic vocal music, discussed immediately before.

[43] *Harmonica musica singulare Dei donum est; cuius praecipuus usus ad cultum Dei destinatus esse debet, sicut exempla piorum Regum docent*, Acta Colloquii, p. 394 (marginal note l).

[44] *Immo maxime mentes piorum ad pietatem, et devote Deo cultum debitum praestandum excitantur, idem*, p. 394 (marginal note m).

[45] *Acta Colloquii*, p. 411.

Et de meipso sancta affirmare possum, ut qui Musica figurali, et organo plurimùm delector, non modò aures sonum percipere, sed animum quoque harmoniâ illa affici mirificè, et vel ad preces, vel ad conciones ardentiore spiritu habendas vel audiendas excitari, quando suavissimâ harmonia canticum Ecclesiasticum vel organo luditur, aut à cantoribus, priusquàm concionator suggestum conscendat, recepta consuetudine, cantari solet: adeoque vim illam divinitus harmoniae inditam, in meipso efficaciter sentire affirmo, de qua ab initio dixisti, quòd Musicae figurali insit. Idem quoque à multis aliis piis viris, etiam Laicis, artis Musicę ignaris audivi, quòd similiter in seipsis experiantur.[46]

And since I have great delight in *musica figuralis* and instrumental music, I can for my own part solemnly confirm that not only do the ears perceive the sound, but the mind is also wonderfully affected by the harmony that is displayed, and it is incited to pray or listen to prayers or sermons with greater enthusiasm when a church song with the sweetest harmony is played on an organ, or, according to usual practice, is sung by the singers, before the preacher ascends the pulpit. Certainly, I can confirm that I perceptibly feel in myself that it is by God's hand that this power has been connected to this harmony, which, according to your statement at the beginning, belongs to *musica figuralis*. Many other pious men, also laymen without knowledge of music, have told me that they experience the same.

It appears that the power of music to which Andreae refers is inherent in music itself. This idea was further substantiated by way of historical proof. With a biblical reference to the history of David, who with his *cithara* drove away the evil spirit of Saul,[47] Andreae pointed out that Saul was cured solely by instrumental music, and this because the music itself was capable of affecting not only his aural senses, but also his mind.[48] This view implied that music as such, independently of its relationship with texts, far from disturbing liturgical practice, is able, on the contrary, to establish a significant religious communication with the personal centre of man, and in this way it contributes to a proper celebration of liturgy. However, according to Andreae, the experience of musical harmony would only be intensified by an understanding of that which was mediated through the music:

Non igitur contemnenda vis est harmoniae Musicae figuralis, quae spiritum Domini malum represit; quae ad animù usque, etiamsi, quod luditur aut cani-

---

[46] *Idem*, p. 411.
[47] 1 Samuel 16.
[48] *Acta Colloquii*, pp. 411-412.

tur, non ab omnibus intelligatur, penetrat. Quam vim multò maiorem in se ex-
periuntur et sentient, qui unâ cum harmonia res quoque sacras, quae canuntur,
intelligent.[49]

One should not hold in contempt the power of harmony of the *musica figuralis*,
which overcame the evil spirit of the Lord. It penetrates the mind, even though
all do not understand what is played or sung. And those who, in addition, understand the sacred things the music is about will experience and perceive this
power as much greater.

From this perspective, music was considered something essentially good
that was to remain integrated in Christian worship, and misuse did not, according to Andreae, and contrary to de Bèze, change its status.

In spite of the divergences between the Lutheran and the reformed
party, Andreae, towards the end of the discussion, could agree with his
counterpart that music belonged to the category of *adiaphoron*:

Sed consensus inter nos est: sua natura adiaphoron esse, in templis organa
Musica habere, aut his carere. Quod in cuiusque Ecclesiae arbitrio est posi-
tum.[50]

But there is agreement between us that its nature is *adiaphoron*, and the organ
may be kept, or dispensed with in the churches. Each church is free to decide.

But, even at this point, the colloquy exposed differences of opinion. The
Lutheran standpoint was characterised by formulations that were not quite
consistent with an interpretation of music as adiaphoratic. Thus Andreae
stated, among other things, that music was *egregia templorum ornamenta:*
modo illis ad celebrationem numinis divini utamur[51] ('an excellent ornament of the Church, if only we use it for the praise of the divine majesty'),
and, further, with reference to Psalm 150, that it was *non modo non prohibi-*
tum, sed expresse mandatum, Psalmo 150 ('not only not prohibited, but
clearly commanded').[52]

De Bèze was justified in making clear that this formulation appeared to
imply that music was covered by a divine command and was thus a necessity in Christian worship. This would mean that leaving out, say, instrumental music in the liturgy, as he was inclined to do, would be reprehensible, a

---

[49] *Idem*, p. 412.
[50] *Idem*, p. 443.
[51] *Idem*, p. 412.
[52] *Idem*, p. 412.

view he found unacceptable. Nor was he convinced by the scriptural basis
of the Lutheran stance, since it dealt with the ceremonial law, relating to the
Old Testament cult which to him had no normative status in the Christian
Church. Andreae agreed that instrumental music was under no special
command, but at the same time he maintained that it was not only covered
by a general command, established out of devotion,[53] but also that it was
approved by God, referring to the evidence of the Psalms.[54] With regard to
vocal music, he similarly called attention to the human voice as 'a most excellent gift' that – through singing – should participate in the praise of
God.[55]

When it comes to the topic of music, the colloquy of Montbéliard exhibits quite different theological profiles, in spite of the declared agreement
at the end. Even if the Calvinist position was presented in a moderate, conciliatory form, it was, after all, characterised by a restrictive and rational
attitude to the liturgical use of the art of music. The Lutheran view was
elaborated in another direction. The positive appraisal of music in its various forms is unmistakable during the discussion. In distinction to the Calvinist attitude, it testifies to the high status of this art within Lutheran liturgical and devotional practice, and reflects a notable openness to the sensuous mediation of spiritual matters.

Another sixteenth-century discussion of controversy worthy of mention was
raised by German Calvinists in Anhalt in 1596.[56] Various elements of Lutheran liturgical practice, such as the use of images, were attacked because
of their alleged theological illegitimacy and incompatibility with the pure
proclamation of the word of God, which was the fundamental concern of
the reformed churches. In this context music was also the object of criticism. The objections were raised specifically against the use of musical instruments, and – on the basis of the criteria of intelligibility – of songs,
which, for musico-artistic reasons or owing to their Latin texts, people
could not understand. This critical position gave rise to a number of replies

---

[53] *Reges veteris Testamenti (…) non speciale mandatum habuisse, ut instrumen-
talem Musicam instituerent in templo, sed pro ipsorum pietate fecerunt hoc ex gen-
erali illo in Thesi nostra positum est, Acta Colloquii*, p. 422.

[54] *Idem*, p. 423.

[55] *Cum igitur vox humana et articulate inter praestantissima dona Dei numeretur,
ideo et ipsa etiam ad laudandum Deum dirigi debet, ne avibus inferiores hac in
parte censeamur, quae suavissimo suo cantu DEVM perpetuo celebrant, idem*,
p. 423.

[56] For a discussion of the Anhalt controversy in relation to music, see J. L. Irwin,
Neither Heart nor Voice Alone, pp. 15-17.

from Lutherans,[57] among them one from the Faculty of Theology of Wittenberg University, which was published in 1597.[58] In this contribution the Wittenberg theologians dealt with, among other things, the question of music. Their defence of music introduced viewpoints that were also present in the Montbéliard colloquy. On the one hand, it was categorised as *adiaphoron* in contradistinction to the reformed position in Anhalt. On the other hand, the status of music in liturgy was given a notably positive assessment. Further, on the basis of scriptural testimony, for instance Psalm 150, it was maintained that the use of musical instruments was in accordance with religious ceremonial tradition in ancient Israel. Even if this Old Testament tradition were not assigned a normative status, it was after all considered indicative of the value of this type of music by the Lutherans. This interpretation was further elaborated with the idea of music as 'a gift of God', a designation that was related to the affective power of instrumental music, also present when this type of music was separated from vocal music.[59] This quality was related to, for instance, the apotropaic function of music, with reference to 1 Samuel 16 (the story of the evil spirit of Saul), but, in particular, to its capability of evoking 'devotion' (*Andacht*). As to the reformed claim for intelligibility in liturgy – with reference to 1 Corinthians 14 – the *sine qua non* in reformed devotional practice, the Lutherans argued that the understanding of instrumental music (organ music) was secured, when the genre (*genus*) of the performed music was clearly established:

> Wenn man nur das genus weiss, so ist es (soviel die Orgeln belanget) gnug und wird damit nicht in wind hinein georgelt. Das genus aber ist, das man weiss, es werden geistliche Lieder, die zu Gottes lob gemachet sind, darauff geschlagen. Wer das weiss, der ergert sich nicht an den Orgeln, welche sonsten eben wol ihre krafft hat Menschliche hertzen zu bewegen, als die Posaune ire kraft hat, wenn man nur Soviel weis, das durch derselben schal entweder zum streit geblasen wird (…) oder andre wichtige ding angezeigt.[60]

> When you only know the *genus*, then this is sufficient (as far as the organs are concerned), and consequently the playing of the organ is not merely bringing the air into motion. Being aware of the *genus* means that you know that the

---

[57] See, for instance, *Erinnerungsschrifft etlicher vom Adel und Staedten an den Durchleuchtigen Hochgebornen Fürsten unnd Herrn Johann Georgen Fürsten zu Anhalt (…) Sampt darauff erfolgten gnediger Verantwortung und erklärung* (Zerbst, 1596), pp. 73-76 (on music).

[58] *Notwendige Antwort auff die im Fürstenthumb Anhalt ohn langsten ausgesprengste hefftige Schrifft* (Wittenberg, 1597).

[59] *Notwendige Antwort*, p. 71.

[60] *Idem*, p. 71.

songs which are played are spiritual, made for the praise of God. He who knows that does not become indignant at the organs that have their power to move human hearts in the same way as the trombone, where you only know as much as that it is through the sound that either combat or other important things are indicated.

In line with this approach, vocal music accompanied by instruments was accepted, even if it implied that people did not understand what was sung. This practice was considered appropriate in a liturgical context, since Scripture testified to the recognition of its use in the liturgical ceremonies of the temple of Israel. The Lutherans did not find scriptural evidence, as did their reformed counterparts, for the assertion that liturgical singing in the temple, accompanied by a wide register of instruments, was intelligible.[61]

These theological disputes not only indicate the conflicting attitudes of the two Protestant denominations with respect to music, but feature at the same time the topical area of music as they mark thematic compartments pointing to recurrent views and perspectives. The Lutheran context is illustrated by a positive appraisal of music that constitutes a basic premise of their musico-theological reflections, in contradistinction to the much more restricted position of the Calvinists. Although not quite consistent with the proposed adiaphoratic interpretation, this elaboration of the topic of music, with the implied idea of music as a central vehicle of communication between God and Man, was to a large extent in conformity with Martin Luther's own views, and was maintained in later historical contexts.

In seventeenth-century Lutheran thought,[62] the topic of music had become consolidated in the intellectual landscape. The Lutheran musico-theological reflections of this period show a number of common features with regard to the division of the subject, viewpoints, and source references, which point to a continuation of the commonplace structure of the considerations on music discussed above. Basic elements of sixteenth-century discourse were taken over, but, at the same time, changing religious, intellectual, and political contexts gave occasion for different accentuations, articulations, and additions. The discussion was determined by the application of accumulated

---

[61] *Idem*, p. 72.

[62] See, for instance, C. Bunners, *Kirchenmusik und Seelenmusik: Studien zu Frömmigkeit und Musik im Luthertum des 17. Jahrhunderts* (Göttingen, 1966); Irwin, *Neither Voice nor Heart Alone*; see also S. R. Havsteen, 'Aspects of Musical Thought in the Seventeenth-Century Lutheran Tradition', in: E. Østrem, J. Fleisher and N. H. Petersen, eds, *The Arts and the Cultural Heritage of Martin Luther* (Copenhagen, 2003), pp. 151-169.

or transmitted mainstream viewpoints and opinions, implying a shared set of coordinates within the topical field. From this perspective, one may say that such topical thinking contributed to, or was a part of, the process of cultural reception as well as of that construction and maintenance of tradition which was a principal constituent in the theological responses to current issues. This approach displays an awareness of confessional identity, which pertains not only to the internal theological clarification of doctrine and practice, but also to the external theological demarcation in relation to other religious communities. The source material covers a variety of literary forms, such as, for instance, prefaces to collections of musical compositions and hymnals, sermons, tracts, and exegetical works, and constitutes convincing evidence of the common nature and structure of the discourse in question.

Seventeenth-century discussions of music may be approached from a number of directions. A good example of a mainstream theological account of music from this period is offered in the reflections of the Lutheran theologian and *Superintendent* from Lüneburg (Northern Germany), Christopher Frick (1577-1640), in his book *Music-Büchlein* (1631),[63] based on two organ sermons delivered at the inauguration of new church organs. An important feature of Frick's considerations, shared by other writers on the subject, is his dependence on the rhetorical genre of argumentation, whose aim was the praise of the *res* in focus of the discourse, i.e. the *laudatio* or *encomium*.[64] This strategy of communication, labelled the *genus demonstrativum* in classical rhetoric, was an important part of the seventeenth-century rhetorical system, and instructions concerning how to organise it were as a rule displayed in the textbooks on this subject. It embraced a particular set of *topoi* or questions to be considered. These points of focus are, for instance, *honestas*, *utilitas*, and, closely related to these, the necessity of the object or phenomenon chosen for presentation. In the account of music given by Christopher Frick, these questions are integrated into the exposition. Thus, for instance, the question of the origin and of the inventors of music belongs to the *topos* of honourableness, and the theme of the various effects of music as well as the question of the purpose of musical practice within the Christian order of life refer to the *topos* of utility.

---

[63] *Music-Büchlein, oder Nützlicher Bericht von dem Uhrsprunge, Gebrauche und Erhaltung Christlicher Music* (Lüneburg, 1631; repr. Leipzig, 1976).

[64] On this subject, see, for instance, J. Dyck, *Athen und Jerusalem: die Tradition der argumentativen Verknüpfung von Bibel und Poesie im 17. und 18. Jahrhundert* (Munich, 1977), pp. 13-23.

To this positive approach is added another *topos* that relates to the question of the despisers and abusers of music, a heading that points, among other things, to the confessional controversy with the Calvinists. It is a notable and recurrent element of seventeenth-century Lutheran discourse to point out the Calvinists' hostile attitude towards music, with reference to the disputes of the sixteenth century, including references to the abovementioned historical incidents of violent excesses that were claimed to have caused the destruction of organs. Against this background, the Lutheran defence of music presents itself emphatically as a statement of confessional identity. Lutherans are categorised as cultivators of music, contrary to their Protestant counterparts. This is clearly the message conveyed by Frick, who outlines the critical stance of the Calvinists, without any sense of the more subtle differences, against the background of statements from, for instance, the *Montbéliard colloquy* and the Anhalt theologians mentioned above.[65]

Frick's defence of music does not need to be elaborated in detail in this context. Suffice it to make some general observations concerning the continuities of the musico-theological discourse. On the one hand, the presence of central elements of the sixteenth-century discourse on music is immediately obvious. Thus, for instance, in parallel with a considerable number of contemporary Lutheran theological writings on the subject, Frick repeats Luther's basic dictum concerning music as a divine gift. From the rhetorical point of view, the introduction of this idea is a development of the abovementioned *topos* of *honestas*, which demands an account of the 'age' (*antiquitas*) and the noble 'origin' (*origo*), in addition to the honourable 'inventors' (*inventores)* of music, in order to establish the pre-eminence of this art. Concordant with more general tendencies in seventeenth-century metaphysico-theological thought, this theme is developed within an all-encompassing, cosmic view. Music was in this perspective interpreted as a phenomenon that, from the very beginning of creation, had been established through divine initiative as a fundamental harmonious structure of being that characterises the various hierarchies of reality, the heavenly, the human, and the natural. Its sonorous realization was considered a reflection of this all-comprising world harmony.[66]

---

[65] *Music-Büchlein*, pp. 30-33.

[66] The cosmic view of music is a heritage of antique philosophical (pythagorean and platonic) speculation that was recontextualised in Christian thought through the Middle Ages, with Boethius as an early key figure. On the idea of world harmony, see, for instance, L. Spitzer, 'Classical and Christian Ideas of World Harmony: Prolegomena to an Interpretation of the Word "Stimmung"', in: *Traditio* 2 (1944), pp. 409-464; 3 (1945), pp. 307-364; R. Dammann, *Der Musikbegriff im deutschen Barock* (Laaber, ³1995), pp. 23-92; S. K. Heninger, *Touches of Sweet Harmony: Pythagorean Cosmology and Renaissance Poetics* (San Marino, CA, 1974).

Closely related to this line of thought, Frick also associates his understanding of the divine quality of music with the notion of the angelic or
heavenly music.[67] The idea, rooted in the Bible and later integrated into the
medieval discourse on music, was also taken up in the Lutheran context,[68]
and emphasised in particular in the seventeenth century. The application of
it was an indication not only of the transcendental or eschatological dimension of music, but also of its divine origin. Within this theological framework, the performance of music was regarded as an activity pointing to the
eternal life, in the theological imagination characterised by a never-ending
musical liturgy.[69] This meant that music was viewed as an anticipation, although in a fragmentary and imperfect form, of the divinely instituted transcendental music. Considered a *praegustus vitae aeternae* ('a foretaste of
the eternal life'), music was assigned an important function on the practical
level in the preparation of man for the life to come, a point that contributes
to its recognition as a significant devotional instrument in the Lutheran
praxis pietatis.

The *utilitas* of music comes across in the idea of the apotropaic function of music, paradigmatically represented with reference to 1 Samuel 16.[70]
In Frick, however, this function is closely connected with the conception of
music as a vehicle for the devotional practice and experience of man. In line
with the sixteenth-century discussion, the devotional role of music is considered central, and it is touched upon in various ways in Frick's account,
but it is here developed in a more extensive way. As was the case in the
Spangenberg text discussed above, it is stated that music contributes to the
maintenance of faith and serves the propagation of the true doctrine. The
function of music or singing in this respect is, according to Frick, based on

---

[67] *Music-Büchlein*, pp. 107-123, 297-340.

[68] The idea of the angelic music is present in Luther's writings, and it is thematised
in Johann Walter's music poems, *Lob und Preis der löblichen Kunst Musica* (1538)
and *Lob und Preis der himmlischen Kunst Musica* (1564), in: J. Walter, *Sämtliche
Werke*, ed. O. Schröder, VI (Kassel, 1953), pp. 153-156, 157-161. For the history of
the idea, see R. Hammerstein, *Die Musik der Engel: Untersuchungen zur Musikanschauung des Mittelalters* (Bern, [2]1990); R. Dammann, *Der Musikbegriff*, pp. 444-
456.

[69] Apart from musico-theological writings, the idea of the angelic or heavenly music
was also represented in hymnal illustrations and on the front pages of music collections; see, for instance, Michael Praetorius (1571-1621), *Musae Sioniae* (1607), in:
Gesamtausgabe der musikalischen Werke von M. Praetorius, ed. F Blume and H.
Költzsch, V (Wolfenbüttel/Berlin, 1937), reproduction of the frontispiece.

[70] *Music-Büchlein*, pp. 75-78. The text is a quotation from the Lutheran theologian
and hymn writer Paul Eber's (1511-1569) preface to a hymn collection by Nikolaus
Herman. The whole text is presented in an appendix to the *Music-Büchlein* (pp. 341-
343), thus underlining the significance of the statement on the value of music.

its ability to impress the proclamation of the gospel into the human mind, the central word being the German verb *einbilden*:

> Aus der Vbung Christlicher aus Gottes Worte genommener Gesänge erfolget dieser Nutz, daß der Mensch solches Wort mit den Gesängen bey sich behält, da er allein ist, neben anderer Arbeit davon singet und also ihm das Wort Gottes tieffer einbildet und von tage zu tage solchem Worte besser nachdenket.[71]

> From the exercise of Christian songs, based on the words of God, follows the profitable effect that man keeps such a word with him together with the songs, when he is alone, in addition to other tasks, sings about it, and thus impresses the word of God more deeply in him, and day by day makes progress in the meditation on such word.

This quality points to the pedagogical and edifying dimension of music, and is explicitly related to the Lutheran practice of hymn singing, and to the crucial role that Luther's hymns have allegedly played in the dissemination of the word of God, in spite of, so Frick claims, the tyranny of the pope.[72]

The idea of music as a necessary sensuous expression of the experience of faith is also present in the seventeenth-century discussion, which includes echoes of Luther's passage on the sonorous expression of the joy of faith from the preface to the Babst hymnal quoted above.[73] But now the idea has become more elaborate and is connected with an impressive metaphor emphasising the anthropological dimension of religious experience. The physical being of man is depicted as an organ. This instrument represents the concordance of all the parts of his body and mirrors the presence of the spirit and the state of peace which Christ has established through the Redemption.[74] In this conception music or singing is made a basic manifestation of the meaning of Lutheran religious practice, implying a special affective tonality that chimes in with the joy associated with the appropriation of the gospel message.

The basically positive appraisal of music that comes to the fore in this seventeenth-century account is further signalled by the indication – in line with Jacob Andreae's stance – that, as an integral part of the praise of God, music is covered by a *Gottes Mandat* ('divine command') with reference to sections from the Psalms of David.[75] Now, this understanding, repeated by

---

[71] *Idem*, p. 185.
[72] *Idem*, pp. 184-185.
[73] *Idem*, p. 60.
[74] *Idem*, pp. 58-59.
[75] *Idem*, pp. 6-7.

many contemporary contributors to the discussion, seems, on the one hand, to be irreconcilable with the interpretation of music as adiaphoratic, maintained by Lutherans into the seventeenth century; on the other hand, to point to a legalistic view of musical practice contrary to basic assumptions in Luther's theological thinking. The tension in the Lutheran position between the pronounced positive attitude towards music and the adiaphoratic interpretation encountered already in Andreae's considerations is definitely also present in the seventeenth-century debate but, in Frick's case, and in consequence, so to speak, of the markedly affirmative attitude to music within the Lutheran tradition, this tension is dissolved in favour of the establishment of music as a necessary institution within Christian worship, which discards the adiaphoratic theme altogether. The legalistic view implied in the reference to a divine command in relation to the religious practice of music is at the same time contradicted by the statement that musical praise is motivated by the redemptive act of God in Christ. In this way, the idea of the necessity of music is to be viewed in the light of the proclamation of the gospel, and within Lutheran religious practice the law is thus transformed into a guide to the articulation of the experience of faith. If this interpretation is correct, it throws new light on the basic Lutheran assumption of a close theological relation between the experience of faith and musical practice.

Frick does not explicitly address the question of the intelligibility of what is presented in musical performances in liturgy. But he assigns a noteworthy importance to the function of music in connection with the proclamation of the word of God. This issue, which appears already in sixteenth-century discourse, was also taken up by other seventeenth-century theological writers. The discussion of this subject reveals different views and tensions among the Lutherans. Some of these, underlining the importance of intelligibility, argue in favour of a restriction in the use of musical artistry for fear of otherwise disturbing the understanding of the word proclaimed within the liturgy.[76]
Another approach, in line with ideas advanced in sixteenth-century discourse, maintained, however, the view that music in itself supported devotional practice independently of its function of textual interpretation. This perception was, for instance, included in the musico-theological reflections

---

[76] An extreme example of this view, close to a Calvinistic attitude, is the *Wächterstimme auß dem verwüsteten Zion: das ist Treuhertzige und nothwendige Entdeckung, auß was Ursachen die vielfaltige Predigt deß Worts Gottes bey Evangelischen Gemeinen wenig zur Bekehrung und Gottseligkeit fruchte und warumb Evangelische Gemeinen bey den häutigen Predigten des heiligen Worts Gottes ungeistlicher und ungöttlicher werdenn* (…) (Frankfurt am Main, 1661), written by Theophil Großgebauer (1627-1661).

put forward by Cunrad Dieterich (1575-1639), *Superintendent* in Ulm, in his *Kirchweyh- oder Gesang-Predigt.*[77] Alluding to statements by Lutheran *Musik-Feinde* ('enemies of music') against the use of *Figural-Gesang* ('polyphonic song'), Dieterich admits that this music is not absolutely necessary, thus intimating an adiaphoratic point of view. At the same time, however, he points out its value within liturgy.[78] In support of this assessment, he refers to the 'openly displayed beauty' associated with the performance of polyphonic music, which he relates to an *aphorismus apostolicus* from 1 Corinthians 14.40, whose claim of a decorous and orderly accomplishment of liturgy[79] often served, in the seventeenth-century theological debate,[80] as a basis for legitimising the use of human ceremonies and for underscoring the importance of the exterior ceremonial form of worship. As an issue associated with the *adiaphora* discussion, the ceremonies in question were not considered as belonging to the essentials of the Christian cult. A widespread agreement existed, however, on the indispensable role they played in respect of the pedagogical and devotional tasks of liturgy.[81] For a number of theologians, the dictum of Saint Paul seemed to relate to the question of the specific constitution, that is, the structure or design of ceremonies. In this way the idea of a decorous (*ehrlich, ehrbar*) and orderly (*ordentlich*) mode of action covered not only an ethico-theological value, but also the very form of appearance pointing to what a later epoch would term the *aesthetic* dimension of ceremonies.[82] Dieterich is in accordance

---

[77] *Die 6. Kirchweyh- oder Gesang-Predigt, darinn vom ersten Ursprung und Brauch des Gesangs in der Christlichen Kirchen summarischer weise discurriret und gehandelt wird, in: D. Cunrad Dieterichs Ulmischer Kirchen Superintendenten Sonderbare Predigten von unterschiedenen Materien hiebevor zu Ulm im Münster gehalten* (Frankfurt am Main/Leipzig, 1669 [first edn 1619-1632]), pp. 220-250.

[78] *Kirchweyh-Predigt,* p. 239.

[79] Dieterich defends his stance as follows: 'umb der offenen Zier willen der Kirchen, damit alles desto ehrlicher und ordentlicher darin zugehe. 1 Cor. 14/40' *(Kirchweyh-Predigt,* p. 239). The Pauline text in question reads in the *Authorized King James Version*: 'Let all things be done decently and in order' (and, in Luther's translation, 'Laßt aber alles ehrbar und ordentlich zugehen'). The text of the Vulgate reads: *omnia autem honeste et secundum ordinem fiant.*

[80] See, further, P. Graff, *Geschichte der Auflösung der alten gottesdienstlichen Formen in der evangelischen Kirche Deutschlands,* I (*Bis zum Eintritt der Aufklärung und des Rationalismus*) (Göttingen, 1939), pp. 1-85; F. Kalb, *Die Lehre vom Kultus der lutherischen Kirche zur Zeit der Orthodoxie* (Berlin, 1959), pp. 90-92.

[81] 2 Corinthians 14.26 also formed part of the theological considerations and was interpreted as pointing to the edifying value of ceremonies.

[82] The Latin equivalents of the German terminology relevant to the 17th-century *adiaphora* discussion are the words *honestum, decorum, ordo,* and derivations from them. For the use of the Latin terms, see, for instance, Balthasar Meisner, *Collegii adiaphoristici Calvinianis oppositi disputatio prima de libertate christiana et adia-*

with this interpretation when he points to and acknowledges *Zierde* ('beauty') as a significant aspect of the liturgical use of music, and emphasises that polyphonic music contributes to making liturgical singing *lieblich* ('mellifluous') and *angenehm* ('enjoyable').[83] However, it has to be kept in mind that the concept of beauty within the framework of the *adiaphora* discussion represents just a general normative idea that did not occasion more detailed instructions concerning artistic design. It implied only the overall prescription for a dignified and unpretentious liturgy, thus paving the way for a variety of artistic realisations.

As to the objection that the 'ordinary man' does not understand what is being performed, Dieterich responds in continuation of the aforesaid reflection – and in line with, for instance, the statements of Jacob Andreae – that, in such a case, music still has an estimable power to move the heart, independently of the proclaimed verbal message.[84] The stance of Cunrad Dieterich, shared by other Lutheran writers of the century, is an instance of the Lutheran inclination towards acceptance and positive evaluation of a broad register of musical manifestations relating to liturgy.

The musico-theological reflections of the sixteenth and seventeenth centuries, presented in this context, point to the effort of deepening the understanding of specificities of liturgical and devotional practices within the Lutheran tradition. As such, they served, one may assume, the ongoing internal theological clarification, and were thus closely connected with establishing an overall confessional identity while at the same time defining a particular element of this confessional identity. As it unfolded during the sixteenth and seventeenth centuries, this enterprise featured a pattern of thinking committed, as we have seen in the selected source material, to a set of recurrent questions, viewpoints, and source references, by which the topical field of music was delineated. The structure of this field and its coordinates were rather stable, but, at the same time, adaptable to concrete historical situations and the prevalent intellectual and religious climate. Against this background, it seems reasonable to describe music not only as a *commonplace* within the Lutherans' theological discourse, but also – in this capacity

---

phoris in genere (Wittenberg, 1618). Rooted in the European rhetorical and philosophical traditions, these concepts carry an aesthetic meaning that the corresponding German vocabulary does not evoke to the same extent. See, for instance, I. Rutherford and U. Mildner, 'Decorum', in: *Historisches Wörterbuch der Rhetorik*, ed. G. Ueding et al., II (Tübingen, 1994), cols. 432-451; B. Wilke and T. Zinsmaier, 'Honestum' in: *Historisches Wörterbuch der Rhetorik*, ed. G. Ueding et al., III (Tübingen, 1996), cols. 1546-1555.
[83] *Kirchweyh-Predigt*, pp. 239-240.
[84] *Idem*, p. 240.

– as a significant element in the construction of confessional identity. A concise manifestation of this point is provided by the account of music in the encyclopaedia *Moralium Gedanensium* (1654),[85] compiled by the Lutheran theologian of controversy Johann Botsack (1600-1674) of Gdansk. In this work we find entries or rubrics like *Cano* and *Musica*, in both cases summing up the *commonplace* knowledge of the subject, outlining the topical field and its various places, including those taken up in this chapter, and pointing to the prominent status of music in the Lutheran tradition as a confessional marker. The specific treatment of music in the work of Botsack is an indicator that this subject was established as a *topos* in the Lutheran intellectual universe.

---

[85] *I.S.N.J. Moralium Gedanensium libri XXX* (Frankfurt am Main, 1655).

THE ROMAN CATHOLIC DOCTRINE ON ABORTION

THE CURIOUS HISTORY OF A COMMONPLACE

Patrick Vandermeersch

Although it is not a specific entry in most dictionaries, the expression 'commonplace' clearly refers to common, indeed, all too common opinions and quotations. It points to statements that everybody should take for granted; to *bons mots*, images, and metaphors that have been repeated so often that they have become obsolete. In a word: a commonplace is a truth, but not an interesting one, for it has become unable to raise objections.

Most encyclopaedias keep silent on the meaning of commonplaces but, as is often the case, the Spanish Encyclopaedia gives us more insight.[1] It reminds us of the fact that the concept of the 'common place' has one of its roots in theology, more precisely in the work of Rudolph Agricola (1443-1483), in his day a famous humanist, now mostly forgotten, except by the University of Groningen, as he was born nearby and lived in the town for many years. He was the secretary of the city council, a good organist, and the builder of the famous great organ of the Martini church. He stands at the centre of an intellectual circle that used to meet in the abbey of Aduard. Although he did not write very much, he was an influential man. He kept in touch with many leading figures of the Renaissance and was especially respected by Erasmus.

Agricola discusses commonplaces (*loci*) in his *De inventione dialectica libri tres* (1479). Basing himself on Cicero, he distinguishes three aspects in every speech: first, it transmits knowledge; second, it aims to convince people; finally, it is intended to provide some pleasure for the listener.[2] At first glance, the first aspect seems to be the most essential one, especially today: many people want to rely only on what is true, 'evidence-based' knowledge. According to Agricola, however, not that many things are self-evident, nor can they become acceptable just through a study of their inner consistency. One is compelled to introduce arguments from outside, and here we meet

---

[1] *Enciclopedia universal ilustrada europeo-americana*, XXXI (Barcelona, n.d.) pp. 563-566; 'lugares communes' can be found within the entry 'lugares' (p. 564), and the reader is immediately referred to 'lugares teológicos' (p. 565).

[2] R. Agricola, *Ecrits sur la dialectique et l'humanisme*, ed. and transl. M. van der Poel (Paris, 1997), pp. 68-83.

the *loci*. They are the external points of view from which one is entitled to make statements about those many things that are not convincing by themselves. As there are a great number of them and one is often forced to rely on arguments taking their point of departure in an external point of view, *loci* should be evaluated critically. Agricola thus proceeds to a listing and an evaluation of twenty-four *loci*. His aim is not so much to outline a complete system of them as to point to the variety of all the different points of view one can adopt in investigating an object.

The term *locus* was taken up by Luther's friend and advisor Philip Melanchthon (1497-1560), who used the words *Loci communes* as the title of a book dealing with the structure and essentials of theological knowledge. Catholic theologians often point to the fact that, despite its title, Melanchthon's book is less a methodological reflection than a catechism.[3] They put Melchior Cano (1509-1560) to the fore, who discussed in his *Loci theologici* the ranking of authorities linked with the distinct sources of theological knowledge. This ranking is very interesting: 1. the Bible; 2. the oral traditions of the apostles; 3. the Catholic Church in its totality; 4. the councils; 5. the Roman Catholic Church in particular; 6. the apostolic fathers; 7. the theologians; 8. ordinary reason; 9. the philosophers; 10. the history of mankind.[4]

However interesting this may be, we will not enter into the debate on the exact order and number of the *loci*. We see, however, what is at stake. In many areas of life, you cannot rely only on what you can know by observation. You also need to rely on authorities. Cano's *loci* are an attempt to differentiate those authorities by ranking them. Commonplaces designate the fact that you should take certain things for granted for, otherwise, you cannot proceed to more elaborated reasoning. On the other hand, you should be critical in the way that you make a reflexive turn questioning the weight of a particular authority.

Today, accepting a truth by sheer obedience is no longer part of our culture. Nevertheless, as Michel Foucault has shown us, there is a more hidden way authority remains present in our minds.[5] Our view of reality has become fragmented, and the distribution of knowledge is not based on an underlying logic. We rely on several discourses that pretend to inform us and indicate the way our behaviour should conform in order to be 'normal'.

---

[3] *Dictionnaire de théologie catholique*, 'lieux théologiques', IX, part 1 (Paris, 1926), cols. 712-747.

[4] M. Cano, *De locis theologicis*, in: *Opera theologica*, I-II (Rome, 1900). The Spanish translation is the only existing one in a modern language: *De locis theologicis*, transl. J. Belda Plans (Madrid, 2006). See, further, B. Körner, *Melchior Cano, De locis theologicis: ein Beitrag zur theologischen Erkenntnislehre* (Graz, 1994).

[5] M. Foucault, *L'Ordre du discours* (Paris, 1971).

Medicine, psychology, biology, sociology, economics, politics, etc., all inform and guide us, but they develop their discourses to a great extent without any concern for other discourses nor for conflict or overlap. For about two hundred years, we have been exposed to a new style of proposing an ideal lifestyle (in fact: teaching morality), and this is linked with the collapse of a religious view based upon a coherent concept of reality. The ways our new discourses interact are incompatible with the traditional religious view that saw everything as a part of a coherent whole. Catholicism especially has been aware of the danger stemming not so much from the autonomy of sciences as from their refusal to accept a well defined place in an overarching system. Late nineteenth-century neo-Thomism was an attempt to counter this proliferation of discourses speaking and teaching about the same reality in different ways.[6]

However, this initiative was not successful. Today, asserting: 'This is not a moral but a psychological problem' sounds like something sensible, although it would have been inconceivable two centuries ago. It would have appeared as silly as if you had said: 'That table is not brown, for it is square'. But times have changed, and so have our commonplaces. The dispersion of knowledges (in the plural) and the new type of guidance given by them is the result of modern *loci*.

Considered in this way, the history of the Catholic doctrine on abortion is an interesting test case of how modern commonplaces work.[7] For most people, it seems obvious that Catholics should consider abortion as murder, which means that they should debate on abortion under the heading of murder, and that possible acceptance of some forms of abortion should comply with the rules adopted for accepting the killing of a human being. Thus one comes to various strange ways of reasoning, e.g. if in some cases the foetus could actually be considered as an 'aggressor', since it could endanger the mother's life. Although it seems strange to deal with a foetus in this way and to apply the categories of 'just war' to it, this is the logical consequence of putting abortion under the heading of 'murder'.[8]

It becomes stranger still when we realise that dealing with abortion under the heading of murder is not at all a traditional, conventional view. On the contrary: here we are in the presence of a very recently constructed 'commonplace', as I will now show. This construction resulted from the fact that religious discourse had to become a separate discourse, resting on

---

[6] See P. Vandermeersch, *Ethiek tussen wetenschap en ideologie* (Leuven, 1987).

[7] For an overview, see J. Connery, *Abortion: The Development of the Roman Catholic Perspective* (Chicago, 1977).

[8] See J. T. Noonan, 'An Almost Absolute Value in History', in: J. T. Noonan, ed., *The Morality of Abortion: Legal and Historical Perspectives* (Cambridge, MA, 1970), pp. 1-59 (p. 40).

its own structure, and was not expected to take its arguments from biology any more, as it used to do. As my aim is not to deal with moral theology, but to use the case merely as an example of how commonplaces work, I will refrain from giving my own opinion on the moral issue of abortion – let me just state that not everything that is *not* a murder is allowed *per se*.

The classical Catholic position on abortion

During the first millennium of Christianity, the statements concerning abortion are rather vague. Without any doubt, it is a sin Christians should not commit, but it is unclear if it is generally considered as murder. There is nothing on abortion in the New Testament, but the topic is present in two early texts, the *Didache* 2.2 and the Epistle of Barnabas 19.5. In both cases, the formulation is nearly identical. In a listing of a rather diverse set of prohibitions, we find the statement: 'you shall not kill a child in the womb and you shall not kill a child when it is born'. In both cases the same two verbs are used to express 'killing' (*ou foneuseis teknon en fthora, ouden genèthen apoktneseis*). Why not use one verb followed by two complements, as various translations do? This is curious.[9]

When Christians adopted the Old Testament only one text on abortion was added to the Biblical corpus. In Exodus 21.22-24 we read, when literally translated: 'If men are fighting and they hurt a pregnant woman and her children come out of her, and there is not a severe injury (*'ason*), the man responsible must pay the compensation demanded of him by the woman's master; he shall hand it over, after arbitration. But if there is a severe injury, you shall give life for life, eye for eye, tooth for tooth, hand for hand, foot for foot, burn for burn, wound for wound, stroke for stroke'.[10] The whole

---

[9] K. Lake translates the *Didache* text as: 'thou shalt not procure abortion, nor commit infanticide' (*The Apostolic Fathers*, 2 vols., transl. K. Lake (Cambridge, MA, 1965), I, pp. 310-313; Barnabas on pp. 402-403). The Attrige edition of the *Didache* makes of it: 'You shall not murder a child, whether by abortion or by killing it once it is born' (H. W. Attrige and K. Niederwimmer, eds, *The Didache: A Commentary*, transl. L. M. Maloney (Minneapolis, 1998), p. 88). The Jefford edition has: 'You shall not murder a child, whether by [procuring its] abortion or by killing it once it is born' (C. N. Jefford, ed., *The Didache in Context: Essays on its Text, History and Transmission* (Leiden, 1995), p. 6).

[10] Translators hesitate about the precise meaning. *The Jerusalem Bible* (New York, 1966) has: 'If, when men come to blows, they hurt a woman who is pregnant and she suffers a miscarriage, though she does not die of it, the man responsible must pay the compensation demanded of him by the woman's master; he shall hand it over, after arbitration. But should she die, you shall give life for life, eye for eye, tooth for tooth, hand for hand, foot for foot, burn for burn, wound for wound, stroke for stroke'. *The New Oxford Annotated Bible* (New York, 1991) has: 'When people

question is to understand precisely what *'ason* means. Surely, it is a severe accident, as we can infer from Genesis 42.4, where the same uncommon verb appears: Jacob is afraid that some *'ason* could happen to Benjamin if he accompanies his brothers to Egypt in order to purchase wheat. Does *'ason* however mean Benjamin's death? This is not clear. However, you could infer from the remaining part of the text on the fighting men in Exodus 21 that there the word refers to the death of someone, as it is said that a life should be given for a life.

This interpretation, however, opens up new difficulties. If *'ason* refers to someone's death, whose death is it? The death of the baby or that of the woman? Early translators have interpreted this differently. The oldest Latin translation (the Vulgate) has understood it unambiguously as the women's life: *sed ipsa vixerit*. The Greek translation of the Septuagint, however, thought of the baby, and added a distinction that was to become common in the Middle Ages: 'when the baby is not yet a perfect copy [of a human being] (*ekseikonismenon*), then the man should pay a financial compensation, but if the child is already a perfect copy, then he should give life for life, [etc.]' An abortion at an early stage of pregnancy is not identical with an abortion at a later stage.

The Greek translation clearly reflects Greek medical views, stemming from Aristotle, according to which the soul has to be understood as the name given to the form of a living being. A form does not exist as a separated 'thing'; it is an aspect of the whole being and presupposes the matter involved in it. Form and matter or – applying the terminology appropriate for human beings – soul and body are two aspects of the same thing. We can only artificially separate them by an operation of our mind, but, in reality, they are intimately linked with each other. They cannot exist separately: that is the core of Aristotelian 'hylemorphism'.[11]

We could list here the statements of various councils, which mostly seem to be aware of the essential difference between an early and a late abortion. However, their aim seems to be primarily directed at standardising the amount of penance imposed on sinners in this realm and not to discuss the ontological status of a foetus. Considered from the amount of penance imposed on the crime, some scholars argue that sometimes abortion is assimilated to murder, sometimes not. One could add that other elements, like

---

who are fighting injure a pregnant woman so that there is a miscarriage, and yet no further harm follows, the one responsible shall be fined what the woman's husband demands, paying as much as the judges determine. If any harm follows, you shall give life for life, eye for eye, tooth for tooth, hand for hand, foot for foot, burn for burn, wound for wound, stripe for stripe'.

[11] See E. Lesky, *Die Zeugungs- und Vererbungslehren der Antike und ihr Nachwirken* (Mainz, 1950), pp. 125-159.

the use of magical practices, intervene in the taxation of the sin and confuse the debate.

In any case, things become much clearer in the Middle Ages, when Aristotelian views on the soul are explicitly adopted and become the cornerstone of the debate on abortion. By then, a human foetus is considered as a human being only once the rational soul has been infused in it. This can only happen once the foetus has the shape of a real human body. The standard formula stems from Peter Lombard and seemed so natural that it deserved no comment from Thomas Aquinas in his commentary on the former's *Sententiae*:

> *Hic quaeri solet de his qui abortum procurant, quando judicentur homicidae, vel non. Tunc puerperium ad homicidum pertinet, quando formatum est et animam habet, ut Augustinus super Exodum asserit. Informe ante puerperium, ubi non est anima viva, lex ad homicidium pertinere noluit.*[12]

At this point we habitually put the question of whether those who perform abortion should be considered as murderers. The foetus can only be the object of a murder when it has been formed and possesses a soul, as Augustine says in his commentary on Exodus [i.e. in the Greek translation quoted above]. The law on murder does not apply to the foetus containing no living soul.

Some might be inclined to say that this argument *ex silentio* is not convincing. Another passage in Aquinas does, however, confirm that the great theologian was convinced that a human foetus was endowed with a human soul only after a certain period of pregnancy. In discussing the embryonic development of Christ, he wonders why the feast of the Annunciation is on March 25, as the infusion of a human soul should normally have happened much later. You would have expected the angel to come at least twice. Discussing medical theories, Thomas concludes that Christ's embryo was configured immediately in a human shape, but on a smaller scale, not much bigger than an ant, so that Mary's pregnancy could last nine months.[13]

There can be no doubt that, for scholastic theology, an embryo became a human being only in the course of pregnancy. For centuries the debate has concerned the identification of the very moment the soul is infused. There

---

[12] Thomas Aquinas, *Scriptum in quartum librum sententiarum magistri Petri Lombardi*, distinctio XXXI, in: *Opera omnia,* VII, ed. I. Nicolai (Parma 1858), p. 952. The transl. is mine.

[13] Thomas Aquinas, *Scriptum in tertium librum sententiarum magistri Petri Lombardi*, distinctio III, quaestio V, art. 2, in: *Opera omnia,* VII, p. 51. See also A. Mitterer, *Dogma und Biologie der heiligen Familie nach dem Weltbild des Hl. Thomas von Aquin und dem der Gegenwart* (Vienna 1952).

have been some rather extreme positions. Some theologians have even stated that this happens only at the very moment of birth, or later still, when the child acquires the ability to speak, providing proof of an operational human, rational soul. Those extreme views were condemned by pope Innocent XI in the list of his sentences against the 'Laxists', the moralists who showed too much understanding, in 1679:

> nr. 34: *Licet procurare abortum ante animationem foetus, ne puella deprehensa gravida occidatur aut infametur.*[14]

> It is permissible to perform an abortion before the foetus receives its soul, so that a pregnant girl would not be killed or lose her reputation.

> nr. 35: *Videtur probabile omnem foetum, quandiu in utero est, carere anima rationali et tunc primum incipere eandem habere, cum paritur, ac consequenter dicendum erit in nullo abortu homocidium committi.*

> It is probable that every foetus does not have a rational soul as long as it is in the womb, and that it starts to be endowed with one only at the moment of birth. As a consequence, one should say that no case of abortion should be called a murder.

However, the condemnation of these extremes did not change anything in the basic sense that there is a fundamental difference between a foetus with and one without a human soul. Even the discoveries relating to the mechanism of procreation in the seventeenth century did not challenge this view. As is well known, as soon as Antony van Leeuwenhoek (1631-1723) had constructed the first microscope, one of his students, John Ham, rushed to his professor in alarm and asked him: 'Look, professor, all those little animals I see! What could this be?' The student had put his own sperm under the microscope, and one can imagine how anxious he became when he saw all those little animals coming out of his genitals.[15] Spermatozoa were discovered and slightly later the ovum, and a quarrel arose on the relation between them. For 'animalculists' the sperm already contained small but complete animals with a little head, and the egg was just a receptacle wherein they grew. For 'ovists', however, everything was already in the ovum, and the male spermatozoon was just a little whip giving the stimulus

---

[14] *Magnum Bullarium Romanum* (Luxemburg, 1727-1748), VII, p. 81. The transl. is mine.

[15] C. Dobell, ed., *Antony van Leeuwenhoek and His 'Little Animals'* (New York, 1960 [1932]).

necessary to start the process of embryo formation. It was not until 1875 that Oscar Hertwig (1849-1922) discovered the fusion between the chromosomes.

Did Leeuwenhoek's discovery put an end to the, by then, current opinion that abortion was not always a murder? Not at all. The traditional view held sway until the end of the nineteenth century. Arguing that, after the fusion, no new break could be identified in the development of a foetus, Catholic medical circles became inclined to adopt the view that every abortion was a murder. This was, however, rejected by many theologians and philosophers. Pointing to the fact that many new cells resulting from the fusion did not get implanted in the uterus, they asked ironically: are they all innocent human beings ending up in limbo, the heavenly place just before heaven where the unbaptised enjoy natural delights, although missing the supernatural delights provided for the Christian just? This place must be overcrowded, with a population much bigger than that of heaven and hell combined! Arguing in this way, the Belgian Cardinal D. Mercier, formerly a professor of philosophy, defends the traditional view in his *Cours de psychologie* and illustrates this with a long quotation from Dante's *Purgatory*.[16]

---

[16] D. Mercier, *Cours de psychologie*, III, part 2 (Louvain, 1912), pp. 329-333. I have added between square brackets the lines that follow in Dante's *Purgatory*, as they are still more explicit:

Anima fatte la virtute attiva
  qual d'una pianta, in tanto differente,
  che questa è in via e quella è già a riva,
tanto ovra poi, che già si move e sente,
  come spungo marino; e indi imprende
  ad organar le posse ond'è semente.
Or si spiega, figliuolo, or si distende
  la virtù ch'è dal cor del generante,
  dove natura a tutte membra intende.
[Ma come d'animal divegna fante,
  non vedi tu ancor: quest'è tal punto,
  che più savio di te fé già errante,
sì che per sua dottrina fé disgiunto
  da l'anima il possibile intelletto,
  perché da lui non vide organo assunto.
Apri a la verità che vienne il petto;
  e sappi che, sì tosto come al feto
  l'articular del cerebro è perfetto,
lo motor primo a lui si volge lieto
  sovra tant'arte di natura, e spira
  spirito novo, di vertù repleto,
che ciò che trova attivo quivi, tira

Still, on November 18, 1974, the Vatican Congregation for the Doctrine of Faith declared in a footnote to its *Declaration on Abortion*, after having referred to recent research in embryology, that the very moment of the infusion of the soul is difficult to define, as there is a continuous process of differentiation of the foetus. The traditional doctrine is not subjected to revision:

> *Haec declaratio consulto quaestionem reliquam facit, quo temporis momento anima spiritualis infundatur. Qua de re ut traditio non est unanima, ita auctores inter se differunt. Nam cum alii affirment id primo vitae tempore fieri, aliis placet hoc non ante fieri, quam germen in sua sede steterit.*[17]

This declaration purposely leaves open the question regarding the precise moment at which the spiritual soul is infused. The tradition is not unanimous on this point, and the authors have different opinions. Some assume this happening already in the first moments of life, while others believe this can only be the case when the germ has taken its proper position.

One might think: there can be no doubt. Even if disagreement is possible, everybody should know what the doctrine of the Catholic Church firmly and steadfastly holds: abortion is wrong, but it is not always murder. Of course, sometimes newspapers and television present things differently, but

---

in sua sustanzia, e fassi un'alma sola,
che vive e sente e sé in sé rigira.]

The active virtue having become a soul, like that of a plant (but in so far different that this is on the way, and that has already arrived) so works then that now it moves and feels, like a sea-fungus; then it proceeds to develop organs for the powers of which it is the germ. Now, son, expands, now distends, the virtue which proceeds from the heart of the begetter, where nature makes provision for all the members. But how from animal it becomes a human being you do not see yet: this is such a point that once it made one wiser than you err, so that in this teaching he separated the possible intellect from the soul because he saw no organ assumed by it. [Open your breast to the truth which is coming, and know that, so soon as in the foetus the articulation of the brain is perfect, the First Mover turns to it with joy over such art of nature, and breathes into it a new spirit replete with virtue, which absorbs that which is active there into its own substance, and makes one single soul which lives and feels and circles on itself.] Dante Allegieri, *La Divina Commedia*: *Purgatorio*, XXV, 52-60, in the bilingual edition *The Divine Comedy*: *Purgatorio*, ed. and transl. C. Singleton (Princeton, 1973) pp. 272-273.

[17] *Quaestio de abortu procurato*, *Acta Apostolicae Sedis* 66 (1974), pp. 730-737, n. 19.

they are so often so badly informed on religious matters.[18] One is, however, very surprised when official textbooks and documents show the same ignorance or – if it is legitimate to suspect this? – when they seem purposely to expound their own tradition differently from how it actually was. The most striking fact is that the most authoritative textbook on Catholic doctrine, Denzinger's *Enchiridion symbolorum, definitionum et declarationum de rebus fidei et morum*, skipped the passages referring to the debate on the moment a foetus becomes a human being from the Vatican declaration of 1974.[19] I could add to this many statements of bishops that are not corrected by statements coming from the Vatican, nor by many theologians, who actually know better but prefer to conceal this aspect of their own tradition by using the vaguer formula of 'sin against life'.

The loci and the authority principle

How should we understand this move and the seemingly purposeful elaboration of a new *locus communis* on abortion since 1974? The motives have not been publicised. One might think that Church officers have recently begun to reason as follows: if, rationally, abortion is not (always) murder, how should we communicate with a public that might be inclined to say: 'If it is not murder it is allowed'? Would it not be better to say 'it is murder' despite the fact that it is not?

But is this not an argument worthy of Machiavelli? Is it permissible to deceive people for the sake of morality? And is it effective? Further on, in this case in particular: is it good moral teaching to give the impression that everything that is not murder is licit? Looking back over the history of Catholic moral teaching, one wonders if the strategy of increasing the number of 'mortal sins', until even silent masturbation in a lonely bed would sentence you to hell, has really provided an improvement of general moral behaviour. In any case, in the second half of the twentieth century we witnessed how this kind of discourse can suddenly collapse. Beginning with A. Hesnard and his *Morale sans péché* (1954),[20] psychotherapists started questioning the (un)healthy nature of Catholic feelings of guilt that made people so afraid of doing wrong that they were no longer capable of striving ac-

---

[18] E.g., the celibacy of the priesthood is often mistakenly thought of as a vow and thus considered the same as the ideal of sexual abstinence typical for a monk. A priest is, however, not a monk, and celibacy is definitely not a vow. It is just a legal prohibition to marry – something that was also applicable to female schoolteachers and air hostesses until some decades ago.

[19] H. Denzinger and P. Hünermann, *Enchiridion symbolorum, definitionum et declarationum de rebus fidei et morum* (Freiburg, [37]1991), §§ 4550-4552.

[20] A. Hesnard, *Morale sans péché* (Paris, 1954).

tively to do good. Without waiting for a new and updated theory of Catholic conscience, many Catholics ceased to practise confession in the late 1960s.[21]

How, then, can people be motivated to behave morally and – as seems to be important in Catholic doctrine which insists on the value of individual conscience – to reflect consciously on moral problems? This is one of the central issues in Catholic moral theology. Staying with the problem of abortion, we meet a very interesting controversy between two popes dealing with this question, in 1585 and 1591 respectively. This debate leaves the discussion on the distinction between an early and a late abortion untouched, but it deals with the various ways of influencing people's behaviour and scruples.

On October 29, 1585, pope Sixtus V declared in his Constitution *Effroenatam* that, henceforth, the same penalties would apply to both cases of abortion. Up until then, an early abortion could be forgiven by a bishop, and the adequate penalty was to be defined by him.[22] But, from this point on, the holy See, to which one already had to refer in the case of a late abortion, would reserve also the absolution of an early abortion for itself. The introductory part of the document, which mentions the reasons for this change, is very harsh and displays a very authoritarian style. It states that the Church has often been compelled to react firmly against the unbridled audacity (*effroenatam audaciam*) of people who dare to transgress the divine law against killing (*divinae legis praeceptum de non occidendo*). This does not, however, mean that the pope equates abortion with murder. The argumentation makes a sideways move. In a rather lengthy passage, the pope fulminates against the lustful cruelty and the cruel lust (*libidinosam impiorum hominum crudelitatem, vel crudelem libidinem*) that prevents a potential human being from growing up and reaching its final destiny in heaven. This lust also impedes an increase in the number of members of the Church.[23]

---

[21] See P. Vandermeersch and H. Westerink, *Godsdienstpsychologie in cultuurhistorisch perspectief* (Amsterdam, 2007), pp. 242-248.

[22] Text in P. Gasparri, ed., *Codicis iuris canonici fontes*, I (Rome, 1923), nr. 165, pp. 308-311.

[23] Here is a partial quotation: *Quis enim non detestetur tam execrandum facinus, per quod nedum corporum, sed quod gravius est, etiam animarum certa jactura sequitur? Quis non gravissimis suppliciis damnet illius impietatem, qui animam Dei imagine insignitam, pro qua redimenda Christus Dominus noster preciosum sanguinem fudit, aeternae capacem beatitudinis, et ad consortium Angelorum destinatam, a beata Dei visione exclusit, reparationem coelestium sedium quantum in ipso fuit impedivit, Deo servitium suae creaturae ademit? qui liberos prius vita privavit, quam illi a natura propriam lucem accipere, aut se materni custodia corporis ab efferata saevitia tegere potuerint? Quis non abhorreat libidinosam impiorum hominum crudelitatem, vel crudelem libidinem, quae eo usque processit, ut etiam venena pro-*

Then the pope comes to his conclusion: he feels compelled partly to inno-
vate, and partly to extend the existing laws on abortion (*vetera jura partim
innovando, partim ampliando*). He has therefore decided to impose the
same penalties for both cases of abortion, prior as well as posterior to the
moment of the infusion of the soul (*abortus foetus immaturi tam animati
quam etiam inanimati, formati vel informis*). In practice, this meant that local bishops were no longer able to forgive the sin of abortion. The cases had
to be sent to Rome before absolution could be given and the imposed penalties became more severe.[24]

Six years later, on May 31, 1591, pope Gregory XIV came back to the
old position in the very lenient text *Sedes Apostolica*.[25] The Church, he
says, should behave like an understanding mother. His predecessor had
been overzealous (*praedecessor noster justitiae zelo accensus*), and the
equation of both penalties had produced an effect opposite to that intended
(*Cum igitur postmodum experientia docuit, ex remedio hujusmodi, non eam
quae sperabatur utilitatem et fructum provenisse, verum potius multis Sa-
tanae malitia* (...)). The lesson to be learnt from this was that Church discipline should rescue people as a physician does, and not by terrorising them.
Thus the pope had decided to return to the old ecclesiastical law.

The text is worthy of quotation:

> *Nos propterea animadvertentes gladium Ecclesiasticae disciplinae, praesertim
> quoad censuras et poenas spirituales, ita exercendum esse ut ad medicinam
> tendat, non ad perniciem animarum; aeternumque Pastorem cujus vices in ter-
> ris gerimur, quantum (divina ejus gratia adjutrice) possumus, imitari volentes,
> qui venit animas hominum salvare non perdere, neminique quantumcumque
> graviter et enormiter deliquerit, viam salutis praeclusit, quin potius ad eam
> assequendam copiosa remedia adhibuit, ac nobis reliquit et simul utilius cen-
> sentes ubi nec de homicidio nec de animato foetu agitur, poenas non imponere
> duriores iis, quae per sacros canones et leges prophanas sunt inflictae* (...).[26]

We have seen that the sword of Church discipline, especially impeachments
and spiritual punishments, must be applied in such a way as to become medicine and so as not to harm souls. We want to imitate the eternal Pastor, in
whose name we serve here on earth, as much as we can (with the aid of divine
grace). He came to save the souls of humans and not to bring them to perdition.

---

*curet ad conceptos foetus intra viscera extinguendos et fundendos, etiam suam pro-
lem prius interire quam vivere, aut si jam vivebat, occidi antequam nasci nefario
scelere moliendo?* (Gasparri, *Codicis*, p. 308).
[24] Noonan, 'An Almost Absolute Value', p. 33.
[25] Gasparri, *Codicis*, nr. 173, pp. 330-331.
[26] Gasparri, *Codicis*, p. 330. My transl.

He did not exclude anybody from salvation, however seriously and heinously he or she took the wrong way. On the contrary, he preferred to provide many remedies to make it possible to gain salvation. Therefore he left it to us to decide, as we thought useful, not to apply more severe punishments than those foreseen in canonical and civil law in those cases where there is no murder, since there is no foetus with a soul.

Is the difference between the two popes just a matter of individual temper? Sixtus was very authoritarian, as required by the lamentable state of Rome when he started his papacy; Gregory was humble and pious. This humble nature, however, did not hamper him from reiterating the excommunication of Henry IV of France, despite the fact that the king of Navarre had meanwhile converted from Protestantism to Catholicism *car Paris vaut bien une messe*. But, instead on focusing on individual psychology, we could perhaps draw attention to an emergent change of mentality concerning moral authority. What would interest me, as a psychologist of religion, is the way this shift in dealing with the moral issue of abortion did not reflect temper alone, but a new awareness of the ways authority figures could guide or even overwhelm people's conscience.

We are discussing a time when Catholicism was refining its techniques for spiritual guidance and confession. Gregory XIV was a good friend of two of the pioneering men in this respect, Carlo Borromeo and Filippo Neri. Although the term 'psychology' was not used commonly, as it is today, it was a period during which psychological power, along with the techniques for making it more effective, were discovered. The most systematic and structural activation of those insights in a secular context was to come later on, with the invention of psychiatry as 'moral treatment' in the eighteenth century and the subsequent discussions of the ethics of psychotherapeutic interventions, as I have discussed elsewhere.[27]

Of course, there was a religious prehistory to this systematic use of psychological manipulation by lay people. According to my knowledge, the basic ideas were laid down in the Jesuits' spirituality that put the religious meaning of individual destiny to the fore and developed specific techniques for education. A topic that deserves further exploration is the new spirituality aimed at the secular clergy and advocated by the Congregation of the Oratory and by the Sulpicians. The presuppositions of the new discipline of pastoral theology, founded in Austria at the end of the eighteenth century, deserve further investigation. Unfortunately, as I am not a historian, I can only express my eagerness to hear more about this part of the psychohistory

---

[27] P. Vandermeersch, ed., *Psychiatrie, godsdienst en gezag: de ontstaansgeschiedenis van de psychiatrie in België als paradigma* (Leuven, 1984).

of Western subjectivity. It would complement the glimpses I have already gained in the course of my inquiry into the history of religious flagellation.[28] It is very typical how this practice shifted from an ecstatic narcissistic ritual in the Middle Ages to an expression of humiliation, but also a strengthening of the personal conscience, in the seventeenth century.

However, this progressive elaboration of a new style of guidance, superseding direct authoritarian talk, did not manage to keep the Church's monopoly as guardian of morality upright. The emergence of new discourses challenged it. When we put the theory of the *loci* into the framework of the cultural history of conscience in the West, we see a clear shift. According to the formulation of Melchior Cano, the *loci* are linked to a hierarchy of authority, but authority is still understood as univocal, as simply a matter of more and less. The universal Church is more important than the Roman Catholic denomination, and this is more important than philosophy, or the history of mankind. In Cano's view, every authority operates in the same public and recognisable way. My hypothesis, that needs to be confirmed by further research, is that, little by little, people became aware that authority is questionable and were invited by the new discourses to claim their freedom.

As a result, the Catholic Church was compelled to present itself as having a discourse of its own, which meant increasingly: an easily recognisable discourse, a separated discourse. In this context the references to the knowledge present in medicine and biology, that had always fostered moral theology, were silently dropped. Puzzled by the bankruptcy of their moral authority, Church officers tried desperately to reintroduce an authoritarian style and therefore chose the most loaded topic in order to impress individual consciences: murder. Unfortunately, by so doing, they forewent the necessary reflection on how to bring people living in the midst of earthly manipulative powers to adequate moral responsibility.

---

[28] P. Vandermeersch, *La Chair de la Passion. Une histoire de foi: la flagellation* (Paris, 2002).

DIE GELERTEN, DIE VERKERTEN

COMMONPLACES IN THE REFORMERS' APOLOGIES FOR THE OVER-TURNING OF ECCLESIASTICAL AUTHORITY

Ninna Jørgensen

In this chapter, the term 'commonplace' stands for a set locution which is embedded in various and changing procedures of persuasion, or moral edification. The emphasis of the investigation rests on the function of popular locutions and imagery in the Reformers' polemical works. As a main thread, the reader will be presented with a discussion of the often used German locution *die gelerten, die verkerten* ('the learned, the perverted/ twisted') and, within the same context, of the biblical imagery that was habitually related to it. By the middle of the Reformation century, the proverb *die gelerten, die verkerten*, with edifying glosses, was integrated into a work that comes very close to constituting a vernacular counterpart to the Latin commonplace books of the sixteenth century surveyed by Ann Moss in her comprehensive monograph,[1] namely Sebastian Franck's *Sprichwoerter* of 1541, one of the first and most substantial publications of its kind in German.[2] Here 'our' saying figures among a range of ten further observations under a heading (wrongly) ascribed to the humanist and pioneering collector of popular proverbs, Henrich Bebel, *In nihil sapiendo iucundissima vita*. Among these we also find the statement that artificial people ('künstler') are the first to be mentioned in Sebastian Brant's *Narrenschiff*.

It is important, at the outset, to note the reasons why anonymous locutions in the vernacular were considered sources of truth by Reformation theologians. In the prologue to his *Sprichwoerter*, Sebastian Franck provides a detailed description of the proverb, which he contrasts to elaborate doctrine in terms of both its form and its function. The proverb is short; it contains the summa or the nucleus of a whole discourse, like in a shrine; it may be subtle, expressing its meaning under cover, through implication. It appeals to every man through its obvious correspondence with experience, as well as with the innate common sense of all mankind. Therefore, it is

---

[1] A. Moss, *Printed Commonplace-Books and the Structuring of Renaissance Thought* (Oxford, 1996), esp. p. 207.
[2] S. Franck, *Sprichwoerter, Schoene, Weise, Herrliche Cluogreden unnd Hoffsprüch* (Frankfurt am Main, 1541; repr. Bern, 1993), p. 145.

more trustworthy than any other sentence, and, as it indicates correct conduct in a self-evident manner, it is, in spite of its brevity, richer in content than a long sermon.[3]

Sebastian Franck was a Lutheran theologian with 'spiritualist' sympathies, and a believer in the inner light of man. But, even to Luther, who is generally considered rather sceptical about the power of reason, Franck's sayings represented evident expressions of life experience. Admittedly, they had to be sieved critically. But, polished as they were by generations of use, and appealing to common sense through plain evidence, they stood in marked contrast to the sophisticated insider language of the scholastics and their far from self-evident argumentation.[4] The extent of Luther's usage of popular sayings was in fact rather wide; he wrote household remedies advocated by members of the respectable middle class in chalk on his wall.[5] In addition, in his mature years, he might sometimes replace the scriptural passage on which he was preaching with a popular locution. This was in accordance with his preaching technique in general; in order to ensure that churchgoers remembered his sermons after they had left church, he made great efforts to concentrate his point in a single sentence, typically a formula from the Creed.[6] For Luther proverbs had a memorable quality and could therefore be useful, although, of course, they were never ranked on the same level as quotations from the Bible.

1. Background

1.1 'Old' doctrine or 'new' doctrine? Or: who are the intruders in the vineyard of the Lord?

In what follows, I shall give a survey of the fundamental theological controversy about old versus new doctrine in its Danish variant. Arguments used in the German and Danish debates were identical, but, because there were significantly fewer participants in the Danish debate, it is a more manageable example given the limited space available here.

The Danish Reformers' attacks on the Catholic Church for having suppressed God's word and hidden it from 'the man in the street' for centuries

---

[3] Franck, *Sprichwoerter*, p. 9.
[4] D.-R. Moser, 'Laiendichtung und Volksdichtung bei Martin Luther', in: L. Grenzmann and K. Stackmann, eds, *Literatur und Laienbildung im Spätmittelalter und in der Reformationszeit* (Stuttgart, 1984), pp. 66-68.
[5] Moser, 'Laiendichtung', p. 66.
[6] N. Jørgensen, '*Sed manet articulus*: Preaching and Catechetical Training in Selected Sermons by the Later Luther', *Studia Theologica: Nordic Journal of Theology* 59 (2005), pp. 38-54.

were met with a vehement voice of opposition from the old Church. Poul Helgesen, a Danish Carmelite, maintained as his refrain that it was absurd to claim that the Holy Ghost had been absent from the Christian community for fourteen or fifteen hundred years and had only just re-entered the stage with the appearance of Martin Luther and his disciples.[7] Helgesen pointed out that Church authorities stood on solid ground, because they relied on a host of martyrs, saints, and Church Fathers in their interpretation of the biblical texts. It would surely be more secure, argued Helgesen, to follow the 'many' of the established order than to join a party, which, in comparison to this solid vehicle – the Church – was like a fifth wheel joined to a carriage.[8]

Helgesen's polemical texts were contributions to this ongoing conflict, and, as his target group was local politicians and citizens, he wrote to them in Danish. His writings moreover included exchanges of opinion with a number of prominent persons, such as Gustav Vasa, King of Sweden, who had engaged, on the Lutheran side, in the debate over controversial theological issues such as the authority of the Bible alone versus the tradition of the Church, and Hans Mikkelsen, mayor of Malmö, who had followed the Danish king Christian II into exile. Mikkelsen was a prime mover in the edition of a Danish New Testament which was smuggled into Denmark as propaganda against the subversive government, which Helgesen had originally supported against the exiled king. In spite of the particular historical context, which is characterised by these personal antagonisms, however, none of the arguments referred to in the debate are unique to the Danish or Swedish Reformation. The Scandinavian examples may, on the contrary, underscore the 'international' character of the Reformation debate in question. In all the parts of Europe touched by the Reformation, we may discern a reading and debating public preoccupied with identical patterns of argumentation. If regarded in isolation as a matter of national history, the nature of the very heated debate between Helgesen and his opponents would perhaps be considered as being rather spontaneous. The assessment will undoubtedly be more accurate if we take into account the use of certain commonplaces, which were marshalled and assigned specific tasks in the debate. Before discussing the actual use of these arguments in the contemporary popular literature, I shall illustrate this point by an observation.

---

[7] See S. Haarløv, *Poul Helgesens teologiske standpunkt og placering i den europæiske humanismebevægelse – set på baggrund af en præsentation af Erasmus af Rotterdams teologiske programskrifter* (Copenhagen, 2007).
[8] P. Helgesen, 'Svar til Hans Mikkelsen (1527)', in: *Povel Eliesens Danske Skrifter, udgivne af Selskabet for Danmarks Kirkehistorie*, ed. C. E. Secher (Copenhagen, 1855), I, pp. 93-94.

In 1528, Poul Helgesen responded to a series of questions posed by Gustav Vasa.[9] The Carmelite steered his course by means of an arrangement of arguments which, down to the last detail, follow John Eck's model refutation of the persistent Protestant claim that the authority of Scripture is prior to that of the Church. Eck's *Enchiridion locorum communium adversus Lutherum et alios hostes ecclesiae* from 1525[10] was the first big effort from the Catholic side to counter Philip Melanchthon's *Loci communes* of 1521 by means of a similar theological commonplace-book of standard references.[11] In the following years, Eck's work was printed and reprinted all over Europe, for instance in Rome, Paris, Cologne, Venice, and Rostock. As he intended, his model arguments seem to have flowed back into 'everyday dispute'. With Eck's work in hand, any theologian with a European outlook could look up further arguments for the dispute against the 'enemy'.

The 'dissolution of heretical objections', on which Helgesen bases his own argument, is found under the heading *De ecclesia et eius auctoritate*. Here, Eck states that the Church precedes the collection of the canonical texts, which the Reformers refer to as their only authority. The decision as to which among the circulating gospels and letters were more 'noble' was made by the principals of the Church. Thus, the Reformers would not even know which texts were canonical, had it not been for the existence of an institution prior to the formation of the canon.[12] In Helgesen's answer to the

---

[9] P. Helgesen, 'Nogre Christelige Suar till the spørsmaall som Koning Gøstaff till Swerigis Rijge lodt wdgaa til sith gantsche Klerfkerij, berammede aff Broder Paulo Hiele, Kjøbenhaffn M.D.xxviii', in: *Povel Eliesens Danske Skrifter*, I, pp. 167-326.

[10] J. Eck, *Enchiridion locorum communium versus Lutheranos et alios hostes ecclesiae (1525-1543)*, ed. P. Fraenkel (Münster, 1979).

[11] See the description of this work by Moss (*Printed Commonplace-Books*, p. 132, and in her chapter in this volume, pp. 1-17).

[12] *Unde haeretico volenti contendere contra ecclesiae instituta et consuetudines, obiiciatur, quibus armis velit contendere contra ecclesiam. Dicturus est: Canonicis scriptures quatuor Evangeliorum, ac Paulinis epistolis. Huic mox obiiciatur: Unde sciat has scripturas esse Canonicas, nisi ex ecclesia? Quare enim credit Evangelium Marci, qui Christum non vidit, esse Canonicum, et non Evangelium Nicodemi, qui vidit et audivit Christum (...) – nisi humiliter confitearis ecclesiae authoritatem cum sancto Augustino (...) 'Evangelio non crederem, nisi authoritas ecclesiae me commoveret'*, Eck, *Enchiridion*, pp. 27-28. ('Therefore, the heretic, who wants to fight the institutions and practices of the Church, is to be countered with the question of with which weapons he wants to fight the Church. He is going to say: with the canonical scriptures of the four Gospels and the Pauline epistles. At once he is to be countered: from where does he know that the Gospel of Mark, who has not seen Christ, is canonical, but not the Gospel of Nicodemus, who has both seen and heard Christ (...) unless you confess humbly with the authority of Saint Augustine (...) "I would not have believed the Gospel, if the authority of the Church had not moved me"').

Swedish king, he argues that of course the Reformers will accept nothing but Holy Scripture, but, if the principals of the Church had not made a distinction between noble and less noble texts, they would not even know what Scripture to refer to. Even the quotation from Augustine used by Helgesen is *verbaliter* the same as in Eck.[13]

The interchange between a standard commonplace-book and the seemingly more spontaneous use of good arguments in the exchange of meanings will not be further discussed here. Helgesen may have found his argument in Eck's book, or, theoretically, it may have been the other way round: Eck's book may itself have used weapons which had already been forged by the defenders of established Church doctrine. The further prospect of integrating commonplaces into the study of ecclesiastical history in the sixteenth century is, however, alluring – whether it be directly, as a result of their diffusion through model reasoning in printed commonplace-books or, more indirectly, as a clue to the working of minds which had been formed through school education.

Even if Eck's objection against the Reformers' unilateral invoking of Scripture undermined its historical credibility, when it came to winning the people's support the defenders of the old order such as Helgesen hit their enemies at their weakest point by pointing to the novelty of the Lutheran doctrine. Already, from a theological perspective, new doctrines were suspicious, and certainly inferior to a tradition which made a virtue of its age. To the common people, a rapid and radical change in religious customs inevitably caused insecurity about salvation and thereby dissension in the parish communities. In accordance with Helgesen's argumentation, his fellow combatants in Germany, notably Hieronymus Emser, conjured up a horrifying perspective in which decisions about the correct reading of the Bible were left to individual choice and arbitrariness. In cases where consultation is necessary, argued Emser, it is more reasonable to trust the 'old and proven' interpreters than the 'newfangled' and 'presumptuous' ones. It is for the individual Christian to decide if he or she will abide by the Holy Fathers, who have left us their heritage with the imprint of their own blood, or follow Luther's new doctrine and tear down everything which the Fathers have left us. Emser concludes this passage with the remark that the day of visitation has apparently come.[14]

---

[13] See Haarløv, *Poul Helgesen*, p. 219.

[14] 'Wo wir auch yemandt in der schrifft glauben sollen und mussen, glauben wir ye billicher, den alten bewerten, dann den nawen vormessen und unbeschnitten. Dach so hab ein yeder die wall oder wilkuer bey ym selber, die auszlegung die uns die heyligen veter, hinder ynen vorlassen, antzuhangen, und bey dem glauben tzu bleiben, bey dem unsere veter, mit vorgiessung yrs bluts, leyb und leben tzugesatzt ha-

It was part of everyday theological knowledge that dissensions would arise before the second coming of Christ. Intruders would cause havoc in His vineyard, intruders who had always been identified, by Church authorities, with heretics, who, like the Reformers, relied on their own interpretation of the Bible against the solid tradition of the Church. In July 1520, this scenario was evoked once more by Pope Leo X in his *Bulla contra errores Martini Lutheri et sequacium* (*Exsurge, Domine*), in which Luther and his followers were identified with wolves trying to destroy the vineyard which Christ had left to Peter and his successors to guard.

The 'frame'[15] which was activated by the guardians of the church, when they repeatedly labelled Luther's doctrine as 'new', was this scenario of havoc caused in the vineyard of the Lord. No wonder, then, if the Reformers were sensitive to the allegation and were eager to 'reframe' it, in order to make the public look at the Catholic theologians as 'recent', measured against the original Apostolic church. The basic argument, so to speak, in this reframing, in which Luther's doctrine was cast as the 'old' and original one, whereas that of the present Church authority was the 'recent' one, was a product of the melting-pot of humanist and Reformed thought which coincided with the formation of a firmly founded identity for the new movement. It had, in fact, been formulated before the edition of the papal bull. Commenting, from the sidelines, on the disputation between Martin Luther and John Eck in Leipzig in 1519, the young Philip Melanchthon, who was no friend of such 'happenings', found that its real significance might have been the public exposure of the distance between the 'old' theology, identical with that of Christ, and the 'new and Aristotelic' artefact:

> (…) *ut palam fieret inter veterem et Christi theologiam ac noviciam et Aristotelicam quantum intersit.*[16]

---

ben. Ader Luters nawe ler nachtzuvolgen, und alles das die alten auffgericht, Widerumb umbtzustossen und tzerreyssen', L. Enders, ed., *Luther und Emser: ihre Streitschriften aus dem Jahre 1521, Flugschriften aus der Reformationszeit*, VIII (Halle, 1890); quotation from <http://www.martinluther.dk/emser04.html>. ('At the points where we should and must believe someone regarding Scripture, we find it more reasonable to believe the old and proven person than the new presumptuous and rough ones. Nevertheless, everybody has the personal choice and option to stick with the interpretation that the ancient Fathers have left to us, and to stay with the belief that they have bequeathed us under the outpouring of their blood, body and life. Or to follow Luther's new teaching and smash and tear down everything which the ancient have established').

[15] See the chapter by D. Cowling in this volume, pp. 113-127.

[16] T. von Kolde, ed., *Die 'Loci communes' Philipp Melanchthons in ihrer Urgestalt nach G. L. Plitt* (Leipzig, ³1900), pp. 24-25. Text in: *Corpus Reformatorum*, ed. C. G. Bretschneider (Halle, 1834), I, p. 88.

This statement clearly indicates the self-perception of the emerging Lutheran movement which was launched by adherents with a humanist background, and was readily employed by authors of polemical pamphlets in the following years. The Reformers contrasted scholastic teaching, which had, in their view, gone astray and become perverted, with true Christian preaching, which they themselves tried to impart to the lay people. In this, they seem to have leant on the Erasmian concept of the 'simple doctrine of Christ'. In this context, the proverbial saying *die Gelehrten, die Verkehrten* was given a new meaning, which would prevail during the formation of the debate in the early years of the Reformation. In what follows, we shall see it evolve through the polemical writings of the Reformers, as well as in their attempts to establish a revised interpretation of history.

1.2 *The German saying: 'die Gelehrten, die Verkehrten'*

In the winter months of the year 1520-1521 – a critical and highly formative period in the course of the Reformation – Martin Luther translated and glossed the *Magnificat* in German. The product, a devotional tract in the style of a 'Christian Prince's mirror', was dedicated to his young princely adherent, John Frederick of Saxony. The tenor of Luther's reading of the text was praise of God's mighty acts in relation to the lowest and poorest people such as, in Luther's perception, the historical Mary must have been, the *Cinderellas* of all secular[17] and religious[18] societies, who are thrown on God's charity alone. In the further exposition, the frustration by God of all who are in possession of temporal or spiritual wealth and position was underscored.

Summing up his glosses on Luke 1.52 ('He has deposed the mighty from their seats'), Luther referred to a number of German proverbial sayings, all of which indicated that the existing order of power and learning of this world was not necessarily identical with the order in God's view. Precisely this phrase, *Deposuit potentes a sede*, has been suggested as a favourite *topos* in endeavours by modern scholars to reconstruct a medieval 'car-

---

[17] M. Luther, *Das Magnificat verdeutschet und ausgelegt, 1520 und 1521*, in: O. Clemen, ed., *Luthers Werke in Auswahl* (repr. Berlin, 1967), II, p. 138, places the emphasis on social conditions and on the fact that the Davidic dynasty was withered and held in contempt.

[18] Clemen, *Luthers Werke in Auswahl*, II, p. 145: the *arm asschen prodlin* is here connected with a reference to the mystical imagery of extreme self-negation and self-deliverance before the mercy of God.

nival culture' with its short-term staging of a 'world turned upside-down',[19] a culture labelled in German as *die verkehrte Welt*.[20] As Luther's cornucopia indicates, a flow of more or less set expressions of mixed biblical and folkloristic origin reflected the many facets and layers of the idea of a reversal of social hierarchies under the auspices of an alternative order, an idea that was not at all popular with the established authorities, whether secular or ecclesiastical. Luther's comments run as follows:

> Daher kumpts, das man mit rechter warheit sagt: Die gelerten die vorkeretenn. Ein furst wiltprett ym hymel. Hie reich dort arm. Denn die gelerten lassen den hohmut yhrs herzen nit, die geweltigen lassen yhr drucken nit, die reychen lassen yhre lust nit.[21]

> From this come the very true sayings: 'The learned, the twisted. One prince is a feast in Heaven. Rich here, poor hereafter'. For the learned people do not abandon the pride of their hearts. The mighty do not abandon their repressions. The rich do not give up their desires.

The rhymed locution quoted first in Luther's gloss, *die gelerten die verkerten,* 'learned people are twisted', seems to have been known in a variety of forms. Luther uses it also in the comparative *je gelehrter, desto verkehrter*, 'the more learned, the more twisted'. From at least 1518, he repeatedly referred to it as a well-known piece of popular wisdom. He later had it noted down in his personal collection of such proverbs, dating from his mature years.[22]

The saying can be traced back to the fifteenth century in German-speaking communities,[23] and contemporaries seem to have recognised it as being German in origin. In the following statement from his prologue to the French Bible of 1555, Sebastian Châtaillon, a native of Savoy, who, besides

---

[19] P. Burke, *Popular Culture in Early Modern Europe* (New York/London, 1978), p. 192; cf. G. M Dreves, 'Zur Geschichte der fête des fous', *Stimmen aus Maria Laach: Katholische Blätter* 47 (1894), pp. 571-587. A *locus classicus* for establishing a whole 'culture' on this biblical verse is *Litterae Odonis episcopi Parisiensis, pro abolendo festo Fatuorum, et restituenda solemnitate circumcisionis Domini (1198)*, in: *Patrologia latina*, ed. J. P. Migne, CCXII, cols. 70A-72C.

[20] Burke, *Popular Culture*, p. 188.

[21] Clemen, II, p. 175.

[22] 'Luthers Sprichwörtersammlung', in: *D. Martin Luthers Werke: kritische Gesamtausgabe* (Weimar, 1914; repr. 1967), LI, p. 645.

[23] C. Gilly, 'Das Sprichwort "Die Gelehrten, die Verkehrten" in der Toleranzliteratur des 16. Jahrhunderts', in: J.-G. Rott and S. L. Verheus, eds, *Anabaptistes et dissidents au XVIe siècle.* (Baden-Baden, 1987), pp. 159-172.

mastering the three ancient languages, was fluent in French, German, and Italian, gave his candid opinion of the kind of reader who, without renouncing worldly wisdom, interprets Scripture as he pleases: 'il deviendra de iour en iour tant plus savant, tant plus méchant, comme dit l'Aleman'[24] ('From day to day he will become more knowledgeable, and more wicked, as the German says'). In a translation of a similar remark by Sebastian Franck concerning the Scribes and Pharisees twisting everything, the same author rendered the meaning of *verkert* by the Latin verb *pervertere*.[25] Apart from betraying the fact that a rhymed *sententia* loses vigour when translated into another language, both translations indicate that the author did not know an original or an equivalent, neither in Latin nor in French.

The locution seems to have reached the peak of its popularity in moral literature which, at the end of the fifteenth century, began to employ the figure of the fool or 'peasant' of late medieval urban plays in order to exhibit the foolishness of all classes in society.[26] The fool was, in this tradition, a representation of the human being as prey to manifold inferior instincts or vices.

Playing on the (rather ambivalent) listing of learned people as first-class fools in the first 'bestseller' of this genre, Sebastian Brant's *Narrenschiff* of 1494, Thomas Murner, a Franciscan, seems to have caught contemporary opinion in the following characterisation from 1512: 'Wir [Pfaffen] sindt die ersten undern gelerten / Die bösen, valschen und verkerten'[27] ('We [the clergy] are the first among the learned / the wicked, false, and perverse').

This saying may, as Bob Scribner has argued, reflect a 'credibility gap' between the pretensions of the clergy and the reality, an anti-clericalism on a wide scale, motivated by many factors. The target of Murner's text was, however, as in the case of Sebastian Brant, all groups in society, because they were all subject to false pretensions, and the aim of his 'sermon' was to make people realise their deviation and improve themselves rather than stir up dormant rebellious passions. Murner belonged to the generation of reform-minded mendicants who chastised society and the Church without mercy, thus unwittingly handing weapons to the future Reformation movement, which he could not follow in its break with the Church. In this enter-

---

[24] *Idem*, p. 159.

[25] *Idem*, p. 163.

[26] E. Catholy, *Das Fastnachtspiel des Spätmittelalters: Gestalt und Funktion* (Tübingen, 1961). *Idem*, *Fastnachtspiel* (Stuttgart, 1966).

[27] Quotation from B. Scribner, 'Antiklerikalismus in Deutschland um 1500', in: F. Seibt and W. Eberhard, eds, *Europa 1500: Integrationsprozesse im Widerstreit: Staaten, Regionen, Personenverbände, Christenheit* (Stuttgart, 1987), pp. 368-382 (p. 370).

prise, the poor preaching of God's word by substandard clergymen (within or outside his own order) must necessarily be the first target. A parallel formulation in his *Schelmenzunft* from the same year illustrates, perhaps more clearly, what was at stake for the Franciscan preacher:

> Ich byn der erst in disser rott / Den ich das Gotss wort dick verspott.
> So ich verkindt das himmelreich / Sag ich dor von so schimpffelich,
> Als ob ich wolt den christen schedigen / Und im von blouwen enten predigen.[28]

> I am the first in this gang / I who blaspheme God's word massively,
> When I proclaim Heaven / I talk about it as abusively as if
> I wanted to harm the Christian / and preach blue geese to him.

The characterisation by Murner of contemporary teaching as 'preaching blue geese' comes very close to the polemical note of the Reformers. According to their own assessments, this abomination was a major reason for revolting against the established church and its 'perverted' clergy. In this context, the saying *die gelerten, die verkerten* denoted the rejection of scholastic teaching along with what was seen as its most harmful by-product, preaching on 'fables' – an expression that might cover almost anything but the Gospel. In this connection, they both identified with learned humanists who faced persecution when questioning scholastic doctrine, and also drew on the more common criticism of substandard preaching launched, to a great extent, by people who, like Murner, remained loyal to the Catholic Church during the genesis of a struggle for life and death in the early twenties of the sixteenth century.

2. Texts

2.1 Two early apologies

When the Reformers were confronted with the accusation that they were overturning the lawful regime of the Church, they interpreted their own position as a result of the 'deposition of the *sedentes*' by God, according to Luther's gloss on Luke 1.52. This 'deposition' was, furthermore, associated with the popular depiction of the poor conditions in which Christ was born in Bethlehem, and contrasted with the arrogance and security of the Jewish leaders, secular as well as religious. Just as Luther insisted on the truthfulness of popular wisdom, the protesters found an extra non-scriptural re-

---

[28] T. Murner, *Schelmenzunft: nach den beiden ältesten Drucken (1512)*, ed. M. Spanier (Halle, [3]1968), p. 7.

source of supporting *dicta* for their enterprise in the commonplaces of everyday language, even if they did not let it become the conclusive word but corroborated it with biblical arguments. Both 'arguments' soon became an integral part of the Reformers' apologies for their alleged subversive activities. This cluster of arguments will be demonstrated by means of an analysis of two early humanist-influenced pamphlets from Germany and Switzerland, both produced in the German pamphlet war that gathered momentum in the years 1520-1521.

A New Apology and Reply for Martin Luther to the Murderous Yells of the Papists, published by a little known but very active pamphleteer called Heinrich von Kettenbach in 1521,[29] is, to the best of my knowledge, the first attempt to formulate a coherent answer on behalf of the Reformation movement in this newly popular forum of debate. Kettenbach was a refugee from the humanist-influenced Franciscan convent of Ulm which produced more than one aggressive controversialist in the early days of the Lutheran Reform movement. We can discern three strategies in Kettenbach's *Apology*, all closely linked together by the assumption that neither power nor learning in the established world are guarantees of true authority.

First, he constructs a martyrology leading all the way back to the 'Jewish' persecution and killing of the Old Testament prophets who announced God's messages in opposition to the inventions of men. These 'Jews' are now represented by the prelates of the Roman Church with their helpers, the priests and monks, who possess a wonderful instrument of persuasion in the person of the executioner with his stake; Kettenbach, with an expression he has, perhaps, invented himself, talks about *uber disputirn* 'over-disputation'.[30] In this connection, the fate of Jan Hus is brought forward as a further testimony to the methods employed by the powerful Church. At this time, the adherents of Luther realistically feared that Luther would share Hus's fate, and Hus became the first non-biblical figure in the Protestant martyrology, in which he remained the most prominent forerunner of anti-Roman protest.

Kettenbach continues with a list of the New Testament men of power who promoted the execution of Jesus; the high priests Annas and Caiaphas, the politicians Pilate and King Herod, and – with a rhymed pun on the German word for 'scribe' – 'The synagogue of the "twisted in Scripture"' (*die Schriftverkehrten* instead of the *Schriftgelehrten*, literally 'learned in Scrip-

---

[29] H. von Kettenbach, *Ein neu Apologia und Verantwortung Martini Luthers wider der Papisten Mordgeschrei*, in: O. Clemen, ed., *Flugschriften aus den ersten Jahren der Reformation*, II (Halle, 1907), pp. 153-175.
[30] Kettenbach, *Apologia*, p. 159.

ture').[31] The pun suggests that the parts may be inverted in a world which, on a more thorough inspection, is showing itself from its reverse side. This perspective forms the second line of argument and responds directly to the allegation that Luther's teaching is 'new':

> Zuo dem v. klagt das lugenhafftig volck, der Luther bring herfür ein new leer unnd ein newen glawben. Darumb einfeltigen sprechen: Ich wil blyben by dem altten glawben unnd myner vorfarn, so sy doch nit wissen den altten, auch nit den newen glawben. Sie wissen nit den altten glawben, den Christus unnd seyne Junger geleert habenn, sy wissen ouch nit den newen glawben, den uns die bepst, prelaten, hochschuoln, Platner, mit hilff Thome, Schoti und narren stultilis erdact unnd furgelegt haben.[32]

> This lying kind [the established Church] complains that Luther produces a new doctrine and a new faith; therefore many simple people say: 'I will stay with the old faith and with my ancestors', although they know neither the old nor the new faith. They do not know the old faith, which Christ and His disciples have taught, and they do not know the new faith, which the pope, the prelates, the universities, and the tonsured have invented and presented to us with the help of Thomas, Scotus, and jester *stultilis*.

According to Kettenbach, the theologians have acted for their own profit; but the lay people should be aware that Luther has now once again produced the pure evangelical truth – this is why, with another pun on the German pronunciation of his name, he is called *luter* (in modern German *lauter*, 'pure'). So the Lutherans are in reality the faction who preach the old, Apostolic, and original faith, whereas the Roman Church is the faction which represents a deviation towards new inventions of men – in other words, scholastic theology.[33]

It is obvious that Kettenbach is here communicating a message which refers to and contradicts such attacks as were brought forward by, for instance, Hieronymus Emser in the passage quoted above. As for the defamation of scholastic theology as the working of selfish fools, we find a close parallel to this alleged substitution of the Holy Scripture by *then skrifft som kallis scholastica theologia* ('the scripture that is called scholastic theology') in 'The Malmö-Book', which is the most important apology by the Reformers in Eastern Denmark. This text is pointedly anti-academic in its

---

[31] *Idem*, p. 167.
[32] *Ibidem*.
[33] *Idem*, pp. 167-168.

approach to the theological enterprise, which is in turn identified with having a training in scholastic theology.[34]

The third strategy proposed in the *Apology* is to point out the similarities between Luther's party and the followers of the historical Jesus, a poor baby born of poor parents and placed in a manger. His first followers were simple men from the countryside, not well-to-do people such as the scribes and the Pharisees who, on the contrary, scorned him. Likewise, Luther's followers are unlearned lay people; only few from the universities and monastic orders listen to him. Kettenbach maintains that this observation is part of the Catholic objections against Luther.[35] But: 'Die Hyrtenn auff dem feld (...) suchten Jesum zuo Betleem in der crippen, die gantz pfaffheit blyb zuo Jherusalem und gingen nit zuo im'[36] ('The shepherds in the field (...) searched for Jesus in the manger at Bethlehem; the whole clergy stayed in Jerusalem and did not go to him'). The biblical narrative corroborates the 'historical' observation that the religious establishment was never a friend of genuine Christianity, which it blacklisted as unworthy of attention, wherever it occurred, even if it be God Himself in the person of Christ.

Exactly this observation formed the nucleus of another pamphlet from the same year, which may be earlier, and may thus have served as an inspiration for the aforementioned text. *On the Old and the New God, Faith and Doctrine*[37] was written by an anonymous author who called himself Judas Nazarei, probably a pseudonym of the mayor of St. Gall, the humanist, polyhistor, and *reformator*, Joachim von Watt (Vadianus). This text has

---

[34] They [the Papists] are trained in 'then skrifft som kallis scholastica theologia (...) de haffde wæredt til store scoler og studia wden landss, eller inden landss, och foedt store naffn, Mesterss naffn og doctoress naffn (...) de som intet andet iblandt de allerbedste lærde have lært end i Aristoteles' og i hedenske poeters bøger (...)', Peder Laurentsen, *Malmøbogen* (*Facsimileudgave*), ed. C. Gierow (Malmö, 1979) ('in the scripture called scholastic theology (...) they have attended great schools and colleges abroad and at home and obtained great names, the names of masters and doctors (...) those who have learned nothing in the company of most learned people than what they have read in the books of Aristotle and pagan poets').

[35] '(...) dem Luther hengt niemant an dann die leyen unnd ungelerten, wenig uss den orden, wenig uss den hosenschuolen, ich solt sagenn uss den hohenschuoln, wenig Thomisten, und ist dannocht Thomas prediger ordens ein Beptslicher held (...)', Kettenbach, *Apologia*, p. 172 ('only lay people and unlearned adhere to Luther, few from the universities, 'sock schools' I mean, few Thomists, in spite of the fact that friar Thomas is a papal hero').

[36] *Ibidem.*

[37] E. Kück, ed., *Judas Nazarei, Vom alten und neuen Gott, Glauben und Lehre (1521)*, *Flugschriften aus der Reformationszeit*, XII (Halle, 1896).

been called 'the first really new Protestant unfolding of history'.[38] The expected readers greeted at the outset may be either God-fearing Christians, seduced people, or obdurate teachers and Pharisees; according to each status the benefit of their reading will be either further edification, conversion, or warning. These expectations should be seen in the light of the good news that God has once more pulled out from its sheath that sword that brings strife to any community. Even if the authorities try to force it back in, it has already, by its glow, opened the eyes of so many that any attempt to restore peace will fail. On the contrary, dissension is now springing up to such an extent that

> das kynd wider seinen vatter, die tochter wyder ire muoter, das hußgesynd under im zwitraechtig, die stifft angsthafft, die Cloester parthyesch, die hochgelerten erstumbt, die schlechten layen hohe wunderbarliche ding reden, eyns do uß, das ander dort uß, daruß eyn gemeines sprichwort erstanden ist: ICH blib by mym alten Got, by mym alten glauben, by der alten leer.[39]

> the child turns against his father, the daughter against her mother, the servants argue with each other, the convents are anxious, the monasteries divided, the learned dumb, the simple lay people speaking strange and wonderful things, one in this, the other in that direction, from which situation a common proverbial saying has arisen: '*I* will stay with my old God, with my old belief, with my old teaching'.

People everywhere, affected by the antagonism of contradictory forms of belief in God, should be enlightened about what are, in reality, the 'old' and the 'new' God, belief, and doctrine. This can be effectuated by recounting the facts of biblical and ecclesiastical history, which is identical to the story of man's blindness since the fall of Adam.

The first and largest part of the pamphlet presents itself as a narrative of universal history along the lines of Augustine, taking its point of departure from the schism between the apostate and the God-fearing creatures in the angelic world. The main protagonist is Lucifer, who tries, through ever new devices, to make Man turn from the only true God. Virtuous, brave people are either persecuted as rebels wanting to establish a 'new' God, or are themselves subject to an exaltation that makes new gods of them. When the

---

[38] Comment by E. Kiepe-Willms on the contribution by G. Benrath, 'Das Verständnis der Kirchengeschichte in der Reformationszeit', in: L. Grenzmann and K. Stackmann, eds, *Literatur und Laienbildung im Spätmittelalter und in der Reformationszeit* (Stuttgart, 1984), pp. 97-109 (p. 111).

[39] Nazarei, *Vom alten und neuen Gott*, pp. 2-3.

author comes to the monastic orders and their founders, the whole phial of humanist wrath is poured out. The Carmelites are not only impertinent enough to maintain that they have been founded by Elijah on the mountain of Carmel, they also claim to have received their cowls from the Holy Virgin. Thomas Aquinas was a diligent, god-fearing theologian, but his works have been elevated to the status of Holy Scripture by his order. As for Saint Francis, he has been so involved in imitations of scenes from the Gospels that the author wonders if the peasant can still distinguish between him and Christ.

As a refrain, the author expresses his worries about the fearfully conservative 'old fools' who 'keep shaking their old grey heads, saying: "What new kind of teaching is this?"'.[40] Thus they seduce the young generation to follow them to the 'secure' positions where the 'many' crowd together, whereby these many form a host of witnesses for the 'old' teaching, which is, in reality, a new one, freshly invented by diabolical devices.

The second part of the tract lists a number of marks by which God and the true doctrine can be acknowledged. In this section, Scripture is presented as the only source of trustworthy knowledge of God. The author moreover displays a strong dislike of any superfluous ceremonies typical of the humanists, who interpreted them not only as signs of superstition, but also as substitutes for a genuine living faith. Scripture is here called the 'mother' of the Church, because all who believe in God base their belief on Scripture, whereby they become 'her children'. So the Catholic Church is, in reality, not identical with the Church, about which 'it is said with a common locution "Outside the Christian church no one can be saved"'.[41] True to his general view, the author lets Cyprian's popularised dictum apply to belief in the word of God, as it is read in Scripture exclusively.

2.2 Narrated Reformation history

Christmas imagery played an important role when Reformation history began to be narrated to the descendants of the Reformers. The notion that God's pure word had been wrung from the darkness of an age of fraud and had been brought to shine by a mere handful of heroic preachers and their predecessors fitted into the well-known narrative of the feeble and vulner-

---

[40] *Idem*, p. 36.

[41] 'Zuom dritten. Der Christlich glaub ist die heilig geschrifft, die heylig gschrifft ist die muoter der Christlichen kirchen (…) Zuom vierden. (…) Daruss moegen wir erkennen das die gemein reden so man spricht "Usserthalb der Cristen kirchen mag niemant selig werden", das es nit mag im grundt verstanden werden vom Pabst und sim bistumb zu Rom', Nazarei, *Vom alten und neuen Gott*, pp. 54-55.

able child in the dark stable at night. Luther's appearance and its impact not only resembled, but formed a new presentation of the divine revelation.

In order to make this point convincingly, the converts had to depict the conditions under the papacy in dark colours. In the heat of the early pamphlet war, protests against confusing the established order with God's ordination drew much of their energy from an internal agreement about the abuses and amorality in the Church. To judge from the assessments of the chroniclers, such an implicit understanding was no longer to be expected in the generations to come. They must therefore be enlightened as to why things had gone wrong after the Incarnation, and a need for a 'new' Christmas thus brought about. This task was, roughly speaking, approached in two ways, as we will now see.

In Friedrich Mecum's (or Myconius's) *Historia reformationis*, published at the beginning of the 1540s, the predominant key of interpretation is provided by biblical and apocalyptic material. The point of contact is Luther's qualification of the pope as the Antichrist, who, according to the prediction in the Gospels, would take his seat in the temple at the end of this world. As this is a New Testament prediction, it must refer to events or even to a definite period under the new dispensation, in other words, to church history. In this context, the coming of Antichrist was not necessarily seen as a sign that the end of the world was drawing close, but conceived of in a more immanent sense, as a possible period of decline in historical time, which might be superseded by a new beginning.

Friedrich Myconius's parents belonged to the wealthier and, in religious terms, more self-confident middle class of the mining districts of Thuringia; he was about ten years younger than Luther. As a young Latin schoolboy he witnessed the selling of indulgences by John Tetzel, and, shortly afterwards, he joined the Franciscan order as a consequence of a religious crisis, which had apparently been triggered by his meeting with Tetztel and his staff, all according to his own testimonies in a letter to a friend.[42] After joining the party of Luther, he became the reformer of Gotha, but had to withdraw prematurely because of poor health; in his remaining years he collected sources for his chronicle.[43]

According to the opening of the narrative of the *Historia reformationis*, the benefit of historical recollection is an enduring respect and thankfulness towards the great persons who have contributed to the well-being of the German nation. Myconius addresses himself conventionally to his children

---

[42] P. Scherffig, *Friedrich Mekum von Lichtenfels: ein Lebensbild aus dem Reformationszeitalter* (Leipzig, 1909).
[43] H. Ulbrich, *Friedrich Mykonius 1490-1546: Lebensbild und neue Funde zum Briefwechsel des Reformators* (Tübingen, 1962), p. 21.

and the inhabitants of the town of Gotha, but obviously he is aiming at all reformed parts of Germany. The chronicle begins with a description of the papal regime and the practices of the Roman Church in the time immediately before Luther's attack on the selling of indulgences. The heading used for this description is 'seduction' ('Wie es im Pabstthum gestanden, und wohin der Endchrist die Christenheit verfuehret'), which was one of the favourite terms used by the Reformers to classify the pastoral care of the contemporary clergy. The diction is almost naïve; Myconius writes, for instance: 'Es war ein greulichs, hesslichs, unflaetigs Thier' ('It [The Catholic Church] was a cruel, hideous, dirty beast').[44] As a comment on this, the true preaching of the gospel by its counterpart is immediately brought into play. According to Myconius, 'The suffering, atonement, death, satisfaction, and payment of Christ' had been hushed up, as long as these things were only preached in terms of a *historia*: 'Do ward Christus Leiden, Erloesen, Sterben, Gnugthun und Bezahlen gar geschwiegen, und nur fuor ein HISTORIA, wie des Ulyssis Meer Fahrt gepredigt: Von den Glauben, dadurch man seines Leidens, Unschuld, Gerechtikeit, Heilikeit, Erbtheils und ewigs Lebens aus lauter Gnaden theilhafft und selig wird, hoeret man nichts'. As the Reformers saw it, the rendering of the text as an account of data without their being taken as an announcement of salvation (the historical sense without its tropological meaning *pro me, pro nobis*), was utterly unfruitful. The vivid exposition of the different unfruitful forms of late medieval piety extends over the rest of chapter one. After this, there follows a historical account of the course of the indulgences affair which triggered the Reformation and Luther's reaction. This affair, it is further stated, forced Luther to bring the Gospel to light. Here the scene changes to the cloister in Wittenberg, which was, according to the chronicler, just being rebuilt at that time, with the result that it consisted of little more than a sheep stable (!), where Luther dwelled and still does.[45] The material was clay and wood, and perhaps twenty people, no more, could stand in the chapel. In conclusion: all over it looked exactly like the pictures that the painters make of the stable in Bethlehem, where Christ was born. And, it is added, the chapel in Prague, in which Johannes Hus preached, likewise was called Bethlehem.[46]

The essence of the story is presented within this framework. In these miserable conditions at Wittenberg, God once more let His dear child be born. This new birth is identical to the new discovery of the Gospel: God let the child be unwrapped from its swaddling-clothes, so that everybody could

---

[44] Friedrich Myconius, *Historia reformationis vom Jahr Christi 1517 bis 1542*, ed. E. S. Cyprian (Gotha, 1715), p. 3. Orthography slightly modernised by the editors.
[45] *Idem*, p. 24.
[46] Paraphrased from Myconius, *Historia reformationis*, p. 25.

see what a lovely little baby Christ was.[47] This 'revelation' (literally: re-
moval of the veil), corresponds to a long and unbroken theological tradition,
in which the veil of Moses is lifted in the new dispensation and God's full
grace thus disclosed.

Myconius continues his narration in the same key. There was no cathe-
dral, and the spirit from the mouth of the Lord had to go forth from a humble dwelling, but, nonetheless, it destroyed the pope.[48] From this house
came also the prompting to open the grave which had been sealed by the
papists in order that Christ should not rise any more.[49] The author returns to
important events which made Luther's success possible, such as the
achievements of Johann Reuchlin and the assignment of Philip Melanchthon to Wittenberg in 1518.[50]

The rest of the chronicle testifies to the further preaching of the word
and the circumstances which accompanied its progress, following the lead
of the Acts of the Apostles. The local Reformation of Gotha, the chronicler's own town, of course receives special attention.

3. *Excursus*

Our investigation has focused so far on two texts drawing on Christmas imagery, both of which were produced by former Franciscans. It is, perhaps,
not irrelevant to investigate whether the recollection that friars had also
once been persecuted by the Apostolic See for preaching the simple Gospel
may have influenced the use of allusions to the Nativity, which became a
predominant feature in the self-perception of the Reformers. In the juxtaposition of a true piety and an invented piety exalted by men, which is so meticulously carried out in *Vom alten und neuen Gott*, it is, almost incidentally, mentioned that Saint Francis – the son of a rich merchant! – was, so
his order maintained, born in a stable and laid in a manger.[51] Admittedly,
this specific product of what seems to have been a Franciscan obsession
with tracking down similarities between the biblical narratives of Christ and
the life of their founder is not yet extant in the authoritative works by late
medieval order members such as *De conformitate vitae beati Francisci ad*

---

[47] 'In dieser armen, elenden jaemmerlichen Capellen hat Gott zu diesen letzten Zei-
ten sein liebes heiliges Evangelium, und das liebe Kindlein Jesus lassen neu geboren
werden; und dasselbe lassen auswickeln, und aller Welt anzeigen, wie ein schoen,
lieblich, troestlich und seeligs Kindlein Jesus sey (...)', *ibidem*.
[48] *Ibidem*.
[49] *Ibidem*.
[50] *Idem*, pp. 25-27.
[51] Nazarei, *Vom alten und neuen Gott*, p. 48.

vitam domini Iesu.[52] The random information that such a feature did exist in the order's legendary material at the time of the Reformation is, however, plausible. If this is so, it helps explain why the idea of the Lutheran movement as a phenomenon similar to the birth in Bethlehem presented itself as such an obvious explanation to the public, as texts such as those by Kettenbach and Myconius suggest.

The other way of dealing with decline in the Apostolic Church was to view it, instead, as a phenomenon regularly recurring in history from the origin of mankind, and handle it in a historical way. This is the case in the Swiss reformer Johannes Kessler's so-called *Sabbata*, or leisure works, which grew under the auspices of his great humanist mentor, the aforementioned Joachim von Watt.[53] In this chronicle, the teaching of Luther is likewise seen as a new beginning, from which the light of God's word can shine forth, after having been neglected for centuries. But the tenor of the narrative is the Platonic allegory of the cave, which the author, in his prologue, employs to illustrate the hesitation of the public to confront the light of the truth.

Johannes Kessler was born in Basel at the beginning of the sixteenth century and belonged to the lower middle class. He studied for about a year in his home city, but broke off in order to go to Wittenberg. On his return, having been convinced by the new evangelical teaching, he decided to give up any aspiration to become a priest and instead became a saddler. Although a lay man, he gathered people around him regularly, preached to them and interpreted Scripture. The magistracy tolerated this, until his success forced it to convince him that he should preach in a church and become, so to speak, more 'magisterial' in his attempts to reform the population. After the Peasants' War he became a teacher at the Latin school and later advanced to higher positions in the administration of the town. His relation to Watt was friendly, but never intimate. He let him monitor and contribute to his chronicle, just as he also let the magistracy sanction the work.[54]

---

[52] Bartholomaeus Pisanus, *De conformitate vitae Beati Francisci ad vitam Domini Iesu*, 2 vols. (Quaracchi, 1906-1912); cf. the characterisation of this work by B. Roest, 'Later Medieval Institutional History', in: D. M. Deliyannis, ed., *Historiography in the Middle Ages* (Leiden, 2003), pp. 277-315 (p. 292): 'The vast and influential "De conformitate beati Francisci ad vitam Domini Iesu" of Bartholomew of Pisa (1390), [which is] (…) fleshing out the by then classic theme of conformity between the lives of Francis and Christ'.

[53] T. Schiess, ed., *Johannes Kesslers 'Sabbata': St. Galler Reformationschronik 1523-1539* (Leipzig, 1911).

[54] Biographical information can be found in the introduction to Schiess, ed., *Johannes Kesslers 'Sabbata'*.

In his chronicle, Kessler narrates episodes in chronological order, but, before he comes to this chronological narrative, Kessler places the Reformation in a broader context. This takes the form of a long prologue addressed to his sons, in which the father, like Myconius, indicates that his descendants will hardly be able to understand and thus appreciate the joy that Luther's contemporaries have felt at his reinstatement of God's word in its rightful place. By means of an exposition of the allegory of the cave from Plato's *Republic*, it is made clear that humankind is an easy prey to darkness and in need of liberation. The allegory is read on several levels; already its pagan author knew of degrees of enlightenment. The Old Testament prophecies of a light shining forth to the people sitting in darkness have finally been fulfilled by eternal light itself, which was brought into the world through the incarnation of Christ and the proclamation of the Gospel. But even if this is an eternal order and may be the fundamental meaning of the metaphor, the image also readily covers conditions under the papacy. In his mercy, God has once again undertaken the task of liberating the prisoners from this cave of darkness 'durch die predig sinen luteren und rainen worts'[55] ('through the proclamation of his pure and clear word'). But the majority of listeners are afraid to accept this:

> Ach, wie schücht der merentail den hellen glanz evangelischer warhait; wie unterschlecht man die ogen ab dem claren verstand, wie Israel ab dem angesicht Mosi; wie mag man sogar nit liden noch dulden, das gesprochen wird: 'Bissher habend ir triegerey allain' (…). [They say] 'wir wellend (irer gedechtnus nach) by dem alten bliben'; item: 'globen wellen wir, was unseren altforderen globt haben'.[56]

> Alas! How the majority shuns the clear radiance of evangelical truth; how the people look to the ground away from clear apprehension, just like Israel did from the countenance of Moses; how people will neither allow nor tolerate that it be said: 'Until now you have only been betrayed' (…). [They say] 'We want to stay with our old faith' (such as they remember it); or else: 'We want to believe what our ancestors believed'.

Just as Christ had forerunners among the Old Testament prophets, the Reformers had their precursors in such people as John Hus.[57] In the time preceding Luther's appearance, the word of God manifested itself in various

---

[55] *Kesslers 'Sabbata'*, p. 6.
[56] *Idem*, pp. 6-7.
[57] *Idem*, pp. 7-8. Cf. I. Wiessmann, *Die St. Galler Reformationschronik des Johannes Kessler (1503-1574)*, dissertation (Bielefeld, 1972).

ways, even in the ridiculing of the Catholic clergy by impertinent individuals. But now, after the 'swan' (as Kessler calls Luther) had begun to sing loudly all over the world, such adaptations to a less developed public life were no longer necessary.

In the second chapter of his chronicle, Kessler offers a survey of the deviation of the Church from its original foundations. In this chapter, Kessler mobilises contemporary critical investigation of history. His enterprise presupposes the awakening consciousness of a historical change, which can be investigated by studying the sources. Historical research had already, in humanist circles, cast suspicion on much of the theoretical foundation of Catholic thought, as represented by the schoolmen, and had rendered papal claims of authority vulnerable to such questions as: how old and how universal were the foundations and honourable institutions of the Church in reality, especially when measured against conditions in the original Apostolic Church? Early in the public debate, Luther had shown that the study of history was a feasible way to disclose the nature of papal authority. He continued to exploit historical sources in his polemical works for the rest of his life, especially when confronted directly with the Roman Church. In the short polemical texts by the pamphleteers from the early 1520s, which we have met until now, we meet this qualification of the established Church as a deviation from the original foundation of the Church by Christ in its abridged form. In his chronicle, however, Kessler found opportunity to elaborate on it.

Hereafter, a rather more annalistic account of Reformation events proper can start, but that is not our concern here.

4. *Concluding remarks*

Although Luther himself on several occasions mobilised the role of the court jester against the overwhelming hegemony of power and learning,[58] it needed more substantial material to corroborate the Reformers' claim that an overthrow of authority had been necessary. This they found in the biblical tradition of the hidden presence of God in apparently poor and simple forms, unworthy of notice. They found a related reversal of values in the exposition of a *verkehrte Welt* as it was reflected in popular moral literature, and, indeed, expressed in the proverbial saying *die gelerten, die verkerten.* This popular proverb became an important feature in the early Protestant

---

[58] Cf. Luther's words in the prologue to his address to the German nobility: '[Ich will] auch einmal hoffnarr werden (...) es hat wohl mehr mal ein nar weysslich geredt (...)', Clemen, *Luthers Werke in Auswahl*, I, pp. 362-364 ('I also want for once to be a court jester (...) more than once a fool has spoken wisely').

rejection of ecclesiastical authority, where it served to underscore the perverted nature of scholastic theology and the repressive use of it by the authorities of the Church. During the confessional life and death struggle of the early 1520s, the proverbial saying *die gelerten, die verkerten* served as a unilateral observation on Catholic (scholastic) teaching. Reproducing a set interpretation, which limited its possible range of meanings, early Reformation polemicists chose to let the saying denote the perversity of scholastic theology. It is a characteristic of the contextualisation practised in the Reformers' polemical texts that it was granted this well-defined, but also limited meaning. They did not pretend to reveal a 'universal' truth about the nature of learned people, but used the proverb (by virtue of its 'universal' validity) as a unilateral condemnation of the 'depraved' scholastics.

Conversely, in Sebastian Franck's 'commonplace-book' of 1541, the proverb was removed from its limited polemical function and reintegrated into a universal moral sphere. In development of this point, which all eleven variants of the saying are used to corroborate, the essence of these mixed expressions is then set out in a short edifying sermon on the vanities of 'worldly wisdom'.[59] This reintegration reflects the quieter pursuit of study by a spokesman of tolerance in the world of religious controversy. According to the survey conducted by Carlos Gilly, a possible further contextualisation of the saying lay exactly with contemporary pleas for religious tolerance.[60] In the end, the application of the saying to the allegedly depraved nature of academically trained theologians turned out to be too hazardous even for the 'established' Reformers.[61]

---

[59] Cf. W. Mieder, 'Das Sprichwörterbuch: ein Überblick zur Parömiographie', in: W. Mieder, *Sprichwort – Wahrwort!? Studien zur Geschichte, Bedeutung und Funktion deutscher Sprichwörter* (Frankfurt am Main, 1992), pp. 37-43 (p. 40).

[60] Gilly, 'Das Sprichwort', p. 163.

[61] Gilly ('Das Sprichwort', pp. 161 and 165) illustrates the Swiss Reformers' rejection of the idea, which was allegedly still maintained by the Anabaptist movement, that the study of the Bible did not require any academic training.

COMMONPLACES AND EVERYDAY WISDOM
IN HENRI ESTIENNE

David Cowling

The vernacular works of the celebrated Hellenist, humanist, and printer Henri Estienne (1531-1598) provide a good case-study for the use of commonplace material in polemical contexts in the later sixteenth century.[1] In what follows, I will understand the 'commonplace' not in its strict and technical sense as an element in a tightly structured compendium of arguments derived from authoritative (typically classical) sources and designed to persuade by means of an appeal to the shared knowledge of an elite, highly educated culture, but rather as a feature of the everyday language and experience of 16th-century readers and writers that typically enjoys low cognitive salience but a correspondingly high potential for persuasion by means of its appeal to 'commonsense' knowledge. That Estienne was able to operate within the learned context can be demonstrated from his own production of commonplace books in the 1570s;[2] his interest in vernacular commonplace compendia is evident in his sustained engagement with French proverbs, which culminated in the publication of *Les Premices*, a collection of vernacular proverbs explicitly arranged in 'lieux communs' (common places).[3] Alongside this explicit engagement with the commonplace tradition, however, Estienne also marshalled material from the everyday experience of his readers in the service of a polemical enterprise. In making the case for the 'defence' of the French language against a perceived influx of words and other linguistic material borrowed from Italy, Estienne consis-

---

[1] The only monograph study to date of Henri Estienne's vernacular production is that of L. Clément, *Henri Estienne et son œuvre française: étude d'histoire littéraire et de philologie* (Paris, 1898; repr. Geneva, 1967). More recent critical work on Estienne is presented in the collective volume *Henri Estienne: actes du colloque organisé à l'Université de Paris-Sorbonne le 12 mars 1987 par le Centre V. L. Saulnier* (Paris, 1988).

[2] For Estienne's own production of commonplace books (the *Virtutum encomia sive de virtutibus: ex poetis et philosophis utrius linguae* of 1573 and the *Parodiae morales* of 1575), see A. Moss, *Printed Commonplace-Books and the Structuring of Renaissance Thought* (Oxford, 1996), pp. 330-332.

[3] H. Estienne, *Les Premices, ou le I livre des proverbes epigrammatizez (...) rengez en lieux communs* ([Geneva], 1594). Estienne claims in his preface that French proverbs have been a topic of interest for him since his youth (fol. a vi^v).

tently privileged, in his persuasive and satirical work, a range of common-place metaphors that were evidently designed to appeal to such ostensibly self-evident concepts as the value of good health, 'purity' (as opposed to harmful adulteration), sound personal and domestic finances, and plain cooking. The choice of such metaphors appears to have been motivated by two factors: first, congruence with the most salient aspects of perceived Italian dominance in financial and fiscal affairs, and influence on courtly fashion and manners; and, secondly, a consideration of 'audience design', in other words, the attempt to tailor the metaphors used to the lived experience of the targeted readership.[4] The effectiveness of such commonplace metaphors may be explained most readily by reference to two important aspects of modern 'cognitivist' metaphor theory, which may be seen to be of relevance to commonplace material more widely, namely the concepts of 'common ground' and 'framing'. 'Common ground' is the contextual information shared by speaker/writer and listener/reader that enables the latter to decode metaphorical utterances accurately, even when the linguistic formulation of the metaphor does not appear to provide all the information needed for successful interpretation. The example given by Raymond Gibbs (1994) is that of a conversation about politics between two speakers of American English: if one refers to a mutual female acquaintance as an 'elephant', this does not, in all likelihood, refer to perceived obesity, but rather serves to indicate that the acquaintance is a member of the Republican party (whose symbol is, of course, an elephant).[5] I would suggest that, in later sixteenth-century France, use of metaphors playing on financial impropriety, extravagance of dress or disguise, immorality of manners, and indigestibility of food all made analogous calls on the 'common ground' of a French readership – not restricted to the persecuted Huguenot population – dissatisfied with the perceived political, financial, and cultural influence of an Italian émigré group and ready to credit them with such vices. The notion of 'framing', as popularised by the cognitivist linguistician George Lakoff in a recent book addressed to Democrat party workers and activists (appropriately entitled *Don't Think of an Elephant! Know Your Values and Frame*

---

[4] See A. Bell, 'Language Style as Audience Design', *Language in Society* 13 (1984), pp. 145-204. Moss notes (*Printed Commonplace-Books*, p. 332) that Estienne expected of the readers of his Latin works such as the *Parodiae morales* a frame of cultural reference as wide as his own; this is clearly not the case in his vernacular output, in which the authority appealed to is that of shared experience.

[5] R. W. Gibbs, *The Poetics of Mind: Figurative Thought, Language, and Understanding* (Cambridge, 1994), pp. 113-114. Compare D. Lee, *Cognitive Linguistics: An Introduction* (Oxford, 2001), p. 12: 'meaning is not a property of utterances but a product of the interaction between an utterance and a human being's "knowledge base"'.

the Debate), attempts to account for the ways in which the parameters of political debate are set in advance, and the odds stacked against the Democrat party, by the deliberate use of metaphorical frames, or 'conceptual structure[s] used in thinking' by their Republican opponents.[6] One example used by Lakoff to illustrate the process of framing and its intended effect on the American electorate is that of former president George W. Bush's mantra of 'tax relief', which started to appear in communiqués from the White House on the day that the president took office. This frame belongs to what Lakoff terms the Rescue scenario, in which 'there is a Hero (the Reliever-of-pain), a Victim (the Afflicted), a Crime (the Affliction), a Villain (the Cause-of-affliction), and a Rescue (the Pain Relief). The Hero is inherently good, the Villain is evil, and the Victim after the Rescue owes gratitude to the Hero'.[7] Each time this frame is activated by use of the term 'tax relief', the view of taxation as an affliction and the Bush administration as the reliever of pain – and therefore a hero deserving of gratitude and voters' support – is reinforced; the task of reframing the debate such that taxation is viewed as a beneficial process guaranteeing social justice, etc., is made all the harder. It is, of course, clear that the notions of framing and of common ground are closely linked, since frames rely, for their effectiveness, on common ground knowledge that is typically taken for granted within a given speech community.[8] To return to the subject-matter of this chapter, we might hypothesise that Henri Estienne, in his eagerness to 'defend' the French language and, indeed, the kingdom itself against Italian influence, attempted to formulate and popularise a set of frames that cast the Italians in the role of a pernicious threat to the purity and integrity of the French language and nation.[9] These frames would be all the more effective if they were based on his

---

[6] G. Lakoff, *Don't Think of an Elephant! Know Your Values and Frame the Debate* (White River Junction, VT, 2004). See also, by the same author, *Moral Politics: What Conservatives Know That Liberals Don't* (Chicago, 1996).

[7] See <http://www.rockridgeinstitute.org/projects/strategic/simple_framing>; last accessed August 4, 2008.

[8] Compare G. Lakoff and M. Turner, *More than Cool Reason: A Field Guide to Poetic Metaphor* (Chicago, 1989), p. 63: 'To the extent that we use a conceptual schema or a conceptual metaphor, we accept its validity. Consequently, when someone else uses it, we are predisposed to accept its validity. For this reason, conventionalized schemas and metaphors have *persuasive* power over us'; G. Lakoff and M. Johnson, *Metaphors We Live by* (Chicago, 1980), p. 129: 'Those [metaphors] that are most alive and most deeply entrenched, efficient, and powerful are those that are so automatic as to be unconscious and effortless'.

[9] For the notion of linguistic purism more generally, and the range of metaphors habitually used by purists, see G. Thomas, *Linguistic Purism* (London, 1991), pp. 19-34.

readers' common ground and reinforced existing anti-Italian prejudices, themselves a commonplace in later sixteenth-century France.

The son of Robert Estienne, the Parisian humanist scholar, printer, and committed adherent of the reformed religion, whose output includes the first printed French-Latin dictionary (1540) and a *Traicté de la grammaire françoise* (1557), the young Henri fled Paris and followed his father to Geneva in 1551 to escape persecution by the Sorbonne and safeguard the succession of the family press.[10] Having taken over his father's press according to the provisions of the latter's will in 1559, Henri proceeded, over the next forty years, to publish a prolific output of humanist and Hellenist material, including an impressive tally of first editions of ancient Greek authors, whom he edited himself.[11] Interspersed among this learned output in Latin and Greek, Estienne published a number of works in the vernacular concerned, directly or indirectly, with contemporary questions of the cultural and, more particularly, linguistic influence of Italy on France. Such questions are addressed in Estienne's celebrated satirical work, the *Apologie pour Hérodote* of 1566, in which a significant number of the vices seen to be afflicting contemporary French society are ascribed to the pernicious influence of alleged Italian immorality and perfidy; the perspective adopted is that of the Protestant critic of Catholic vices.[12] Already in the *Traicté de la conformité du langage françois avec le grec* of 1565, however, Estienne had concentrated his fire on those who, he asserts, adulterate the 'purity' of the French language through the introduction of foreign words. The prefatory material to this text is significant not only as Estienne's first contribution to a debate on the legitimacy of linguistic borrowing into French from other (competing)

---

[10] For a biography of Henri Estienne, see L. Feugère, *Essai sur la vie et les œuvres de Henri Estienne* (Paris, 1853).

[11] For an edition of Estienne's scholarly prefaces to his editions of classical works, see J. Kecskeméti, B. Boudou, and H. Cazes, *La France des Humanistes: Henri II Estienne, éditeur et écrivain* (Turnhout, 2003). As Cazes remarks in her introduction (p. xii), Estienne's vernacular works frequently arise from his editorial practice as spin-offs from these prefaces; his desire to 'defend' French from foreign influence is clearly rooted in his efforts to restore the correct (classical) usage of the Greek language and free it of the 'abuse' that it has suffered at the hands of lesser scholars (*idem*, p. xxxiii; pp. 94-95).

[12] *Apologie pour Hérodote: satire de la société au XVIe siècle*, ed. P. Ristelhuber, 2 vols. (Paris, 1879; repr. Geneva, 1969). See also B. Boudou, *Mars et les Muses dans 'L'Apologie pour Hérodote' d'Henri Estienne* (Geneva, 2000). Specific vices attributed to the Italians are sodomy (*Apologie*, I, 175) and bestiality (I, 177), blasphemy (I, 188; II, 75) and imprecations (I, 201), charlatanism and pick-pocketing (I, 211), confidence tricks (I, 212-213), bankruptcy (I, 249), and political assassination (I, 353), none of which, or so we are to believe, existed in France prior to the Italian influence.

vernaculars that can be traced back to Du Bellay's *Deffence et Illustration de la langue françoyse* (1549) and, beyond it, to Sperone Speroni's *Dialogo delle lingue* (1542), where the object of debate and discussion was, ironically, Tuscan, but also for the metaphors that are marshalled in support of Estienne's arguments. All the metaphors selected for inclusion here can be found elsewhere in Estienne's anti-Italian corpus in more elaborated form; what is significant is that they are all drawn from or appeal to the everyday experience of Estienne and his readers. In his dedicatory letter to Henri de Mesmes, a royal *maître des requêtes* and parliamentarian favourable to humanist scholars, to whom he had already dedicated a number of works,[13] Estienne explains that he owes the genesis of his present work on the 'desordre' (disorder) and 'abus' (abuse) that can currently be perceived in the French language to the return of a mysterious malady that has afflicted him three times, and that has caused him to seek out new activities, just as those who are 'degoustez des viandes ordinaires' (disgusted by their ordinary food) seek out fresh culinary pleasures.[14] On this third occasion, the loss of Estienne's wife has diverted him from the normal course of his scholarly work and has caused him to write a rather different work from the one initially promised to his patron. The analogy chosen, which is presented as a kind of epic simile, likens the author to a merchant who has been blown off course and is now forced to change his plans, hoping nonetheless that he will make more 'profit' from these new activities than he would have done from the habitual ones.[15] The habitual task in this context is Estienne's

---

[13] See J. Balsamo, *Les Rencontres des Muses: italianisme et anti-italianisme dans les Lettres françaises de la fin du XVIe siècle* (Geneva, 1992), p. 52.

[14] H. Estienne, *Conformité du langage françois avec le grec*, ed. L. Feugère (Paris, 1853; repr. Geneva, 1970), pp. 12-14. See also the facsimile edition *Traicté de la Conformité du language françois avec le grec (1565) suivi de De Latinitate falso suspecta (1576) et de Project du livre intitulé: De la precellence du langage françois (1579)* (Geneva, 1972). Estienne had already declared in the preface to his edition of Sextus Empiricus (1562), also addressed to Henri de Mesmes, that a fever had made him allergic to the reading of literary texts (Kecskeméti, *La France des Humanistes*, p. xlv).

[15] Estienne, *Conformité*, ed. Feugère, pp. 13-14: 'il m'en est pris comme aux marchands qui, selon le lieu auquel la tempeste les a jettez, sont contraincts de faire autre emploitte qu'ils ne deliberoyent. Mais Dieu veuille qu'au reste il m'en prenne aussi comme à aucuns d'eux, qui se trouvent avoir plus faict de prouffit sur ce à quoy ils n'avoyent pensé, qu'ils n'eussent faict en poursuivant leurs traffiques accoustumees. Or, tout le prouffit que je preten, est que les lecteurs reçoivent quelque contentement de mon labeur' ('the same fate befell me as those merchants who, depending on the place where the storm has washed them up, are forced to do different business from that which they had planned. But, God willing, I will emulate some of them, who manage to derive more profit from this unforeseen business than from

monumental *Thesaurus linguae graecae*, which finally appeared in 1572 and virtually bankrupted its compiler.[16] The work that Estienne now offers Henri de Mesmes, himself an accomplished classical scholar, and, ironically, a connoisseur of contemporary Italian literature,[17] is couched as an attack on those courtiers who, through ignorance or the desire for novelty, claim for themselves the privilege of legitimising 'bastard' French words and of naturalising foreign ones.[18] As Henry Heller has recently demonstrated, antipathy verging on xenophobia directed towards Italian immigrants, which had originated in humanist circles as a counterblast to Petrarch's infamous assertion that 'oratores et poetae extra Italiam non quaerantur' ('orators and poets should not be sought outside Italy'), spread in the course of the sixteenth century to merchants, Huguenots, the nobility, and, finally, the urban Catholic population.[19] Estienne seeks to harness these widespread, indeed, commonplace xenophobic sentiments for his campaign to rid the French language of such 'bastardised' or 'foreign' words; in so doing, of course, he uses the contemporary debate about the desirability of purity in language as a means of catalysing hostility towards the Italian Catholic faction at the court of France, whose manners he would go on to lambast in the *Apologie pour Hérodote* and other works, and towards Italian immigrants more generally. The immigration frame brings with it a series of shared presuppositions: foreign words entering a language, like human immigrants, require naturalisation if they are to be given leave to remain; their presence in the country may lead to interbreeding with the native popula-

---

their normal trade. For the only profit that I aspire to is that my readers derive some pleasure from my work'). All translations are my own.

[16] See Feugère, *Essai*, p. 93.

[17] See Balsamo, *Les Rencontres des Muses*, p. 52.

[18] Estienne, *Conformité*, ed. Feugère, p. 14: 'j'ay tousjours eu ceste opinion, que la cour estoit la forge des mots nouveaux, et puis le palais de Paris leur donnoit la trempe: et que le grand desordre qui est en nostre langage, procede, pour la pluspart, de ce que MM. les courtisans se donnent le privilege de legitimer les mots françois bastards, et naturalizer les estrangers' ('I have always been of the opinion that the court was the forge of new words, and that the *Palais* tempered them; I also believe that the great disorder that is afflicting our language derives largely from the fact that our friends the courtiers give themselves the right to legitimise bastard French words, and to naturalise foreign words').

[19] H. Heller, *Anti-Italianism in Sixteenth-Century France* (Toronto, 2003), p. 3. The quotation is from Petrarch's *Seniles*, IX. 1; for Franco-Italian rivalry, see F. Simone, *Umanesimo, Rinascimento, Barocco in Francia* (Milan, 1968), p. 86; N. Mann, 'Humanisme et patriotisme en France au quinzième siècle', *Cahiers de l'Association Internationale des Etudes Françaises* 23 (1971), p. 60; L. Sozzi, 'La Polémique anti-italienne dans l'œuvre narrative d'Henri Estienne', in *Henri Estienne*, p. 100; Balsamo, *Les Rencontres des Muses*, pp. 32-33, 37.

tion, producing 'bastards'. Thus what is ostensibly a contribution to a linguistic debate is designed to tap into a set of beliefs about the desirability (or otherwise) of mass immigration and the threat posed to established kinship structures by widespread bastardy. Conclusions such as these are favoured by the 'entailments' (logical consequences) of the metaphors themselves, which lend themselves to certain – typically conventionalised – modes of reasoning.[20]

The preface to the *Conformité* sets out Estienne's ideological position in the linguistic debate and, through its choice of metaphors, situates that position in the lived experience of the readership. Modern theoreticians of metaphor have noted the effectiveness of metaphor as a persuasive tool precisely because it is able to tap into and reinforce conventional modes of thought, to appeal to the already-known as a means of apprehending the abstract or the ineffable.[21] By himself selecting a frame of reference that is both appropriate to his own circumstances and familiar to his readership, Henri Estienne attempts to bolster his polemical message with an appeal to the ostensibly self-evident 'truth' of the terms in which it is couched. The first frame activated is that of food and cooking. Estienne concedes that the thesis espoused in the *Conformité*, namely that French, of all the modern vernaculars, most closely approaches Greek, 'la roine des langues' ('the queen of languages'), has been found to be 'fort cru' ('entirely raw') and 'de dure digestion' ('difficult to digest') by foreigners, while compatriots have, of course, found it 'de bon goust et de bonne digestion' ('of good taste and easy to digest').[22] This frame will be taken up in later works as a means of arguing that foreign words are – literally – unpalatable to patriotic Frenchmen. The equation between words and people, already activated by the 'immigration' frame, finds more elaborate expression in a lengthy section of the preface devoted to a description of the kind of language that Estienne will *not* be discussing in his treatise:

> Mais avant qu'entrer en matiere, je veulx bien advertir les lecteurs que mon intention n'est pas de parler de ce language françois bigarré, et qui change tous les jours de livrée, selon que la fantasie prend ou à M. le courtisan, ou à M. du palais, de l'accoustrer. Je ne preten point aussi parler de ce françois desguizé, masqué, sophistiqué, fardé et affecté à l'appetit de tous autres, qui sont aussi curieux de nouveauté en leur parler comme en leurs accoustremens. Je laisse

---

[20] For metaphorical 'entailments' in cognitivist metaphor theory, see Z. Kövecses, *Metaphor: A Practical Introduction* (Oxford, 2002), pp. 93-105.

[21] See, for instance, Lakoff and Johnson, *Metaphors We Live by*, p. 157. This ability of metaphor has, of course, long been recognised in the exegetical tradition.

[22] Estienne, *Conformité*, ed. Feugère, p. 17.

apart ce françois italianizé et espagnolizé; car ce françois ainsi desguisé, en
changeant de robbe, a quant et quant perdu, pour le moins en partie,
l'accointance qu'il avoit avec ce beau et riche language grec. (Estienne, *Conformité*, ed. Feugère, p. 20)

But, before I begin, I wish to warn my readers that I do not intend to refer to
that gaudy form of the French language that changes its livery every day depending on how our friend the courtier or our friend the lawyer choose to dress
it up. Nor will I be referring to the kind of French that is disguised, masked, affected, made up, and confected according to the wishes of all those other people
who are as obsessed with novelty in their speech as they are with novelty in
their clothes. I shall leave to one side the French that is italianised and hispan-
ised. The reason for this is that this disguised French, by changing its dress, has
at the same time lost (at least in part) the similarity that it used to display with
the rich and beautiful Greek language.

By deploying the frames of extravagant dress and disguise, Estienne makes
an appeal both to a well established tradition of French anti-aulic satire and,
in particular, to Huguenot disapprobation of the perceived excesses of the
French royal court, dominated (as popular opinion held) by the arch-
Catholic faction around the Queen Mother, Catherine de' Medici.[23] In the
same way that frequent changes of 'livery' were seen as a symptom of the
supposed moral degeneracy of the French court and of the financial profli-
gacy of its courtiers (fuelled by loans from Italian financiers), supposedly
unnecessary changes to the language, specifically the borrowing of words
from the modern vernaculars, as opposed to Greek, Latin, and earlier states
of the French language itself, are presented as inherently undesirable and,
indeed, harmful to it, since they distort its 'true' nature. This notion of distortion, which relies for its effectiveness on the frame of masking and its
overwhelmingly negative connotations for a readership suspicious of lavish
court entertainment and the figure of the Italian 'charlatan', has an additional ideological burden, as is made clear in Estienne's reference to Greek:
by masking the close linguistic relationship that Estienne (whose knowledge
of Greek was unparalleled in the period) claimed to perceive between that
language and French, Italian influence prevents French from assuming its
rightful position in the hierarchy of languages as a close relative of Greek.
No-one could argue, of course, that Italian was not closer to Latin than
French was; Estienne's aim is to circumvent this difficulty by asserting,

---

[23] For anti-aulic satire in France, see P. M. Smith, *The Anti-Courtier Trend in Sixteenth Century French Literature* (Geneva, 1966); criticisms of extravagant dress
and disguise are discussed on pp. 51, 61, 84-85, and 157.

with copious if rather (to a modern eye) unconvincing examples, that French was far closer to Greek than Italian ever could be. Aside from the obvious prestige that could be acquired for French through such an argument, there is a deeper ideological basis for the comparison between French and Greek: the latter is characterised as lending words to all other languages and borrowing words from none.[24] Ignoring the clear historical and cultural reasons for this state of affairs (he prefers to concentrate on Greek's facility in the creation of neologisms), Estienne chooses to associate linguistic prestige - or 'preeminence' - with what we might call a positive balance of payments in the international market.[25] This conception is underpinned by a further important frame, that of borrowing, which is also of immediate relevance both to contemporary Franco-Italian relations and to the everyday experience of Estienne's readership. The common ground knowledge to which the metaphor of borrowing was designed to appeal would have included, in 1565, widespread discontent at the perceived role of expatriate Italian financiers, some of whom lent huge sums to the French Crown in return for tax-farming privileges and other benefits. The infamous *Grand Parti* of Lyon, organised by Cardinal François de Tournon in 1555 as a means of funding the foreign wars and lavish domestic expenditure of Henri II, had relied heavily on the banks of Lyon (effectively an Italian monopoly in this period); its collapse two years later, which bankrupted a large number of widows and orphans who relied on such schemes as the only way of making inherited capital work for them, was widely decried as the fault of the Italian bankers.[26] In the light of such recent events, and the well documented anti-Italian sentiment that they had engendered, Estienne's deployment of the frame of borrowing has an obvious political, as opposed to merely linguistic, resonance. The form is which he chooses to make the point, however, is clearly designed to appeal to his readers' everyday experience:

---

[24] *Idem*, p. 19: '[le grec] est si riche en toutes sortes de mots, et mesmes en ce qui concerne les arts tant liberaulx que mechanicques, qu'il en preste à tous autres langages et n'en emprunte de pas un' ('Greek is so rich in all sorts of words, and especially as regards the liberal and mechanical arts, that it lends to all other languages and does not have to borrow from any').

[25] For the proto-mercantilist notions underpinning this conception, see D. Cowling, '"Neither a Borrower nor a Lender be": Linguistic Mercantilism in Renaissance France', in: A. Musolff and J. Zinken, eds, *Metaphor and Discourse* (Basingstoke, 2009), pp. 190-204; P. Desan, *L'Imaginaire économique de la Renaissance* (Mont-de-Marsan, 1993), p. 110. For early mercantilism in France more generally, see Desan, *L'Imaginaire économique*, 1993, p. 11; Heller, *Anti-Italianism*, pp. 212-218.

[26] See Heller, *Anti-Italianism*, p. 31; also H. Hauser, 'La Crise de 1557-1559 et le bouleversement des fortunes', in: *Mélanges offerts à M. Abel Lefranc par ses élèves et ses amis* (Paris, 1936), pp. 307-319.

(...) s'il fault venir aux emprunts, pourquoy ne ferons-nous plustost cest honneur aux deux langues anciennes, la grecque et la latine, desquelles nous tenons
desja la plus grande part de nostre parler, qu'aux modernes, qui sont, sauf leur
honneur, inferieures à la nostre? (...) Mais il nous en prend comme aux mauvais
mesnagers, qui, pour avoir plustost faict, empruntent de leurs voisins ce qu'ils
trouveroyent chez eux s'ils vouloyent prendre la peine de le cercher.[27]

if we do have to borrow, why do we not reserve that honour for the two ancient
languages, Greek and Latin, from which we already derive the greater part of
our speech, rather than extend it to the modern vernaculars, which are, dare I
say it, inferior to our own? (...) But we are like the sort of poor householder
who, in order to save time, borrows things from his neighbours that he would
have found at home if only he had bothered to look for them.

Borrowing, for Estienne, implies an unequal relationship between debtor
and creditor, with the latter in a position of strength, and all reasonable steps
should be taken to avoid it; the French should seek to apply the same standards of thrift and prudent domestic management to their language as they
do to their own households.[28] The homely and apparently self-evident nature of these formulations belies the skill with which such commonplaces of
everyday life (perceived, perhaps, in a more acute form in the context of the
nascent mercantilism of later sixteenth-century France) are applied to an
ideologically and confessionally loaded 'defence' of the French language
against foreign influence. If Estienne's warnings are not heeded, he asserts,
then he fears that the French language, which has previously enjoyed such
'vogue' and 'credit', will be unable to pay back its creditors and will be
obliged to 'faire un tour de banqueroutier' ('declare bankruptcy'): the sol-
vency of the language depends on its ability to repay more loan words to the

---

[27] Estienne, *Conformité*, ed. Feugère, pp. 21-22. An identical formulation can be
found in the *Apologie pour Hérodote* the following year: '(...) avons faict un tour de
mesnagers à contrepoil, allans emprunter chez nos voisins ce que nous pouvions
trouver chez nous (voire qui eust esté meilleur), si nous eussions voulu prendre la
peine de le cercher' ('we have become like wrong-headed householders by going
and borrowing from our neighbours what we could have found at home (and indeed
of higher quality) had we taken the trouble to look for it'), Estienne, *Apologie pour
Hérodote*, ed. Ristelhuber, II, p. 137. A similar sentiment had been expressed by the
humanist printer Etienne Dolet, complaining at Francis I's patronage of the Italian
Giulio Camillo (*Correspondance: répertoire analytique et chronologique suivi du
texte de ses lettres latines*, ed. C. Longeon (Geneva, 1982), p. 100).
[28] For Estienne's own financial problems in the 1570s, which were exacerbated by
the stagnation of the Genevan economy, a general shortage of money, and high rates
of interest, see O. Reverdin, 'Henri Estienne à Genève', in: *Henri Estienne*, pp. 21-
42 (pp. 31-32).

Italians than it has taken from them.[29] (There is an unconscious – or deliberate? – irony in these lines: the terms *vogue*, *credit* and *banqueroute* are all words borrowed from Italian.)

All of the frames activated in the preface to the *Traicté de la conformité du langage françois avec le grec* can be found in more elaborated form in Estienne's later – and more celebrated – satirical attack on the perceived affectations of the italianising courtiers of Henri III, the *Deux Dialogues du nouveau langage françois italianizé et autrement desguizé, principalement entre les courtisans de ce temps* of 1578.[30] In the meantime, of course, the Saint Bartholomew's Day massacre of August 24, 1572, during which at least three thousand Huguenots were killed in Paris alone, had considerably worsened relations between Catholics and Protestants and, indeed, the expatriate Italian community and French public opinion, which held the Queen Mother and her entourage primarily responsible for this 'crime italien'.[31] This hardening of attitudes is perhaps perceptible in Estienne's introduction of a further frame to add to those already deployed in the *Conformité*, namely that of sorcery. French courtiers who seek, for personal gain or through a love of novelty for its own sake, to imitate the Italian faction around the Queen Mother are decried in the *Deux Dialogues* as parrots or as donkeys, or criticised for 'larding' their speech with foreign elements ('lardons italiens') or with herbs picked from the gardens of Italy; such individuals are described as sick and, as such, lacking the discernment (taste) necessary to distinguish good linguistic usage (food) from bad. More seriously, this lack of discernment is also ascribed to the fact that such courtiers are 'ensorcelez' (bewitched):

> Il faut bien dire qu'ils soyent ensorcelez, de laisser des mots qui sont de leur langue naturelle et maternelle, et lesquels ils entendent bien, pour en prendre

---

[29] Estienne, *Conformité*, ed. Feugère, p. 32. The seriousness of the problem of bankruptcy in the period and its unpopularity with the Third Estate are indicated by the demands made at successive Estates-General in 1560 and 1576 that those found guilty of fraudulent bankruptcy should be 'punis extraordinairement et capitalement' ('punished extraordinarily for a capital offence'); see Hauser, 'La Crise de 1557-1559', p. 319. It should be noticed that the Third Estate was particularly hostile to Italian financial and fiscal influence during the period, demanding a curb on naturalisations and the exclusion of foreigners from all but wholesale business in 1576 (see Heller, *Anti-Italianism*, pp. 140-153).

[30] There is an excellent modern edition of this text by P. M. Smith (Geneva, 1980).

[31] See Heller, *Anti-Italianism*, p. 114. It is ironic that anti-Italian rioting had taken place in Paris as recently as two months before the massacre, the Venetian ambassador at the court of France having reported in 1569 that Italians had not been safe on the streets of Paris for two years (Heller, *Anti-Italianism*, p. 80).

des estrangers, lesquels ils n'entendent qu'à demi, et ne sçavent prononcer qu'à demi. (Estienne, *Deux Dialogues*, ed. Smith, p. 88)

> They are clearly bewitched, since they reject words that belong to their own natural and maternal language, and that they fully understand, in order to borrow foreign words that they only half understand, and that they can only half pronounce.

The only way to 'cure' an affected courtier of this kind, according to Estienne, is to remove him from the environment of the court, in which the presence of Italians reinforces the 'ensorcellement' that is denounced above. The common ground knowledge on which this frame is based goes right to the heart of the religious conflicts of the later sixteenth century. The anonymous Huguenot (perhaps Estienne himself) who had written the *Discours merveilleux de la vie, actions et deportements de Catherine de Médicis, Royne-mère* (1575), a scurrilous attack on the Queen Mother and her alleged attempts to divide and exterminate the French nobility, had made much of rumours of Catherine's close connections with necromancers and poisoners.[32] Indeed, a strikingly similar range of commonplace metaphors are used in the *Discours* in the support of an overtly polemical argument that seeks to discredit Catherine's claim to exert political power: instead of caring for her subjects like a true prince, who has the role of father and doctor, Catherine, in her desire for financial gain inherited from her Medici lineage – 'une maison de marchand eslevée par usures' ('a merchant family elevated through usury'), acts like a 'malicieux barbier' who never binds up a wound; she now tries to persuade French Catholics that their Huguenot compatriots are 'bastards' and rebels to the Crown.[33] In his final appeal to the Catholic nobles of France, the author of the *Discours* returns to the frame of bastardy in order to emphasise that Catholics and Huguenots are linked by shared birth and nationhood, and that all are 'vrais François' ('true Frenchmen').[34] The *Deux Dialogues* end with the call for all foreign words that cannot find an advocate for their retention to be 'banished' from the kingdom of France (along, presumably, with those that have introduced them), and with what appears to be a coded reference to the pernicious in-

---

[32] The *Discours* is edited by N. Cazauran (Geneva, 1995); see pp. 31-54 for questions of authorship and attribution (Cazauran's view is that Henri Estienne acted as *remanieur* for a second edition of the text in 1576). Clément (*Henri Estienne*, p. 32) suggests a collaboration between Estienne and Innocent Gentillet, author of a *Discours contre Nicolas Machiavel* that appeared in 1576.

[33] *Discours merveilleux*, ed. Cazauran, pp. 131, 181, 183, 263-265, 269.

[34] *Idem*, p. 279.

fluence of the alleged sorceress Catherine de' Medici on her courtiers.[35] In this respect at least, Estienne's attack on the linguistic excesses of French courtiers reads like a contribution to Huguenot polemic.

There is another important respect in which Estienne's linguistic theory, which itself made a significant contribution to the genesis of linguistic purism in France, is grounded in the ideology of the reformed religion. In the preface to the *Traicté de la conformité du langage françois avec le grec*, Estienne had, after having rejected the affected and 'disguised' language of the courtiers as a worthy object of study, announced that his treatise would consider only the French that was 'pur et simple, n'ayant rien de fard ni d'affectation, lequel M. le courtisan n'a point encores changé à sa guise, et qui ne tient rien d'emprunt des langues modernes'[36] ('pure and simple, without make-up or affectation, the sort of language that our friend the courtier has not yet changed to suit himself, and that has no borrowings from the modern vernaculars'). A similar conception is found in the Calvinist pastor Pierre Viret's *Disputations Chrestiennes, touchant l'estat des trepassez, faites par dialogues*, printed by Jean Gerard in Geneva with a prefatory epistle by Jean Calvin in 1544.[37] In his own preface, Viret defends his decision to write in French and not Latin by arguing that the Holy Spirit, although it does not reject eloquence outright, much prefers 'simplicité de langage' to 'eloquence pompeuse' (p. 35); those who practise the latter are no more than 'magpies' or 'parrots' who lack good judgement and, in their insatiable desire for novelty, forge a new language that contains half understood elements of Latin and French (p. 36). Such 'affectateurs de langage' even go so far as to 'mendier et desrober les langues estrangeres' ('beg and steal from foreign languages', *ibidem*).[38] More seriously, their preference for showy eloquence leads them to neglect the study of the Scriptures for

---

[35] *Deux Dialogues*, ed. Smith, pp. 418-419 ('bannissement' of foreign words) and 439 ('ensorcellement'). For polemical Huguenot attacks against Catherine as a witch and Italians as parasitical leeches sucking the blood of the body politic, see C. Wells, 'Leeches on the Body Politic: Xenophobia and Witchcraft in Early Modern French Political Thought', *French Historical Studies* 22 (1999), pp. 351-377.

[36] Estienne, *Conformité*, ed. Feugère, p. 20.

[37] I have consulted the 1552 edition.

[38] The metaphor of begging words from foreign languages is also found in the twelfth chapter of the second book of Du Bellay's *Deffence et Illustration de la langue françoyse* of 1549: 'Pourquoy donques sommes nous si grands admirateurs d'autruy? Pourquoy sommes nous tant iniques à nous mesmes? Pourquoy mandions nous les langues etrangeres, comme si nous avions honte d'user de la nostre?' ('Why are we such great admirers of other peoples? Why are we so hard on ourselves? Why do we beg [words] from foreign languages, as if we were ashamed to make use of our own?'), *La Deffence, et illustration de la langue françoyse (1549)*, ed. J.-C. Monferran (Geneva, 2001), p. 174.

that of the authors of pagan Antiquity, with predictably disastrous consequences. Linguistic practice and morality are thus closely linked for Viret,
as they are for Estienne, who writes frequently of the 'dépravation' of the
French language at the hands of the (depraved) courtiers of Catherine de'
Medici.[39] Viret judges that those who practise such affected language are
themselves ill, and that they lack the ability to distinguish good food from
bad, or to see that the best language is that which is 'simple et sans fard'
('simple and without make-up', pp. 40-41). Without necessarily wishing to
establish a verifiable intertextual relationship between Viret's *Disputations
Chrestiennes* and Estienne's later works, I would argue that Estienne's own
particular brand of linguistic theory owes much to such avowedly Calvinist
conceptions of language; what is most striking, however, is that Estienne's
appeal to the everyday knowledge of his readers, and specifically to knowledge that is associated with the running of a middle-class household, can
also be found in Viret's *Disputations*. A discussion of Purgatory is introduced by a long comparison in which it is likened to a laundry, in which
souls, like dirty clothes, are put out to air, washed, cleaned and steamed (p.
145). Estienne's readership, like that of Viret, appears most susceptible to
argumentation of this kind, in which everyday competences are brought to
bear on the analysis of complex phenomena. The commonplace frames activated in such argumentation were intended by the authors to provide a
powerful model not just for the interpretation of their texts, but also for political action in defence of the purity and integrity of France itself.

  While it cannot be argued that Estienne's vernacular polemics draw directly on commonplace books of the kind discussed by Ann Moss in this
volume, it is, I hope, clear that his vernacular writings make an appeal to a
body of knowledge that, although not grounded in the learned tradition, enjoyed a similar level of authority among his readers and was designed to
strike a chord with those who felt disadvantaged or disenfranchised by perceived Italian influence in both courtly and commercial circles. Indeed, it
could be argued that 'frames', as understood by modern cognitivist theoreticians of metaphor, function in a way analogous to the analytical categories
of the commonplace tradition by focusing attention on one – typically conventionalised – aspect of a controversial topic while simultaneously occlud-
ing other aspects of it. In this respect, they recall the Ciceronian image of

---

[39] For 'dépravation' as a key concept for Estienne's linguistic judgements in his
Précellence du langage françois of 1579, see P. Swiggers, 'Français, italien (et
espagnol): un concours de "précellence" chez Henri Estienne', in: G. Holtus, J.
Kramer and W. Schweickard, eds, *Italica et Romanica: Festschrift für Max Pfister
zum 65. Geburtstag*, II (Tübingen, 1997), pp. 297-311 (p. 303, n. 1).

the lattice (*transenna*)[40] insofar as they create structure in a complex domain of experience while at the same time hiding parts of it: the exclusive emphasis on the risks inherent in international trade and the supposed ignorance of parrot-like courtiers conceals the possible benefit to be derived from cultural exchange and downplays the linguistic sophistication of bilingual speakers.[41] A skilful polemicist such as Henri Estienne exploited precisely this interplay between disclosure and occlusion in order to encourage his readers to conceptualise the problem of linguistic and cultural borrowing in exclusively negative terms and, ultimately, to turn this conceptualisation into a new commonplace. While it is clear that Estienne failed to stem the immediate tide of Italian borrowing, the hostile French reaction to linguistic borrowing from English in the late 20th century would seem to bear out the long-term success of this persuasive enterprise.[42]

---

[40] For a discussion of this image, found in the *De oratore*, I. 35. 162, see T. Cave, *The Cornucopian Text: Problems of Writing in the French Renaissance* (Oxford, 1979), p. 122.

[41] For a reading of Estienne's *Deux Dialogues* that addresses questions of bilingualism and code-switching, see D. Cowling, 'Henri Estienne and the Problem of French-Italian Code-Switching in Sixteenth-Century France', in: W. Ayres-Bennett and M. C. Jones, eds, *The French Language and Questions of Identity* (Oxford, 2007), pp. 162-170.

[42] For the influence of Estienne on 20th-century French linguistic purists, see D. Hornsby, 'Patriotism and Linguistic Purism in France: *Deux Dialogues dans le nouveau langage françois* [sic] and *Parlez-vous Franglais?*', *Journal of European Studies* 28 (1998), pp. 331-354.

ROYAL AUTHORITY AND COMMONPLACE SIMILITUDES IN FRENCH NATURAL-PHILOSOPHICAL POETRY

DUCHESNE'S *GRAND MIROIR DU MONDE* AND DU BARTAS'S *SEPMAINE*

Kathryn Banks

Commonplace metaphors and royal authority in natural-philosophical poetry

During the turbulent final decades of the sixteenth century in France, royal authority was profoundly challenged. At the same time, Guillaume de Saluste Du Bartas's *Sepmaine, ou la creation du monde* (*The Week or the Creation of the World*) became an unprecedented publishing phenomenon, and inspired a number of imitations. The genre spawned by the *Sepmaine* has primarily natural-philosophical and religious concerns, and only very recently have any of its contributions to political debate been analysed.[1] However, dotted about in these long poems are polemical representations of royal authority and of the relationship between kings and their subjects, topics which were a source of intense anxiety in late sixteenth-century France. This discussion of monarchy within natural-philosophical poems is dependent upon the very common analogy between nature and human society, between the natural world and the societal one. The underlying similarity between nature and society was the foundation of a wide variety of more specific analogies, such as those between the human body and the body politic, between animal communities and human societies, or between the sun and the king. These are 'commonplaces' in the sense that they represent common cultural material in late sixteenth-century France, and, furthermore, were the basis for various similitudes – in the sense of particular instances

---

[1] See my *Cosmos and Image in the Renaissance: French Love Lyric and Natural-Philosophical Poetry* (Oxford, 2008), chapt. 2, pp. 64-80, 87-90. See also J.-R. Fanlo, 'La Matière de l'œuvre: à propos du "premier jour"', *Cahiers textuel* 13 (1993), pp. 115-131; Banks, 'Interpretations of the Body Politic and of Natural Bodies in Late Sixteenth-Century France', in: A. Musolff and J. Zinken, eds, *Metaphor and Discourse* (Basingstoke, 2009), pp. 205-218.

of making and developing likenesses[2] – which appeared in commonplace books.[3]

As I have shown elsewhere, Du Bartas makes a provocative and controversial argument against nascent absolutism by formulating the body politic analogy in an original way.[4] Several poets who imitated both Du Bartas's style and his presentation of the world through a Biblical lens furthermore shared his practice of evoking political concerns through commonplace analogies between the natural and the societal. This chapter will examine, alongside Du Bartas's *Sepmaine*, Joseph Duchesne's *Grand Miroir du monde*. Like Du Bartas's poem, Duchesne's *Grand Miroir* depicts the created cosmos, whereas others of Du Bartas's imitators, such as Jude Serclier and Michel Quillian, focus upon the apocalypse.[5] Moreover, comparing Duchesne's depiction of kingship with that of Du Bartas is particularly interesting since, although both men were Huguenots in the service of Henri de Navarre, Duchesne wrote a decade later than Du Bartas, when a fundamental shift had taken place in the debate about kingship and Navarre's relationship to it. As I shall go on to explain, when Du Bartas was writing the *Sepmaine*, royal authority was undermined by some elements of Protestant political thought and by armies led by Navarre; by contrast, a decade later, it was challenged less by Protestants than by hard-line Catholics, and Navarre was next in line to the throne. Furthermore, both Du Bartas and Duchesne emphasise the validity of arguments from nature, lending weight to their use of commonplace analogies between the natural and the human worlds, and thus to their depictions of kingship. On the seventh 'day' of his *Sepmaine* (which is structured by the Creation narrative as re-

---

[2] For Erasmus and Rudolph Agricola, similitudes operated primarily in rhetoric, although they constituted a place of humanist dialectic; by the third quarter of the sixteenth century, though, they were 'being secured to the chains of reason supplied by Aristotelian logic' (A. Moss, 'Thinking Through Similitudes', paper delivered at the fifty-first annual meeting of the Renaissance Society of America, University of Cambridge, April 7, 2005); see also Moss's contribution to this volume, pp. 1-17 (pp. 11-12).

[3] For example, one comparison for the monarch collected by Erasmus in a commonplace book of similitudes is – like some I will discuss from poetry – based upon the sun's bestowal of heat and light upon humankind: *Ut sol non alius est pauperi, alius diviti, sed omnibus communis: Ita princeps personam spectare non debet, sed rem* ('Just as the sun is no different towards the poor man or towards the rich man but is the same towards all, so the prince must not pay attention to status but to reality'; cited from Conrad Lycosthenes's re-organisation of the *Parabolae* (Lyon, 1614), p. 96, my transl.).

[4] Banks, *Cosmos*, chapt. 2, pp. 64-80, 87-90.

[5] M. Quillian, *La Derniere Semaine ou consommation du monde* (Paris, 1596); J. Serclier, *Le Grand Tombeau du monde, ou jugement final* (Lyon, 1606).

counted in Genesis), Du Bartas revisits the Creation of the previous six days and emphasises the importance of the natural world in providing lessons for the human one, and then proceeds to dedicate the second half of his seventh 'day' to such lessons.[6] Similarly, Duchesne states that humankind should be ashamed, given the loyalty and love manifested by animals, and then goes on to give humanity a series of lessons in fidelity from the animal kingdom.[7] Turning to manifestations of hatred or aggression in animals, Duchesne finds lessons for humanity there too.[8] In short, natural-philosophical poetry in the style of Du Bartas was one of those Renaissance discourses in which similarity was a central epistemological category, and the similarity between the natural and the societal or political was an important one. Indeed, while the representation of the natural world is justified for these poets by its status as an image of its Creator (as Du Bartas says explicitly and Duchesne's title suggests), it seems also to be validated by its ability to provide lessons for human society.

The *Grand Miroir* was first published in 1587. Then, in 1593, when controversy concerning monarchy and Navarre had become extremely acute, an enlarged edition was published which made even greater use of commonplace analogies to form arguments about kingship. I would argue that the 1593 edition, in common with some apocalyptic poetry, bears witness to an increasing politicisation of the genre popularised by Du Bartas; it also allows us to trace the representation of kingship – by a Huguenot in the service of Navarre – over the years during which the League most radically challenged royal authority while Navarre fought to conquer what, after 1589, he considered his own kingdom. However, these issues are beyond the scope of this study, which will analyse Duchesne's 1587 depiction of royal authority through commonplaces, namely the similarities of kings both to the sun and also to 'royal' animals, in this case the ichneumon.[9] I will compare this to Du Bartas's use of similar commonplaces to construct a very different depiction of kingship, a difference that can be attributed at least in part to the changing political climate in the 1580s. Finally, I will analyse more directly what this comparison can tell us about the functioning of commonplace analogies, both in general and in natural-philosophical po-

---

[6] G. de Saluste Du Bartas, *La Sepmaine*, in: U. T. Holmes, J. C. Lyons, R. W. Linker, et al., eds, *The Works of Guillaume De Salluste Sieur Du Bartas* (Chapel Hill, 1935-1940), II, pp. 193-440 (Day VII, ll. 435-716).

[7] J. Duchesne, *Le Grand Miroir du monde* (Lyon, 1587), pp. 147-150. All citations from the *Grand Miroir* are from this edition, except where reference is explicitly made to the 1593 edition.

[8] Duchesne, *Le Grand Miroir*, pp. 150-153. See also the 1593 edition, p. 577.

[9] Duchesne also compares kings to the four cosmic elements (*Le Grand Miroir*, pp. 157-159).

etry in particular. However, before doing so, it will be useful to remind the reader of some late sixteenth-century French history, placing the focus upon the crucial question of royal authority in the period up to 1587.

Royal authority in late sixteenth-century France

The latter decades of the sixteenth century witnessed profound challenges to the French monarchy, in the form of active resistance, criticism of the king, and theoretical elaborations of limits upon royal power. In the wake of the St. Bartholomew's Day Massacre of 1572, in which the royal family were implicated, Protestant 'monarchomachs'[10] argued that royal power was constitutionally limited, and that kings who abused their power could legitimately be resisted. These ideas were influential amongst moderate Catholics as well as Protestants. The fifth civil war (1575-1576) saw Protestants and Catholic *Malcontents* (under the leadership of Navarre and Condé) raising armies together in open rebellion against the king, Henri III. In the south and west, institutions, usually called *assemblées politiques*, developed to lead resistance to royal authority. Du Bartas wrote his *Sepmaine* in this context, beginning its composition at least as early as 1574 and first publishing it in 1578.[11] Meanwhile, in 1576, he became Navarre's *écuyer tranchant* and fought in his service, as well as participating in the Academy at the Court of Navarre and serving there as a kind of court poet.[12]

From the late 1570s, hard-line Catholics also challenged royal authority, with consequences which would be of much greater magnitude. The relatively far-reaching concessions made to the Protestants in the 1576 Peace of Monsieur implied for many that their new king was not committed to defeating heresy. For the first time, a Catholic League was organised on a national level to fight the Huguenots independently of the crown. The League's oath demanded full allegiance to the head of the League, thus undermining the primacy of fidelity to the king.[13] The League was initially short-lived, but reappeared in 1584 following the death of the duke of Anjou, which placed Navarre, a Protestant, next in line to the throne, at least according to the customary rules of succession. The new League of 1584 had far greater membership than before, comprising not only an association of nobles but also an urban organisation that would be larger and more visi-

---

[10] For example, François Hotman (*Francogallia*, 1573) and Théodore de Bèze (*Du Droit des magistrats*, 1574).

[11] Du Bartas, *Works*, I, p. 12.

[12] Du Bartas, *Works*, I, pp. 11-12; F. A. Yates, *The French Academies of the Sixteenth Century* (London, 1947), p. 123, n. 3.

[13] F. J. Baumgartner, *Radical Reactionaries: The Political Thought of the French Catholic League* (Geneva, 1976), pp. 55-56.

ble. It was motivated by a desire to prevent Navarre's accession as well as to protect Catholicism more generally; it also wished to maintain – in the face of the increasing intrusion of the monarchy – the privileges and freedoms of the clergy, the nobility, and the members of the city communes.[14] Meanwhile, Navarre – who, despite leading troops against royal armies, had been careful to protest his fidelity to the king – portrayed his goals as identical to those of the royal family, presenting the League as their common enemy, as well as that of religion and of France.[15]

At the same time, France was beset by serious social and economic problems. Its civil populations witnessed violence at a 'dramatically elevated point of intensity', which relativised even the atrocities of the earlier wars, and which was perceived as an 'inhuman' and unprecedented 'predation';[16] armed bands of robbers infested the countryside engaging in pillage and assault.[17] Economically, too, France was in crisis, and royal policy in this area alienated almost every segment of society.[18] Taxes caused discontent, especially since the king was seen to bestow great opulence upon a very small number of the *noblesse moyenne,* his *mignons*; this was criticised even by moderate observers, and was a consistent theme in League pamphlets after 1585.[19] The king also bestowed upon his favourites honours including the governorships of towns. In addition, while many nobles were in a poor financial situation, it had become increasingly difficult to obtain credit, and tax-collectors and money-lenders – often resented all the more since they were Italian – made good profits.[20]

Furthermore, Henri III failed to satisfy the keenly-felt need for a strong leader; he seemed to escape into 'cloistered unreality' rather than to confront the challenges facing him in any sustained or coherent manner.[21] Great importance was placed upon the king's presence to his subjects, one of the

---

[14] Baumgartner, *Radical Reactionaries*, pp. 32-33, 56; J. Barbey, *Etre roi: le roi et son gouvernement en France de Clovis à Louis XVI* (Paris, 1992), pp. 246-253; H. A. Lloyd, *The State, France, and the Sixteenth Century* (London, 1983), pp. 134-144.

[15] J. Garrisson, *Henri IV* (Paris, 1984), pp. 112-127.

[16] D. Crouzet, 'Le Règne de Henri III et la violence collective', in: R. Sauzet, ed., *Henri III et son temps* (Paris, 1992), pp. 211-225 (pp. 211, 212, my transl.).

[17] J. H. M. Salmon, *Society in Crisis: France in the Sixteenth Century* (London, 1975), esp. pp. 207-211.

[18] Salmon, *Society*, p. 196.

[19] Baumgartner, *Radical Reactionaries*, pp. 30-34.

[20] Salmon, *Society*, pp. 206-216. See also the chapter by D. Cowling in this volume, pp. 113-127.

[21] N. M. Sutherland, 'Henri III, The Guises and the Huguenots', in: K. Cameron, ed., *From Valois to Bourbon: Dynasty, State and Society in Early Modern France* (Exeter, 1989), pp. 21-34 (p. 22).

'essential resources of royal authority',[22] but, as Jacques-Auguste de Thou complained, Henri 'never gets on a horse or shows himself to his people as his predecessors have always done'.[23] Nor did he live up to the ideal of the *roi guerrier* (warrior king),[24] an integral part of the French ideology of kingship.[25] Accused of engaging in homosexuality with his elegant *mignons*, he was perceived to lack virility and military prowess;[26] moreover, he was repeatedly forced into humiliating capitulations.

By the end of 1584, the League held the northern and eastern part of France, as well as most large towns in the country.[27] In the 1585 Treaty of Nemours, Henri III complied with many of the League's demands, revoking all the former edicts of pacification, forbidding the practice of Protestantism, and urging French Catholics not to recognise Navarre as his successor. This did not restore the king's authority or enable him to take over the Guise war-machine: he was obliged to surrender key towns to the League, and, furthermore, various League forces attempted to impose the Treaty of Nemours by force, acting under the leadership of Henri de Guise rather than that of the king. In response, the union of Protestants and moderate Catholics was reborn under the leadership of Navarre, Condé, and Montmorency, and Navarre criticised a peace made with 'rebels' at the expense of 'obedient subjects' and with 'foreigners' at the expense of 'the princes of the blood'.[28]

Navarre's supporters and the League engaged in a particularly intense war of pamphlets in 1585. Moderate Catholics – including several powerful nobles between 1585 and 1587 – flooded to Navarre's side,[29] motivated by a concern for France and the fundamental laws that defined it, as well as by Gallicanism.[30] Furthermore, in the face of increasingly severe threats to monarchy, a growing number considered strong royal power to be the safest option, adopting 'a sceptical and quietist form of stoic moral and political thought (...) hostile to any justifications of political activism or resistance'.[31]

---

[22] J. Boutier, A. Dewerpe, and D. Nordman, *Un Tour de France royal: le voyage de Charles IX (1564-1566)* (Paris, 1984), p. 293, my transl..
[23] Quoted and transl. in M. P. Holt, *The French Wars of Religion, 1562-1629* (Cambridge, 1995), p. 102.
[24] Sutherland, 'Henri III', pp. 23, 22.
[25] Barbey, *Etre roi*, pp. 229-234.
[26] A. Jouanna, 'Faveur et Favoris: l'exemple des mignons d'Henri III', in: Sauzet, ed., *Henri III*, pp. 155-165.
[27] D. Buisseret, *Henry IV* (London, 1984), p. 17.
[28] Quoted and transl. in Buisseret, *Henry IV*, pp. 18-19.
[29] Buisseret, *Henry IV*, pp. 18-21.
[30] Garrisson, *Henri IV*, pp. 123-125.
[31] Q. Skinner, 'Montaigne and Stoicism', in: *The Foundations of Modern Political Thought* (Cambridge, 1978), II, pp. 275-284 (p. 276).

A new emphasis was placed upon loyalty and obedience to the king,[32] and upon recent and increasingly absolutist theories of monarchy.[33] Meanwhile, Navarre strengthened his reputation as a strong leader and military commander.[34]

1587 saw Navarre's famous victory over royal troops at Coutras. In the same year a memo circulated between Leaguer towns which made loyalty to the king conditional upon his fighting heresy, while casting into grave doubt whether he had done so; the conditions were being created for May 12, 1588, the Day of the Barricades, when the king would flee Paris, leaving the town and its institutions of government in the hands of the League. It is in this atmosphere that Joseph Duchesne published his *Grand Miroir du monde*. The poem is dedicated to Navarre, and the dedicatory epistle expresses confidence that the poem will be well received, citing the warm welcome accorded to the poet by Navarre upon his last visit to Gascony as evidence that Navarre will also welcome his poem. This is an indication of Duchesne's attempt to gain a post with Navarre; he was successful in this attempt and thus able to describe himself in the 1593 edition of his poem as a 'Conseiller et Medecin ordinaire du Roy' ('Adviser and Physician to the King'). In his 1587 preface to the reader, Duchesne stated that he had started the poem about three years earlier. He therefore wrote it in the years between 1584 and 1587, when royal authority was very much weakened by a reinvigorated League, and when Navarre was allying himself with royalty more closely than ever before and beginning to garner more support as heir to the throne.

The sun-king

While nature had both positive and negative examples for humanity, the heavens – as the most perfect part of the universe, seeming almost to partake of divinity – were to be emulated. In other words, if the king was similar to the sun, then it was incumbent upon him to be as similar to the sun as possible. Indeed, during the civil wars the activities of the Palace Academy and court festivities aimed to replicate cosmic harmony in the French kingdom and to reproduce the just monarchy.[35] The natural-philosophical poetry of Du Bartas and Duchesne explores how kings need to behave in order to realise this ideal: the similarity between sun and king is elaborated to show

---

[32] Barbey, *Etre roi*, pp. 243-245.
[33] Salmon, *Society*, pp. 216-218.
[34] Buisseret, *Henry IV*, pp. 15-25.
[35] Yates, *The French Academies*, esp. pp. 36-76, 118-122, 236-274.

how kings might act in order to emulate, in their kingdoms, the heavenly
relationships between the sun and the universe.

The image of the sun had an obvious potential to glorify the king; it
was, of course, commonly used for God. Unsurprisingly, then, it was to be
most famously associated with the absolutist king par excellence, Louis
XIV. It became popular in France in the sixteenth century, the period during
which concepts of absolute royal power were elaborated and negotiated.[36]
However, Du Bartas employs the comparison with the sun to castigate kings
who fail to live up to their solar counterparts. Like his use of the body politic analogy, it is concerned with kings who do not take adequate care of all
of their subjects, and contains thinly veiled criticism of the French king.
However, whereas the former focuses on royal massacre, the latter is concerned with favouritism, with some subjects being looked after much better
than others.

Du Bartas does not explicitly name Henri III, but he contrasts the sun
with 'those kings' who neglect their royal responsibilities by enriching a
few members of their court at the expense of the rest of their people, and by
spending all of their time in one region while 'abandoning' to 'unwise
princes' the government of the rest of the provinces. This description certainly recalls contemporary perceptions of Henri III's favours, both of opulence and of governorships. References to *voluptez* ('sensual pleasures') and
apas[37] further bring to mind the insinuations made about the sexual nature
of Henri's attraction to his favourites. 'That sort of king', Du Bartas suggests, fails to live up to the image of monarchy inscribed in the heavens,
since the sun makes its presence felt throughout its 'kingdom', visiting all
areas within a day, and greeting its subjects:

> Je veux, o cler flambeau, chanter que tu n'es pas
>
> De ces rois qui, pipez par les flateurs apas
>
> D'un ou deux de leur court, tout un peuple apauvrissent
>
> A fin que de ses biens deux ou trois s'enrichissent;
>
> Qui, charmez des douceurs de mille voluptez,
>
> Ne hantent, partiaux, qu'une de leurs citez,

---

[36] Barbey, *Etre roi*, p. 191.

[37] This term can have a sexual meaning, denoting the 'female charms which excite
male desire', a sense which the *Grand Robert* dates to the beginning of the seventeenth century. In addition, the *Robert Historique* explains that the term already had
the figurative meaning (as opposed to its literal meaning of the bait used to catch an
animal) of 'ce qui attire' ('that which attracts') as early as 1549; E. Huguet's *Dictionnaire de la langue française du seizième siècle* (7 vols, Paris, 1925–1967, I,
pp. 252-253) explains, giving an example from love lyric, that the verb *appaster*
could mean *séduire* (*to seduce*).

Et n'aymans qu'un païs, à de mal-sages princes
Abandonnent le soin du reste des provinces,
Car à chaque pays dans l'espace d'un jour
Tu donnes le bon-soir, tu donnes le bon-jour.[38]

I want, oh bright flame, to sing that you are not one of / Those kings, who deceived by the flattering lures / Of one or two of their court, impoverish a whole people, / So that two or three get richer from their wealth; / Who, charmed by the sweetnesses of a thousand pleasures of the senses, / Frequent, being partial, only one of their towns, / And loving only one region, to unwise princes / Abandon the care of the rest of their provinces, / For to every region in the space of a day / You say good evening, you say good day.

After thus evoking the sun's passage through the sky during the course of a day, Du Bartas proceeds to describe the seasons (IV, 599-646). He admits that, at any one time of the year, some receive more of the sun's heat than others and thus experience spring while others experience autumn. However, the sun nonetheless bestows its bounty equally upon all areas of its 'kingdom': it varies its path each day so that the various areas receive increased amounts of the sun's heat 'in turn' ('de rang' (600), 'par ordre alternatif' (602)).

Duchesne's discussion of the sun also depicts a 'king' travelling around his 'kingdom' and also describes how the seasons are dependent upon the sun's gift of heat. Like Du Bartas, Duchesne refers to the constellations through which the sun passes and, in his description of spring, mentions the birds, Cupid, and the relationship between Zephyrus and Flora. However, whereas Du Bartas observes that different places all experience spring in turn, for Duchesne, spring is itself a place, and it gains the special attentions of the sun-king. Spring is a town into which the king makes a royal entry, and to which he grants particularly generous privileges:

Muse, mon cher souci, dicte-moy quelque vers,
Pour pouvoir saluer l'œil beau de l'univers:
Uranie aide-moy à celebrer l'entree
Du beau Latonien à la face doree.
Desja l'astré Mouton, au poil d'or tout frisé,

---

[38] *La Sepmaine*, 'Day' IV, ll. 585-594. This is the text from 1578. In the 1581 edition, the king abandoned 'towns' to 'base people' ('des personnes viles') rather than 'provinces' to 'unwise princes', a transformation probably motivated by disapproval of the relatively low social status of the *mignons*; the sense of *vil* is social as well as moral, and could be opposed to *noble*. All translations are my own, and prioritise the goal of comprehension by the modern reader of English.

A de belle verdeur son portail lambrissé,
Où ses beaux estendarts, pour accroistre la joye,
Tous semés de bourgeons, le Mois guerrier desploye,
Tandis que ce grand Prince, une fois tous les ans,
Passe par la cité de son aimé Printemps.
Oyez chanter Iö, voyez comme les rues
Des champs, des bois, des prés, y sont toutes tendues
De tapis fleuronnés, de mille et mille fleurs,
Enrichis de l'esmail de leurs belles couleurs.
        Voyez comme desja on parfume la place
Du logis du Taureau, dedans lequel il passe:
        Quel honneur luy feront les deux Amycleans,
Les deux Bessons couplés, eschevins du Printemps?
Ils luy vont au devant en pompe et à la file,
Avec eux tout l'honneur de leur Maison de Ville:
Ceux qui vont tout devant les Freres estoilés,
C'est l'escadron leger des Menestriers aislés,
Qui, en lieu de haut-bois, de clairons, de trompettes,
Font retentir tout l'air avec leurs chansonnettes.
Zephire vient apres, et s'attend, le mignard,
Recevoir de sa Flore un gracieux regard.
L'Amour marche à costé, et avec eux apporte
Le Poile tout brodé de fleurs de toute sorte.
Voyez comme desia ils descouvrent leurs chefs,
Font hommage à leur Roy, lui presentent les clefs
De leur belle Cité, et le Roy, d'une veuë
Toute agreable aussi, ses bons sujets saluë,
Et, Prince liberal, confirme de nouveau
Les privileges deus de droict au Renouveau,
Sur toute autre saison, lui ottroyant puissance
D'accroistre, conserver, et de donner naissance
Aux choses d'ici bas : le tout signé du seing
Des accords, des odeurs, et de l'air plus serain.
(*Le Grand Miroir*, pp. 128-130)

Muse, my tender care, dictate me some verses, / So that I can greet the handsome eye of the universe: / Urania help me to celebrate the entry / Of the handsome Latonian[39] with the golden face. / Already the starry Ram, with its golden
hair all curly / Has decorated its gate with beautiful greenery, / Where the war-

---

[39] Apollo.

rior Month (March),[40] to increase the joy, / Unfurls its beautiful standards, all strewn with buds, / While this great Prince, once every year, / Passes through the town of his beloved Spring. / Hear them sing 'Io', see how the paths, / Of the fields, the woods, the meadows, there are all bedecked / With tapestries thick with blossom, with thousand upon thousand of flowers, / Enriched with the variegation of their beautiful colours. / See how already they perfume the square / Of the dwelling of the Bull, through which he passes: / What honour will be done to him by the two Amycleans, / The two Twins lodged together,[41] *eschevins*[42] of Spring? / They march before him with ceremony and in line, / With them all the honour of their Town Hall: / Those who march just before the starry Brothers, / Are the light squadron of winged Minstrels, / Who, in place of oboes, of clarions, of trumpets, / Make all the air echo with their sweet songs. / Zephyrus comes next, and trusts, the charming one, / That he will receive from his Flora a gracious gaze. / Love[43] walks next to them, and with them carries / The ceremonial canopy all embroidered with all sorts of flowers. / See how already they uncover their heads, / Pay homage to their King, present him with the keys / To their beautiful Town, and the King, looking / Just as kindly (on them), greets his good subjects, / And, bountiful Prince, confirms again / The privileges due by right to Spring, / Over every other season, granting it the power / To increase, preserve, and give birth / To the things here below: all this signed with the signature / Of agreements, of scents, and of more peaceful air.

The privileges of sixteenth-century French towns varied, but those granted to the town of Spring seem particularly generous, giving it creative powers above any other season. Thus, whereas Du Bartas used the comparison between king and sun to suggest that all subjects and all places should be treated equally by the king, Duchesne uses it with precisely the opposite sense: it is 'natural', following the example of the heavens, that some towns have special privileges, just as spring is granted particular rights by the sun. These privileges are 'due by right' to the town of Spring.

However, the king's confirmation of privileges seems to reflect an equally positive attitude on the part of the town towards its king. Kings often did confirm a town's privileges during a royal entry, as if in thanks for the welcome accorded. However, during the civil wars, towns which had failed to manifest sufficient loyalty to the king did not always have their privileges renewed; this had been the subject of protest in Paris, for exam-

---

[40] The French word for March is *mars* which also, as in English, designates the Roman god of war; hence the 'warrior month' signifies March.
[41] Castor and Pollux, the constellation of Gemini.
[42] (In most northern towns) elected figures presided over by a *maire*.
[43] Cupid.

ple, where the League dominated the Bureau of the *Hôtel de Ville*, the mu-
nicipal government, and thus was able to thwart the king in his dealings
with the city.[44] It seems difficult to imagine, though, that the town of Spring
could have been anything but entirely loyal. Royal entries were intended to
demonstrate the 'eagerness, respect and joy' inspired by the king in his subjects,[45] and the citizens of Spring show ample evidence of these. The celebration is explicitly a source of 'joie' ('joy'), and the eagerness of the inhabitants to welcome their king is demonstrated by the repetition of 'déjà'
('already'): they are keen to play their roles in the celebrations as soon as
possible. The town authorities honour the king in the customary fashion, by
processing before him and bearing a ceremonial canopy for him. They demonstrate their respect by immediately removing their hats and paying homage to him, and their obedience is represented symbolically in the usual
way; that is, by handing him the keys to their town. Finally, while French
towns during royal entries were generously bedecked with triumphal arches,
theatrical scenes, and other sorts of painted or sculpted decorations, Spring
is beautifully decorated with buds, flowers, colours, and scents, while the
birds sing like minstrels ('Menestriers aislés').

In short, Spring forms a striking contrast to those towns which, in 1587,
were already allied with the League and clearly challenging the king's authority. While the League demanded the renewal of privileges, the example
of Spring shows that privileges are confirmed for those 'good subjects' who
eagerly welcome and obey their king; privileges cannot be demanded, it
seems, but rather have to be earned. Just as, through its display of colours,
buds, and scents, the spring celebrates most the sun's presence, and has the
special privilege of being more productive and creative than the other seasons, so towns that celebrate their king will be rewarded by him. Duchesne
does not say explicitly that disloyal towns will be less well rewarded, and
abandons his analogy with royalty when he discusses the sun's role in the
other seasons; nonetheless, whereas he aligns the privileges of obedient
towns with spring's power over life and growth, once the sun has 'galloped'
through summer in five lines, the poet emphasises the association of autumn
and winter with death and finitude (pp. 132-134).

Several lexical items in the passage bear meaning in relation to both nature and politics, thus operating on both levels of the analogy. For example
'entrée' is both an astronomical term and a political one, considered proper
to denote the 'entry' of the sun into a constellation as well as that of a king
into a town. 'Esmail' and 'fleuronnés' arguably both evoke human decora-

---

[44] Baumgartner, *Radical Reactionaries*, pp. 32-33, 42-43, 56; Barbey, *Etre roi*,
pp. 246-253; Lloyd, *The State*, pp. 134-144.
[45] Boutier, *Un Tour*, pp. 293-294, my transl.

tion as well as natural splendour: *esmail* referred both to the diverse colouring of flowers and also to enamel; *fleuronner* meant *to blossom* but also evokes *fleuron* which, according to Cotgrave,[46] designated primarily a fleuron, a flower-shaped ornament used in architecture, which, of course, would be a particularly pertinent symbol in a celebration of a French monarch. This trait is particularly strong in the final line quoted above. 'Accords' refer both to the harmonious relations that exist in the heavens – to cosmic harmony – and also to agreements or treaties, a meaning which is all the more present here given that the 'accords' are 'signed'. Similarly 'serain' implies both a cosmos without meteorological disturbances and also the 'peace' obtaining between the king and the subjects of an obedient town like Spring. *Odeur*, which had a much wider range of meanings than *scent*,[47] could refer to the way in which an action was interpreted, for example by the king,[48] and thus suggests here both the cosmic beauty of spring and also political harmony. This lexical practice arguably strengthens the persuasive and epistemological weight of the comparison between sun and king: the fact that 'entrée' designates both a royal entry and a solar one increases the sense of similarity between the two, the sense that they are essentially examples of the same phenomenon, but occurring in different domains; the term 'accord', by designating both cosmic harmony and political agreement, reinforces the implication that the latter should mirror the former.[49]

Royal entries routinely made use of cosmic imagery and mythological heroes to elevate the king's status. Duchesne's analogy provides an account of how a king should behave in order properly to correspond to his cosmic counterpart. His suggestion that kings should reward obedience contrasts with the French king's reaction to the League: as Navarre put it, the 1585 Treaty of Nemours rewarded rebellion. Duchesne strongly suggests that – in order to live up to the heavenly ideal of kingship – the king ought to ally himself with his 'good subjects' rather than his rebellious ones. Furthermore, Duchesne presents the sun-king making his presence felt to his subjects. Royal entries reaffirmed royal authority and symbolically enacted the

---

[46] R. Cotgrave, *A Dictionarie of the French and English Tongues* (London: Adam Islip, 1611), unpaginated.

[47] Banks, *Cosmos*, pp. 51-55 (p. 54).

[48] In one of his many letters to the king during 1570 and 1571, Navarre feared that his actions might be presented to the king in such a way as to make the latter receive them 'de mauvaise odeur' ('with a bad *odeur*'): quoted by Garrisson, *Henri IV*, p. 48.

[49] Du Bartas also – and often to a more extreme degree – uses lexical items which bear meaning in relation to both levels of a comparison, thus making it hard to dissociate the two levels (see Banks, *Cosmos*, chapt. 1-2).

(ideal) relationship between king and town. They had been extensively employed during a long royal tour of France in 1564-1566, intended to strengthen the position of a young Charles IX following the first of the civil wars; they also presented Navarre, a Protestant, as an integral part of the royal family.[50] While, in 1587, Henri III seemed distant from his subjects and was singularly failing to exert his authority, Duchesne linguistically enacted the royal entry, along with its affirmation of royal power and of the bond between king and subject; like the many reports of actual entries, the poem re-presents the already highly symbolic ritual but, in Duchesne's case, in the absence of any 'original' event.

For both Du Bartas and Duchesne, then, the image of the travelling sun-king provided a foil for the problematic functioning of monarchy in France. Both poets employed a rhetorical strategy dependent upon the commonplace notion of a relationship of analogy and emulation between the earth and the heavens, appealing to the notion that the functioning of the heavens must be the right one, and that the human world should mirror the heavenly world. Both poets suggest that the king should make his presence felt in his kingdom. However, whereas Du Bartas is highly critical of the monarchy, in the late 1580s Duchesne was more concerned to bolster royal authority than to undermine it. He uses the same commonplace as Du Bartas in order to focus on the behaviour of subjects as well as kings, depicting at length the idealised obedient subjects of Spring. Thus Duchesne linguistically reaffirms the bond between monarch and subjects, representing it as one of loyalty and obedience.

The ichneumon: the ruthless 'roi guerrier' and the enemies of the 'bien public'

While the depiction of the sun affirms royal authority, that of the ichneumon (pp. 151-153) calls for it to be vigorously asserted. Comparing the king to an ichneumon was not as common as comparing him to the sun. Du Bartas had discussed the ichneumon without referring to kingship (*Works*, VI, pp. 235-266), and so Duchesne politicises a subject that was not political in the earlier poem. However, comparisons between human society and the animal world were common, as were, more specifically, those between kings and 'royal' animals, although dolphins, eagles, and bees were more usual choices. Duchesne introduces the ichneumon as a 'Rat Pharaonien', which, as Goulart observes in his commentary to the 1593 revised edition of

---

[50] Garrisson, *Henri IV*, pp. 32-34.

the *Grand Miroir* (p. 413), is like calling the creature a 'royal rat', since Pharaoh was the title of the ancient Egyptian kings.[51]

The ichneumon is a small animal closely related to the mongoose. Yet, in Pliny's account in his *Natural History* (VIII. 36-37), it cleverly defeated both snakes and crocodiles; it created a 'coat of armour' from mud in order to withstand the snake's attack, and it darted down the sleeping crocodile's throat in order to consume the larger animal from within.[52] In Duchesne's *Grand Miroir*, the ichneumon, like the sun, is presented as one of nature's positive examples. The ichneumon, as depicted by Duchesne, is a brave fighter and a skilful 'military' tactician. The poet tells us that he has chosen to end book 4 with this creature, since any retreat should be led by 'le chef plus vaillant' ('the most valiant leader'). Duchesne makes use of the notion of a creature able, through cunning strategy, to defeat animals much bigger than itself. He contrasts the small size of the ichneumon with the greatness of its soul or spirit, apostrophising the 'petit animal magnanime de cœur' ('small animal great in soul').[53] This 'royal' animal is celebrated for its ability to defeat forces apparently greater than itself, if not through might then through diligence ('Si non avec la force, avec son industrie'), and employing wisdom ('sagesse') and bravery ('brave cœur').

On the other hand, the ichneumon is described as 'cruel' and depicted as ruthless and determined. It seeks out and destroys the eggs of its enemies, as well as waging war upon older members of the species; it gnaws snakes' heads or drowns them, and kills the crocodile by eating its liver and drinking its blood until it is entirely hollow. Moreover, the ichneumon takes pleasure in defeating its enemies, 'feasting' on the crocodile's liver and 'joyfully making merry' as it consumes its body from within.[54] However, all this violence is in a worthy cause: Duchesne tells us that snakes and crocodiles would otherwise make Egypt uninhabitable.

Duchesne hints throughout this discussion that the behaviour of this 'royal' animal has – or should have – a human equivalent. The ichneumon

---

[51] The ichneumon was often called a *rat de Pharaon*, for example in Jacques Amyot's popular translation of Plutarch's *Moralia*; however, Duchesne's slightly different formulation potentially has rather different connotations, as Goulart highlights.

[52] See also Plutarch's *Moralia*, 966d and Aristotle's *Historia animalium*, 612a 16.

[53] 'Magnanime' meant 'noble-souled' (whereas its modern meaning is 'generous'). Its meaning was thus closer to that of its Latin root (*magnus animus*), and Duchesne appears to have this Latin root in mind here, given the juxtaposition of the ichneumon's small size with its 'cœur' described as 'magnanime'.

[54] '[S]e festoye, / A ton mortel regret des lobes de ton foye, / S'abbruve de ton sang, et s'esgaye, joyeux, / Dans ton corps, jusqu'à tant qu'il l'ait rendu tout creux' (p. 152).

is described as acting 'pour le bien du public' ('for the public good'), an expression which would more normally be used with reference to human society than the natural world, and which indeed was frequently used precisely to justify recourse to arms during the wars, being employed by both the League and supporters of Navarre in the mid-1580s.[55] Furthermore, the ichneumon's violent action sounds very much like military activity, since Duchesne consistently uses vocabulary pertinent to human battle: 'livrant encor bataille' ('engaging battle again'); 'l'attache, et l'assaut' ('attacks him and assails him'); 'la sentinelle' ('the sentry'); 's'armant' ('arming himself'); 'soudain il eschelle / Le fort Crocodilois, et se fourre dedans / Par l'huis plus dissolu' ('suddenly he scales the Crocodilian fort, and penetrates it by the loosest gate'); 'donnant ainsi l'alarme' ('raising the alarm'); 'ce nouvel assaut' ('this new attack'). Furthermore, not only is the ichneumon anthropomorphised as a courageous leader ('le chef plus vaillant'), as we have seen, but also the crocodile is represented anthropomorphically as 'ce grand Brigand d'aguet' ('this huge Brigand on the look-out'); more generally, crocodiles and snakes were two of many animals used by authors of pamphlets to characterise their opponents.[56]

Thus, by celebrating the actions of this 'royal' animal, Duchesne provides an ideal portrait of a king. The king, Duchesne suggests, should be a brave and skilful military leader, seeking out enemies of the public good in order to destroy them ruthlessly and even joyfully. With bravery, determination, and military cunning, the poet implies, the king can defeat even enemies who appear to be more powerful than himself. The powerful enemies of the king who spring readily to mind are of course the League, who, from the point of view of Navarre, and of many Protestants or Catholics of a *politique*[57] persuasion, were indeed enemies of the king and of the public good. The ideal portrait of a king relentlessly pursuing his clever military strategies differs strikingly from contemporary perceptions of Henri III as a weak leader whose lack of coherent long-term strategy and military skill enabled the League to grow rapidly in strength and effectively to call the shots: whereas Henri III seemed to ignore problems until forced defensively into action, the ichneumon attacks first as a preventative measure. The king of Navarre and heir to the throne of France, on the other hand, had military

---

[55] A. Jouanna, *Le Devoir de révolte: la noblesse française et la gestation de l'État moderne, 1559-1661* (Paris, 1989), esp. pp. 192-193.

[56] J. Pineaux, 'La Métaphore animale dans quelques pamphlets du XVIe siècle', in: *Le Pamphlet en France au XVIe siècle* (Paris, 1983), pp. 35-45.

[57] Those who emphasised the need to ensure the survival of the commonwealth, dubbed *politiques* by the most militant Catholics, a term intended to suggest that they placed political considerations above religion.

skills and qualities which made him fit the image of the ichneumon much more satisfactorily.

Duchesne then proceeds, in the concluding lines of book 4, to make his lesson for kings explicit, stating that they should follow the ichneumon's example by banishing trouble-makers from their realms. He also relates the lesson to France specifically, saying that such an action could provide a solution to France's problems. Furthermore, he indicates more clearly the identity of the 'crocodiles' and 'snakes' in France:

> Vous devriez imiter, ô vous Rois, et vous Princes,
> L'ichneumon genereux, chassans de vos provinces,
> Ceste espece d'Aspics que l'on nomme Cracheurs,
> Ces contempteurs de Dieu, tous ces blasphemateurs
> Qui crachent vers le ciel, une poison meschante
> Qui sort à tout propos de leur bouche puante:
> Vous devriez depeupler, de larrons, de meurtriers,
> De brigands inhumains, d'avares, usuriers,
> De gens aime-procés, trestous vrais Crocodiles,
> Vos forests, vos chemins, vos palais et vos villes.
> Ainsi les belles fleurs de l'immortalité
> Couronneroyent vos fronts, ainsi de mon costé
> J'aurois encor un jour de revoir esperance,
> Avec plus de seurté le repos de la France.

> You should imitate, o Kings and Princes, / The noble ichneumon, chasing from your provinces, / That species of Asp which one calls Spitters, / Those contemptors of God, all those blasphemers / Who spit towards the heavens an evil poison / Which comes out in relation to all subjects from their stinking mouths: / You should rid of thieves, of murderers, / Of inhuman brigands, of the greedy, moneylenders, / Of lovers of law-courts, just so many true Crocodiles, / Your forests, your paths, your palaces, and your towns. / Thus the beautiful flowers of immortality / Would crown your foreheads, thus as for me / I would one day have again the hope / To see again with more security the respite of France.

Duchesne states quite explicitly that France would benefit from a king who shared the qualities of the ichneumon, and used them to defeat France's enemies (as defined by Duchesne). His use of the conditional ('I would have (…) hope') implies that France does not yet have such a king. He thus provides an account of how Henri III – and perhaps his successor – ought to behave in order to alleviate France's problems. Since Navarre shared the ichneumon's 'military' skills, the ideal of kingship promoted by the poet is one which would support his patron's suitability for the throne.

The argument that France requires a warrior king could weigh in the balance for Catholics wavering between the needs of the Catholic religion and the need for a strong monarch.

Duchesne wrote these lines amid a rhetorical struggle to determine who was acting in the interests of the public good and who was undermining it. In 1585, Henri III had promised to rid France of Protestants, but Duchesne's analogy suggests that the real enemies of the public good – those who really deserve to be banished from the kingdom – are those who resemble crocodiles and 'spitting' snakes ('Cracheurs'), those committing violent crimes or 'spitting' blasphemy. More precisely, the 'crocodiles' and 'snakes' include 'blasphemers' who 'spit poison', calling to mind the acrimonious words issuing from Leaguer pulpits and propaganda,[58] perceived, for example by Navarre, as undermining religion as well as the king. The 'thieves', 'murderers', and 'brigands' recall those romping lawlessly through France, and the adjective 'inhuman' applied to the brigands voices the strong contemporary perception of them as inhuman predators, particularly thanks to the analogy with crocodiles, which, earlier in the discussion, were anthropomorphised precisely as 'brigands'; murderers and thieves could also bring to mind those attempting to enforce the Nemours treaty. Duchesne's 'greedy people' could evoke the fiscal officers and money-lenders making huge profits, or perhaps the king's favourites receiving extravagant gifts; the money-lenders are also given an individual mention. Ridding the French territory of the financiers and usurers might have seemed to Duchesne all the more appropriate, given that many were Italian.[59] As for the lovers of law-courts, it was a common complaint that, thanks to the open sale of judicial office, France had too many lawyers and too much litigation,[60] and Duchesne may have been aware of the strong presence of dissatisfied lawyers in Catholic urban agitation.[61] In short, Duchesne suggests that the king could solve France's troubles by strongly exerting his authority over all of these 'true crocodiles'.

---

[58] Most of the Parisian clergy, according to contemporary accounts, actively supported the Paris Sixteen (the most powerful cell of the urban League); they comprised its 'most effective weapon', thanks to their power over popular opinion (Baumgartner, *Radical Reactionaries*, pp. 41-42).

[59] See the chapter by D. Cowling in this volume, pp. 113-127.

[60] Salmon, *Society*, pp. 78-79.

[61] Salmon, *Society*, pp. 247-257; *idem*, 'The Paris Sixteen, 1584-1594: The Social Analysis of a Revolutionary Movement', in: J. H. M. Salmon, *Renaissance and Revolt: Essays in the Intellectual and Social History of Early Modern France* (Cambridge, 1987), pp. 235-266.

Conclusions

1. Commonplaces and authority: similitudes as creative 'thinking tools'

The depictions of kingship by Du Bartas and Duchesne are both dependent upon the same underlying analogy between nature and society. More specifically, both poets discuss the king's relationship with his kingdom by depicting the sun travelling through the constellations and ordering the seasons. Both poets find it helpful to depict the ideal monarch greeting his subjects and making his presence felt. However, whereas, for Du Bartas, the example of the sun implies that the king should govern over all areas of his kingdom in the same way and treat all his subjects equally, for Duchesne solar monarchy suggests that kings employ discernment in order to treat subjects appropriately in accordance with their merits. Furthermore, while the loyal inhabitants of Spring should be rewarded, another example from the natural world demonstrates that enemies of the king and of the public good – those powerful enemies who 'spit' poison and engage in inhuman violence – should be decisively quashed, with perseverance, bravery, cunning, and perhaps even cruelty and joy; by contrast, in the aftermath of the St. Bartholomew's Day Massacre, Du Bartas had used an example from the natural world to warn against the propensity of kings violently to crush their subjects, and thus to suggest (with the Protestant monarchomachs) that royal power should be reined in.[62]

Therefore, while commonplace analogies might (in some discourses at least) have set the parameters of political debate, they did not bear a fixed meaning that rendered them useful only to proponents of a particular view. While analogies undoubtedly shaped interpretations of events, conversely they were themselves shaped by (contemporary apprehensions of) events. In the terms of Kuhnian paradigms,[63] similitudes between nature and society shaped the sorts of 'questions' asked about royal authority in the final decades of the sixteenth century but did not shape the 'answers' found. Similitudes were part of the linguistic *outillage mental* of late sixteenth-century

---

[62] Banks, *Cosmos*, chapt. 2, pp. 64-80.

[63] In the history of science, T. S. Kuhn's concept of the 'paradigm' has been used to denote a set of basic beliefs which determine the terms of the questions posed at a given moment. See Kuhn's *Structure of Scientific Revolutions* (Chicago, [2]1970) and, for an overview of the varied notions of the 'paradigm', J. Golinski, *Making Natural Knowledge: Constructivism and the History of Science* (Cambridge, 1998), pp. 14-27.

France, but this *outillage mental* shaped a framework of conceptual possibilities rather than defining one of rigid concepts.[64]

As Ann Moss states in this volume, commonplaces 'constituted in effect the cultural matrix of early modern Europe', yet could be exploited 'to manoeuvre authoritative argument' against commonly-held opinions (pp. 5-6). In the case of similitudes, as distinct from other sorts of commonplace, emphasis should be placed upon the latter, that is, upon their creative potential in the service of a variety of contradictory opinions: while any commonplace might be used in diverse and contradictory ways, the similitude seems particularly rich in creative potential. Indeed, in her discussion of the predilection of preachers for the similitude, Moss states that similitudes provided an 'abundance of opportunities to diversify' (p. 11). Thus similitudes may be more versatile than the metaphors which they develop. Where, as in the depiction of the sun-king, the implications of an analogy are unfolded at some length, diverse arguments can be constructed, for example about kingship. In other words, 'glossing' a similarity enabled a writer to some extent to determine its interpretation rather than be bound by the interpretations which were most commonly applied to it.

2. Analogy and genre: politics in natural-philosophical poetry

In natural-philosophical poetry, political comment appeared in a discussion of the cosmos and thus avoided 'censorship', not only in any literal sense, but also in that readers were not forewarned of the political content they would encounter. Political arguments grounded in nature, while they were used in other discourses, also gained potency from their inclusion within a genre which insistently presents the natural world as a source of lessons for humanity, as both an image of the human world and an ideal to which it should aspire: as we have seen, this is both stated explicitly and implied through the use of lexical items which bear meaning in relation to both levels of an analogy.

Moreover, the potentially very powerful role played by the development of similitudes means that the genre of poetry inaugurated by the *Sepmaine* can perform a particularly interesting function in relation to commonplaces and authority. Of course analogies between the natural and the political were precisely commonplace, and were by no means employed only in Christian natural-philosophical poetry. However, this particular genre *invited* the detailed 'unfolding' of similitudes. Du Bartas's language –

---

[64] See L. Febvre's *Problème de l'incroyance au XVIe siècle* (Paris, 1942) and, on *outillage mental* as productive as well as restrictive, Banks, *Cosmos and Image*, pp. 4, 23n, and *passim*.

considered a paradigm of a style often termed 'baroque' – is flamboyantly imagistic.[65] Furthermore, he considered that his poem was, in part, an epic,[66] and used comparisons in the epic style, that is, developing them at length and focussing as much on the subject used for comparison (for example, the king) as on the initial subject-matter (the sun). In addition, Du Bartas was inventive in his use of epic comparisons, whereas some other poets, such as Du Bartas's very well-known contemporary, Ronsard, tended to draw their epic comparisons directly from ancient texts.[67] Duchesne often shares Du Bartas's stylistic practice with relation to comparisons.

Thus, thanks to the generic specificities of their use of similitudes, Du Bartas and Duchesne are able to explore at length – and, crucially, to shape – the implications of the commonplace analogies employed. As a result, Du Bartas voiced an original and polemical formulation of the body politic, and Duchesne similarly used comparisons between the king, the sun, and a royal animal in innovative and provocative ways. Thanks to, first, a particular poetic style and, secondly, commonplace analogies based on nature, politics was explored in natural-philosophical poetry, a departure from more usual genres of political commentary. Du Bartas and Duchesne apparently hope that poetry might play some role in achieving societal harmony, not simply through the musicality of poetry – considered by some as a potential means of facilitating the descent of heavenly harmony upon France[68] – but rather through the provision of specific lessons as to how harmony can be achieved; in the fraught final decades of the sixteenth century, an important part of this was negotiating the relationship between kings and subjects.

---

[65] On images in the 'baroque' aesthetic, see A. Baïche, *La Naissance du baroque français: poésie et image de la Pléiade à Jean de La Ceppède* (Toulouse, 1976); W. Floeck, *Esthétique de la diversité: pour une histoire du baroque littéraire en France*, transl. by G. Floret (Paris, 1989), pp. 80-141. On Du Bartas's relation to this aesthetic, see B. Braunrot, *Imagination poétique chez Du Bartas: éléments de sensibilité baroque dans la Création du Monde* (Chapel Hill, 1973).

[66] *Brief Advertissement sur sa première et seconde Sepmaine* (1584), in *Works*, I, pp. 218-224 (p. 220).

[67] A. E. Creore, 'Ronsard, Du Bartas, and the Homeric Comparison', *Comparative Literature* 3 (1951), pp. 152-159.

[68] Yates, *The French Academies*, pp. 36-76. Duchesne himself discusses the power of harmony, and wishes he knew a song which could affect the 'deaf atheists' (*Le Grand Miroir*, pp. 130-131).

TO TAKE IN A TOWN WITH GENTLE WORDS[1]

THE USE OF *LOCI* IN THE ANTWERP ENTRY OF 1549

Stijn Bussels

A striking application of Ann Moss's understanding of the early modern concept of commonplace, as discussed in her chapter in this volume, can be found in the joyous entry of Charles V and his son and successor Philip into Antwerp on September 10, 1549. The town clerk and renowned humanist Cornelius Grapheus was responsible for the inscriptions on the triumphal arches and *tableaux vivants*. It is not entirely certain that Grapheus collected commonplaces or consulted commonplace books, but he definitely used phrases from authoritative authors as subject-matter for the inscriptions on the *tableaux vivants* and triumphal arches alongside the entry route.

In a large inscription on a *tableau* where Philip was at the centre of attention, for example, the prince was welcomed as follows: 'At last you are come, yet now we may presently behold your long desired face'.[2] Originally, these verses come from Aeneas's father, Anchises. In the sixth book of Virgil's *Aeneid*, the Trojan hero descends into the Underworld and is greeted by his departed father. Although this particular context is far removed from the joyous entry – certainly, the metropolis of commerce had no interest in resembling the underworld – the phrasing was designed to fit the important occasion. The use of verses derived from the famous Roman poet created a high-level communication between the educated Antwerp burghers and the Habsburgs. As Moss points out, it will have created a bond, as everyone who could understand the reference must have felt part of

---

[1] These words come from Shakespeare's *Coriolanus* of c.1607 (III. ii. 59) and are spoken by Volumnia to prompt her son and brilliant general Coriolanus to make maximum use of eloquence to convince the citizens of Rome, who are in revolt against him, of his integrity and military and political competence.

[2] This inscription on an Antwerp *tableau* was originally in Latin, but was translated into Dutch by Grapheus in the official account of the entry: 'Emmer sydij commen, men mach doch nu, u langbegeerde aensicht tegewoirdichlijck aenschouwen' (C. Grapheus, *De seer wonderlijcke schoone Triumphelijcke Incompst, van den hooghmogenden Prince Philips, Prince van Spaignen, Caroli des vijfden, Keysers sone* (…) *inde stads van Antwerpen, Anno M.LLLLL.XLJX* (Antwerp, 1550), fol. E^v). The English transl. of this account is mine.

'a community of shared points of reference, core texts, and common practice'.[3]

This chapter, however, will not use this strict understanding of the concept of commonplace. By contrast, I want to change the focus and concentrate on non-verbal communication. I intend to demonstrate that the concept
central to this volume is of interest not only in terms of its strict definition
within the context of the grammar class, but also in the discussion of visual
representations. I will therefore concentrate on the antique concept of *locus*,
which can be used as a synonym of 'commonplace', but also has the additional meaning of dialectical strategy, part of a series of standard questions
that offer persuasive arguments.

By relating both these senses of *locus* to the Antwerp entry, I will focus
on the specific way the organising municipality, the *magistraat*, tried to reinforce the established order by repeating its central message about the
competence of the Habsburgs and itself. Within this discourse, I will analyse the invention and the elocution of the arguments and finally, in order to
see how the arguments were delivered, I will also look at the performance.
Taking my point of departure for these three steps in the creation process of
the entry, which can be linked to the rhetorical phases of *inventio*, *elocutio*,
and *actio*, I will try to demonstrate that the municipality addressed the audience at different levels of understanding.

However, let us first place the entry in a broader context and start one
year earlier, when Philip and his suite embarked in Barcelona, with Genoa
as their final destination, in order to begin a solemn tour through the territories under indirect and direct Habsburg command. After visiting many cities
in northern Italy and some in the Holy Roman Empire, Philip met his father
in the capital of the Netherlands, Brussels. Together they visited the most
important cities in the Netherlands. In the first place, they aimed for Louvain. There the prince had to take the oaths of the *Blijde Inkomst* ('Joyous
Entry'). These oaths dated back to 1356, when Johanna of Brabant had to
acknowledge the rights of the Brabantine cities of Louvain, Brussels, Antwerp, 's-Hertogenbosch, Nijvel, and Tienen.[4] Two hundred years later, the
oaths had been extended to the Netherlands as a whole. Despite this broad
authority, the oaths had to be repeated in every important city. The political
ritual, organised and largely financed by the municipalities, was similar
everywhere. Outside the gates, the prince had to swear to respect the civic
privileges. Thereafter, the keys of the town were handed over to Philip.
Then he, his father, and their retinue processed into the city, preceded by

---

[3] A. Moss, chapter in this volume, pp. 1-17 (p. 6).
[4] A. Vranckx, 'De Blijde Inkomst van 3 januari 1356 en ons publiek recht', *Standen
en Landen* 16 (1958), pp. 145-164 (p. 153).

the civic representatives. They walked through the centre following an official entry route decorated with *tableaux vivants* and triumphal arches that
honoured symbolically the Habsburgs, the city, and their renewed relationship. The following day, the prince swore the oaths of the Joyous Entry. Finally, this union between the future monarch and the city was celebrated
with banquets, tournaments, and firework displays.

For several years, the Spanish nobleman and humanist Juan Christoval
Calvete de Estrella recorded this journey. In his account, *El Felicissimo
Viaje del muy Alto y muy Poderoso Principe Don Phelippe*, he describes the
Antwerp entry at greatest length and with greatest enthusiasm.[5] This cannot
come as a surprise, knowing that Antwerp was the most important trading
city of the Netherlands, if not of northern Europe. This extraordinary status
can also be seen in a second account by the hand of the chief organiser, the
Antwerp town clerk and renowned humanist Cornelius Grapheus. In his introduction to the official account, *De seer wonderlijcke schoone
Triumphelijcke Incompst van (…) Prince Philips (…) inde stads van
Antwerpen*, he proudly emphasises the exceptional display of wealth and the
high tempo in which everything was arranged.[6] The accompanying pictures
of the *tableaux vivants* and triumphal arches, designed by the Renaissance
artist Pieter Coecke van Aelst, make Grapheus's pride comprehensible.

In his introduction, Grapheus also emphasises the diverse group of
people that gathered to see the prince and the emperor: '(…) daer
[Antwerpen] gecommen sijnde (…) de geheele stadt, de overste, de
gemeynte, de edelen, de coopluyden, de natien, ende alderley vremdelingen
der geheelder werelt tot deser stadt toe vloeyende, so te voete, so te peerde,
boven maten costelijck, boven maten chierlijck' ('[When the prince arrived
in Antwerp] the whole city, the rulers, the community, the noblemen, the
traders, the trade nations, and divers foreigners from the whole world
flowed together on foot or on horseback, all richly and elegantly dressed').[7]
It goes without saying that a royal entry was not an everyday occurrence.
For the average citizen, it could be the chance of a lifetime to witness the
glamour of the highest ranks in society and to see the glitter of the
ephemeral constructions and spectacles. Therefore, time and again,
thousands of people assembled to gape in admiration at the impressive

---

[5] For an overview of all the ephemeral constructions of the Antwerp entry, see W.
Kuyper, *The Triumphant Entry of Renaissance Architecture into the Netherlands:
The Joyeuse Entrée of Philip of Spain into Antwerp in 1549, Renaissance and Mannerist Architecture in the Low Countries from 1530 to 1630* (Alphen aan den Rijn,
1994), chapt. 1; S. Bussels, *Van macht en mensenwerk: retorica als performatieve
strategie in de Antwerpse intocht van 1549* (Ghent, unpublished PhD, 2005).
[6] Grapheus, *Triumphelijcke Incompst*, fol. Aiii^v.
[7] *Ibidem.*

display of wealth. In this, the Antwerp entry was surely no exception. Moreover, the Antwerp crowd did not escape the notice of Calvete de Estrella, who was nevertheless well used to attending events that generated great public interest.[8]

Although the mass of onlookers is noticed by both Grapheus and Calvete de Estrella, the Antwerp entry cannot be seen as an uncomplicated mass medium. Admittedly, many people attended the spectacle, but the question can be asked if most people were able to understand what they saw. The participation of Grapheus as chief organiser demonstrates that the humanist influence on the programme was vital. The town clerk is associated with Erasmus as his friend and follower.[9] Later in this chapter, I will deal with Erasmus's influence on the entry in more detail. Here I can already indicate that one needed a humanist education to understand thoroughly the complex antique allegories, heroes, and gods on the *tableaux vivants* and the triumphal arches. Many people will only have noticed the glitter and glamour surrounding the entry. Did they, however, fail to notice the entire civic discourse about the Habsburgs, the city, and their relationship?

We may turn for an answer to classical rhetoric, for it had to deal with the same problem of communication and public differentiation. An orator had to be able to convince professional judges and politicians, but also a jury of common citizens. Therefore, the handbooks of rhetoric suggest incorporating many layers of persuasion into one discourse. Cicero, for example, writes in his *De oratore* (55 BC) that teaching (*docere*) is confined to those who share the knowledge of the orator, but that moving (*movere*) and pleasing (*delectare*) have a far broader range, for these rhetorical tasks have their effect on the masses and even on strangers:

> (...) *verba enim neminem movent nisi cum qui eiusdem linguae societate coniunctus est, sententiaeque saepe acutae non acutorum hominum sensus praetervolant: actio, quae prae se motum animi fert, omnes movet; eisdem enim omnium animi motibus concitantur et eos eisdem notis et in aliis agnoscunt et in se ipsi indicant.*

---

[8] J. C. Calvete de Estrella, El *Felicissimo Viaje del muy Alto y muy Poderoso Principe Don Phelippe, Hijo del Emperador Don Carlos Quinto Maximo, desde España a sus tierras de la baxa Alemaña: con la descripcion de todos los Estados de Brabante y Flandes* (Antwerp, 1552), fol. 288[r].

[9] M. De Schepper, 'Humanism and humanists', in: J. Van Der Stock, ed., *Antwerp: Story of a Metropolis, 16th- 17th Century* (Gent, 1993), pp. 97-103; F. Prims, 'Het eigen werk van Cornelis Grapheus (1482-1558)', *Antwerpiensia* 12 (1938), pp. 172-184.

(...) for words influence nobody but the person allied to the speaker by sharing the same language, and clever ideas frequently outfly the understanding of people who are not clever, whereas delivery, which gives the emotion of the mind expression, influences everybody, for the same emotions are felt by all people and they both recognize them in others and manifest them in themselves by the same marks. (III. lix. 223)[10]

Using this concept, I will now illustrate the different levels of persuasion at work in the Antwerp entry. This implies that our central point of view is quite unusual. Traditional research on royal entries starts from an aesthetic point of view or an iconographical-political analysis. By focussing on the entry's ability to reach a broad audience, I want not only to examine the figures on the *tableaux vivants* and the triumphal arches, but also to look at the entry as a public spectacle. There must have been, for example, much attention paid to the living presence of the actors on the stages and certainly to the Habsburgs in the procession, but also to the festivities after the entry.[11]

In order to discuss the different ways in which the Antwerp entry responded to the tasks of *docere*, *movere*, and *delectare*, I will approach the entry as a *laudatio* for the Habsburgs and Antwerp, through which the municipality took the opportunity to strengthen the established order. In doing so, I will draw on the classical theory of rhetoric and look at the arguments that were put forward in the rhetorical phase of the *inventio*, and at how these arguments were phrased in the *elocutio* and performed in the *actio*. This method of analysis is not only an interesting 21st-century method for investigating the broad reach of an early modern discourse. As we will soon see, it was also a popular early modern heuristic device.

---

[10] Cicero, *De oratore, Book III* (...), transl. by H. Rackham (Cambridge, MA, 1942), pp. 178-179.

[11] See, for a similar focus, M. A. Meadow, 'Ritual and Civic Identity in Philip II's 1549 Antwerp *Blijde Incompst*', in: R. Falkenburg, J. De Jong, M. Meadow, B. Ramakers and H. Roodenburg, eds, *Hof-, Staat- en Stadsceremonies, Nederlands Kunsthistorisch Jaarboek* 49 (1999), pp. 37-67; W. Eisler, 'Celestial Harmonies and Hapsburg Rule: Levels of Meaning in a Triumphal Arch for Philip II in Antwerp, 1549', in: B. Wisch and S. Scott Munshower, eds, *'All the World's a Stage...': Art and Pageantry in the Renaissance and Baroque*, part 1: *Triumphal Celebrations and the Rituals of Statecraft* (Pennsylvania, 1990), pp. 333-356; Bussels, *Van macht en mensenwerk*.

'Loci' as standard questions

The orator first had to go through the *inventio*-phase to find appropriate arguments for his discourse. The handbooks of rhetoric helped him by providing a series of standard questions, the so-called *loci* (or the Greek *topoi*), which the orator had to go through. Every question that could be answered yielded him a new argument. According to Bart Ramakers, the highly influential amateur actors and dramatists of the so-called Chambers of Rhetoric used this antique frame of *loci* to substantiate the message their plays conveyed.[12] In his *De inventione dialectica* of 1479, Rudolf Agricola also started from the rhetorical *loci*. He invented a device of twenty-four questions as a universally valid parameter for every kind of scientific research, subsequently further elaborated by, among others, Erasmus, Melanchthon, Vives, Sturm, and Ramus.[13]

For our purposes, it is interesting to look at the specific questions the orator had to ask in order to honour someone in a *laudatio*. In his *Institutio oratoria* (94-95 AD), Quintilian gives the most elaborated precepts (III. vii. 10-15). He distinguishes three different clusters: *loci* that aim at arguments dealing with the time before the central figure of the speech lived, such as his/her descent; *loci* that provide arguments concerning his/her body, such as beauty and power; and *loci* that supply arguments about his/her character and career. Although the organising municipality also praised Charles and Antwerp, I want to concentrate here on the filling of the *loci* with arguments in honour of Philip, who had to be cogently introduced, honoured, and legitimised as future monarch. Having said that, the first cluster of *loci* already praises both Philip and Charles, for the organisers could evidently

---

[12] B. Ramakers, 'Tonen en betogen: de dramaturgie van de Rotterdamse spelen van 1561', in: *'De rhetorijcke in vele manieren'*, *Spiegel der Letteren* 43 (2001), p. 182. Cf. A. C. G. Fleurkens, *Stichtelijke lust: de toneelspelen van D. V. Coornhert (1522-1590) als middelen tot het geven van morele instructie* (Hilversum, 1994), pp. 65-117.

[13] M. Cogan, 'Rodolphus Agricola and the Semantic Revolutions of the History of Invention', *Rhetorica* 2 (1984), pp. 163-194; T. M. Conley, *Rhetoric in the European Tradition* (Chicago/London, 1990), pp. 124-132; P. Desan, *Naissance de la méthode (Machiavel, La Ramée, Bodin, Montaigne, Descartes)* (Paris, 1987), p. 14; J.-C. Margolin, 'L'Apogée de la rhétorique humaniste (1500-1536)', in: M. Fumaroli, ed., *Histoire de la rhétorique dans l'Europe moderne, 1450-1950* (Paris, 1999), pp. 198-209; J. Monfasani, 'Humanism and Rhetoric', in: A. Rabil Jr., ed., *Renaissance Humanism: Foundations, Forms, and Legacy* (Philadelphia, 1988), pp. 196-197; W. Schmidt-Biggemann, *Topica Universalis: eine Modellgeschichte humanistischer und barocker Wissenschaft* (Hamburg, 1983), pp. 2-66; C. Vasoli, 'L'Humanisme rhétorique en Italie au XVe siècle', in: M. Fumaroli, ed., *Histoire de la rhétorique dans l'Europe moderne, 1450-1950* (Paris, 1999), pp. 81-129.

honour them both by linking the prince's descent with his father's merits.[14] Moreover, by so doing, the municipality underlined the logic of continuity and with the same argument even legitimised its own power. Just as there was a succession from father to son in the Habsburg context, the same mighty families were in power in Antwerp. This dynastic argument was seen many times throughout the entry and most clearly on a *tableau vivant* in which Philip stood next to his Burgundian-Habsburg ancestors (Ill. 1). Actors represented Philip the Good, Charles the Bold, Mary of Burgundy, Maximilian of Austria, Philip the Handsome, and Charles V. An inscription underscored the fact that Charles's succession by Philip would not change relations with the city: 'Met hoe ongeloofelijcker gunste, uwe voervaderen, grootmachtige Prince, de stadt Antwerpen altoos bemint, gheholpen, ende vervordert hebben, is eenen iegelijcken wel bekent. (…) het welcke sy met ongetwijfelder hopen betroudt, dat ghy hun voetstappen navolgende desgelijcx oock doen sult' ('It is well known to everyone, powerful Prince, that your ancestors have always loved, helped, and promoted Antwerp with unbelievable grace. (…) So Antwerp trusts with indubitable hope that you will follow their example').[15]

The specific succession from Charles to Philip, on the other hand, is clearly visualised in the triumphal arch that the Spanish nation had erected along the entry route (Ill. 2). A round temple of Janus constituted the centre of attention. On the left, a statue of Augustus closed a door, in keeping with Roman tradition, in order to indicate a time of peace. On the right, statues of Charles and Philip did the same. In the first place, this showed that the Habsburgs could be compared with the most prominent Roman emperor (see below). Secondly, this made it clear that Charles ruled peacefully (this was a humanist dream and far from reality) and that it was believed that his future successor would do the same. To convey this idea, the father was leading his son by the hand with paternal solicitude and was even looking back to make sure that the youngster was able to follow in his wake.

---

[14] Erasmus, among others, presents this *locus* as an ideal opportunity to assess the competence of the future monarch. In the introduction to his *Institutio principis christiani* or *The Education of a Christian prince* (1516), he writes to his pupil, the young Charles: (…) *denique tot undique te maiorum tuorum circumstant exempla, ut omnibus certissima spes sit Carolum aliquando praestaturum, quod a patre tuo Philippo dudum expectabat orbis*; Erasmus, *Opera omnia* (Amsterdam, 1974), IV, I. 134. '(…) above all so many are the examples which you see around you from among your ancestors, that we all expect with confidence to see Charles one day perform what the world lately looked for from your father Philip'; Erasmus, 'Institutio principis christiani', in: A. H. T. Levi, ed., *Collected Works of Erasmus*, XXVII (Toronto, 1986), p. 204.
[15] Grapheus, *Triumphelijcke Incompst*, fol. Mii[v].

The second cluster of *loci* concentrated on the body. Looking back at the picture of the *tableau vivant* of the Burgundian-Habsburg dynasty, we see that the prince was represented in a powerful and proud posture (Ill. 1). Although it is hard to verify, we can assume that the youngster in the solemn procession will have made the same impression. According to Grapheus, the splendour with which the Habsburgs showed themselves to the Antwerp audience was beyond words: 'Met wat state, met wat menichte des Edeldoms, ende groote Personagien, dese dry aengetreden zijn, kanmen dat gedencken, danmen hier int cort soude connen bescriven' ('In what state, in what a company of Nobleness and high Personages they stepped forward is impossible to describe in this short description').[16] In the procession, the Habsburgs used the opportunity personally to exhibit their corporality as an argument for laudation. There was no mediation through a civic representation. This self-presentation also featured in the tournament held on the day after the entry. Calvete de Estrella writes that Philip wanted to pay his respects to the city and the organisers of the entry and decided to join the joust.[17] The prince showed himself as one of the bravest knights in the combats. Thanks to the young Habsburger, his quadrille was able to gain the victory: 'El Principe mostrò su gran valor aquel dia, que sue vno delos, que mejor justaron y mas lanças ronpieron, aunque muchos lo hizieron muy bien de entranbas partes, mas el Principe de Piamonte llevò la gloria en todo con su quadrilla' ('On that day, the prince showed his great valour, as he jousted as one of the best and broke the most lances. Although everyone did his utmost, the quadrille of the prince of Piedmont [and of Philip] won the day').[18] Although we have to be wary of the subjective tone – Calvete de Estrella will surely have tried to please his master – we can still accept that the setting of the tournament will have allowed the prince maximum opportunity for the display of power.[19]

---

[16] Grapheus, *Triumphelijcke Incompst*, fol. Ciiii[r].

[17] 'El Principe de España por honrrar la fiesta; y dar contentamiento à aquellos dela villa, quiso ser vno delos dela quadrilla d'el Principe de Piamonte' ('The Prince of Spain wanted to honour the festivities and to satisfy the citizens. He therefore asked to be part of the quadrille of the prince of Piedmont'). Calvete de Estrella, *El Felicissimo Viaje*, IV, fol. 258[r].

[18] Calvete de Estrella, *El Felicissimo Viaje*, IV, fol. 259[r].

[19] Juliet Barker sees in the late Middle Ages an increasing importance of glitter and glamour in the tournaments, and Roy Strong sees a continuation of this evolution in the early modern period, where the special setting strongly dominated the game: J. R. V. Barker, *The Tournament in England 1100-1400* (Woodbridge, 1986, ²2003), pp. 84-111; R. Strong, *Art and Power: Renaissance Festivals* (Suffolk, 1973), pp. 11-16.

Finally, the standard rhetorical questions put forward arguments about character and career. In distinction to the other two clusters of *loci*, this cluster aimed at characteristics that the central person owes entirely to himself. For this reason, Quintilian evaluates this cluster as the most important (III. vii. 15). In the early modern period, the same thought was expressed in, among others, Machiavelli's *Discorsi* (1513-1520) in a clear distinction between *Fortuna* and *Virtù*. Bearing in mind Philip's age, it will come as no surprise that his accomplishments were not the central focus of attention in the entry, but, strangely enough, nor were the 'valiant actions' of Charles. Only one *tableau* took a specific military exploit as its subject by representing the war with the Muslims (Ill. 3). Calvete de Estrella writes:

> (...) el Emperador y Principe armados de resplandecientes arma con sus insignias Imperiales y Reales: yuan delante como huyendo demiedo d'ellos muchos armados en habito de Turcos, Alarabes, Moros y Genizaros. Estauan alos pies d'el Emperador y Principe ciertas Princesas presas con crueles cadenas, rogandoles con muchas lagrimas, que las librassen de aquela seruidumbre y largo catiuerio.[20]

> The emperor and the prince were dressed in brilliant armour with imperial and royal insignia. They pursued a fleeing terrified group of armed Turks, Arabs, Moors, and Janissaries. At the feet of Charles and Philip lay captured princesses who were cruelly shackled in heavy chains and begged with tears in their eyes to be liberated from subjection and slavery.

Once again, the reporter draws attention to the panoply of the Habsburgs dressed in royal military costumes while chasing off a 'bunch of infidels' (to use the terms found in the accounts). It had its effect, since the enemies all tried to get away as soon as possible through a small door in the corner of the scene. At the feet of the Habsburgs lay chained girls representing the territories under Muslim command. The *tableau* thus represented, in visual form, Charles's initiative to start a war of 'liberation' on the southern Mediterranean seaboard and on the borders of south-east and central Europe. Philip was urged to continue his father's work by means of an inscription that read: 'Der vaderlijcker vromicheyt voerbeelde, is den sone een stercke vermanige' ('The paternal pious example is a strong stimulus for the son').[21] This *tableau*, however, is the only one in the Antwerp entry with a specific reference to imperial feats of arms. The municipality referred to feats which were, in the eyes of the citizens of Antwerp, rather uncompro-

---

[20] Calvete de Estrella, *El Felicissimo Viaje*, IV, fol. 243^r.
[21] Grapheus, *Triumphelijcke Incompst*, fol. K^v.

mised, since the 'Turkish tyranny' was of no direct concern for them. Although the Ottoman army was at the gates of Vienna in 1529, and financial contributions had to be paid, the war had no devastating impact in the Netherlands.

This, however, cannot be said of the scourge of the war against the French. The attack on Antwerp in 1542 by the Guelder commander Maarten van Rossum was still fresh in the memory. As an ally of the French, van Rossum wanted to besiege the city and hand her over to Francis I. His plan was not carried out, because the Guelder had to flee when the Habsburg troops arrived.[22] Seven years after these events, no one had forgotten the attack: Calvete de Estrella's exhaustive reference is significant.[23] The Antwerp municipality, however, wanted to avoid any reference to these dark moments on such a joyous day.[24] This omission was all the more proper because relations between the Habsburgs and the Valois were reasonably good in 1549.[25]

The Antwerp *tableaux* were also silent about Charles's battles against the Protestants in the Holy Roman Empire. His victory over Elector John Frederick of Saxony near Mühlberg was a famous feat and was often represented, for example in Titian's equestrian portrait of Charles (1548). The fact that this campaign was not shown in the entry can be linked with the important role played by the Lutherans in the Antwerp economy. It would have been most ill-advised to shock these vital trading partners with images of a battle against their brothers in faith.[26]

---

[22] W. Blockmans, *Keizer Karel: de utopie van het keizerschap, 1500-1558* (Leuven, 2000), pp. 81-82.

[23] Calvete de Estrella, *El Felicissimo Viaje*, IV, fol. 222^r.

[24] Representations of the victories over the French were, however, common. They were, for example, a popular theme for paintings in the houses of the Antwerp higher classes; M. Martens and N. Peeters, 'Antwerp Painting before Iconoclasm: Considerations on the Quantification of Taste', in: S. Cavaciocchi, ed., *Economia e Arte Secc. XIII-XVIII: atti della 'Trentatreesima Settimana di Studi' 30 aprile–4 maggio 2001* (Florence, 2002), p. 85.

[25] Calvete de Estrella writes how Philip met the French king at the beginning of his voyage in Aigues-Mortes. The Habsburger even signed a treaty to underline the (temporary) good relationship. Calvete de Estrella, *El Felicissimo Viaje*, IV, fol. 8^v.

[26] Here the entry into this trading city is an exception in the whole series of entries of Charles and Philip. In Lille, for example, the persecution of Protestants was clearly represented in the *tableaux vivants*. In his *Art and Power*, Roy Strong writes: 'But the changing mood of the times found disturbing expression in tableaux of religion at Lille, where the themes of incipient counter-reform were manifest in a forthright statement. While Charles and Philip stood within the Temple of Virtue, below yawned a gaping hell-mouth inhabited by the figure of Martin Luther. Further on, the figure of the Catholic Church was to be seen treading Heresy underfoot, attended by pope and emperor as the shield of the faith, while nearby Luther and

In the triumphal arch of the Genoese trade nation, the battle against the Protestants was nevertheless visualised, although in guarded terms. A painting high in the ceiling showed 'heretical scientists' being burned, yet without any specific reference to their faith. The arch had the same focus as the *tableau* just mentioned. Once again, Turks were shown as blameworthy in a central panel where *Victoria* increased Philip's bellicosity (Ill. 4). With bloodstained hands and defeated Turks at her feet, she reached out for the young prince.[27] The Ottomans constituted a serious impediment to Genoese commercial interests. Because of the seizure of Constantinople one hundred years before the Antwerp entry, the Genoese had gradually lost many southern Mediterranean contacts. Driving back the Turks would be a boon for their mercantile interests.

Although the Spanish triumphal arch was, as we have already seen, centrally concerned with urging the prince to a policy of peace, it showed Charles's actions against the Ottomans too. In one of the passageways, a picture showed how the Turks fled at the mere mention of his name. Further on, the two pillars at the front referred to Charles's device 'Plus oultre' that could also be seen on top of the Genoese arch and was also represented a dozen times on the long series of pilasters that followed the entire entry route. It articulated the idea of the unremitting expansion of Habsburg power, for, by surpassing Hercules' pillars at the Straits of Gibraltar, Charles went further than his antique predecessors had ever done.[28]

Loci as fixed formulae

This device leads us to the second step in our analysis, which starts from the rhetorical phase of *elocutio*. The arguments put forward by the standard questions of the *inventio* had to be phrased carefully. In this regard, most studies discuss the problem of comprehensibility of the Antwerp entry. For the humanistic discourse had excluded generally known biblical and Chris-

---

Zwingli rubbed shoulders with Julian the Apostate, Simon Magus, Arius and Hus, as vanquished heretics. The tableaux anticipated the events of the rest of the century' (Strong, *Art and Power*, pp. 88-89).

[27] 'Tenia desnudos los braços y los manos tendidas y sangrientas delos, que estauan degollados y heridos, alos quales con grande ira pisaua: por el habito se conocian, que eran Turcos' ('[Victoria] bared her arms and stretched out her hands to the prince. She was entirely covered with the blood of wounded and mauled enemies whom she held under her feet disapprovingly, and who could be recognised by their dress as Turks'), Calvete de Estrella, *El Felicissimo Viaje*, IV, fol. 232ʳ.

[28] M. Bataillon, 'Plus oultre: la cour découvre le nouveau monde', in: J. Jacquot, ed., *Les Fêtes de la Renaissance*, II: *Fêtes et cérémonies au temps de Charles Quint* (Paris, 1960), pp. 13-27.

tian personages in favour of antique heroes, allegories, and gods. The onlooker had to be schooled in the *studia humanitatis* to decipher the phrasing of the arguments.[29]

However, we can nuance this statement by looking at the frequent use of fixed formulae such as the imperial device. The general public was still engaged at a certain level, as 'Plus oultre' was repeated very often.[30] Here, we reach another use of the term *locus*, namely the concept of the cliché. In Antiquity and the early modern period, the negative connotations of 'hackneyed' and 'overworked' do not yet apply.[31] A device is a clear example of such a cliché that, in spite of its complex form, gives expression to imperial competence and power for a broad public. By mean of its continuous repetition, few people will have had difficulty in linking the firmness of the pillars with Charles's policy.

We can look back at the chained princesses at the feet of Charles and Philip and notice another kind of fixed formula. The accounts tell us that they represented the cities and regions under Muslim slavery, namely *Bithinia, Pamphilia, Graecia, Assyria, Palestina, Aegyptus, Phaenicia, Arabia, Numidia, Aethiopia, Hierosolyma, Constantinopolis*, and *Damascus*. It was a common practice to represent cities and regions by means of personifications. If we look carefully at the picture of the stage, however, it is not likely that many people knew which actress represented which city or region (Ill. 3). It is more probable that they will have seen that the girls as a whole represented the assembled group of suppressed Muslim territories.

The majority of the onlookers will have interpreted the fleeing oppressors in the same way. Although the accounts single them out as specific Muslim rulers, Turks, Arabs, Moors, and Janissaries, most onlookers will probably have seen them as one coherent group, since they were represented with a similar outer appearance. It was not only in the Antwerp entry that the Muslim world was generalised as having bad sovereigns. The Muslims were an accepted cliché employed to represent slavery, heresy, and

---

[29] See H. Soly, 'Plechtige intochten in de steden van de Zuidelijke Nederlanden tijdens de overgang van Middeleeuwen naar Nieuwe Tijd: communicatie, propaganda, spektakel', *Tijdschrift voor Geschiedenis* 97 (1984), pp. 341-361.

[30] K. J. Höltgen, 'The Ruler Between Two Columns: Imperial Aspirations and Political Iconography from the Emperor Charles V to William of Orange', in: M. Bath, P. F. Campa and D. S. Russell, eds, *Emblem Studies in Honor of Peter M. Daly* (Baden-Baden, 2002), pp. 143-213.

[31] For Antiquity, see, among others, S. B. Blinn and M. Garrett, 'Aristotelian *Topoi* as a Cross-Cultural Analytical Tool', *Philosophy and Rhetoric* 26 (1993), pp. 93-112; M. C. Leff, 'The Topics of Argumentative Invention in Latin Rhetorical Theory from Cicero to Boethius', *Rhetorica* 1 (1983), pp. 23-44. For the early modern Netherlands, see, among others, Fleurkens, *Stichtelijke lust*, pp. 95-103.

tyranny. In the *Querela pacis* of 1517, a fierce pacifist such as Erasmus did not reject a war against them. His goddess of peace does not speak with one voice about this kind of war.[32] Although the European monarchs are charged with the responsibility of avoiding it, *Pax* can understand certain grounds for war. The worst thing that can happen to the people is the terror of tyrants such as the Muslim rulers. They have to be countered with all possible means. It is, however, not clearly substantiated why the Muslim rulers were tyrannical, neither in the Antwerp *tableaux* and triumphal arches, nor in Erasmus's writings. We may instead see the image of the Turks (and Arabs, who were often linked with them) as a stock formula to represent bad government without having to mention any specific European counterexample.

The same kind of cliché was used to represent good government. We have already seen devices representing in visual form political firmness and success. The Antwerp municipality went even further by visualising the specific competence of Charles and Philip in a triumphal arch next to the Grand Place (Ill. 5). Once again, they made reference to Antiquity by having the Habsburgs support the world upon their shoulders, just as Hercules and Atlas had once supported the heavenly firmament. A simple comparison is out of the question, for, in classical myth, the latter two heroes had quarrelled as neither of them wanted to bear the eternal weight. This did not match the central theme of the entry, namely the joyous transfer of power between Charles and Philip. We can, moreover, interpret the antique heroes as a cliché which expressed Habsburg political power. According to Gordon Teskey in *Allegory and Violence*, early modern artists gratefully used the antique gods and heroes for 'their role in the conjoining of political authority to spiritually resonant cultural forms'.[33] By using Greek and Roman myth to express royal power, the creators of the arch conveyed an aura of eternal power. So the monarchs enjoyed a portion of the inapproachability

---

[32] *Quod si hic fatalis est humani ingenii morbu, ut prorsus absque bellis durare effunditur, tametsi praestabatet hos doctrina, bene factis uitaeque innocentia ad Christi religionem allicere, quam armis adoriri. Attamen si bellum, ut diximis, omnino uteri non potest, illud certe leuius sit malum, quam sic impie Christianos inter se committi collidique.* Erasmus, *Opera omnia*, IV, I. 90; 'But perhaps it is the fatal malady of Human nature to be quite unable to carry on without wars. If so, why is this evil passion not let loose upon the Turks? Of course it used to be thought preferable, even in their case, to win them over to the religion of Christ by teaching and by the example of good deeds and a blameless life rather than by mounting an armed attack. But if war, as we said, is not wholly avoidable, that kind would be a lesser evil than the present unholy conflicts and clashes between Christians', Erasmus, *Querela Pacis*, p. 314.
[33] G. Teskey, *Allegory and Violence* (Ithaca, 1996), p. 79.

of their fictive representatives. In our case, the Antwerp municipality made it clear that the rule of the Habsburgs was everlasting and overpowering. Therefore, the antique heroes were the ideal representations thanks to their denotation of force, valour, and perseverance.

Concept and cliché, though, had a complex interrelation. The differences were explicitly emphasised. The subscription underscored that 'Hercules ende den grooten Atlas sijn al bueselen, dese twee sijn de gene die des geheelen werelts last waerachtelijck op hun schouderen dragen' ('Hercules and the big Atlas were both triflers. These two [Charles and Philip] are the ones that really support the whole worldly burden upon their shoulders').[34] Although the latter were still indebted to the former in order to acquire a legendary renown, the antique heroes did not express the concept of regal power, for Charles and Philip were put on the arch to represent, through their own physical presence and appearance, Habsburg supremacy.

In the tournament mentioned above, Philip personified the commonplace expression of Habsburg power to an even greater extent. By joining the joust and proving his stout-heartedness, he placed himself in the tradition of the brave knights of the legendary King Arthur and Amadis de Gaule. By 1549, it was definitely clear that tournaments no longer served as a means of settling a dispute, but as a way of flaunting skills and bravery. Therefore, the tournaments were increasingly staged as a play wherein the monarch often played the leading part as the ultimate rescuer.[35] One of the most famous chivalric spectacles ever held took place in Binche some months before the Antwerp entry. It immediately became a fixed point of reference. Something was 'más brava que las fiestas de Bains'.[36] In one of the jousts, Philip was concealed as Beltenebros, a former disguise of Amadis, and took up arms against the evil wizard Norabroc (by reversing the letters of this name, one got the name of the noble Spanish actor who played this character). After many ordeals, the Habsburg prince defeated the wizard and restored peace and order.[37]

---

[34] Grapheus, *Triumphelijcke Incompst*, fol. Lii^v.

[35] E. Van Den Neste, *Tournois, joutes, pas d'armes dans les villes de Flandre à la fin du Moyen âge (1300-1486)* (Paris, 1996), pp. 136-137; E. Lecuppre-Desjardin, *La Ville des cérémonies: essai sur la communication politique dans les anciens Pays-Bas bourguignons* (Turnhout, 2004), pp. 200-210.

[36] Strong, *Art and Power*, p. 91.

[37] E. Peters, '1549 Knight's Game at Binche: Constructing Philip II's Ideal Identity in a Ritual of Honor', in: R. Falkenburg, J. De Jong, M. Meadow, B. Ramakers and H. Roodenburg, eds, *Hof-, Staat- en Stadsceremonies, Nederlands Kunsthistorisch Jaarboek* 49 (1999), pp. 11-35.

Fixed formulae performed

Although the Antwerp tournament was less explicitly staged than the one in Binche, it would still have been hard for the common audience to have a full understanding of the comings and goings of the different groups of knights. The more the joust evolved into a propaganda show, the more the rules became complex, ritualised, and situational. Therefore, the large crowd that was viewing the tournament will in the first place have noticed the skilful and elegant bodies of the youngsters, for the accounts make clear that the prince and his retinue did not restrain themselves from showing off. With this, we arrive at our last phase of analysis, namely the *actio*-phase, where our attention will be directed to the specific visual clichés used to deliver the phrased arguments. Which fixed formulas were used in the corporeal performances of the actors and the corporeal representations on the paintings and statues?

Neither Grapheus nor Calvete de Estrella give a clear description of the physical self-presentation of Philip in the tournament. Once again, we have to resort to the description and the illustration of a *tableau vivant*. Let us look more specifically at the stage where the prince's device 'Nec spe, nec metu' was represented (Ill. 6). Just like Charles's 'Plus oultre', it was a concrete and preset phrasing of the argument that the prince was suitable for his future task. Neither hope, nor fear led him; he chose the right way independently. On the right of the staging of Philip, *Spes* pulled at his mantle and, on the left, *Metus*. Fortunately, four women stood by the prince. They were the allegories of Constancy, Fidelity, Force, and Magnanimity. In that way, the municipality represented the need for a steady government. For most bystanders, problems would have occurred in distinguishing the winged girl and the old man alongside Philip as *Spes* and *Metus*, not to mention the naming of the four women flanking the prince as the political virtues of *Constantia, Fiducia, Fortitudo*, and *Magnanimitas*. It is, however, plausible that most bystanders will have recognised the representation of Philip himself. Grapheus writes that the actor who played the prince looked like him. He 'resembled the prince in every respect' ('onse Prince, den levenden over al gelijcke').[38] The crown and the elegant dress will have helped this identification.

What is interesting for the *actio*-phase of our analysis is the specific way in which Philip's body was used in performance. This will probably not have gone unnoticed by the bystanders. Grapheus writes explicitly that the prince was staged in all masculine force on a block of stone, showing

---

[38] Grapheus, *Triumphelijcke Incompst*, fol. Miii^r.

how he remained standing in spite of his attackers.[39] Just like the firmness of the pillars of Charles's 'Plus oultre' and Philip's firmness in the tournament, the inflexibility of the staged prince was a cliché which expressed his competence. Few people, however, would relate this scene to its intrinsic reference to the Stoic political ideal of Constancy that became more and more popular in humanistic milieus.[40] Most bystanders would just have seen the primary subject of the *tableau*, a strong young man.

In addition to this gesture of sturdiness, the actor also represented masculinity through his dress. In his *De civilitate morum puerilium* or *On Good Manners for Boys* of 1530, Erasmus prescribes that a boy should be careful not to cultivate his outer appearance excessively, in order to maintain his decency: 'It is boorish to go about with one's hair uncombed: it should be neat, but not as elaborate as a girl's coiffure'.[41] In due modesty, beauty could be aimed at by women, but men had to strive for dignity and authority. To give too much attention to one's looks was as bad as to give too little attention. In the same belief, the organisers of the entry chose to represent Philip as a decently dressed youngster and not as a naked David or Adonis, although both were nevertheless very popular figures in contemporary painting and sculpture.

This does not exclude the fact that Philip will have demonstrated masculine appeal. In the first place, there was the traditional jerkin with puffed sleeves which accentuated the muscular chest and upper arms. Secondly, the prince wore a pair of knickerbockers. These accentuated his sexuality, as, in mid-sixteenth century, the codpiece was given a prominent place in the design of these trousers. The codpiece was originally a piece of cloth which made it easier for a man to urinate. At the beginning of the sixteenth century, it became a protective garment in the imperial army. Later on, noblemen used it to show their military strength and their connection with the Habsburgs. Once adopted at other courts and in the cities in the mid-sixteenth century, it became a fixed visual formula expressing male power.[42]

---

[39] '[Onse Prince] staende met een manlijck wesen op eenen viercantigen steen, van drije voeten hooge, wordt ten beyden sijden met sinen mantel herwarts ende derwaerts getrocken', Grapheus, *Triumphelijcke Incompst*, fol. Miii[r].

[40] P.-F. Moreau, 'Les Trois Etapes du stoïcisme moderne', in: P.-F. Moreau, ed., *Le Stoïcisme au XVIe et au XVIIe siècle: le retour des philosophies antiques à l'âge classique* (Paris, 1999), pp. 11-27.

[41] Erasmus, *Opera omnia*, IV, I. 864; transl. in Erasmus, 'De civilitate', p. 277.

[42] In her paper 'Codpieces and Manly Display' at the annual meeting of the Renaissance Society of America in San Francisco in 2006, Carole Collier Frick made this historical evolution clear. She also drew attention to Europe's first encounters with

The examples in the visual arts are legion. Artists such as Bruegel, Seisenegger, Bronzino, and Pontormo used the codpiece as a clear *locus* for representing manly strength. A fine example is the latter's portrait of a young *Halberdier* of the 1530s (Ill. 7). His codpiece is even more prominent than Philip's, and there is a striking difference in form, as the soldier has bound his penis conspicuously (perhaps in an attempt to represent an erection). This constrictive garment primarily underlined the male power of youngsters such as Philip and the *halberdier*. Noticing the *halberdier*'s fine gesture and restrained expression, however, an elegant sensuality also seems to be have been conveyed. This same synthesis between strength and elegance can be found in Jeffery Persels's discussion of Rabelais's oeuvre, in which the codpiece is connected with humanist concepts of refined manliness:

> More than mere association with a newly homocentric universe, Humanism could perhaps be viewed fruitfully as, for lack of a neutral term, 'vir-centric' – a moral program represented in and through the male body. For Rabelais, chronicler of its intellectual victory and acute observer of the sociocultural moment, it is forcefully represented in and through the codpiece.[43]

We can now focus on the female clothing and its link with femininity in order to identify fixed visual expressions. When we look at the actresses representing the allegories of good government behind the firm prince, it is striking that the designer of the illustrations, Pieter Coecke, depicts their theatre costumes as transparent veils over a well-pronounced body. This is most apparent in the actress to Philip's right, whose breasts are accentuated by the tight-fitting fabric. In other *tableaux*, some actresses even revealed their breasts, as in the one in which the nine Joys triumph over the six Miseries (Ill. 8). This observation may lead to the question of whether the transparent veil and the emphasis on the breasts were general clichés de-

---

'primitive' New World males, which led to an overt sartorial reaction on the part of European men that transformed the utilitarian codpiece into a masculine display.

[43] J. C. Persels, 'Bragueta Humanistica, or Humanism's Codpiece', *Sixteenth Century Journal* 28 (1997), pp. 79-99 (p. 99). On the other hand, the codpiece is a new *locus* for the representation of sexual power. Persels refers to a passage in which Panurge drives an opponent into a tight spot with sexual intimidation. This is done in a virtuous game with a codpiece and an orange. Rabelais writes: 'Whereat Panurge pulled out his long codpiece with its silken lock and extended it a cubit and a half, and held it in the air with his left hand, and with his right took his orange, threw it in the air several times, and on the eighth hid it in his right fist, very quietly holding it up; then he began to shake his fine codpiece, showing it to Thaumaste' (quoted in Persels, 'Bragueta Humanistica', p. 80).

signed to arouse an erotic response in the onlookers.[44] To answer this, we may turn to Renaissance painting, where the veiled and revealed female body was prominent. According to the Italian art historian Mario Perniola in 'Between Clothing and Nudity', Renaissance artists had a strong awareness of the erotic potential of the female body.[45] One clear example is the depiction of the popular theme of the suicide of Lucretia by artists such as Dürer, Baldung Grien, Van Cleve, and Cranach. Time and again, Lucretia reveals her breasts. A knife is planted in between them. Soon that knife will do its deadly work, leading Lucretia into suicide, saving her honour, increasing the will for a revolution, and dismissing the last violent king of Rome, whose son had raped her. In spite of her imminent suicide, depictions of Lucretia's body are still very explicit. Cranach's depiction of 1533 is exemplary (Ill. 9). Although we should resist the temptation to project our own responses onto a sixteenth-century viewer, it is hard to imagine that this picture could have failed to produce an erotic response. The knife is not depicted as the deadly instrument it is in the antique heroic story. It is transformed into an ornamental object that goes well with the attractive necklace and the fine-looking haircut. The blade does not give the impression of being made of mortal steel, but seems rather fragile and crystalline. Moreover, the transparent veil decorates Lucretia's body in such a manner that it does not conceal it at all. In an elegant gesture, the Roman woman even accentuates her genitals by placing the see-through veil over them without covering them up. It seems that Cranach's Lucretia is less concerned with her coming suicide than with her sensuous appearance in the eyes of the onlooker. We can conclude, then, that the painter uses the same means as the organisers of the entry, namely the visual commonplaces of the transparent veil and the uncovered breasts.

In addition to the visual display of 'masculine' strength and 'feminine' sensuality with the aid of predetermined means, another concept was remarkably prominent during the Antwerp entry, namely the motif of the triumph, which was itself represented by means of fixed formulae. The Roman custom of honouring a successful general or emperor with a solemn entry through the *Via Sacra* onto the *Forum Romanum* inspired this motif significantly.[46] Moreover, for Titus, Septimius Severus, and Constantine, triumphal arches of stone were built to commemorate their victories for eternity.

---

[44] See C. Breward, *The Culture of Fashion: A New History of Fashionable Dress* (Manchester/New York, 1995), pp. 69-73.

[45] M. Perniola, 'Between Clothing and Nudity', in: M. Feher, R. Naddaff and N. Tazi, eds, *Fragments for a History of the Human Body*, 3 vols. (New York, 1989), II, pp. 237-265.

[46] M. Beard, J. North and S. Price, *Religions of Rome* (Cambridge, 1998), pp. 44-45.

When, in 1536, the pope and the citizens of Rome granted Charles the privilege of entering Rome in the very same way, these antique monuments were at the centre of attention. They were covered with inscriptions that linked the Habsburg with his Roman forebears.[47]

For the same reason, the Antwerp organisers erected triumphal arches with antique decorations, such as winged Victory figures, triumphal wreaths, and palms, along with the classical architectural orders, clearly shown, among others, in the arch that contained the *tableau* of 'Nec spe, nec metu' discussed above (Ill. 6). Thanks to Sebastiano Serlio's mid-sixteenth-century *Architettura* and Coecke's early translation into Dutch, French, and German, these motifs became an increasingly popular commonplace for expressing imperial, royal, and civic power visually. The Antwerp entry and its illustrated official account are important early disseminators of this classical style.[48]

In 'Charles V and the Idea of the Empire', Frances Yates explains how the triumph motif became a fixed theme in the laudation of the Habsburgs. The comparison with the Roman emperors conveyed the Habsburgs' desire to follow Caesar and Augustus and rule the whole world. Certainly, this ambition was an unattainable phantom, but nonetheless highly influential. World dominion on the Roman model was not only an important propaganda theme for the Habsburgs, it later grasped the rest of Europe too. Yates writes: 'It is precisely as a phantom that Charles's empire was of importance, because it raised again the imperial idea and spread it through Europe in the symbolism of its propaganda'.[49] Charles's device 'Plus oultre' went even further in this direction. As we have already seen, it was a proper *locus* for expressing a sense of *aemulatio* towards the Romans. At the beginning of Charles's reign, Habsburg propaganda substantiated this with conquests in Europe and north Africa. Later in his career, this device came to refer to territorial expansions in America and the Ottoman Empire.[50] Political emulation was consistently visualised and the Roman emperors overshadowed.

This sense of *aemulatio* was also represented visually during the entry by other means. Let us take a final look at the Spanish arch. The central

---

[47] Strong, *Art and Power*, p. 83.

[48] H. De La Fontaine Verwcy, *Humanisten, dwepers en rebellen in de zestiende eeuw* (Amsterdam, 1975), p. 55.

[49] F. A. Yates, 'Charles V and the Idea of the Empire', in *Astraea: The Imperial Theme in the Sixteenth Century* (London, 1975), p. 1.

[50] K. J. Höltgen, 'The Ruler Between Two Columns: Imperial Aspirations and Political Iconography from the Emperor Charles V to William of Orange', in: M. Bath, P. F. Campa and D. S. Russell, eds, *Emblem Studies in Honor of Peter M. Daly* (Baden-Baden, 2002), pp. 143-168.

building was inspired by the Roman circular temple. This was clearly pre-
scribed and depicted in Serlio's treatise and Coecke's translation (Ill. 2 and
10). The dome, the obelisks, the use of four orders for the columns, and the
rustica style of the basement are clearly inspired by these books. The triumphal arch, however, represents an attempt to change and emulate the previous design, for instance by adding antique *colossi*, a balustrade around the
dome, and a trumpet-like vault.

    This architectural emulation fitted closely with the message the Spanish
wanted to convey. As already mentioned, the arch made it clear that Philip's
reign would be characterised by peace and could therefore be compared
with the reign of his father and of Augustus; what is more, however, the
imperial dream of world dominion was literally unrolled for the benefit of
the prince. Two angels (it is unclear whether they were actors or mechanical) descended spectacularly and spread out a piece of satin with a text in
Latin, given here in Grapheus's translation: 'Voerwaer tis een groot ende
seker voerteecken dat ghi, o Prince, Coninck der Spaenscher Natien, sult
wesen des werelts eenich Monarcha, gemerct dat uwe macht is toecom-
mende so groot, dat sy haer sonder eynde strecken sal aan het hoochste tot
onderste der eerden' ('Truly, it is a great and certain sign that you, o Prince,
King of the Spanish Nation, will be the only Monarch of the world, given
that your future might is so great that it will spread from the highest to the
lowest parts of the world').[51]

    It is probable that many bystanders were not able to read and under-
stand the Latin text. They would, however, have been impressed by all glitter and glamour, for it was not only the textual discourse that was used to
convince the people by means of clichés such as allegories, devices, and he-
raldic references. Visual discourse was also used throughout. Visual clichés
had the task of convincing the onlookers that the Habsburgs and the municipality were rightly invested with their high responsibilities To that end,
firm columns were erected, antique triumphal arches reconstructed, actors
and actresses attractively dressed, and, finally, angels came down from the
very heavens.

---

[51] Grapheus, *Triumphelijcke Incompst,* fols. Eiiii^v-f.F^r.

1. The Burgundian-Habsburg dynasty, in: Cornelius Grapheus, *Spectaculorum in susceptione Philippi* (...) *mirificus apparatus* (Antwerp, 1550), fol. M4ᵛ (UGent Res.1190).

2. Detail from the triumphal arch of the Spanish trade nation, in: *Idem*, fol. F2^{v}-F3^{r}.

3. Philip and Charles chase away the Islamic enemy, in: *Idem,* fol. K6ᵛ.

4. Frans Floris, *Victoria*, 1552 (Rotterdam, Museum Boymans Van Beuningen, inv. Bdh 3528, H.4).

5. Philip and Charles as Hercules and Atlas, in: C. Grapheus, *Spectaculorum* (...) *apparatus,* fol. M3ᵛ.

Tota alt.
ped.lxv.
Latitudo
pe.xxxv.

N 2

6. Philip led by neither Fear nor Hope, in: *Idem,* fol. N2ʳ.

7. Pontormo, *Portrait of a Halberdier (Francesco Guardi?)*, 1528-1530, oil on panel, 92 x 72 cm (Los Angeles, The J. Paul Getty Museum).

8. Detail of the tableau with the nine joys and six miseries, in: C. Grapheus, *Spectaculorum (...) apparatus,* fol. I4^v.

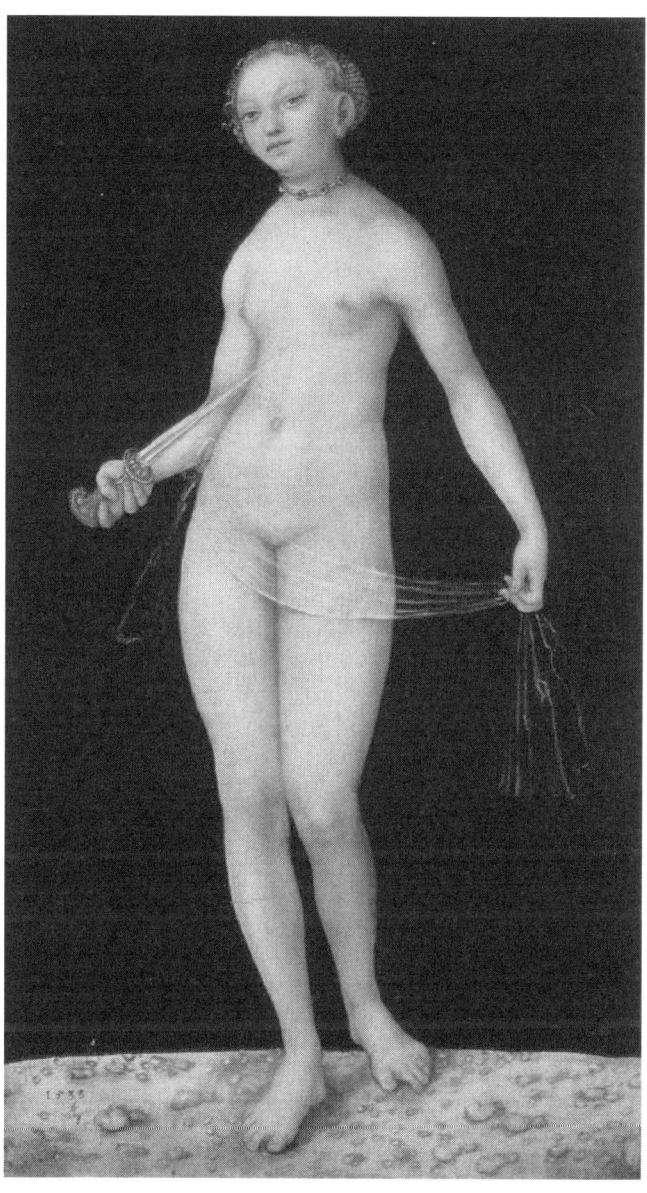

9. Lucas Cranach the Elder, *Lucretia*, 1533 (Staatliche Museen zu Berlin, Gemälde-galerie).

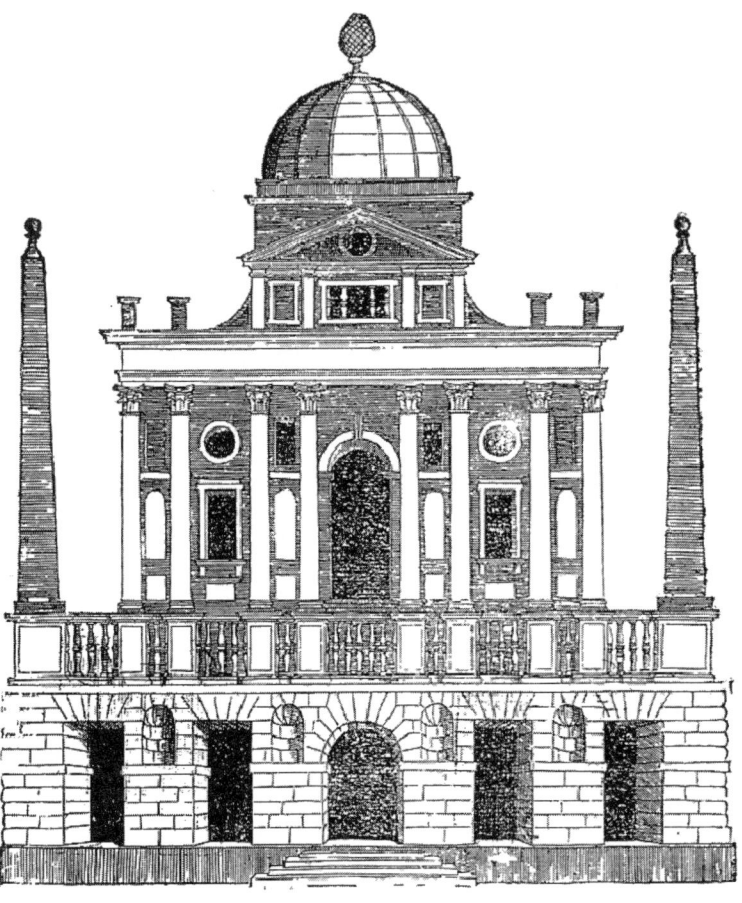

10. *Tempio Sacro,* in: Pieter Coecke Van Aelst, *De boecken van Architecturen Sebastiani Serlii* (Antwerp, 1553), fol. lv.

ITALIAN ACTORS AS AGENTS OF REBELLION AGAINST COMMONPLACES IN THE AGE OF COUNTER-REFORMATION

Philiep Bossier

The fascinating dossier of early modern female performance in Italy has a double link with the fundamental study of the way an almost parallel culture of commonplaces is functioning at a large scale in the context of emerging vernacular literary systems in Europe. On the one hand, the first generation of professional actresses (c.1560) need to affirm themselves in the context of negative commonplaces against their newborn presence on the stage. So they construct a rhetorical system of reference to the first examples of professional acting in the early 1530s, in which – by contrast – one can observe how exclusively male performers try both to isolate and to protect their acting style as an autonomous artistic activity. On the other hand, they wish to deconstruct negative a-priori judgement towards explicit female exposure in public places. So they try to explore all the possibilities of ambivalence both in drama and by using the codification of female beauty in the dominant neo-petrarchan culture in which they live. As a result, a new attitude of public fascination regarding female poetic beauty on the stage gradually replaces the former rejection of the same. The important thing is that, in doing so, female performers use various patterns of standardised culture in order to maintain their position as a more visible presence in dominant court politics. They use as an open repertoire the unwritten techniques of professional performance skills. They take advantage of the existence of a certain number of stock characters in the major Renaissance dramas from two decades before. The ambiguity of these characters is so much part of the structure of the text that they can be used in the most various and even contradictory ways of depicting reality. Should we accept as a guideline the proposal for a general and complete definition of 'commonplaces' offered by Ann Moss, then we can immediately confirm its application – albeit in a particular way – to the question of actors as agents of rebellion in the era of the Counter Reformation:

> [...] commonplaces are cultural material with both past and present currency within a given language community; their reference is to opinions commonly accepted as valid; they are deployed primarily as tools for argument in dis-

course designed to promote and reinforce culturally sanctioned modes of thought; and, furthermore, commonplace propositions have a ritualised character that makes of them recognisable modes of communication coded for universal reception, be it as familiar forms of verbal expression, hackneyed metaphors, normative rules, or recurring patterns.[1]

Indeed, in the case of the Italian professional theatre system, the actors' search for dynamic commonplaces within the repertoire is there to stabilise and to reinforce those dramatic and scenic conventions that allow them to seduce the audience on a permanent basis: in doing so, they counter-balance the static or 'frozen' cultural material of both past and present traditions which still survive in some performance models of a non-professional kind, i.e. those practised by dilettante actors on stage and in the marketplaces. In synthesis, the way the new generation of comedians interfere with the contemporary system of commonplaces shows us that, in fact, they occupy a strong position in what we could call an 'intermediate culture' between dynamic and static commonplaces and, as a consequence, between standardised patterns of repertoire and their continuous need for *aggiornamento*. The power and persuasion coming from such a comfortable culture-in-between, immune from direct attacks, has an almost immediate impact on other participants in the literary society still condemned to an isolated, peripheral or even 'invisible' position. Indeed, the attractiveness of an intermediate position between two types of commonplaces will be explored by the first female writers: following the example of their colleagues on stage, a new generation of writers advocating professional skill will try out similar rhetorical strategies in order to give new shape to established tradition. The second consequence is that the remaining male actors will meet in their female fellows the best placed advocates and ambassadors to promote both in Italy and beyond a way of organising theatre that will come to be the dominant practice in subsequent years: a system based on regular companies of both men and women travelling from court to court by implementing the *stagione* model of organising theatre. As will be demonstrated in this chapter, commonplaces occupy a strategic position in the transformation of European dramatic conventions.

Ambassadors of intermediate cultures: Italian actresses on the early modern stage

The importance of female performance as a structural element in early modern European theatre has only quite recently been brought to the atten-

---

[1] See A. Moss's chapter in this volume, pp. 1-17 (p. 1).

tion of international scholarship.[2] Two main fields of research can be recognised in this specific area of cultural studies. On the one hand, starting from around the 1980s, new historical insights in Italy have made it possible to analyse the phenomenon of contrasting performance practices in the Cinquecento, usually gathered under the eighteenth-century anachronism of *commedia dell'arte*, as an interesting expression of poetic choice which characterises the dynamic culture of the late Renaissance in Italy.[3] Indeed, the *commedia dell'arte* often deals with the question of how to translate into practical form the many attempts to standardise models drawn from Plato, Aristotle, Horace and Cicero through Cinquecento fusion.[4] On the other hand, in recent times gender studies have made a real contribution to the more detailed investigation of exceptional instances of female presence in the literary hierarchy of early modern Europe.[5]

Notwithstanding the scientific results of both approaches, the study of women's activity on the stage is still suffering from a certain number of omissions, especially in terms of method. Indeed, the investigation of women's presence is predominantly linked with the reconstruction of what we could call the *vitae* of exceptional personalities in a male-dominated literary system.[6] Secondly, women's practice is mainly viewed as a specific area of cultural production, which functions as a counterforce against all kinds of dominant practices. As a result, what is striking in the research is the emphasis on individual destiny as well as on the functioning of a counter-model in society. In a way, both approaches underscore the notion

---

[2] For an excellent recent overview see A. MacNeil, *Music and Women of the Commedia dell'Arte in the Late Sixteenth Century* (Oxford, 2003). A standard encyclopaedic reference is G. Duby and M. Perrot, eds, *Histoire des femmes en Occident* (Paris, 1991-). The most complete and systematic treatment can be found in L. Timmermans, *L'Accès des femmes à la culture sous l'Ancien Régime* (Paris, 2005).

[3] The term *commedia dell'arte* was introduced by the Italian playwright Carlo Goldoni. Contemporary sixteenth-century denominations are: *commedia di zanni, teatro di comici*, or *commedia improvvisa*.

[4] See P. Bossier, *'Ambasciatore della risa': la commedia dell'arte nel secondo Cinquecento (1545-1590)* (Florence, 2004).

[5] One of the most important achievements is the publication of original early modern French or Italian texts with critical commentaries and an up-to-date bibliography in M. L. King and A. Rabil Jr., series eds, *The Other Voice in Early Modern Europe* (Chicago/London, University of Chicago Press).

[6] Not surprisingly, the series mentioned in note 5 is dedicated to the rehabilitation of singular voices such as Olympia Morata, Jacqueline Pascal, Isotta Nogarola, Madeleine de Scudéry and many others. However, while attempts have been made to catalogue every single cultural contribution made by these forgotten female authors, less attention has been paid to the particular functioning of these voices in a broader context.

that female activity on stage was an exceptional event or even a peripheral voice in culture. In this chapter, I would like to investigate an alternative methodological approach in which both approaches should be reconsidered from the perspective of a singular practice occurring in relation to a broader network of relationships within the cultural system. In doing so, an analytical perspective is added to existing research by proposing a framework of cultural dynamics taken as a whole: the nature of individual female performance is to be seen as part of a general shift within the cultural system.

What is true for this specific area of research in early modern performance is also valid for state-of-the-art research in most areas of Renaissance studies. Indeed, in most histories of literature, the Italian Renaissance is still presented as either a continuous construction of static and strict norms or a succession of rigid and very precise models of court literature, all of which were to become, sooner or later, the basis for high culture in the principal capitals of Europe. To list some of these: the implementation of a literary system based on vernacular expression and the *auctoritas* of Trecento foundational texts (Boccaccio for prose, Petrarch for poetry); the outlining of the behaviour of the ideal courtier starting with Castiglione; the codification of the political treatise based on Machiavelli; the choice of a new kind of novel based on Ariosto's invention of a soap-opera-like structuring of plot and sub-plots in his *Orlando Furioso*; the centralisation of baroque imagination in Tasso's *Jerusalem Delivered*; the professionalisation of modern theatre; and the 'invention' of the opera as a new form of art established by the end of the century. As a consequence of the rigidity of these models, some eccentric personalities such as Pietro Aretino, Michelangelo Buonarroti, Gaspara Stampa and Benvenuto Cellini are still quite difficult to place within them, as the models are based on a belief in unambiguous meaning and one-dimensional choice as regulating principles in society. Such a traditional and orthodox positioning of authors and texts might be considered to be altogether too rigid. After all, cultural reality and early documents seem to stress that norm and anti-norm do not always have to exclude one another. They might even be co-present in one and the same text, cultural event, scenic prototype or stage convention. For the Italian Renaissance, the shaping of ambiguity in literary products was as much a structuring principle as the simple codification of literary norms. To a certain extent, and of course subject to time constraints, the representation of moral dignity and apparently repulsive behaviour could coexist. For example, within an aesthetic portrayal of beauty in the painting of naked bodies, explicit sexuality could be appropriate; or in certain genres of drama, serene human perfection could be pictured as being compatible with more impulsive desires of the senses. Such possibilities depend on the extent to which we perceive the hierarchies of the aesthetic canon in the Renaissance to be flexible and open. In this way, an accurate study of the ambiguous stage characters and the way their qualities are transmitted by female performers might contribute to a descriptive analysis of the internal dynamics of the literary system of the period between Humanism and the Baroque.

Cultural mediation and the theatre system in the Italian Renaissance

Recent literary studies have focused predominantly on specific principles of cultural dynamics.[7] Itamar Even-Zohar's polysystem theory, for example, focuses on how in a certain period of its evolution a literary system can undergo pressure to transform itself into an alternative series of norms with a new kind of stability.[8] With his concept of the 'rhetoric of diffraction', Fabio Finotti has also made a particular contribution to the general discussion of contradictory movements in Italian Renaissance literature.[9] These were especially operative after the codification of language and aesthetics by Pietro Bembo in his *Prose della volgar lingua* (*Prose of the Vernacular Language,* Venice, 1525) – a provocative text that was only accepted after a lengthy debate conducted throughout the Italian peninsula. Finotti argues that the core principle of literary development at the time concerns the way in which the initial model of classical court literature is 'diffracted' into a varied and dynamic set of alternative, though not oppositional, expressions of the same prototype.

In addition to utilising these interpretations, I would like to argue that the concept of the 'cultural mediator', together with that of 'rebellion against static commonplaces' can be of use for our understanding of the dynamics of the literary process. The notions of 'cultural mediator', and of the more traditional 'counter-model', can be fruitfully combined when reconsidering female performance on stage as an expression of more general tendencies, developments and changes within the cultural hierarchy of Renaissance Italy, rather than as one of the strategies to promote a particular group in society – in this case, actresses. In fact, from the moment actresses be-

---

[7] See P. Bossier, '"Le verbe puissant et princier": bref aperçu de la dynamique littéraire à la Renaissance italienne', in: B. Van den Bossche et al., eds, *'Innumerevoli contrasti d'innesti': la poesia del Novecento (e altro): miscellanea in onore di Franco Musarra*, II (Louvain/Florence, 2007), pp. 675-689.

[8] I. Even-Zohar, *Papers in Historical Poetics* (Tel Aviv, 1978); idem, 'Polysystem Theory', *Poetics Today* 1 (1979), pp. 287-310, idem, *Polysystem Studies, Poetics Today* 11 no. 1 (1990, themed volume).

[9] F. Finotti, *Retorica della diffrazione: Bembo, Aretino, Giulio Romano e Tasso, letteratura e scena cortigiana* (Florence, 2004).

came active in the Italian theatre in the 1560s,[10] they do not seem to support individual fate or fortune nor even gender-related ambition, but instead to promote, initially, a group-oriented quality of performance.[11] Actresses presented themselves as ambassadors of a stage practice seen as a whole, that is, in the way new professional drama was to be guaranteed, from that moment on, by the dramaturgical choices of theatre companies which travelled from one marketplace to another and from one court festivity to another, especially in northern and central Italy (Venice, Mantua, Ferrara, Florence).[12] As a result, actresses became a symbol of a new theatre model, based on professionalism and new market strategies, in order to construct a strong basis for themselves within the main culture of late Renaissance Italy, in which courts used theatrical performance as part of their cultural politics.

In this way actresses could even reach powerful positions within the context of pre-Baroque theatre in Italy. Female performers spoke, acted and performed in the name of (and certainly on behalf of) their male colleagues, who had been active on the stage as full-time professionals since the 1540s,[13] and, as such, they were mediators of a practice that needed to be defended, strengthened and recognised in the cultural system. However, and

---

[10] A rather amusing modern toy for research is the website 'Commedia dell'Arte Women Timeline', which presents the first evidence of female acting around the sixties of the Cinquecento: 'Lucrezia signs contract in Roma as a professional actress'. See <http://www.isebastiani.com/Timelines/Timeline-Women.html>, last accessed November 20, 2006. See also A. Evain, *L'Apparition des actrices professionnelles en Europe* (Paris, 2001).

[11] It is striking that the most recent contributions on the *commedia dell'arte* focus on a new chronological presentation of the phenomenon of professional acting: the initial period of small companies, the first ventures of big companies abroad, the international market for Italian troupes placed under the supervision of a female actress, and the period of the written traces of the companies (scenarios, dramatic texts, letters). As a consequence, the moment actresses became responsible for the working of a company is nowadays considered as a watershed in theatre chronology in the Italian Renaissance.

[12] These dramaturgical choices are linked to professionalism: working with contracts, the indication of the period of performance, renting and housing of theatres, conventions of travelling, protecting 'copyright' and theatre direction, etc.

[13] It is now accepted that comedians promoted themselves as being 'different', in opposition to regular court tricksters or occasional performers at court. The most accurate norm to distinguish the new professional acting from the former is the way new performers chose to work with written contracts within which all the members of the troupe as well as their main responsibilities are named. The first known contract was used in Padua in 1545. See 'Commedia dell'Arte troupes Timeline' at <http://www.isebastiani.com/Timelines/Timeline-Troupes-a.html>, last accessed November 20, 2006.

this is very striking, these actresses tried to reintegrate even older practices into their new kind of performance in a more explicit way than male actors. Female specialists in the professional theatre from the 1560s-1580s tried to assemble, in a historically oriented perspective, the legacy of individual performers who had worked at the start of the century, and whose activities had been fundamentally important as a result of their focus on the acquired skills of theatre practice (for instance, the dramaturgy of Angelo Beolco called Ruzante (d. 1542) or of his associate in art, Zuan Polo, d. 1541). They were therefore mediators of a cultural past that was to be re-actualised for the sake of an emerging profession in its fight against negative commonplaces. Vincenza Armani, Vittoria Piisimi and Isabella Andreini (1562-1604) were representatives of this new model of performance within the cultural system of the late Renaissance. This model was based on the actresses' mediation of both previous and contemporary structures and norms, in which they focused on previously established, distinctive ways of acting that had been initiated by male performers in the 1530s (although the latter had not founded structured troupes performing on an annual basis), as well as on contemporary norms, by trying to create a new image of female presence on the stage which explored female beauty, attractiveness and fascination, especially through their voices and declamation.

The blossoming of female performance is not an isolated phenomenon. It is not only a central part of the establishment of a new kind of profession within the cultural hierarchy of the Italian Renaissance, but also represents certain underlying patterns of cultural change characteristic of this specific period in Italian history. The growing importance of female actresses is first of all connected with a broader process of professionalisation of the arts in Italy, in which practices that had formerly been linked to individuals were now presented as the affair of a specialised group of people. This process can be characterised by a restricted set of features: a new social activity settling into the economic framework of the marketplace by the introduction of a leading – albeit provocative – model capable of promoting an entire profession; the presentation of the profession as having a past of its own; the picturing of the profession as entering the present stage from a new perspective and thus breaking with its glorious past; and the aim to deconstruct the negative a priori attitude which society held towards public performance.

Secondly, the introduction of women onto the Italian stage corresponds to the ultimate phase of the until then predominant model of poetry and self-consciousness, that is, the various ways in which Petrarch's *Canzoniere* was used and reused in artistic manifestations. In contrast to previous interpretations of Petrarch, those of the 1560s-1580s concentrate much more on the elusive shape of beauty, on the physical presence of the body and on the exploration of the senses. We can observe this in paintings, but also in a new kind of performance on the stage, embodied by female beauty and thematic ambivalence.

A third underlying cultural pattern marks the beginning of a new period of the Italian Renaissance in the 1560s, a period officially marked by the conclusion of the Council of Trent (1545-1563). From this time onwards, aesthetic choices were discussed much more, and polemics were more frequently concerned with practical considerations, such as the influence of theatre on the public, the impact of body language on the stage, and the need for written texts as a prerequisite for controlling the process of literary creativity by means of censorship. In fact, an attempt to control the production of culture was not the exclusive preoccupation of the ecclesiastical authorities. A similar development can be discerned in the increasing power of academies, professional corporations and in the ethical deontology within poetics, in which, of course, commonplace interpretations based on tradition were still very active.

As a consequence of these patterns of cultural transition, there was a real need for poetic strategies from within the field. The ambivalences derived from the comedic tradition of the past and the coexistence of oppositional practices could barely be tolerated any longer. It is, for example, emblematic that Torquato Tasso's striking but provocative masterpiece, *Jerusalem Delivered*, had to be rewritten several times due to pressure from the Church. This was not only because its religious content was linked to erotic staging, but also because it was unusual in not respecting harmony and equilibrium in style and composition, qualities that were so important for canonical works of art. Within such a context, cultural mediation could function as an active principle. The mediation of traditional authorities, as well as canonical, petrarchan standards of beauty, was of strategic importance to the emerging professionalisation of theatrical performance. The same applies to the more than occasional attempts to rebel against mainstream orthodoxy. From the first half of the sixteenth century onwards, the passage from the dominant position of the high Renaissance codification of art to a more ambivalent position is marked by a series of mutations that result in this process of professionalisation.

When hierarchies undergo serious pressure, rigid cultural delimitations become less and less stable. As a result, the opposition between low and high culture becomes less explicit and a larger area is created in between, which is open to all kinds of influences from outside the established culture. This is exactly what happened within Italian theatrical performance. The canonical court theatre (1500-1540), basically administered by members of the court or by the princely aristocracy, was gradually replaced (1540-1560) by a model from non-official culture, that is, coming directly from carnival or from oral performances practised in the public marketplace. As a result, skills from popular and oral performance were gradually introduced within the borders of the dominant model of written culture. The integration of skills coming from a popular tradition of theatre (such as carnival) into the performances of the professional troupes was typical of the time. It is likely that, in order to be recognised as a value within this new social context, or even in order to mask the mixture of popular and courtly expression, a new model of intermediate culture was introduced: the actress performing litera- ture on the stage by translating the petrarchan codification of beauty and female fascination into new standards, in co-operation with the male come- dians who continued to work in the tradition of popular comedy using the vernacular.

Following this interpretation, as surprising and provocative as it might sound, the actress's arrival (in the 1560s) on a stage that was already occu- pied by artists in search of professional skills is illustrative of a real need for mediation between the high and low strata of art at this stage of cultural evolution. It is not surprising that the actress is almost always pictured, in addition to her theatrical performance, in the context of standardised activi- ties concerning court literature: as a performer declaiming poetry, as a woman of letters, or as a *cortigiana* or *meretrix honesta* offering a venue for literary debates.[14] Being an ambassador of a new intermediate culture, the *comica* (as the actress-*cortigiana* is called in contemporary writings) was – for a certain time at least – surrounded in the public psyche by a mystical aura. Needless to say, this fascinating power of ambiguity on stage and as a public person was immediately explored by actresses such as Isabella An- dreini, who elevated her status in society to the highest level ever achieved by a non-member of court – as is evidenced by the praise of renowned poets such as Tasso and Guarini.[15] The roots of this ambiguity in performance and perception, however, lay in the subgenre of the *comedia* and its use of char- acters with multiple and contradictory identities on the stage. Ambiguity, humour, parody and rebellion against cultural commonplaces in Renais- sance comedy were to a certain extent indicative of changes in the public acceptance of a leading culture phenomenon.

---

[14] It is most significant that Isabella Andreini, in addition to her career as a per- former, was active as a publisher of texts. Indeed, with her *Mirtilla* (1588) she con- tributed, as one of the first female authors, to the success of the pastoral as a new genre in the Italian Renaissance. After her death, her husband and troupe companion Francesco Andreini published her *Letters* in 1607, an exquisite example of how new professionals integrated the established (i.e. petrarchan) norm of the past in order to continue their innovative work on the basis of accepted written material, incorporat- ing this into their scenic, less easily accepted, production.

[15] Indeed both authors, authorities in vernacular poetry and drama, wrote poems in admiration of the actress's abilities to portray a scene.

The mediation of ambivalence: prototypes in comedy

For modern research, the conventional watershed of 1508 has been established as the canonical starting point for a new dramatic literature in the
vernacular in Renaissance Italy. Indeed, with *La Cassaria* (The Coffin), the
first of Ludovico Ariosto's *comedie nuove* – Italy's new comedies – the
prestigious avant-garde court of Ferrara gave the official signal of the emergence of a new kind of elite culture. From the first decade of the sixteenth
century onwards, the cultural politics of the most innovative princes (the
dukes of D'Este in Ferrara, the Gonzagas in Mantua, the dukes of Montefel-
tro in Italy's first Renaissance-built palace – 1480 – in Urbino) was no
longer exclusively concentrated on the imitation of classical texts from the
Latin and Greek repertoire. Instead, the classical model now became a
source of inspiration for an original literature, written in Italian, and in
which linguistic self-consciousness was a leading principle. This was the
birth of the *comedia*, in which dramatic plot, choice of characters and stage
setting continued to be inspired by Latin playwrights such as Plautus or,
even more, Terence, albeit within a new context with specific references to
the cultural, political and social changes in early sixteenth-century Italy.

The use of theatrical *prototypes* formed a striking characteristic of this
production of texts in the vernacular. Within a large but at the same time
always repetitive standard setting of characters in this new kind of comedy,
some pieces seemed to function between the 'elastic' borderlines of their
definition-in-context. As a result, the characters were more flexible in their
'stage' behaviour, and seemed more difficult to incorporate into simple one-
dimensional interpretations of the type of person being portrayed. Moreover, these characters appealed to the audience in order to achieve more
than a superficial, basic and exclusively linear reception of the scenes represented on stage. In short, in framing a very dynamic presence both in their
physical movements on the stage and between the lines of the written text,
these particular prototypes seemed to resist the literal interpretations of the
contemporary cultural codes.

Within the stock of characters, some functioned in a more ambivalent
way than others. First of all, the pedant, absent from the Latin or Greek
models generally used as inspiration for the newly written texts for court
entertainment, was a new subject on the Renaissance stage. As a theatre
figure, he started to be used frequently from this cultural period onwards
and seemed to function on more than one level in the literary codification of
the *comedia*. Also, a second prototype can be identified as a frequent character in all the multiple variants of the early comedy, which, as a rule, always started from the usual and expected standard formula: the almost an-

cestral antagonism between tender young lovers longing for marriage and the narrow-minded but strong (because rich) world of older men and women opposed to this project, yet happily countered in their destructive aim by the intercession of an intermediate class of match-making servants. This Italian version of the Latin *servus* was based on former classical models, but also integrated its contemporary, more popular and regional variant, the so-called *zanni* (a Venetian abbreviation of 'Giovanni', Italy's 'Mr Everybody'): a rude young man from the countryside of the Bergamasque mountains looking for a job as a street porter in the magnificent harbour of the Republic of Venice and willing to exceed any limit to obtain his goals of sex, money and, most importantly, food. The third stock character producing ambiguity within the text was the prologue, who was a theatrical invention on the threshold between text and paratext, introducing the audience to the argument about to be played. As such, he was the written instance both inside and outside the text, as any actor would be who steps in or out of their role. Nevertheless, he did not completely fit with the comedy as a whole, as at a certain moment he left the scene.

All these figures could express quite contrasting values. The pedant was the ultimate survivor and defender of antique Latin culture: he was the prototype of the teacher, pictured in relationship to the pupil, and was the focus for both transmitting consciousness of authority and acquiring knowledge. On the other hand, the pedant was continuously exposed to ridicule because of his lack of contemporary knowledge, his inappropriate language, which he did not seem to understand, his imperviousness to the sexual innuendo of his discourse and, on the moral side, his suspected susceptibility to an 'impure' attitude towards his male students. The same kind of double picture applied to the *zanni* as a predecessor of the *Harlequin*: on the one hand, he stood for the stupid, rough and undistinguished fellow whom people could easily use for their own ends, but who still generally overcomes his opponents by exploiting all the talents he possesses as the ideal trickster.[16] In the play, however, he was the symbol of inventiveness and of a fresh, new take on problem solving. The two characters were the extreme opposites of each other: the latter symbolising all that can be dynamic and

---

[16] As the *zanni* is a ridiculous mask coming from the mountains behind the rich Veneto area with Venice as the cultural epicentre, Harlequin is nowadays considered as the aesthetic improvement of his more peasant-like and rough ancestor in the tradition. Harlequin's dramatic destiny would become significant internationally due to the performances of Tristano Martinelli, his brother and other members of his troupe during the 1570s-1580s in France and abroad. For the specific importance of Harlequin-Martinelli in northern Europe, see W. Schrickx, 'Commedia dell'Arte Players in Antwerp in 1576: Drusiano and Tristano Martinelli', *Theatre Research International* 1 (1976), pp. 79-86.

new in society, with the creation of a new kind of language, and the former representing the old-fashioned and sterile model of communication which was losing its predominant position in the now bilingual (Latin/Italian) community of intellectuals and artists.

If it is true that the coexistence of contrasting principles, as personified by the characters of the new Italian comedy, was constructed upon the same basis of scenic ambivalence, then it is interesting to note how ambivalence also becomes a functional principle in the aesthetics of early modern Italy. Using a large spectrum of contrasting significations, ambivalence is then located as a counter-value to empty commonplace interpretations based on oppositional notions such as bad versus good, stupid versus intelligent, master versus servant, or victim versus winner. Indeed, the way theatre used characters whose definitions, within the text, were ambiguous, shows us how important open rather than rigid definitions were in Renaissance society. This insight certainly offers a better understanding of the complicated interaction between norm and exception in sixteenth-century culture.

From the moment of their arrival on the scene, actresses were involved in the above-mentioned work of portraying these forms of scenic ambiguity. They did this by shaping a character that was difficult to define according to the simple and linear modes of interpretation which had been employed by their predecessors. As did the stock characters of the prologue, the *zanni* and the pedant, with whom the public in the meantime were becoming familiar, actresses' roles, given their non-linear nature, had the effect of producing troubling significations on the stage. As a result, the audience was invited to react in the most inventive way possible. This is the reason why some members of the audience, following the ecclesiastical authorities, did not accept the public exposure of unmasked female beauty and bodies, confusing the role of the actress with that of the prostitute, selling her body for money. Others, however, were capable of a more reflective reading of the theatrical signs and went as far as to interpret the actress's presence as a reincarnation of the sublime idea of beauty and magnificence in nature.

A rebellion against poetic convention: the example of Maddalena Campiglia

Negative commonplace attitudes towards female acting are based on the traditional confusion between 'public performance' and 'public woman'. Significantly, people who opposed the introduction of professional theatre on a permanent basis in early modern society used this very confusion to condemn public theatre as such. A very interesting aspect of research is the question of how *the female pastoral drama* in early modern Italy was to confirm this general evolution. Indeed, I have already mentioned the pastoral experience of Isabella Andreini's *Mirtilla* (1588), which can be considered as a way of positioning herself as an author in her own right. The same is true for *Flori*, a very significant text (also 1588) by the Vicenza-born noblewoman Maddelena Campiglia (1533-1595). What we can detect behind the use of the typical format of the pastoral comedy is the way the female author allows herself to deal, albeit behind the mask of scenic metaphor and double-bind in the text, with contemporary matters, such as marriage, female writers or the capacity to organise one's life freely. It is very striking that Campiglia uses the same strategies of embedded ambivalence we have already noted in the actresses' work. Just like actresses, this author shows her literary professionalism by using all the possibilities offered by literary texts: metaphors, implicitness, appeal to the audience, reference to established authority (Petrarch, once again, in the poems that precede the pastoral play). For all these reasons, Maddalena Campiglia occupies an emblematic position in the rich panorama of the cultural changes of the end of the *Cinquecento*. Her choice to practise a specific kind of literary genre is not a casual one: by implementing her text both within a traditional framework (the pastoral drama) and some not yet standardised borderlines (the female pastoral drama), *Flori* is pictured by the author as a text which does not fit in any standard classification. In fact, she prefers to work with a genre *in statu nascendi*: for one reason, this position as an open text allows a lot of freedom for the author; for another, this fits perfectly with the central theme of her writing: giving 'birth' to a text is like giving life to a child, whose (literary) parenthood (as a woman) is here to be defended. So, what is recommended in such a situation is reference to a currently accepted cultural pattern. At the same time, this opportunity of ambivalence in genre patterns can be employed in a very useful way. Campiglia thus acts in a double way. On the one hand, reference to classical literature allows her to deal here with established *auctoritates* like Virgil or Tasso. On the other, pastoral drama creates the opportunity to formulate some statements of her own regarding the central nucleus of this textual tradition, i.e. the glorification of a wedding in an idyllic universe as the conclusive moment of restoration of peace and harmony after a previous period of turbulence all due to the devastating power of Eros. Most significantly, the use of two contrasting principles in both dedicatory letters accompanying her text is a confirmation of the underlying rhetorical strategy based on a double reading of the same standard pattern: one completely conventional letter is presented to a male dedicatee, and another, in contrast, completely non-conformist, to a female companion. To Lady Isabella Pallavicino Lupi, Marchioness of Soragna, she writes:

Sono tuttavia sicurissima che, sendo ella tanto virile nei pensieri e nelle opposizioni quanto donna nel bellissimo sembiante e negli onestissimi portamenti,
aggradirà questo mio rozzo parto, e la viva candidezza del cuore con che lo ac-
compagno. Sogliono tutte le madri d'oggidi, dovendo far comparir fuori le loro
figlie, comporle nella più leggiarda maniera che si sanno imaginare, ricercando
a questo effetto i più riposti e astrusi cantoni dell'arte; che a me non giova di
fare, procurando più tosto d'allontanarmi dall'ordinario costume donnesco.

But I am quite sure that you will be gracious enough to be pleased with this
poor offspring of mine and with the keen and heartfelt affection that accompanies it, for I know you to be as virile in your thoughts and deeds as you are
feminine in your beauty and the honesty of your manners. Mothers today, when
they are sending their daughters out into the world, always dress them in the
finest way possible, drawing on all the most recondite and abstruse artifices at
their disposal. But this is not my way; on the contrary, I seek to depart from the
normal habits of woman ['l'ordinario costume donnesco'].[17]

As a counterpart, she addresses – albeit by stressing the conventional 'obligation' of this move – 'The most illustrious Lord Curzio Gonzaga' with the
following: both a continuation of the previous image of the text as child and
a reformulation of it with the addition of literary commonplace in referring
to established authority. At its start, the letter follows convention:

Non mi pareva d'aver per aventura sodisfatto al debito del desiderio mio se,
mandando in luce questa mia favola boscareccia sotto il celebre nome della Si-
gnora Marchesa Pallavicina Lupi, non la raccomandavan'anco a Vostra Signoria Illustrissima, il cui valore è solo celato ai pochi stimatori della virtù.

Your Excellency, I felt that I should not have satisfied the obligation of my desire if I had sent this pastoral play of mine out into the world under the famous
name of the Marchioness Isabella Pallavicino Lupi without at the same time en-
trusting it to your Lordship, whose valor is known to all those who prize virtue.[18]

Right after this initial, somehow sterile respect of ceremony, she comes to
rebel against literary commonplace when she invokes once more 'her own
way', intelligently interwoven with a small network of traditional references
as guarantees for this unusual practice:

---

[17] M. Campiglia, *Flori, A Pastoral Drama: A Bilingual Edition*, ed. V. Cox and L.
Sampson (Chicago/London, 2004), pp. 44-45.
[18] Campiglia, *Flori*, pp. 46-47.

So che le opposizioni saranno molte; ma di questa sola far dovrei stima, che fatto avessi meglio spendere il tempo in scritti spirituali, si come avea cominciato, sviando la mente da qualunque vano pensiero; se da Sant'Agostino data non me ne fosse licenza con affermar che ogni sorte di virtù allontana l'uomo dai vizi. Confesso parimente che la favola sia più secondo l'intenzion mia che le regole di coloro che hanno insegnato l'arte di questi poemi, perché gli episodi che si sono inseriti superano di lunghezza l'azion principale. Tuttavia, (...) ed essendone state composte da persone di qualche nome altre ancora, senza la piena osservazione dei precetti d'Aristotele e degli avvertimenti dataci dai commentatori della sua poetica, io credero' che questa, fatta da donna, e da donna forse poco atta a simile impresa, debba esser letta se non con lode, almeno con sopportazione.

I know the poem will attract criticisms for all kinds of motives, but the only one I am prepared to take seriously is this: that it would be better for me to devote my time to writing religious works, as I have done in the past, and to turn my attention away from all worldly considerations. I feel myself absolved on this score, however, by none more then St Augustine, who maintained that all forms of virtuous activity serve to preserve us from vice. For the rest, I confess freely that I have composed the plot of this play more in accordance with my own tastes than with the prescriptions of those who have written theoretically on the genre of pastoral, for the various digressive episodes that have been introduced in fact occupy more space in the play than the principal action. In any case, (…) I am not the first to compose such a play without following to the letter the precepts of Aristotle and the recommendations of his commentators; indeed, there are writers of some renown who are guilty of this same transgression. In view of this, it seems to me that a play written by a mere woman (and a woman, perhaps, ill-fitted for such an enterprise), deserves to be received, if not with generosity, at least with tolerance.[19]

To conclude comes her provocative proposal of her text as her own natural daughter, of course once more a commonplace in its own right, but presented here as a weapon of both self-consciousness and auto-legitimatisation of literary paternity/maternity:

Accresca dunque Vostra Signoria (...) il primo obbligo che le tengo (...), con questo secondo, degnandosi gradire il mio picciolo dono (...). Poiché non le posso dar cosa più cara di questa mia figlia, vera figlia, e naturale, di che principalmente mi godo.

---

[19] Campiglia, *Flori*, pp. 47-49.

But I hope, nonetheless, that you will grant me the further favour of accepting this little gift. (…) For I have nothing to give dearer to me than this daughter of mine: this true and natural daughter, the apple of my eye.[20]

As has been discussed in this paper, three elements of cultural change are here linked together in the same way that female performers managed to put them together: the mediation of culture, the inscription of ambivalence or multi-interpretation, and the need to defend an alternative system in order to create new dynamics within the contemporary culture.

As a conclusion, the ascension of female performance by the 1560s in Italy can be interpreted as answering a structural need for mediation inherent in the literary field that resulted from a fading of the highly normative phase of Renaissance literature. Actresses played an important mediating role in the fusion of cultures within an openly structured space, and at the same time took a stand against negative, commonplace attitudes. Before conquering the rest of Europe as the ultimate demonstration of professional and modern theatre, female performance served an aim that far exceeded that suggested by the traditional interpretation of this phenomenon as merely the promotion of a non-male alternative voice in Renaissance society. In the same way, female practice on the stage and in writing shows us the fundamental importance of the culture of commonplaces as a crossroads of both sanctioned modes of thought and reference, and their being a starting-point for cultural renewal.

---

[20] *Ibidem.*

COMMONPLACES IN RELIGIOUS UPBRINGING IN SIXTEENTH-CENTURY ITALIAN YOUTH CONFRATERNITIES

IACOPO ANSALDI AND THE *COMPAGNIA DELL'ARCANGELO RAFFAELLO*

Nils Holger Petersen[1]

This chapter is concerned with the use of particular strategies for the basic religious education of boys in sixteenth-century Italy. These strategies were related to newly formulated Jesuit practices for religious teaching of the unlearned but also have roots in practices introduced before the reformations of the sixteenth century.

I want to emphasise and discuss the use of 'commonplaces' in the practice of teaching doctrine in the late sixteenth century through a presentation of the *Dottrina cristiana* published by Iacopo Ansaldi in 1585 and other contextually relevant information. The term 'commonplace' had, of course, a specific use at this time: the *loci communes* representing specific (rhetorical) traditions pertaining to the organisation of general knowledge and the teaching thereof.[2] Neither the traditions for organising knowledge nor the way one traditionally drew up lists of authorities as support for the presented *loci* in commonplace-books can be found in the same systematic way in the printed books for the elementary teaching of catechism, usually entitled *dottrina cristiana*. However, it may be possible to see the use of com-

---

[1] The research for this chapter has been carried out in collaboration with Dr Eyolf Østrem at the *Centre for the Study of the Cultural Heritage of Medieval Rituals* funded by the Danish National Research Foundation as a part of a joint project concerning *lauda* singing in the late Renaissance. See E. Østrem and N. H. Petersen, 'The Singing of *Laude* and Musical Sensibilities in Early Seventeenth-Century Confraternity Devotion', Parts I and II, *The Journal of Religious History* 28 (2004), pp. 276-291, and 29 (2005), pp. 163-176; E. Østrem and N. H. Petersen, *Medieval Ritual and Early Modern Music: The Devotional Practice of Lauda Singing in Late-Renaissance Italy* (Turnhout, 2008). Although the material dealt with in this chapter is covered in more detail in our recent book, Eyolf Østrem is not, of course, responsible for this chapter, but it could not have been written without our collaboration, from which I have profited immensely.

[2] See A. Moss, *Printed Commonplace-Books and the Structuring of Renaissance Thought* (Oxford, 1996).

monly accepted notions and claims in a book for doctrinal teaching as a kind of generalised *loci communes* and thus to compare the uses in *dottrine cristiane* of notions and claims with well-established semantic meanings – referring to traditional musical thought and church music practices so as to establish authority – to the use of Latin commonplace-books and their function in Renaissance thought. In what follows, the term 'commonplace' will be employed in an extended way and broadly used in three areas in which the teaching of Christian doctrine can be said to build on such basic notions, claims, and authorisation: on the level of contents, on an 'aesthetic' level concerning poetry and music, and on the level of arguments for the role of music and song in teaching.

From its early years, the Jesuit order was concerned with the question of religious – and other – education. The most spectacular Jesuit contribution to European culture in the early modern period may very likely have been their schools. Along the way, the Jesuits developed new educational methods which also included the writing and use of school dramas and music. This had a fundamental impact on the further development of the European theatre. Formal school education had not been foreseen as a part of the Jesuit programme from the very beginning, but this task was taken up within the first decade after papal approval of the order. By contrast, the concern for the basic instruction of children and unlearned adults in Christian doctrine was fundamental to the movement even before it was formally established. The early constitutive Jesuit documents emphasise this task, and apparently Ignatius of Loyola had practised such teaching already in 1526. The *Formula of the Institute*, one of the fundamental documents of the order, which was written up in 1540 and revised in 1550, already in the first edition indicates as one of the main purposes of the order 'the instruction of young and uneducated persons in Christianity'.[3] The influence of Lutheran catechism on the Jesuit practices must be noted, although it seems that their catechisms were not normally polemical.[4]

Although not polemical, the teaching practices to which I am referring had further purposes pertaining to the Counter-Reformation beside the fundamental aim of 'giving instruction in Christian living and practice': they were also meant to secure the Catholic Christendom and devotion and – with the same ultimate purpose – to fight heresy.[5]

The Jesuit concern with upbringing and education had important ramifications also for the religious teaching practices more generally in religious

---

[3] See J. W. O'Malley, *The First Jesuits* (Cambridge, MA, 1993), pp. 4-5 and 115-126 (p. 116).
[4] O'Malley, *The First Jesuits*, pp. 115-116 and 124.
[5] See O'Malley, *The First Jesuits*, pp. 125-126.

institutions of the Catholic Church in the later sixteenth century, including the so-called youth confraternities. This is the situation which will be discussed in the following, mainly through the example of Ansaldi's *Dottrina*.

However, it should be remembered that, at this time, youth confraternities had a long and well-established tradition of religious instruction. Indeed, the Jesuit concern with religious instruction should probably be seen as part of long-standing Catholic traditions which they emphasised and developed further.

During the fifteenth century, youth confraternities for boys of between approximately 13 and 24 years of age were established first in Florence. The interest in providing institutions for the religious upbringing of youths was seemingly connected to a new orientation which placed hope and trust in adolescents as a separate group. Most of these youth confraternities were so-called *laudesi* confraternities: they had religious ritual and devotional singing as their main objective.

The rise of devotional singing in the vernacular in Tuscany and Umbria from the thirteenth century in the wake of religious revivals had given rise to large repertories of songs connected to lay confraternities, in the beginning monophonic but later also polyphonic; the individual item is usually referred to as a *lauda*. These confraternities – and also the youth confraternities from the fifteenth century onwards – were usually (more or less consistently) affiliated with one of the mendicant orders and were also to a high degree active in religious processions and productions of so-called *sacre rappresentazioni*, religious plays which would also incorporate the singing of *laude*.[6] Richard Trexler – in a seminal article – has pointed to the role of the Florentine youth confraternities as mediating a traditional culture of public politico-religious manifestation and the 'new world of political authoritarianism':

> These grave boys represented on the one side a world of private virtues, but on the other a hope of public salvation for families whose survival had been cus-

---

[6] C. Barr, *The Monophonic Lauda and the Lay Religious Confraternities of Tuscany and Umbria in the Late Middle Ages* (Kalamazoo, MI, 1981), pp. 27-28; C. Barr, 'Music and Spectacle in Confraternity Drama of Fifteenth-Century Florence: The Reconstruction of a Theatrical Event', in: T. Verdon and J. Henderson, eds, *Christianity and the Renaissance: Image and Religious Imagination in the Quattrocento* (Syracuse, NY, 1990), pp. 376-404 (pp. 389-390); N. Newbegin, 'Politics in the *Sacre rappresentazioni* of Lorenzo's Florence', in: M. Mallett and N. Mann, eds, *Lorenzo the Magnificent: Culture and Politics* (London, 1996), pp. 117-130 (p. 119).

tomarily tied to processional prestige. To do this successfully, youthful asceticism, not boyish miscreance was the order of the early Florentine Renaissance.[7]

In Trexler's view, the youth confraternities had the primary task to 'remove the boys from the chaos and spontaneity of the street, and to provide a leisure-time activity under competent direction which would aid the formation of a pious character'.[8] It is not surprising, then, that instruction in the basics of Christian belief was important to these companies. Indeed, it seems likely that the concrete task of teaching basic Christianity to the young played an important role in the decision to establish a youth confraternity. What is known as the first Florentine youth confraternity, the *Compagnia dell'Arcangelo Raffaello* (founded in 1411), was later claimed (in the seventeenth century) – although documentation for this is not extant – to have been founded out of a personal commitment to teach Christian doctrine to youths.[9] In 1435, the Florentine humanist and general of the Camaldolan order – a branch of Benedictine monasticism – Ambrogio Traversari, although not specifically mentioning the teaching of the doctrine, wrote to Pope Eugenius IV (exiled in Florence) about the institution of youth confraternities, that the leaders of the city were 'pleased to send their sons to be nourished in this school and to be educated in this school of Christian virtue.'[10]

The *Compagnia dell'Arcangelo Raffaello* soon gave rise to another youth confraternity in Florence: the *Compagnia della Purificazione della Vergine Maria e di San Zanobi*, which in 1427 was hived off from its mother-confraternity. The earliest preserved statutes for this new confraternity were copied in 1439 and are still extant.[11] They contain precise descriptions of a catechetical programme demanding that the Ten Commandments, the twelve articles of faith, the seven mortal sins, the five bodily senses, the seven acts of mercy, the seven sacraments, the Paternoster, and the Ave Maria should be learned by heart by all members of the confraternity.[12]

---

[7] R. C. Trexler, 'Ritual in Florence: Adolescence and Salvation in the Renaissance', in: C. Trinkaus and H. A. Oberman, eds, *The Pursuit of Holiness in Late Medieval and Renaissance Religion* (Leiden, 1974), pp. 200-264 (p. 264).

[8] Trexler, 'Ritual in Florence', p. 210.

[9] K. Eisenbichler, *The Boys of the Archangel Raphael: A Youth Confraternity in Florence, 1411-1785* (Toronto, 1998), p. 128.

[10] Transl. by Trexler, 'Ritual in Florence', p. 209, and quoted in Eisenbichler, *The Boys*, p. 29.

[11] L. Polizzotto, *Children of the Promise: The Confraternity of the Purification and the Socialization of Youths in Florence 1427-1785* (Oxford, 2004), pp. 24-25 and 347-355.

[12] Polizzotto, *Children of the Promise*, p. 33.

In 1417, Bishop Nicolò Albergati had reformed the youths of the *Compagnia di S. Girolamo* in Bologna, giving them a catechism with much the same topics and elements as just mentioned.[13]

In the Post-Tridentine era, the teaching of Christian doctrine received a new emphasis in the Florentine sodalities which, however, ultimately removed the Christian doctrine from the realm of traditional youth confraternities into newly founded schools of Christian doctrine, *scuole della dottrina cristiana*, which, in principle, were to be established in all parishes. This attempt to bring the catechetical programme – as well as other devotional practices hitherto performed by lay confraternities – under a strict ecclesiastical control can be seen as part of an implementation of the reforms of the Council of Trent followed up by a local Florentine council in 1573.[14] It seems to have been a lengthy process: in 1585 only six such schools had come into being in Florence.[15] Konrad Eisenbichler has called attention to synods convoked by Archbishop Alessandro de' Medici in 1610 and 1619 demanding, among other things, that the teaching of Christian doctrine should henceforth take place in the parish.[16] As late as the mid-seventeenth century, however, the teaching of Christian doctrine is documented in the *Compagnia dell'Arcangelo Raffaello*, and it is mentioned in the revised statutes of the company which were approved by the archbishop in 1636, specifically referring to a printed *dottrina cristiana* (of 1584) apparently composed by the confraternity but no longer extant.[17]

In 1577, the archbishop had appointed the layman Iacopo Ansaldi, guardian of the above-mentioned youth confraternity of the Purification 1580-1585, to oversee the teaching of Christian doctrine in all boys' schools and companies in the diocese. In 1585, Ansaldi published his *dottrina cristiana*, which he himself described as being a revised edition of a Jesuit catechism by Giacomo Ledesma. Two years earlier, he had published a compilation of catechetical texts for the Purification confraternity in the form of

---

[13] N. Terpstra, *Lay Confraternities and Civic Religion in Renaissance Bologna* (Cambridge, 1995), p. 21; Eisenbichler, *The Boys*, p. 128.

[14] G. Aranci, *Formazione religiosa e santità laicale a Firenze tra cinque e seicento: Ippolito Galantini fondatore della congregazione di San Francesco della dottrina cristiana di Firenze (1565-1620)* (Florence, 1997), p. 113; Polizzotto, *Children of the Promise*, pp. 230-233.

[15] Polizzotto, *Children of the Promise*, p. 232; Aranci, *Formazione religiosa*, p. 117.

[16] K. Eisenbichler, 'Italian Youth Confraternities in an Age of Reform', in: J. P. Donnelly and M. W. Maher, eds, *Confraternities and Catholic Reform in Italy, France, and Spain* (Kirksville, MO, 1999), pp. 27-44 (p. 42); idem, *The Boys*, pp. 93-95 and 135-137. See also Aranci, *Formazione religiosa*, pp. 125-129, quoting synodal decisions (p. 126).

[17] Eisenbichler, *The Boys*, pp. 129 and 135.

the *Discorsi spirituali et civili, Secondo il Cathecismo per instruttione de Giovani desiderosi far profitto nella vita Spirituale et Civile.*[18]

The records of the company of the Archangel Raphael tell that on July 28, 1585 the priest Jacopo Genovese and Iacopo Ansaldi were sent by the archbishop to visit the company. Apparently the point was to command the confraternity to teach Christian doctrine in accordance with the general policy which Ansaldi represented. According to the entry, the assistant substitute guardian father Nicholò Antifassi answered that they would continue their ordinary practice reading a tablet containing the doctrine aloud every day and sometimes giving a lesson based on it.[19]

Eisenbichler understands the visit as insulting to the confraternity with its 'own long tradition in such teaching and learning', but believes the confraternity to have won the day, since no instructor to teach doctrine at the company was appointed by Ansaldi.[20]

The teaching of doctrine in the confraternity is highlighted by an earlier entry in the confraternity *ricordi* (for Pentecost Sunday, 1582) which refers to a printed sheet of paper – seemingly a doctrinal tablet such as the one mentioned in Antifassi's answer. The record mentions how one of the youths gave a lesson on *carità*, the third of the theological virtues (faith, hope, and charity). Also a play is briefly introduced, and – highly unusually – a (part of the) text is given in the entry.[21] The play stages a youth playing Tobias; he is first encountered in a dialogue with another youth of the confraternity who appears as rather disillusioned by its general state: 'Giá son' sett'anni che con poco frutto / io fei l'entrata in questa santa casa' ('It has already been seven years with only little benefit since I started in this holy house').[22]

---

[18] See Aranci, *Formazione religiosa*, pp. 103-107; Polizzotto, *Children of the Promise*, pp. 229-230; Eisenbichler, *The Boys*, pp. 133-134.

[19] This entry is found in the *ricordi* of the Archangel Raphael confraternity, preserved at the *Archivio di Stato*, Florence, under the shelfmark *Compagnie religiose soppresse da Pietro Leopoldo* (henceforth CRS) 155-165. These manuscripts have been consulted at the Archivio di Stato di Firenze during several visits to the archives between 1999 and 2005. See CRS 162, 22 (*olim* 21), fol. 66^v. This entry is also transcribed in Aranci, *Formazione religiosa*, p. 376 (reading Antisassi instead of Antifassi), and paraphrased and discussed in Eisenbichler, *The Boys*, pp. 132-133.

[20] Eisenbichler, *The Boys*, pp. 132-133, quotation on p. 132.

[21] The entry is in CRS 162, 22 (*olim* 21), fols. 12^v-15^r. It is transcribed in Aranci, *Formazione religiosa*, pp. 349-360.

[22] CRS 162, 22 (*olim* 21), fol. 13^r; Aranci, *Formazione religiosa*, p. 351. For a further description and discussion of the play, see also Eisenbichler, *The Boys*, pp. 205-207.

The dialogue leads to an intercession which prompts the arrival of the figure of the Archangel Raphael who is accompanied by two angels and a choir singing in polyphony, *un coro di Musica*.[23] The didactic culmination of the play is clearly situated in the lines of the Archangel Raphael, who lets the accompanying angels hand out a printed sheet (*una carta stampata*) to everyone; its contents are described in the introduction to the play. Among other things, the Archangel Raphael has this to say about the paper:

> Ciascuno studi questo, ognun' impari
> Per questo il modo del' viver Christiano
> Per che questa non è se non la legge
> Di Christo e di sua Chiesa a qual ciascuno
> Che desia di salvarsi è obligato.[24]

> Let everyone study this, let everyone learn
> through this the ways of a Christian life,
> because this is nothing but the law
> of Christ and of his Church, to which everyone
> who wishes to be saved is beholden.

In the following lines, Raphael reproaches the youths for having neglected this:

> Mediante questa di già i nostri antichi
> Lasciorno al' mondo di lo' buon' odore
> E ordinaron bene, ma voi dismesso
> Havevi, che ogni giorno rosinasse
> Negl'orecchi d'ognun' questi precetti
> Acciò che ognuno li ritenesse a mente.
> Come volevi voi, che stessi in piede
> Quest'edifitio, senza Pietra?
> Su la quale è fondato questo luogo
> Fatto per introdurre i giovanetti
> Nella strada d'Iddio pe suoi precetti.[25]

---

[23] CRS 162, 22 (*olim* 21), fol. 14ᵛ; Aranci, *Formazione religiosa*, p. 358. For the mention of the choir, see fol. 12ᵛ; Aranci, *Formazione religiosa*, p. 350. Concerning the term *musica* at the time, see Østrem and Petersen, 'The Singing of *Laude*', I, pp. 292-293.

[24] CRS 162, 22 (*olim* 21), fol. 15ʳ; Aranci, *Formazione religiosa*, pp. 358-359. English translation from Eisenbichler, *The Boys*, p. 130.

[25] CRS 162, 22 (*olim* 21), fol. 15ʳ; Aranci, *Formazione religiosa*, p. 359. English translation from Eisenbichler, *The Boys*, p. 130.

Through this your forerunners already
left in the world good reputation of themselves
and they commanded well, and you have
lapsed in this, that every day there should resound
in your ears each of these precepts
so that each of you may keep them in his mind.
What did you expect? That this building
would stand without this stone,
[this stone] on which this place was founded,
for the purpose of introducing young men
into the path of God through his precepts?

The contents of the paper sheet are indicated in the introduction to the play:

Li XII Articoli della fede: Credo in deum Patrem omnipotentem, creatorem celi et terre, et quel che seque: I X comandamenti della legge; I VII sacramenti della Chiesa; le III virtù Teologali; le IV virtù Cardinali; i VII doni dello Spirito Santo; i XII frutti dello Spirito Santo; i II comandamenti della Carità; le VII opere di Misericordia Temporali; li VII peccati Mortali.
Segue di là [fol. 13ʳ]
Le 4 cose di dee ricordare contento il Christiano; Li V sentimenti del Corpo. Li comandamenti della Chiesa; Le cose da osservari dal' buon Christiano; Le VI peccati contro lo spirito Santo; Le otto Beatitudini.
LAUS DEO[26]

The twelve articles of faith: I believe in God the Father almighty, creator of heaven and earth, and what follows [The Apostles' Creed]; the Ten Commandments; the seven sacraments of the Church; the three theological virtues; the four cardinal virtues; the seven gifts of the Holy Spirit; the twelve fruits of the Holy Spirit; the two commandments of charity; the seven temporal works of mercy, the seven mortal sins.
Continuing [next page]
The four things a Christian must always keep in mind; the five senses of the body; the commandments of the Church, the precepts a good Christian must observe; the six sins against the Holy Spirit; the eight Beatitudes.

Although not exactly the same as in the early statutes of the confraternity of the Purification, nor, as we shall see, in the *dottrina* of Jacopo Ansaldi, the

---

[26] CRS 162, 22 (*olim* 21), fols. 12ᵛ-13ʳ; Aranci, *Formazione religiosa*, p. 350. See also Eisenbichler, *The Boys*, p. 130.

contents of the paper sheet described in the record for Pentecost 1582 consists of a list of basic items of the Catholic faith with the same function as the above mentioned tablet in the entry from July 1585.

As Eyolf Østrem and I have argued, it is not clear whether the company was seen to have neglected the *dottrina cristiana* at the time of the visit of Ansaldi and Genovese, as Eisenbichler seems to suggest.[27] The 1582 entry could indicate a renewal of the Archangel Raphael confraternity's commitment to teach the doctrine to the youths at that time. Possibly Ansaldi in 1585 simply acknowledged the teaching efforts of the company which – as mentioned – had also printed a Christian doctrine in 1584.

If the 1582 entry indicates a renewal of the confraternity's practice of teaching Christian doctrine, it deserves attention that this renewal was announced through a play where also music figured prominently. Twice there is specific mention of the singing of a madrigal, although no information is offered about the texts or music for these madrigals, sung during the play and afterwards.[28] This brings to mind what several scholars have pointed out: that the *sacre rappresentazioni* of youth confraternities constituted a fundamental didactic tool. As emphasised by, for example, Polizzotto, Eisenbichler, and Newbegin, this was doubtless the case in the fifteenth century, but the significance of the *rappresentazioni* remained to a high degree also after the Council of Trent, although the general attitude of ecclesiastical authorities had become more critical towards such practices.[29]

The described educational event in 1582 seems to have been a creative response to the recent demands for doctrinal teaching in religious commonplace formulae.

Although no precise information concerning the teaching in the confraternity during the following years is to be found, not least the descriptions of the tablets in 1582 and 1585 and the reference to the printing of a book for doctrinal teaching in 1584 make it likely that the teaching would have followed the same basic principles found in Ansaldi's *dottrina cristiana*. Further, remarks about the catechism in the 1636 statutes point to the employment of elementary musical recitation for its teaching, just as we shall see in Ansaldi's *dottrina*.[30]

---

[27] Eisenbichler, *The Boys*, p. 132; Østrem and Petersen, *Medieval Ritual and Early Modern Music*, pp. 143-144.

[28] CRS 162, 22 (*olim* 21), fols. 12^v, 14^v, and 15^r; Aranci, *Formazione religiosa*, pp. 350, 358, and 360.

[29] Polizzotto, *Children of the Promise*, pp. 77-96 and 208-224; Eisenbichler, *The Boys*, pp. 198-234, esp. pp. 198, 221, and 224; Newbegin, 'Politics in the *Sacre rappresentazioni*', p. 119.

[30] Eisenbichler, *The Boys*, p. 135.

In view of Ansaldi's position in Florence in the 1580s, his book must be considered as representative of the fundamental and prevailing materials and ideas about doctrinal teaching to boys. The small book contains the 'doctrine' mainly in the form of an account of basic Christian beliefs and claims, given by way of a dialogue between a teacher and a student, *La Dottrina Per Dialogo, & per Canto, ò per salmeggiare* ('The doctrine through dialogue and to be sung or chanted in the manner of psalms'). This is anticipated by an *Introduttione alla dottrina* consisting primarily of a few basic texts, the *Pater noster*, the *Ave Maria*, the *Credo in Deum Patrem omnipotentem* (the Apostles' Creed), and the *Confiteor*, all of which are given in Latin.[31] First, however, the book presents several didactic introductions about the purpose of the teaching of the doctrine and the methods to be used in this teaching as well as a section citing grants of indulgence by Pope Pius V (1566-1572) and Pope Gregory XIII (1572-1585) for the teaching or learning of Christian doctrine. After the sections containing the doctrine, the book presents sections containing the order for the Vespers of the Virgin Mary, the Litanies of the Virgin Mary, and Litanies of Saints; these sections again are all in Latin. There follow two sections of Italian *laude*: *Laude Da cantarsi* ('*Laude* to be sung') and *Lodi Da Cantarsi per i fanciulli della Dottrina Cristiana* ('Praises to be sung by the children for the Christian doctrine'). There follows, finally, a section on Christian manners.[32]

What is particularly interesting in this context is that the dialogue concerning the *dottrina* is meant to be sung or chanted; there are, however, no melodies or indications of how to sing it. As previously mentioned, Ansaldi's *Dottrina cristiana* is based to a large extent on previous catechetical publications, primarily the work of the Jesuit Giacomo, or Diego, Ledesma (1524-1575), who is mentioned in the letter of dedication to the archbishop as well as in one of the introductory sections. Under the Latin headline *Quasi modo geniti infantes lac concupiscite* ('Like newborn infants, long for the milk'), doubtless refering to 1 Peter 2.2, *sicut modo geniti infantes rationale sine dolo lac concupiscite ut in eo crescatis in salutem*

---

[31] Note that the Apostles' Creed seems to have been given in Latin also in the printed sheet at the confraternity of the Archangel Raphael in 1582; see n. 26 above.

[32] The book has been consulted at the Biblioteca Nazionale, Florence, at shelf mark Misc. 10.2 (in the Magliabechiano collection): I. Ansaldi, *Dottrina cristiana. Nuovamente Ristampata, & publicata per ordine dell'Illustriss. & Reverendiss. Cardinal di Firenze. Da insegnarsi, & esercitarsi dalli Curati, & Guardiani delle Compagnie de' Fanciulli della suo Diocesi per publica utilità.* (Florence, 1585). Excerpts from some of the introductions are reprinted in Aranci, *Formazione religiosa*, appendix I, nos. 7-8, pp. 363-367. See also Eisenbichler, *The Boys*, pp. 133-134; Polizotto, *Children of the Promise*, pp. 230-231.

('Like newborn infants, long for the pure, spiritual milk, so that by it you may grow into salvation') − probably by way of the beginning of the text for the Mass Introit on the first Sunday after Easter, *Quasimodo geniti infantes, alleluia: rationabiles sine dolo, lac concupiscite*[33] − Ansaldi refers to the publication of his book as reprinting Ledesma's *Dottrina* so that the doctrine can be sung:

> (...) per poterla cantare, ò salmeggiare à Cori, ò solo con certe Laudi spirituali secondo l'opportunità. Perche questo s'è fatto per più ragioni.[34]

> (…) so that it can be sung or chanted jointly or solo in conjunction with certain spiritual *laude* according to the occasion. This has been done for several reasons.

In the words of John O'Malley, Ledesma 'was another great architect of the educational program for the Jesuit schools'. He was influenced by Petrus Canisius (1521-1597) and published a *Dottrina christiana* with instructions for doctrinal teaching in 1573; this was reprinted several times.[35] Towards the end of his *Quasi modo* section, Ansaldi refers to two *Doctrines* by Ledesma: the *Dottrina piccola*, the 'small doctrine' and the *Dottrina grande*, the 'big doctrine'. For Ansaldi, they correspond to spring and autumn, the first for small children, the second for the older and more mature. What is presented in Ansaldi's 1585 edition is the 'spring'. Although he announced it, no edition by Ansaldi of the big doctrine is known.[36]

The idea of singing or chanting the doctrinal statements of the catechisms goes back to Jesuit catechetical practices in the 1550s. Such a practice of teaching Christian doctrine in song was confirmed at the First General Congregation of the order.[37] It is further corroborated by a document, *Avvisi per li nostri prencipalmente: del modo de insegnare la dottrina*

---

[33] M. Sodi, and A. M. Triacca, eds, *Missale Romanum: editio princeps (1570), edizione anastatica, introduzione e appendice* (The Vatican, 1998), p. 364.

[34] Ansaldi, *Dottrina cristiana*, p. 12. Also in Aranci, *Formazione religiosa*, p. 366. Aranci reprints the letter of dedication as well as the *Quasi modo* section *(idem,* pp. 363-367).

[35] O'Malley, *The First Jesuits*, p. 124. Concerning Ledesma's methods, see Østrem and Petersen, *Medieval Ritual and Early Modern Music*, pp. 57-65. See, further, Aranci's discussion of the close relation between Ansaldi's volume and Ledesma's two *Dottrine*, to which Ansaldi makes explicit reference in his dedication to the Archbishop of Florence, Cardinal Alessandro de' Medici (Aranci, *Formazione religiosa*, pp. 103-106).

[36] Ansaldi, *Dottrina cristiana*, pp. 15-16; Aranci, *Formazione religiosa*, pp. 366-367, see also p. 106.

[37] O'Malley, *The First Jesuits*, pp. 121-122.

christiana alli nostri scolari et al popolo, 'Notices Mainly for our Members: On the Manner of Teaching Christian Doctrine to our Students and to the People', contained in a small volume, probably authored by Giacomo Ledesma between 1560 and 1565, which is kept in the *Archivio generale della Compagnia di Gesù*. In chapter 3 (*Del principio et modo di incominciare ad insegnar la Dottrina Christiana*, 'On the Principle and Manner of Beginning to Teach the Christian Doctrine'), it is clearly stated that the doctrine is sung as a matter of course.[38] Concerning the first lesson, we read – among other points – that it must be explained why the doctrine is taught by song:

> (...) cioè perché li putti così più facilmente imparano, et che quelli che non sanno parlare et quelli che non sanno leggere, et li rozzi d'ingegno, rustici, donne, etc. et perché più si conferma la memoria et perché in luogo di canzoni brutte che si sogliono cantare, si cantino cose sante e buone, et vi habbiamo essempio nella primitiva chiesa che cantavano hinni matutini et vespertini, et per lodare Iddio in ogni modo, et anche per queste et simili altre cause hoggi dì canta la chiesa le cose sacre.[39]

> (...) this is because the boys can more easily learn it, and because those who are not able to speak and those who are not able to read and the untalented, the peasants, women, etc., can more readily memorise it, and because instead of bad songs which they used to sing, they will sing something holy and good; and there is the example of the early Church where hymns were sung in the morning and the evening and to praise God in all ways, and for these and other similar reasons also today the Church sings the holy matters.[40]

These are fundamentally the same reasons given in Ansaldi's *Quasi modo* section, formulated in a slightly different way and divided into ten, not always consistently disjunct, points:

1. The doctrine is more easily learned and remembered.
2. Children and youths are happier to learn.
3. Those who can hardly speak or read can learn through singing.
4. It is less time-consuming since all sing at the same time and willingly.
5. It helps to avoid wicked songs (*cattivi canti*).
6. Those who hear the singing without attending the teaching will learn it.

---

[38] The text is introduced and reprinted in Aranci, *Formazione religiosa*, pp. 343-349 (p. 346).
[39] Aranci, *Formazione religiosa*, pp. 346-347.
[40] My translation.

7. Through the songs, they learn to sing doctrine and praise God.
8. It belongs to the practice of the Catholic Church. Ansaldi refers to the night office, the divine office, and the use of hymns, psalms, and canticles. In particular, there is mention of the praises of the three 'boys' (*putti*) in the furnace (Daniel 3) teaching the world a longing for singing, blessing, and praising God.
9. The singing of doctrine imitates the Angels in Heaven who continuously sing 'Holy Holy' to God. Reference is made to the entrance of Jesus into Jerusalem, to King David, and to Saint Paul's exhortations to sing hymns.
10. Practices in Florence show the impact of the singing of the boys, girls, women, etc., who not only stay at home to sing *laude* but publicly perform the spiritual songs (*le Laudi spirituali*), going around like choirs of angels, 'et con queste dolcezze si levano da infinite cattive usanze mundane' ('and with these sweet practices removing infinite amounts of bad worldly practices').[41]

It is obvious that Ansaldi does not present new arguments. He relies on authority and tradition in a way that may be compared to the commonplace-books but also shows clear differences. There is no strictly formalised way of arranging quotations from earlier authorities. Whereas quotations or commonplaces in commonplace-books were gathered under headings,[42] Ansaldi simply calls upon the authority of traditional catechisms written by well-known theologians by mentioning their works as standing behind his own. He points to 'le Dottrine del Ledesma, et la Dottrina Fiorentina, quella di Bologna, et altre Dottrine, et Catechismi fatti da famosissimi Padri Teologi Cattolici' ('the Doctrines of Ledesma, the Florentine Doctrine, the one from Bologna, and other Doctrines and Catechisms written by famous Catholic Theologian Fathers').[43] The references are of a general nature, normally not given as quotations; as ultimate authorities, Ansaldi, unsurprisingly, refers to biblical statements and to the practices of the Church. Some of the biblical references, especially concerning the imitation of the song of the angels and the notion of *dolcezza* ('sweetness') as a characteristic for spiritual song, have roots in liturgical commentary at least as far back as Carolingian times.[44] Although there is no consistent systematic organiza-

---

[41] Ansaldi, *Dottrina cristiana*, pp. 10-15; Aranci, *Formazione religiosa*, p. 366. See further the general contextualization in Østrem and Petersen, *Medieval Ritual and Early Modern Music*, pp. 43-86, esp. pp. 63-69.

[42] Moss, *Printed Commonplace-Books*, Preface, p. v.

[43] Ansaldi, *Dottrina cristiana*, p. 16; Aranci, *Formazione religiosa*, p. 367.

[44] See A. Ekenberg, *Cur cantatur: die Funktionen des liturgischen Gesanges nach den Autoren der Karolingerzeit* (Stockholm, 1987), e.g. pp. 42-46, 51, and 171-178; also N. H. Petersen, 'Carolingian Music, Ritual, and Theology', in: N. H. Petersen,

tion of *loci*, there is standardisation involved. The above cited arguments for using song as a means for teaching the doctrine are used again and again in printed books for the doctrine and in prefaces for printed collections of *laude* in very similar formulations. As already pointed out, in the end the fundamental authorities are always the same: the Church and its practices, and the Fathers, and then in practice also previous books for teaching the doctrine.[45]

After the introductory explanatory texts and the *Introduttione alla dottrina*, the basic Latin doctrinal texts, the dialogical doctrine begins in the following manner:

> INCOMINCIA LA DOTTRINA Per Dialogo, & per Canto, ò per salmeggiare.
> M.   Cominciamo nel nome del Sig. Iddio.
>   Sere voi Cristiano?
> D.   Sono per gratia del N Sig. Giesù Cristo.
> M.   Che cosa è Cristiano?
> D.   Il Cristian'e per gratia: Del nostro Signor Giesù Cristo.
>   Et è suo discepolo: E vero imitatore: Ch'essendo battezzato: Crede, e fa profession della sua legge.
> M.   Che intendete voi che sia Cristo?
> D.   E vero Dio, & vero Huomo.[46]

> HERE BEGINS THE DOCTRINE in Dialogue and in Song, or Chanted like Psalms.
> Teacher: Let us begin with the name of the Lord God.
>   Are you a Christian?
> Student: I am by the grace of our Lord Jesus Christ.
> Teacher: What does it mean to be a Christian?
> Student: One can only be a Christian by the grace of our Lord Jesus Christ.
>   A Christian is his disciple. Indeed, his imitator. This is what it means to be baptised: Believe, and profess his law.
> Teacher: What do you think of Christ?
> Student: He is true God and true Man.

M. B. Bruun, J. Llewellyn, and E. Østrem, eds, *The Appearances of Medieval Rituals: The Play of Construction and Modification* (Turnhout, 2004), pp. 13-31 (pp. 20-21).

[45] A list very similar to the one cited here from Ansaldi's book is quoted (and translated) from a preface to a *lauda* collection intended for the teaching of the doctrine (Milan 1576) in Østrem and Petersen, *Medieval Ritual and Early Modern Music*, pp. 43-44.

[46] Ansaldi, *Dottrina cristiana*, p. 25.

From the rubric *Per Dialogo, & per Canto, ò per salmeggiare*, 'in dialogue and in song, or chanted in the manner of psalms', it seems likely that this must have been carried out in a recitativic formulaic chanting as in the psalmody of the divine office. This seems to be corroborated by the consistent claims in the Jesuit tradition that the sung doctrine made it easy for non-educated children (and/or women) to carry it out in praxis and that this actually 'worked'.

A collection of *laude* from the early seventeenth century, printed in Naples, contains, in a final appendix, two pages of short and simple musical formulae under the heading *Compendio delle cose più necessarie della Dottrina Christiana* ('Compendium of things necessary for the Christian Doctrine').[47] The compendium lists basic texts for doctrine, among them the Apostles' Creed, the Pater noster, the Ten Commandments, and further texts of the kind found in the catechetical writings of the fifteenth and sixteenth centuries. The texts listed for the use of *dottrina christiana* are all given in Italian, the Creed and the Pater noster in both Latin and Italian. All the texts are divided up into short lines, each of them carrying a number which refers to one of the melodic formulae printed on the last two pages of the book. In this way, it becomes possible to piece together the melodies for all the various texts. Needless to say, the melodies constructed in such a way are very simple. There is no indication, in the Naples book, of melodies for a doctrine in dialogue. It does, however, give a hint of how one could arrange simple settings of almost any text by way of a formulaic melodic system. It appears as a fairly crude device, but one that has much in common with the way modern musicologists have tried to understand at least certain early settings of liturgical music as formulaic in its structure.[48]

The poems and musical settings for the *laude* constitute a very different area from the traditional materials of doctrine. As mentioned, the *lauda* became a part of the traditions of the Church during the later Middle Ages by way of the religious revivals of the thirteenth century and the confraternities which seem to have grown out of these popular movements.[49] What is

---

[47] T. Longo, ed., *Lodi et Canzonette spirituali* (Naples, 1608), the last part of the book, pp. 14-24 (the last pages lack pagination). For a discussion and exemplification of this compendium, see Østrem and Petersen, *Medieval Ritual and Early Modern Music*, pp. 61-65. In this context, it is important to note that the title page contains the emblem of the Society of Jesus.

[48] L. Treitler, *With Voice and Pen* (Oxford, 2003), esp. pp. 186-201.

[49] See above n. 6. I further refer to B. Wilson, *Music and Merchants: The Laudesi Companies of Republican Florence* (Oxford, 1992) and M. Dürrer, *Altitalienische Laudenmelodien: das einstimmige Repertoire der Handschriften Cortona und Florenz*, 2 vols. (Kassel, 1996).

mainly important to note is that, by the fifteenth century, the *lauda* had become a devotional art form to which high ranking poets of the day contributed. The *lauda* had its most important place in confraternity devotions but, as mentioned earlier, the involvement of confraternities – and among these prominently the youth confraternities – in public rituals and performances, notably the *sacre rappresentazioni*, in the city meant that the *lauda* was also heard outside the more or less secluded rituals of the confraternities.

One of the most commonly sung *laude* of the fifteenth century was the *Giesù, Giesù, Giesù, ognun chiami Giesù* by the Florentine poet Feo Belcari (1410-1484). It is found in many collections of *laude*, also those pertaining to *dottrina christiana* and included among the *lodi* for the children in Ansaldi's volume.[50] The commonly employed melody in *lauda* collections, such as, for instance, the influential collection of Serafino Razzi from 1563, is adapted from a carnival song from the 1470s, as Patrick Macey has argued.[51] Ansaldi's book, unfortunately, gives no melodic information at any point, but the books for teaching doctrine generally give one same musical setting, different from Razzi's.[52] Here is the text of the first stanza:

Giesù, Giesù, Giesù,
Ognun chiami Giesù.
Chiamate questo nome
col core e colla mente,
E sentirete come,
Egli è dolce e clemente,
Chi 'l chiama fedelmente,
Sente nel cor Giesù.[53]

Jesus, Jesus, Jesus,
let everyone cry out Jesus.
Call this name
with heart and mind,

---

[50] Ansaldi, *Dottrina cristiana*, pp. 84-86, in which seven stanzas are printed.

[51] P. Macey, *Bonfire Songs: Savonarola's Musical Legacy* (Oxford, 1998), pp. 44-47. See also n. 52 below.

[52] See Østrem and Petersen, *Medieval Ritual and Early Modern Music*, pp. 114-115; however, the musical setting (pertaining to *dottrina* books) given in figure 16 (p. 114) is not from Ansaldi's *Dottrina cristiana* as indicated in the caption and in footn. 40 (p. 115). Mistakenly, Ansaldi's work was indicated here instead of the correct reference: *Lodi devote per uso della Dottrina Christiana* (Genoa, 1589), pp. 2-3, cf. n. 39 on p. 113.

[53] Translation quoted from Macey, *Bonfire Songs*, p. 47. The abovementioned musical setting found in Razzi's collection is transcribed on p. 45.

and experience how
it is sweet and merciful;
whoever calls it faithfully,
feels Jesus in his heart.

Commonplace imagery stands out in this text: heart and mind, sweet and merciful, as well as, of course, the use of the name of Jesus itself as a meaningful exclamation in its own right; the latter explained by reference to the medieval and Catholic devotion to the Holy Name of Jesus which can be traced back to the Council of Lyons in 1274 and was propagated by confraternities also in Florence.[54] Belcari was the most important poet of *laude* in fifteenth-century Florence and belonged to the Company of San Zanobi.[55]

The single stanza given here may stand as representative of the literary *lauda* style at the time which remained dominant also in the sixteenth century. The late medieval or Renaissance tradition of devotional *laude* includes more or less similar texts by literary figures of the fifteenth century who were generally perceived as radically different: the statesman, businessman, and poet Lorenzo the Magnificent (1449-1492) and the controversial religious reformer Girolamo Savonarola (1452-1498). The poems of the songs of this repertory relate not only to traditional theological concepts but also to established patterns of emotional expressions which, in their particular religious contexts, were doubtless semantically meaningful and not considered as mere clichés. This follows from our knowledge of the individual social contexts in which the *laude* were sung: devotional confraternity rituals (offices and processions) and devotional doctrinal teaching in addition to private devotions. In all such contexts, the *laude* were used as a medium for active religious participation of laymen with an emphasis on their own responsibility for their salvation. There is a continuity to be seen here with the revivals of the thirteenth century which brought about the *lauda* singing in the first place.[56]

Girolamo Savonarola's predilection for popular *lauda* singing and his occasional denunciations of polyphonic 'art song' in sermons from the time of his – unofficial – rule in Florence (c.1494-1498) form at least part of the background for the general sixteenth-century decline in the professional polyphonic confraternity *lauda* traditions, which may seem connected to the

---

[54] See the article 'Society of the Holy Name' in The Catholic Encyclopedia Online, <http://www.catholic.org/encyclopedia/>, last accessed October 25, 2008.
[55] Wilson, *Music and Merchants*, p. 176.
[56] See Wilson, *Music and Merchants*, pp. 183-192; Østrem and Petersen, *Medieval Ritual and Early Modern Music*, pp. 15-42 (esp. pp. 40-42) and 119-63 (esp. pp. 119-21).

general Florentine crisis in the early decades of the century.[57] Patrick Macey
has shown how the simple, monophonic or homophonic, Savonarolan *lauda*
tradition became dominant in the sixteenth century in basic accordance with
prevalent views on music in the Catholic reform movement. The Florentine
Dominican friar, and biographer of Savonarola, Serafino Razzi (1531-1611)
published his first collection of *laude*, the *Libro primo delle laudi spirituali*
in 1563. In the same year, Giovanni Animuccia (1500-1571) published his
first collection of *laude* in Rome. The continuity between Razzi's volume
and the Roman *lauda* tradition of the Oratorians of Filippo Neri (1515-
1595), in which Giovanni Animuccia was strongly involved as their first
maestro di cappella (from the 1550s until his death), has been underlined in
recent scholarship.[58]

In the records of the *Compagnia dell'Arcangelo Raffaello* there is a
scarceness of indications concerning the singing of *laude*. This can be explained in a number of ways and does not necessarily mean that *lauda* singing was a rare event. On the contrary, it seems likely that certain practices
were so common as only rarely to have led to any specific mention in the
records. This is the impression one gets from some of the preserved information about the activities of the confraternity. From 1563 to 1785 (when
three out of the four oldest youth confraternities, including the Archangel
Raphael, were closed), the *ricordi* of the Archangel Raphael confraternity
are preserved for most years. These records are kept in the State Archives of
Florence together with the preserved statutes of the company. However, due
to the flood in Florence in 1557, the earliest extant statutes from 1468 are so
damaged by water as to be almost completely illegible. A readable and even
certified copy of the 1468 statutes from 1560 has, however, been preserved.
As mentioned earlier, completely revised statutes were made in 1636; these
are also extant.[59]

---

[57] Concerning Savonarola and music, the most important recent contribution is
Macey, *Bonfire Songs*. For the early sixteenth-century decline, see Wilson, *Music
and Merchants*, pp. 87-88, 126-127, and 220-221; Barr, *The Monophonic Lauda*,
p. 30. For a discussion of the so-called 'crisis' theory, see N. Eckstein, 'The Religious Confraternities of High Renaissance Florence: Crisis or Continuity', in: F. W.
Kent and C. Zika, eds, *Rituals, Images, and Words: Varieties of Cultural Expression
in Late Medieval and Early Modern Europe* (Turnhout, 2005), pp. 9-32.

[58] H. E. Smither, *A History of the Oratorio*, I (Chapel Hill, 1977), pp. 37-57; Macey,
Bonfire Songs, pp. 135-149; I. Fenlon, *Music and Culture in Late Renaissance Italy*
(Oxford, 2002), chapt. 3, pp. 44-66; Østrem and Petersen, *Medieval Ritual and
Early Modern Music*, pp. 87-112.

[59] Archivio di Stato, Florence: The statutes (of 1468, 1560, and 1636) are found under the shelfmark Capitoli delle CRS 882, 752, and 627. See also notes 17 and 19
above.

Devotional singing played an important role in the life of the confraternity from its beginning. As underlined by Eisenbichler, the 1468 statutes, as known via the 1560 copy, refer primarily to the singing of Latin hymns and canticles (the *Te Deum*, the *Magnificat*, and so forth), whereas the singing of *laude* is not strongly emphasised. The reason for this may be, as Eisenbichler suggests, that the educational purpose of a youth confraternity entailed a stronger emphasis on Latin singing.[60] This would accord well with the prevalence of Latin materials in the teaching of the doctrine as treated above.[61]

However, in chapter eight of the 1560 statutes, identical to those of 1468, describing the meetings of the confraternity, the *tornata*, the singing of *laude* as a standard practice, is mentioned before the beginning of the service: one of the youths is supposed to read from the Bible on the guardian father's command or to sing a *lauda* or a psalm.[62] The following chapter, giving the general order of the service, also states that *laude*, among other devotional items, are sung when 'it pleases the guardian father'.[63]

In the 1636 statutes, by contrast, the singing of *laude* is not mentioned at all. Instead, the singing of psalms is repeatedly mentioned as well as other references to the traditional Latin liturgy, such as the Office of the Dead and the celebration of the Eucharist. This may well reflect the implementation of attitudes from the Catholic reform movement, but it does not follow that *laude* were not performed.[64]

During the sixteenth century, music and musical education seem to have become increasingly important for the confraternity. Generally, performances of music and drama seem to have been essential to at least the oldest youth confraternities in Florence. This comes to the fore in remarkable ways, not the least in the records of the Archangel Raphael confraternity. Around 1600, leading Florentine intellectuals and musicians were members of, or closely associated with, the confraternity and contributed to its sometimes lavishly produced ceremonies, which, at times, also featured productions of sacred representations. Musico-dramatic performances, as it seems in the new *stilo rappresentativo* developed in the Florentine academies of the late sixteenth century under the sponsorships of Giovanni Bardi and Jacopo Corsi, were carried out in the confraternity at least since 1585, that is thirteen years before Jacopo Peri's and Ottavio Rinuccini's

---

[60] See Eisenbichler, *The Boys*, pp. 236-238.
[61] See n. 31 above.
[62] Capitoli delle CRS 752, fol. 8^r. See also Eisenbichler, *The Boys*, p. 139.
[63] CRS 752, fol. 8^v.
[64] Capitoli delle CRS 627, esp. xxv-xxviii. See Eisenbichler, *The Boys*, pp. 141-143, cf. pp. 108 and 238.

Dafne, probably performed in Florence in 1598 and traditionally claimed as 'the first opera'.[65]

Also, as a part of the so-called *tornata,* the traditional devotional meetings in the Raffaello confraternity, artful music appears often and is recognised as such with obvious joy and pride by the scribes of the *ricordi.* This has been recognised by scholars for some time. However, Eyolf Østrem and I have recently discussed what can be described as the aesthetics of religious rituals in the Arcangelo Raffaello confraternity, as it comes to the fore through entries in the *ricordi* of the company.[66] Certain changes around 1600 seem to make such 'religious aesthetics' more pronounced after c.1600, but the records also show the importance of artful music already in the 1580s as an integral part of the rituals. By the late sixteenth century, to be a member of the Arcangelo Raffaello also meant being part of an intellectual and cultural elite. Its members included an impressive range of artists in all arts.[67] The role of artistry in the *ricordi* of the confraternity of the Archangel Raphael shows that this confraternity cannot readily be seen as covered by the Savonarolan legacy. The complaints of Serafino Razzi in his second published collection of *laude* (with annotations), the *Santuario di laudi* from 1609, about the lack of devotion of the 'moderni' could well have been directed against practices such as those reflected in the *ricordi* of the Archangel Raphael confraternity (Razzi refers to himself in the third person):

---

[65] Eisenbichler, *The Boys,* esp. pp. 235-236; J. W. Hill, 'Oratory Music in Florence, I: Recitar Cantando, 1583-1655', *Acta Musicologica* 51 (1979), pp. 108-136, esp. pp. 110-112; E. Strainchamps, 'Music in a Florentine Confraternity: The Memorial Madrigals for Jacopo Corsi in the Company of the Archangel Raphael', in: K. Eisenbichler, ed, *Crossing the Boundaries: Christian Piety and the Arts in Italian Medieval and Renaissance Confraternities* (Kalamazoo, MI, 1991), pp. 161-178; N. H. Petersen, 'Intermedial Strategy and Spirituality in the Emerging Opera: Gagliano's *Dafne* and Confraternity Devotion', in: E. Hedling and U.-B. Lagerroth, eds, *Cultural Functions of Intermedial Exploration* (Amsterdam, 2002), pp. 75-86; Østrem and Petersen, 'The Singing of Laude', I, p. 279. For a general (traditional) history of the beginnings of opera, see R. Donington, *The Rise of Opera* (London, 1981) and F. W. Sternfeld, *The Birth of Opera* (Oxford, 1993). For a presentation of the newfound knowledge as well as a discussion of the implications, see Østrem and Petersen, *Medieval Ritual and Early Modern Music,* pp. 201-256.

[66] Østrem and Petersen, 'The Singing of *Laude*', I-II, esp. I, pp. 287-297. See also Østrem and Petersen, *Medieval Ritual and Early Modern Music,* pp. 130-36; Eisenbichler, *The Boys,* pp. 198-269, chapts. 16-19 on theatre, music, and art in the confraternity; Hill, 'Oratory Music in Florence, I'.

[67] Eisenbichler, *The Boys,* p. 123.

Diremo ancora, come il Padre Fra Serafino Razzi pregato questo anno 1603 ha composto tre hinni latini, con tutto l'altro officio di questa serva di Dio per sua divozione, e per sodisfare alla pia mente di chi appresso di lui ne ha fatto instanza, e per recitarlo privatamente che ben sappiamo i moderni oggi per lo piu desiderare cose squisitissime, & in cui sia piu elevazione, che divozione, e che piu habbiano di scolorosità, e difficultà a intendersi, che di semplicità christiana, e di pietà popolare.[68]

We will also recount how the Father Fra Serafino Razzi, upon request in the year 1603, composed three Latin hymns with all the rest of the office for this servant of God [i.e. Margarita da Città di Castello], for her devotion and to satisfy the pious mind of him who had requested it, and to be recited in private; for we know well that the moderns today mostly desire the most exquisite things, where there is more elevation than devotion; which are colourless and difficult to understand, and lack Christian simplicity and popular piety.

The sudden and unprecedented frequency with which what must have been simple traditional monophonic *laude* are mentioned in the *ricordi* during the summer of 1632 in connection with the teaching of Christian doctrine by Lorenzo Vanni in the confraternity deserves a brief comment in this context.[69] These records may describe a particularly important example of something that, in more or less similar ways, had gone on at least since the early or mid-1580s (as discussed previously). The descriptions of the teaching in these records accord well with the impressions of the doctrinal teaching in Ansaldi's book and the Jesuit traditions as discussed above. In view of the events recorded in 1582 and 1585 – and the reference in the 1636 statutes to the *dottrina* book of the confraternity from 1584 – it seems unlikely that teaching sessions in accordance with such descriptions should not have occurred frequently in the later 1580s and 1590s.

On the other hand, the doctrinal event on Pentecost Sunday, 1582 seems to show an altogether different approach to such teaching, although it is in complete agreement with the demands of the ecclesiastical authorities concerning the basic contents.[70] This approach was clearly very much in

---

[68] Razzi, *Santuario di laudi* (Florence, 1609), p. 224. See Østrem and Petersen, 'The Singing', II, p. 171, from where the translation is taken. See also Østrem and Petersen, *Medieval Ritual and Early Modern Music*, p. 76.

[69] CRS 162, 24 (*olim* 23), fol. 41[r] (Sunday May 23), fol. 41[v] (Sunday May 30), fol. 42[r] (Sundays June 13 and 20), fol. 42[v] (Sundays June 27 and July 4), and fol. 43[r] (Sunday July 11). See the general discussion of Vanni's teaching activities in the confraternity in Eisenbichler, *The Boys*, pp. 134-136, and a fuller discussion of the entries in Østrem and Petersen, *Medieval Ritual and Early Modern Music*, 146-48.

[70] See above, n. 21-26.

line with the confraternity's traditional emphasis on drama, artful music, and other artistry. It seems that the confraternity continued to see its devotional uses of artful music and drama as its most important activities; one may speculate that the commonplaces of *dottrina cristiana* in the newly demanded forms may have been understood to be necessary but less rewarding, less richly formulated, in other words closer to religious cliché. By 1632, however, since doctrinal instruction had for the most part been taken over by the *scuole della dottrina cristiana*, such activities may have been seen in a new light again.

CHOREOGRAPHY AS COMMONPLACE

Barbara Ravelhofer[1]

> (...) mas gloriosa es
> La destreza de los pies
> Que la fuerça de las manos.
> (Francisco Navarro, 1642)[2]

In the early modern period, the commonplace was basically destined for literary rather than non-verbal communication, as Ann Moss reminds us in the
present collection; it belonged to the elite domain of the grammar class,
where boys learnt to arrange knowledge by writing. For Moss, the commonplace book had a particular influence on developing minds; it 'tended to
foster the assumption that all knowledge could be plotted onto a preconceived moral grid'.[3] While it is important to remember this more rigorous
initial definition of the commonplace, we should ask whether more flexible
approaches and uses became current in the course of the sixteenth century.
In mid-sixteenth-century England, for instance, a 'commonplace' also denoted a common topic, a statement taken for granted, a stock theme, or even
a platitude.[4] If the commonplace can be universalised, embracing all knowledge, why should it be restricted to the verbal, especially given the spatial
semantics of the term itself?

Locus communis, *lieu commun*, *Gemeinplatz*, *topos*: since Antiquity,
European thought has connected the abstract notion of 'something shared by
many' with the notion of space. The visual arts offer a fertile ground for
commonplaces: we could think of Serlian stage design, which provided visual templates for centuries of theatre performance to come; or we might
admire the golden section, instantly understood to signify beauty, in Renaissance book design, Vesalian anatomy, and Da Vinci's studies. Rhetoric
rests on spatial logic (*dispositio*) to order language. The common*place* –

---

[1] I would like to thank Richard Sugg for his comments on this essay.
[2] 'More glorious than the force of hand is the dexterity of the foot.' Don Francisco
Navarro, dedicatory poem, in Juan Esquivel Navarro, *Discursos sobre el arte del
dançado* (Sevilla, 1642; facs. edn Valencia, *s.d.*), no pag. I would like to thank
Richard Sugg for his comments on this essay.
[3] A. Moss, chapter in this volume, pp. 1-17 (p. 3).
[4] *The Oxford English Dictionary*, 2nd edn, 'commonplace', section 5, documented
since 1560; <http://dictionary.oed.com>, last accessed February 21, 2007.

whether visual or textual – is the focal point where all meaning converges, and, from this moral high ground, it aspires to quintessential, authoritative direction. Despite its name, suggestive of stasis, the commonplace is therefore strangely mobile and active. In light of this, it seems worthwhile to investigate a discipline which is, in its expressivity, often compared to language, and which involves both location and direction: dance.

In early modern Europe, dance was considered an important social accomplishment, practised with solicitous energy and passionately debated by both apologists and detractors. In the opinion of enthusiasts, the splendour of dance even defied worldly power: 'more glorious than the force of hand is the dexterity of the foot', proclaimed Francisco Navarro in a book celebrating the achievements of court dancers under the reign of Philip IV of Spain. Many such comments of French, English, German, Spanish, and Italian provenance have survived, which in itself attests to the eminent role of dancing between the fifteenth and seventeenth century. Literature on the subject espoused a number of commonplace notions, of which I will investigate a few here: dance as a socialising force which turned practitioners into better people; the dangers of speed and the benefits of moderate movement; and, finally, dance-as-silent-language. First I will sketch with a few broad brushstrokes an impression of cross-European attitudes towards dancing, with particular attention to dancing as an educational discipline. Then I will move on to three influential Italian professionals. Domenico da Piacenza was a fifteenth-century choreographer active in Ferrara and Milan; his compositions circulated in manuscript and attracted a number of followers in Northern Italy.[5] Fabritio Caroso, a famous sixteenth-century dancing master from Sermoneta (a town south of Rome), developed many practical and theoretical insights in the course of his long career, which led to sumptuous illustrated volumes greatly admired by his peers. Bernardino Stefonio, a Jesuit scholar and playwright, composed ground-breaking dance theatre in Rome in the 1590s and early 1600s. Stefonio's ideas spawned a critical debate well beyond his Roman College, and his works saw multiple editions in several countries. Domenico, Caroso, and Stefonio enjoyed an excellent reputation in their time. Their creative engagement with kinetic commonplaces will be the topic of the latter part of this essay.

---

[5] On Domenico's influence upon later choreographers see G. Ebreo, *De pratica seu arte tripudii*, ed. B. Sparti (Oxford, 1993); A. W. Smith, ed., *Fifteenth-Century Dance and Music: Twelve Transcribed Italian Treatises and Collections in the Tradition of Domenico da Piacenza*, 2 vols. (Stuyvesant, 1995).

Dance as a socialising force

Learning to dance may be a solitary exercise for one's own pleasure, but often the art involves interaction with one or several partners. Therefore a dance lesson inculcates social conditioning: it promotes an awareness of one's audience, consideration of partners, and a proper carriage and deportment according to the expectations of everybody present. Dancers learn about their place not only in the dance space but also within the wider community. For this reason, classical thought placed great emphasis on movement, its role in education, and its place in the social fabric. Plato defined education as a 'disciplined state of pleasures and pains' – a state of equilibrium between hardship and relaxation which might translate as a healthy balance between work and leisure within a community.[6] In this respect, dance was considered particularly helpful. In Plato's utopian Republic, music and gymnastics formed part of the ideal citizen's education, as they served both body and spirit, engendering a sense for and appreciation of harmony.[7] The training of the body culminated, ideally, in the goodness of the soul. Bodily exercise was believed to inculcate virtue, and thus, in Plato's vision, both boys and girls learned to dance under the direction of special masters.[8] But it had to be the right kind of dance: 'all postures and melodies connected with goodness of soul or body (...) are good, and those connected with badness universally the reverse'.[9] 'Good' dances were recognised as such by being orderly and having a beneficial social purpose. Of the orderly kind Plato recommended two particular genres: the martial pyrrhic dance, which prepared the performer for action on the battlefield, and *emmelia*, the dance of peace, which was said to engender a sense of well-being and equanimity. Other genres, however, were declared 'unfit for a citizen'; among these being burlesque and bacchanalian kinds, as they smacked of excess. Interestingly, these dances were deliberately attributed to slaves and 'hired aliens', as if Plato had sought to expurgate improper motion from the enfranchised community of his *polis*.[10] Aristotle held the firm opinion that gesture was indicative of one's character and betrayed

---

[6] *Laws*, II. 653c, in: *The Collected Dialogues of Plato Including the Letters*, ed. E. Hamilton and H. Cairns (Princeton, 1963).
[7] *The Republic*, III. 412a-b.
[8] *Laws*, VII. 791c, VII. 813b.
[9] *Laws*, II. 655b.
[10] *Laws*, VII. 815-816.

one's soul; possibly echoing Plato, he considered disorderly movements un-natural.[11]

Adopting deep-rooted notions going back to Classical Antiquity, early modern dance theory established a catalogue of commendable as well as undesirable kinds of posture and movement when it attempted to socialise the dancing body.[12] Choreographic patterns and dance rules therefore offer fertile ground for the investigation of the kinetic commonplace and its function as social control mechanism. In Western Europe, the earliest choreographies date back to the mid-fifteenth century and are of French, Burgundian, or Italian origin. Evidence for institutionalised dancing emerges for the first time in fifteenth-century Italy, where we find dance lessons as part of a comprehensive school curriculum in the cities of Mantua and Ferrara. As Jennifer Nevile shows, one of the most famous humanist schools in fifteenth-century Italy, Vittorino da Feltre's Mantuan establishment, offered instruction to its pupils by 'saltatores'.[13]

It was widely held that education should begin at a very young age, so as to form a still malleable individual. Dancing became integral to the didactic programme, since it balanced mental with physical exercise and lightened the learning process with a playful note. In *The Boke Named the Governour* (first published 1531), one of the earliest English educational treatises, the author, Sir Thomas Elyot, recommended sweetening moral lessons with pleasant diversions. Because 'the studie of vertue is tediouse for the more parte to them that do florisshe in yonge yeres', Elyot suggested dancing as a saving device, for here the virtue of prudence could be 'founden out and well perceyved' by dancers and their audience. Dancing, in Elyot's view, turned everybody into 'diligent beholders and markers'.[14] As *The Governour* demonstrates, the art provided a collective learning experience, for it involved not only performers but also bystanders – hence its

---

[11] Aristotle, *On the Heavens*, 307a3-5, *On the Soul*, 406a30-406b1, *Nicomachean Ethics*, 1128a12-13, in: *The Complete Works of Aristotle*, ed. J. Barnes, 2 vols. (Princeton, 1984), I, pp. 493, 647; II, p. 1780.

[12] See, for instance, G. Vigarello, 'The Upward Training of the Body from the Age of Chivalry to Courtly Civility', in: M. Feher, R. Naddaff, and N. Tazi, eds, *Fragments for a History of the Human Body: Part Two* (New York, 1989), pp. 148-199.

[13] J. Nevile, *The Eloquent Body: Dance and Humanist Culture in Fifteenth-Century Italy* (Bloomington, 2004), p. 20.

[14] Sir Thomas Elyot, *The Boke Named the Governour* (London, 1531), fol. 84ᵛ. On children performers, see also B. Ravelhofer, '"Virgin Wax" and "Hairy Men-Monsters": Unstable Movement Codes in the Stuart Masque', in: D. Bevington and P. Holbrook, eds, *The Politics of the Stuart Court Masque* (Cambridge, 1998), pp. 244-272.

attractiveness as a social tool, and the training of those 'in young years', evidenced across early modern Europe.

In Italian as much as English and German households of the better sort, children had hardly begun to walk when they were dispatched to dancing classes. From the age of four, little Lavinia Guasco was subjected to a strict regimen of dancing and singing, algebra and arithmetic, calligraphy, counterpoint theory, complicated board games, the practice of several musical instruments, and the perusal of relevant literature such as *Galateo* and *Il Cortegiano*. Tears flowed. As her father ruefully acknowledged, 'I was held to be the most importunate and perhaps the most tyrannical father that any daughter ever had, (...) admonishing, shouting, threatening, and at times beating you'. In the end, however, the pains paid off when Lavinia departed, only eleven years old, for Turin to serve the Duchess of Savoy.[15] Lavinia might be called a professional courtier, but even children who were not raised to make a living knew how to dance from an early age. Isabella d'Este performed to public acclaim when she was seven years old.[16] Children's ballets were an accepted art form in early modern Europe. In 1660s Nuremberg, for instance, the musician Jacob Lang orchestrated a spectacle with sixty boys and girls ranging in age from six to twelve, who performed as shepherds, knights and dwarves, hobby horses, and the four continents.[17] 'Give me a child until he is seven and I will give you the man', Saint Francis Xavier is alleged to have said, and, true to this principle, social and theatrical dancing became a staple of Jesuit instruction in the sixteenth and seventeenth centuries. As the 1586 *Ratio Studiorum* (which governed practice in Jesuit colleges) proposed, the performance of drama (which often involved ballet) could be used to kindle interest in scholarly subjects, and it even had an empathic effect:

> Our students and their parents become wonderfully enthusiastic, and at the same time become very much attached to our Society, when we train the boys

---

[15] Annibal Guasco, *Discourse to Lady Lavinia his Daughter*, ed. and transl. P. Osborn (Chicago, 2003), p. 51.

[16] *Fifteenth-Century Dance and Music*, ed. Smith, p. xxi; E. Southern, 'A Prima Ballerina of the Fifteenth Century', in: A. Dhu Shapiro and P. Benjamin, eds, *Music and Context: Essays for John M. Ward* (Cambridge, MA, 1985), pp. 183-197.

[17] J. M. L. [Jacob Lang?], *Kurtzer Entwurff eines anmuthigen Kinder-Ballets* (Nuremberg, 1668). An engraving illustrating this ballet survives in the Stadtbibliothek, Nuremberg, and is reproduced in H. Zirnbauer, *Musik in der alten Reichsstadt Nürnberg* (Nuremberg, *s.d.*), p. 61.

to show the results of their study, their acting ability, and their ready memory, on the stage.[18]

In England, dance was initially taught to young members of elite households on an individual basis. From the late sixteenth century, however, dancing became a curricular fixture for a wider constituency, notably at London's Inns of Court (although lessons were not given in-house but farmed out to dancing schools nearby, which, by all accounts, 'st[a]nke of sweat most abominably'[19]). An ambitious timetable of the Restoration period detailed how young gentlemen lawyers were to be profitably disciplined: 'From 9 to 11. Ad Arma. Carry on harmless acts of manhood, fencing, dancing etc.',[20] while observers pointed out that 'these Exercises of Dancing' were 'much conducing to the making of gentlemen more fit for their Books at other times'.[21] Throughout the sixteenth and seventeenth centuries, the students lived up to their reputation as excellent dancers in public shows. Some Inns of Court masques were presented before a very select audience, including royalty; such performances often amounted to a broadly affirmative celebration of monarchic politics, the analogy between beautiful, well-timed movement and well-behaved subject being obvious.[22] One of the most famous productions, James Shirley's *The Triumph of Peace* (1634), addressed the lawyers as 'the Ornament of our Nation' and highlighted their mandate to present their 'duties to their royall Maiesties, (...) to celebrate, by this humble tender of Your hearts, and services, the happinesse of our Kingdome, so blest in the present governement'.[23] Masques also ex-

---

[18] Cited from W. H. McCabe, *An Introduction to the Jesuit Theater*, ed. L. Oldani (St Louis, 1983), p. 13.

[19] Verdict of Sir Thomas Overbury (d. 1613), who entered Middle Temple in 1598. Cited from M. Vale, *The Gentleman's Recreations: Accomplishments and Pastimes of the English Gentleman 1580-1630* (Cambridge, 1977), p. 89.

[20] Edward Waterhous's scheme from 1663 but based on long practice at Gray's Inn. Cited from W. R. Prest, *The Inns of Court under Elizabeth I and the Early Stuarts, 1590-1640* (London, 1972), pp. 139-140.

[21] William Dugdale's view, in J. P. Cunningham, *Dancing in the Inns of Court* (London, 1965), p. 4.

[22] Masques should, however, not simply be read as blunt propaganda instruments but events that might on occasion offer tactful criticism of political orthodoxies. See K. Sharpe, *Criticism and Compliment: The Politics of Literature in the England of Charles I* (Cambridge, 1987).

[23] James Shirley, *The Triumph of Peace* (London, 1633 [1634]), sig. a2[r-v], 'To the Foure Equall and Honourable Societies, the Innes of Court'. One should not be misled by Shirley's grovelling preface; although meaning to be supportive of the Stuart monarchy, the spectacle itself voices subtle criticism of the masque form as royal panegyric.

tended their didacticism from the dancing commoner to the audience, 'to make the Spectators understanders', as the English court poet Ben Jonson famously put it – a mode of thinking reminiscent of Elyot's earlier insights.[24] Yet others harboured less charitable thoughts about such 'humble tenders'. Shirley's and Jonson's contemporary Robert Bolton – a prominent preacher and Puritan writer connected with works such as *The Carnall Professor* (1634) – regarded the 'worthy houses of Law' as a place destined 'for great and honourable actions, for the publike good, and the continuance of the glory and happinesse of this Kingdome'; yet, alas, 'they licentiously dissolve[d] into wicked vanities and pleasures', with 'abominable spectacles' which were 'the grand empoysoners of grace (...) and all manly resolution'. For Bolton, the Inns had ended up as '*Schooles of lewdnesse* and *Sinkes of all sins*', to which dancing had contributed in no mean fashion.[25] We see, then, that the commonplace notion of dance as a positive educational tool did not go unchallenged.

In France, the most blatant attempts at turning pastimes into socially purposeful activities occurred in the seventeenth century. A flurry of treatises dealt with the history, theory, and practice of dance and spectacle, usually coming up with the generous conclusion that such arts offered profit as much as delight.[26] Proposals for French academies to reform society often included a balletic element. Antoine de Pluvinel, *haute école* expert under Louis XIII, suggested the nationwide establishment of institutions to take care of idle young 'gentils hommes' in an 'escole de vertu': inmates were to be drilled in horsemanship and dancing next to military skills, history, and maths.[27] The idea that dancing could serve to discipline its performers was famously endorsed by Richelieu, and put to practice in the court ballets which marshalled the aristocracy's energy under Louis XIV. We need to ask whether choreographies in *ballets de cour* or 'schools of virtue' eventually

---

[24] In the court masque *Loves Triumph Through Callipolis* (London, 1630 [1631]), sig. A2ʳ.

[25] Robert Bolton, *A Discourse about the State of True Happinesse* (London, 1611 and seq.; 1638 edn), pp. 73-74. *The Carnall Professor. Discovering the Wofull Slavery of a Man Guided by the Flesh* (London, 1634) bears Bolton's name on the title-page but this attribution has been questioned (ESTC 3225).

[26] Best known are Monsieur de Saint-Hubert, *La Manière de composer et faire réussir les ballets* (Paris, 1641; facs. edn Geneva, 1993), and C.-F. Ménestrier, *Des ballets anciens et modernes selon les règles du théâtre* (Paris, 1682; facs. edn Geneva, 1972).

[27] *L'Instruction du Roy en l'exercice de monter à cheval* (Paris, 1627), pp. 199-206, p. 202. The work first appeared in 1625 and was corrected by Pluvinel's pupil René de Menou. An academy after Pluvinel's ideas had been founded as far back as 1584; see Giles Worsley's fine essay 'The History of "haute école" in England', *The Court Historian* 6 (2001), pp. 29-47 (p. 36).

led to the orderly performance of the political subject. Dancers were and are, after all, individuals who might have approached their task with a sense of irony.[28] The limits of physical education were caricatured in certain English comedies of the mid-seventeenth century, where megalomaniacal dancing masters boasted that they kept the populace from rebellion by the flick of a foot – yet diabolical master plans to transform a whole nation by way of choreography ended in failure.[29]

Even though contested and ridiculed, the idea that the practice of dancing was somehow conducive to the formation of a good person, an accomplished, well-rounded individual, or a model subject persisted. Pre-1700 dance literature conveys the acute impression of tightly cued social gatherings where the tiniest details were carefully registered and evaluated by an occasionally merciless audience. Sixteenth- and seventeenth-century dance books are replete with instructions as to how to sit down, how to greet one's company, what kinds of gestures to use depending on the status of the addressee, or how much time to spend on taking off one's gloves (no longer than it took to pray one 'Ave Maria', and one should never ever pull them off with one's teeth, according to Fabritio Caroso[30]). This also raised expectations with regard to the teachers and performers themselves: not only were they supposed to excel on stage, but ideally they should lead exemplary lives. As late as the eighteenth century, the celebrated French court dancer Vestris maintained that a great dancer had to be virtuous; an observation which deeply impressed the German poet and essayist Heinrich Heine, who regarded it as a profound truth.[31]

Order in speed: Domenico da Piacenza

Let us now return to the origins of the theoretical debate on dancing in the fifteenth century. Possibly because dance was not regarded as a serious pursuit at that time, the earliest tracts on choreographies and their meaning stress the intellectual demands of the art, and hence adduce frequent analogies to language, logic, and philosophy. Quattrocento authors developed

---

[28] This has been argued in recent criticism; for instance, by Mark Franko in *Dance as Text: Ideologies of the Baroque Body* (Cambridge, 1993).

[29] Monsieur Galliard, in the Caroline comedy *The Varietie* (c.1641, pub. London, 1649), attributed to William Cavendish and James Shirley. Shirley specialised in control-freak dancing masters; his comedy *The Ball* (perf. 1632, pub. London, 1639) would be another, though less extreme, example.

[30] F. Caroso, *Nobiltà di dame* (Venice, 1600), p. 67, avertimento II.

[31] 'Ein großer Tänzer muß tugendhaft sein' (Heinrich Heine, letter from Paris, February 7, 1842, in: G. Brandstetter, ed., *Aufforderung zum Tanz: Geschichten und Gedichte* (Stuttgart, 1993), p. 31).

conscious links to classical authority and placed themselves within a wider humanist discourse. Domenico da Piacenza, a dancing master associated with the Este and Sforza families, composed 'De arte saltandi', an influential treatise on the art of dancing in the vernacular (despite its title), probably some time before 1463. For Domenico, dance was 'a refined demonstration of as much intellect and effort as one can find'.[32] Furthermore, Domenico was acutely aware of the social dimension of dance: it was important not only to take care of oneself but of one's partner, and one needed to know about the social connotation of certain steps and genres.

Order was very important in Domenico's work – not only in technical but also in ethical terms. Domenico developed the idea of *misura* – a complex concept which encompassed the notions of 'dancing mode', 'decorum', and 'sense of proportion'. Nevile argues convincingly that Domenico's ethos – and choreographic practice – corresponded to that of contemporary architects (such as Leon Battista Alberti) who believed that geometric order led to moral virtue.[33] Domenico's dances are sometimes characterised by a geometric grid or a linear axis.[34] Dancers often begin a step sequence with the left foot and end it with the right one. Very often one group imitates the movement of the preceding group, or movements to the left are executed towards the right in a mirroring manner. Frequently dancers return to their original positions at the end of the dance. This is also a common pattern of sixteenth- and seventeenth-century Italian courtly dance.

Domenico further recommended *maniera*, a smooth execution which eschewed extremes. *Maniera* and *misura* – both in the sense of rhythmical and spatial proportion and Aristotelian moderation – must animate the choreographic *and* the social performance. A fine dancer should move 'like a gondola (...) propelled by two oars through the waves when the sea is calm'.[35] The wonderfully poised image conveys a sense of effortless balance. Here the individual is at peace with the world that surrounds him (or her; the fifteenth century saw a number of famous female performers, notably in Italy). It is an image which makes readers almost forget that rules govern the course of the gondola.

Taking his cue from Aristotle, Domenico developed a technical terminology which distinguished between 'natural' and 'accidental' move-

---

[32] Domenico, 'De arte saltandi', parallel text with transl. in *Fifteenth-Century Dance and Music*, ed. Smith, I, chapt. 1, ll. 21-22. On the date of the treatise see I, pp. 7, 111.

[33] Nevile, *The Eloquent Body*, pp. 120-121.

[34] Nevile offers compelling examples of dances imitating the geometric design of Medici gardens (*The Eloquent Body*, pp. 123-125).

[35] Domenico, 'De arte saltandi', in *Fifteenth-Century Dance and Music*, ed. Smith, chapt. 1, ll. 16-25; chapt. 3, ll. 47-48; chapt. 7, l. 77.

ments.[36] The former were supposedly found in nature and were part of people's basic kinetic repertoire, such as single and double steps. Interestingly,
Domenico also placed in this group some kinds of movement which a modern reader might not immediately identify as 'natural': would the inclusion
of *riverentia* (a kneeling movement) imply that it is an inborn human characteristic to show respect or even deference by way of movement? Would
Domenico thereby suggest that one should accept existing hierarchies? 'Accidental' movements, on the other hand, simply served to ornament existing
'natural' movements; here Domenico mentioned the *frappamento* (tap) or
scorsa (scurrying step). In terms of tempo, Domenico's 'accidental' movements (not all but many) tend to require less time than 'natural' ones.
Tempo also informs Domenico's generic distinction of dances and steps in
several types of *misura*: the slowest was *bassadanza*, followed by the more
animated *quadernaria, saltarello*, and (fastest of all) the *piva*:

> I am *bassadanza*, queen of the *misure*, and deserve to wear the crown. Few un-
> derstand my performance. Whoever in dance or in music uses me, blessings
> from the heavens are offered.
> (...)
> I am called *piva* and am the saddest of the *misure*, because I am used by the vil-
> lagers in the country.[37]

These kinetic distinctions are not simply represented in strictly choreographic terms. Domenico humanises his *misure* and endows them with a
particular social status and intellectual capacity. The *misure* speak to the
reader, opening a dialogue between the dance and the prospective performer.

---

[36] Apart from the *Nicomachean Ethics*, Domenico was probably familiar with Aristotle's *Aesthetics*, if not other works as well. Domenico could have drawn upon Aristotelian terms from a number of texts, both on physics and ethical topics (indeed
both are related in his oeuvre). Smith prefers the translation 'incidental movements'
for 'motti acidentalli' (*Fifteenth-Century Dance and Music*, ed. Smith, I, p. 11 and
chapt. 8-9).

[37] 'De arte saltandi', chapt. 11, ll. 202-218, transl. A. W. Smith. It is sometimes difficult to distinguish between a whole dance, sections of a dance, and individual
steps. *Misura* is a charged term: it could mean 'mode', 'dance', 'sense of proportion', or 'a way of counting mathematically the speed of your performance'. 'Saltarello' can be an entire dance, but it is also a quick jump. With the *misure* as outlined above Domenico may also mean dance modes, i.e. when he tells the reader to
perform a certain step sequence in the mode of the *bassadanza*, he means that this
sequence should be danced slowly in a 6/8 rhythm. If the reader is told to dance the
same step sequence in the *saltarello* mode, it is performed more quickly.

The Socratic dialogue was, incidentally, a favourite mode of communication in early modern dance books which informed readers about choreographies and proper deportment; commonly such dialogues evolved, charged with full-flavoured practical advice, between a teacher and his pupil. Thus in Fabritio Caroso's sixteenth-century dance book *Nobiltà di dame* (1600):

> *Disciple.* Please go on to describe each of the abovementioned headings, so that I shall know how to teach them to my womenfolk.
> *Master.* (...) Be careful not to adopt the habit of some who first draw their bodies back while bending deeply, and then thrust their bodies forward (a movement so unseemly that, were I to say what it resembles, everyone would die laughing). Still others bend so very straight down and then rise, that they truly resemble a hen about to lay an egg.[38]

This example of Socratic dialogue builds upon common knowledge. Dance treatises devised in this manner seek to involve the reader by using analogies and examples from everyday life. Such discursive strategies turn reading (and possibly performing) into an inclusive experience, perhaps similar to that of singing psalms, whose melody and content everybody knows.

Domenico's *misure* are exceptional in going a step further (as it were) and addressing the reader directly. No go-between (either teacher or disciple) obscures the immediate appeal of the dance. The courtly *bassadanza* is the first to offer direct interpretation and application. The slowest of all *misure*, the *bassadanza*, calls herself 'queen'. Domenico's hint that the slow movement might be nobler than the fast one corresponds to a kinetic trope in the iconography of medieval and early modern Western rulers who are usually depicted motionless.[39] The *bassadanza* appeals to reason and even lures her listeners with an epiphany: those able to understand or, better yet, perform this majestic mode are promised heavenly grace. In contrast, the *piva* is relegated to the periphery, the village. Domenico later adds with disapproval that the *piva* was popular in dances performed by tipsy revellers in

---

[38] F. Caroso, *Nobiltà di dame*, ed. and transl. J. Sutton and F. M. Walker (New York, 1995), pp. 140-141.

[39] B. Ravelhofer, '*Histrio* and Historian: Imperial Symbolism in the *Gedechtnus* Works of Maximilian I', in: R. Suntrup, J. Veenstra and A. Bollmann, eds, *The Mediation of Symbol in Late Medieval and Early Modern Times* (Frankfurt am Main, 2005), pp. 257-273. A similar argument on slowness as dignified and quickness being the domain of actors or servants is also developed in Nevile, p. 98, who states that Italian art of the Renaissance depicted elite women with very little movement.

the late hours of festivals.[40] His remarks are reminiscent of Plato's objection
to bacchanalian dancing. The *piva* appeals to the dionysian, not the rational
mind. Domenico's idea of the quick movement as a cypher for uncontrolled,
dangerous behaviour marks an important early stage in a long-standing debate, which gives rise to a pervasive commonplace in Western thought as-
sociating the fast with the pantomimic, histrionic, licentious, and socially
transgressive. Castiglione regarded lively jumps and turns as something better exercised in private or in theatricals; on all other public occasions he advised his readers to 'keepe a certain dignitie, tempred (...) with a handsome
and sightly sweetnesse of gestures'. A courtier should be careful about entering 'into that swiftnesse of feet and doubled footinges, that we see are
very comely in oure *Barletta* [a professional dancer]' as this was 'unsee-
mely for a Gentilman'.[41] Della Casa's *Galateo* (first pub. 1558) concurred:
only grooms rushed about panting and sweating.[42] In seventeenth-century
England, masques invested grotesque dancers with gesticulating movements, while physiologists such as Thomas Wright juxtaposed the 'harlots',
discernible 'by the light and wanton motions of their eyes and gestures',
with 'honest matrons' known 'by their grave and chaste looks'.[43] The stage
fury became the kinetic stock-in-trade figure embodying violent evil in bal-
let-opera all over Europe. And later, the fatal effects of the dynamic waltz, a
visible expression of uncontrollable passion, were denounced in Goethe's
Sorrows of Young Werther and Byron's diatribes on the topic. It comes as
no surprise that, when Kierkegaard looked for the quintessential expression
of the demonic, he considered ballet and chose a satanic leap:

> The most terrible words that sound from the abyss of evil would not be able to
> produce an effect like that of the suddenness of the leap that lies within the con-
> fines of the mimical. (...) The horror that seizes one upon seeing Mephistophe-
> les leap in through the window and freeze in the position of the leap![44]

---

[40] 'De arte saltandi', in *Fifteenth-Century Dance and Music*, ed. Smith, chapt. 14,
ll. 322-324.

[41] Quoted from the first English transl. of Baldassare Castiglione's *Il Cortegiano* by
Thomas Hoby, *The Courtyer* (London, 1561), bk. 2, sig. Miii^r.

[42] 'Non dèe l'uomo nobile correre per via né troppo affrettarsi, ché ciò conviene a
palafreniere e non a gentiluomo, senza che l'uomo s'affanna e suda ed ansa (...)',
Giovanni della Casa, *Galateo*, ed. S. Prandi (Turin, 1994), p. 80.

[43] Thomas Wright (d. 1624), *The Passions of the Mind in General*, ed. W. W. Newbold (New York, 1986), bk. 1, chapt. 7, p. 110.

[44] Kierkegaard had seen Antoine Bournonville's ballet *Faust* (performed in Copenhagen in 1832), where the choreographer himself danced as Mephistopheles; deeply
impressed by Bournonville's leap, Kierkegaard noted in his journal that 'the demonic is namely the sudden', a notion he further developed in *The Concept of Anxiety* (1844). Søren Kierkegaard, *The Concept of Anxiety: A Simple Psychologically*

The leap precedes the fall, as Milton knew so well. One does wonder whether Kierkegaard knew *Paradise Lost*, where Satan peers into the abyss before he takes flight, only to drop 'ten thousand fathom deep'. Milton's terrifying lines evoke stasis and movement at the same time. Satan is, as the misplaced preposition of direction indicates, already falling while still gazing:

> Into this wild abyss the wary fiend
> Stood on the brink of hell and looked a while,
> Pondering his voyage (...).[45]

Satan's fiendish leap is a universe away from Renaissance dance ethics and aesthetics. In all things there was a natural goodness, Domenico had contended, with reference to Aristotle, whose idea of the golden mean (prevalent in the *Nicomachean Ethics*) he espoused in his own work: 'being moderate saves one'.[46] In Milton's postlapsarian grammar, Satan is/moves out of order, beyond redemption.

Mute rhetoric: Fabritio Caroso and Bernardino Stefonio

While the appeal of Domenico's art lay in its deceptive simplicity, dance manuals from the sixteenth century onwards tended towards a more ostentatious, display-oriented approach.[47] Dancing masters foregrounded the idea of performance as physical persuasion, and, to this end, elaborated on the analogy between movement and language by turning dance itself into text, or 'Rhetorique muette', as Thoinot Arbeau, a churchman and dance expert living in Langres near Dijon, famously put it in his treatise *Orchésographie* (1589).[48] Best known at the time were, perhaps, Fabritio Caroso's dance

---

Orienting Deliberation on the Dogmatic Issue of Hereditary Sin, ed. and transl. R. Thomte and A. Anderson (Princeton, 1980), pp. 131, 250. I have replaced the translator's 'remain stationary' with 'freeze'. See also *Aufforderung zum Tanz*, ed. Brandstetter, p. 409.

[45] John Milton, *Paradise Lost*, ed. A. Fowler (London, 1971), bk 2, ll. 917-919. Fowler calls Milton's sentence a 'fine passage of mimetic syntax' (p. 132).

[46] 'De arte saltandi', in *Fifteenth-Century Dance and Music*, ed. Smith, chapt.1, ll. 15-16; chapt. 7, ll. 74-75.

[47] On this transition, usually deplored in dance criticism, see in particular R. zur Lippe, *Naturbeherrschung am Menschen*, 2 vols. (Frankfurt am Main, 1974, [2]1981).

[48] Thoinot Arbeau [Jehan Tabourot], *Orchesographie et traicté en forme de dialogue, par lequel toutes personnes peuvent facilement apprendre & practiquer l'honneste exercice des dances [Orchésographie]* (Langres, 1589), fol. 5[v]. A prolific number of studies have commented on this analogy. See, for instance, Franko,

books, printed in Venice in 1581 and 1600, and reprinted in Rome as late as 1630.[49] Caroso's colleagues thought highly of him. According to the prominent Milanese choreographer Cesare Negri, whose creations were performed before the Spanish Infanta, Caroso could not be praised highly enough for his beautiful dances. In particular, Negri extolled Caroso's *Il Ballarino* (1581), dedicated to Bianca Cappello de' Medici, Grand Duchess of Tuscany, as 'a most beautiful book, a testimony of [the author's] splendid and illustrious valour'; Negri used the work as a point of reference by which he measured his own publications.[50] Caroso's revised version of *Il Ballarino*, *Nobiltà di dame*, included detailed step instructions, choreographies, music in lute tablature, and poems, as well as engravings showing stills of dancing couples. Furthermore the work stylised the performance itself into a mute 'pedalogue'[51] which participants practised with steps inspired by classical metre. The rhythm of poetry translated directly into legwork, Caroso argued – after all, poetry drew upon the concept of verse feet:

> the immortal poet Ovid demonstrated this well in his verse (for one calls that joining of feet a *caesura*), so that when scanning one of his pentameter lines we find first a dactyl, then a spondee, and finally a *caesura*, and here we stop a little.[52]

This might be an appropriate moment to stop a little and recall one of the early modern definitions of the commonplace book: a preconceived grid on which knowledge could be plotted. For Caroso invented a choreography, called *Contrapasso Nuovo*, which combined text with movement and literary theory. *Contrapasso Nuovo* applied Ovidian versification to the dance floor; in the printed version of the dance, an engraving illustrates the nexus between movement and language (see Ill. 1).[53] Like the verbal commonplace, the dance was the outcome of long critical reflection on practice, for *Nobiltà di dame* represented the *summa* of Caroso's fifty years of professional experience. Like the verbal commonplace, *Contrapasso Nuovo* was an elite creation, addressing a connoisseur audience. Caroso dedicated his dance to Lady Cornelia Orsina Cesi with a poem. This poem stated, in a

---

Dance as Text; S. R. Cohen, *Art, Dance, and the Body in French Culture of the Ancien Régime* (Cambridge, 2000).

[49] F. Caroso, *Il Ballarino* (Venice, 1581) and its revised sequel, *Nobiltà di dame* (1600); *idem, Raccolta di varij Balli* (Rome, 1630), a reprint of *Nobiltà di dame*.

[50] 'Un bellissimo libro, testimonio del suo valore ben chiaro, & illustre' (Cesare Negri, *Le Gratie d'amore* (Milan, 1602; facs. edn Bologna, 1983), pp. 2, 4).

[51] For 'pedalogo [pedalogue]' see *Nobiltà di dame* (1600), *Laura Suave*, p. 115.

[52] *Nobiltà di dame*, transl. Sutton, 'Passo Puntato Semigrave', p. 102.

[53] *Nobiltà di dame* (1600), pp. 240-244, *Contrapasso Nuovo*.

somewhat self-deprecatory manner, that words were not enough to praise the lady's virtues ('che non bastano à ciò voci, e parole', *Nobiltà di dame*, p. 240). The greater the need, then, to immortalise her rosy cheeks in a dance, and to illustrate her beauty with an abstract floor pattern printed on the subsequent page of *Nobiltà di dame*.

The pattern shows three ladies (D for 'dame') and three gentlemen (C for 'cavalieri') arranged in a circle. They gaze at the rose in the centre; trajectories towards the centre signal the direction of the gaze. Once set in motion, the dancers weave along an interlaced path (one undulating line for the ladies, the other for the gentlemen), the rose always remaining the hub of the action that wheels about it. Caroso praised his creation as 'fatto con vera Regola, perfetta Theorica, & Mathematica' (*Nobiltà di dame*, p. 243), a beautiful geometric structure pulsating with the rhythms gleaned from Ovid, the *spondeo* (– –) and *dattile* (– vv). Within the choreography, the *spondeo* translates into two simple steps ('passi semibrevi'), and the *dattile* into a 'seguito' (a triple step with a possible emphasis on the first step – here Caroso bends his own rules to create a dactyl, as the 'seguito' is usually executed in anapaestic rhythm, vv –). All this evolves around the rose, which, placed at the centre, offers not simply spatial but also moral and aesthetic orientation. Would the rose be the grid on which the dancers' movements could be plotted? Could we read the title of the dance as commonplace heading, with the subject matter provided by the danced performance? Lady Cesi's symbolic presence animates the entire choreography, giving the performers a model to aim at. Geometric and rhythmical order may direct those who understand the dance to her virtues. To my knowledge, no other pre-1700 choreographic illustration makes the connection between geometric order, beauty, and moral accomplishment as apparent as does Caroso's *Contrapasso Nuovo*.

While Caroso intended his dance for performance on any social occasion, Bernardino Stefonio was more specifically interested in the role of dancing in the theatre. This became evident in Stefonio's immensely successful Jesuit school play *Crispus*. First staged in 1597, the tragedy saw many subsequent performances and eight editions in France, Italy, and the Netherlands between 1601 and 1634.[54] A christianised, all-male adaptation of Seneca's *Hippolytus*, *Crispus* showed the tribulations of its eponymous hero, fatally pursued by his lustful stepmother, consort of the Roman emperor Constantine (as Louis Oldani and Victor Yanitelli aptly put it, 'for educating youth in dutiful citizenship and personal responsibility, tragic en-

---

[54] M. Fumaroli, 'Le *Crispus* et la *Flavia* du P. Bernardino Stefonio S. J.: contribution à l'histoire du théâtre au Collegio Romano (1597-1628)', in: J. Jacquot and E. Konigson, eds, *Les Fêtes de la Renaissance*, III (Paris, 1975), pp. 505-524.

counters with historic heroism best suited the positive indoctrination of love of one's country'[55]). A version presented twice in Naples in 1603 involved four choreographies executed by sixteen college students.[56] Illustrations showing the floor tracks of these four dances were included in an edition commemorating the Naples performances which appeared one year later. These choreographies conformed to the humanist concept of *ut pictura poesis*, at the heart of the Jesuit quest to teach by pleasure and emotional involvement.[57]

What exactly might a boy have learnt when dancing these patterns? Both Stefonio and his Neapolitan publisher regarded the choreographies as a revival of Greek *emmelia*[58] – hence they were meant to promote, in some way, social behaviour in times of peace. As Stefonio observed, dancing could, just like preaching, melt the hardened heart, especially if aided by the trappings of theatre, and nothing gave so much pleasure as jointly experiencing a calamity from a safe distance in a group.[59] To that end, Stefonio's dances rehearsed a number of easily recognisable emblematic commonplaces. The eagle (Ill. 2) – main figure of the first ballet – represented empire, the constant quest for honour and the defiance of misfortune (the Roman eagle was frequently alluded to in the course of the play). The third choral dance (Ill. 3) involved more taxing guesswork for the audience, as it evolved around a perspectival grid which visualised how fame – or rumour

---

[55] L. J. Oldani and V. R. Yanitelli, 'Jesuit Theater in Italy: Its Entrances and Exit', *Italica* 76 (1999), pp. 18-32 (p. 25).

[56] Fumaroli, 'Le *Crispus*', p. 515. For a good overview of choreographies in the style of *Crispus*, see O. di Tondo, '"Leggiadrìa di ballo et di gesti": alcune osservazioni sulla danza negli intermedi e nel primo melodramma tra XVI e XVII secolo', in: A. Chiarle, ed., *L'Arte della danza ai tempi di Claudio Monteverdi* (Turin, 1996), pp. 189-226; B. Stefonio, *Crispus: Tragoedia*, eds L. Strappini and L. Trenti (Rome, 1998).

[57] Fumaroli, 'Le *Crispus*', p. 515.

[58] Stefonio's and the publisher's comments were considered sufficiently important to be included in a range of later editions, including that of Urbeveterum (Civitavecchia), 1620; all further quotations are taken from this edition. For 'emmelia' see Stefonio's preface, sig. a3ᵛ: *Illa tantopere laudata schemata veterum saltationum, et omnem Tragoedorum Emmeliam ob oculos expressam vidimus, è Romanorum litteris, ac vetere Graecia repetitam: in versu concentum, in concentu tempus, in tempore corporum motum, ac statum, in motu, statuque figuram, in figura cum rebus agendis sententiam congruentem, omnemque conversionem cuiusque modi flexus ad dexteram, ac laevam, scitè praeeuntem Coryphaeum aptè consequentis in seriem Chori* (*Crispus*, printer's address to the reader, sig. [a6ʳ⁻ᵛ]).

[59] *Quod pectus ita ferreum est, ut non illud expugnet Orchestra, Logeum, Thymele, choragium, emmelia* (...) (*Crispus*, sig. a3ᵛ); *interdum non est turpe, cum multitudine sentire: et in parte felicitatis est, communem calamitatem sequi* (*Crispus*, sig. a4ᵛ).

– could spread from a single source to the borders of the universe. The young performers tried to embody acoustic airwaves, as it were.

The last dance, a labyrinthine, cross-shaped choreography (Ill. 4), represented the human condition and the need for Christian guidance. As the Chorus lamented, 'you who are happy, fear the hand of God which overturns the greatest empires in a brief moment'.[60] This insight was exemplified in the character of Crispus, first fêted by the Roman people and then accepting his execution with serene equanimity, his last thoughts firmly devoted to Jesus. In Marc Fumaroli's reading, the final dance expressed the idea that Christ had, through his incarnation, descended to the labyrinth of this world; by his exemplary, arduous passage he had shown humankind the way to salvation.[61] The performance of the labyrinth, then, did not simply emulate the play's main character; it led to physical as well as mental *imitatio Christi*.

The illustrations do raise some questions about choreographic practice, though. It does not take much to read the *printed* image of an eagle as 'empire'. Yet how easy is it for sixteen dancers to compose such an image by sequential action? The printed designs amount to a cumulative representation, showing not a snapshot of the dances but their total impression created in the course of several minutes. What the audience saw at any point in the performance was a partial, incomplete view of the whole scheme. Witnessing the dances must have stimulated much speculation on the part of observers. Were the patterns painted on the dance floor (similar to the labyrinths one can see in medieval cathedrals, traced by the faithful),[62] to facilitate the reading of the dance? If so, Stefonio must have found a method of removing these floor patterns after each performance in order to make space for the next ballet. Were the dances explained in a note handed out to the audience?[63] Or did Stefonio proceed without any further guidance, hoping that allusions in the spoken text as to eagles, labyrinths, and the miserable state of humankind would do the trick? A challenge could have added to the pleasure of learning. A thrill of discovery might have been in store for an audience which attentively followed the boys' *tableaux vivants* and meandering lines, and thus slowly worked out the emerging shapes and meanings of a choreography, making connections between spoken text and moving illustration. On the other hand we should consider the possibility that Stefo-

---

[60] *Dei / Summa momento brevi / Regna vertentem manum, / Quisquis es felix, time* (*Crispus*, p. 108; my transl.).

[61] Fumaroli, 'Le *Crispus*', pp. 523-524.

[62] A standard work is P. R. Doob, *The Idea of the Labyrinth from Classical Antiquity through the Middle Ages* (Ithaca, 1990).

[63] Two programmes for *Crispus* survive (Fumaroli, 'Le *Crispus*', p. 517), but we have no further details about the specific Naples performances.

nio chose illustrations in a printed version of his play precisely because the dances had not been sufficiently clear to spectators during performance.

Jesuit ballet banked on the pleasures of lived knowledge, or what modern pedagogical theory calls situational learning, in which a holistic experience enhances the memorising of subject matter. Stefonio's choreographies sought to inculcate an abstract virtue by physical enactment and emotional appeal. In performance, the boys were living their faith. Dancing the complicated passages of the labyrinth, they were made physically aware that, even if a situation seemed chaotic, a higher order was at work, and things would eventually come to a resolution. Even more, Stefonio extended his instructions to a reading audience. The printed choreography can be traced with the reader's eye and there unfold its didactic potential.

Conclusion

In early modern Europe, dance had ethical implications which were recognised by choreographers, practitioners, and observers alike, and alertly glossed by opponents of the art. Convinced that human passions could be inferred from bodily action, humanist authors argued for a conscious grooming of manners and movements, and polemicists clamoured loudly for the regulation or abolition of dancing. The question remains whether kinetic lessons – both on paper and on the stage – actually achieved the desired learning outcome. Were Stefonio's boys frustrated by the discipline of Jesuit ballet, or did they feel elated because they had mastered a difficult formation? A visual commonplace such as the labyrinth could have helped emblematically versed audiences (and readers) to decode a complex choreography, but would this have led to greater faith in a universal, benevolent higher order?

We do not know to what extent the prescriptive advice of dance manuals was representative of the movements on the dance floors of Rome, Prague, Munich, or London. Perhaps works such as Caroso's polished encyclopaedias represent an elite departure from more widely practised, unscripted forms of kinetic behaviour, now lost to us. What such treatises do tell us, however, is that, irrespective of country or century, authors in favour of dancing endorsed its qualities by recourse to a number of commonplaces, such as order and proportion, or a supposedly natural catalogue of movements which came to humankind by default. Dancing masters accepted as a given the dance's social functionality, its usefulness for regulated communication, and its capacity to make people happy with their station in life. The concept of the orderly dancer as a good example to the beholder informed early modern spectacle all over Europe. This essay has also given some space to claims to the contrary, which suggests that commonplaces endorsing dancing as a positive activity were consciously employed to shore up a discipline under attack. Such strategies trusted in the moral authority of the commonplace: long-established truisms bolstered by classical authority served as effective ammunition against polemicists.

The labyrinth, once invoked by poets and choreographers and traced by performers in cathedrals and stately Neapolitan palazzi, can still be a moral maze. The faux pas, first introduced into English in the 1670s to denote a compromising act, has become common conversational currency.[64] Dance scenes which visualise social relationships belong to Western literature's living tradition, whether we think of the charged ballroom atmosphere in Tolstoy's novels, the decadent Sicilian *valse* in Lampedusa's *Il Gattopardo*, or the delicate steps of Rita Dove's poetic protagonists. It seems interesting that even word-processing programmes now use commands such as 'go to', 'move' and 'track change'. Early modern dance literature (*in utramque partem*) encouraged thinking about dance in new contexts. The pedalogic pedagogues of the sixteenth and seventeenth centuries contributed to a common dissemination of pseudo-choreographic expressions still in use to-day.

---

[64] In W. Wycherley, *The Plain Dealer* (1676), and englished in about 1700 as 'false step' (*The Oxford English Dictionary*, online version <http://dictionary.oed.com>, last accessed February 1, 2007).

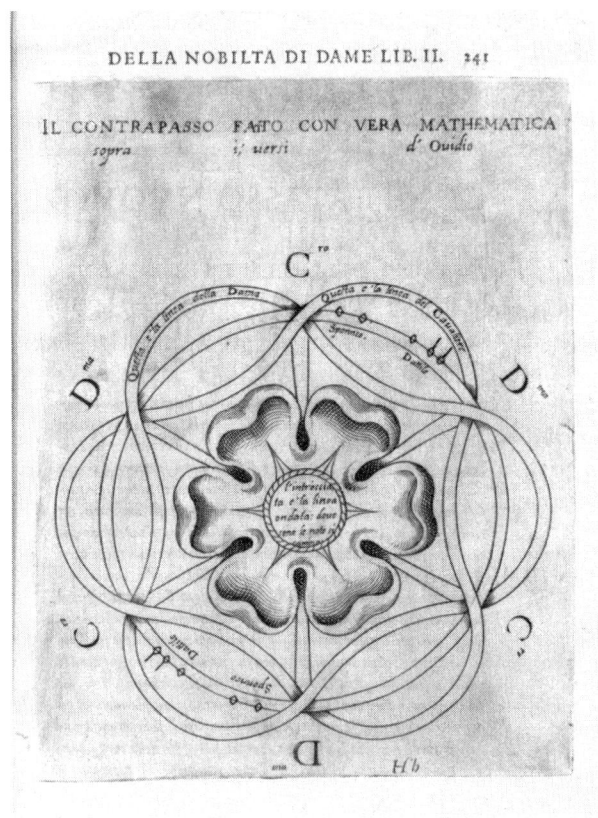

1. Illustration to *Contrapasso Nuovo*, in F. Caroso, *Nobiltà di dame* (1600), p. 241. British Library, shelfmark C.7.d.12. © The British Library. All rights reserved.

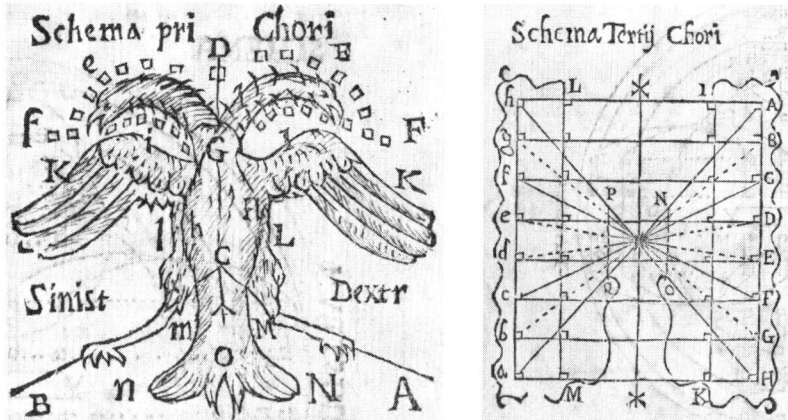

2 and 3. B. Stefonio, *Crispus* (Naples, 1604). University of Chicago Library, Special Collections Research Center, shelfmark PA8585.S64C9 1604. Eagle and Fame choreographies, appended to the play. The eagle's contours have been lovingly accentuated in ink by an early reader. The positions of the sixteen dancers are indicated by the sixteen letters A to Q.

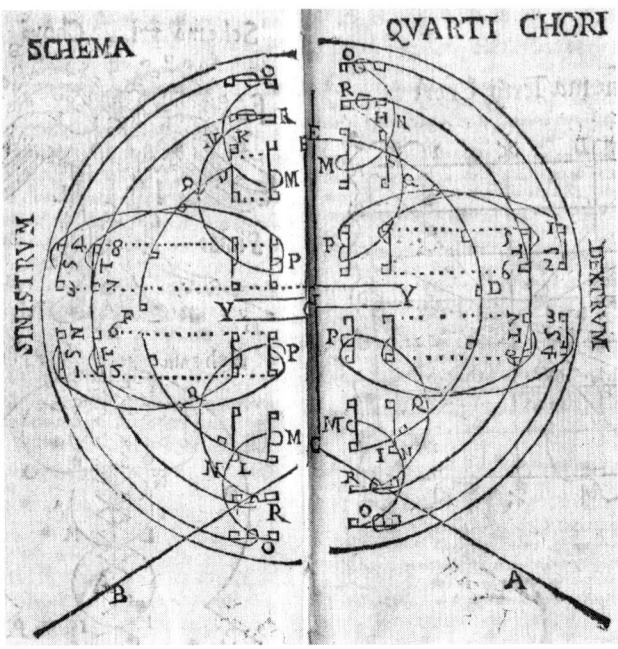

4. Final dance in *Crispus*. University of Chicago Library, Special Collections Research Center.

COMMONPLACES IN *CENDRILLON* AND *PEAU D'ANE*

BETWEEN ACADEMIC DISPUTE, FOLKLORE MAGIC, AND MORAL INSTRUCTION[1]

Mette B. Bruun

Introduction

In terms of date, this contribution rests on the verge of our volume. The texts of interest, Charles Perrault's *Cendrillon* and *Peau d'Ane* (1690s), are late compared to the pivotal concern with the reformations of the sixteenth century. In terms of topic, however, it is suggested that a study of these two texts may shed some light on the ways in which commonplaces may have been employed for religious instruction in the aftermath of the Counter-Reformation's concern with the edification of lay people, and also add some further perspectives to our spectrum of notions and understandings of 'the commonplace'.

Our point of departure is provided by a conception of commonplace which belongs within Ann Moss's introductory identification of the flexible and inclusive, indeed 'elastic', understanding of the term. The *topoi* examined here are, recasting Moss's words, 'cultural material with both past and present currency';[2] indeed, Perrault stresses and exploits exactly the ability of these *topoi* to work over time, and even to accommodate modifications of a contemporary flavour. Furthermore, we will place our focus on their deployment 'primarily as tools for argument in discourse designed to promote and reinforce culturally sanctioned modes of thought',[3] and argue that, through his appropriation of fairytale commonplaces, Perrault champions a particular cultural and religious ethos.

For a *topos* to function as 'common', it must imply a degree of either formal or semantic stability. Fairytales offer useful material for the study of this stable connotative cargo of the commonplace and the ways in which it is negotiated and adapted. On the one hand, they are composed of conven-

---

[1] This work forms part of a project carried out at the Centre for the Study of the Cultural Heritage of Medieval Rituals, funded by the Danish National Research Foundation.
[2] A. Moss, chapter in this volume, pp. 1-17 (p. 1).
[3] *Ibidem.*

tional elements such as auxiliary animals, supernatural villains, deep forests, parental poverty, eating and sleeping, trials and feats. On the other hand, however, the tales are independent narratives; they exhibit an individual fashioning of customary traits and are steeped in specific historical contexts. Some of them even appear as an author's autonomous work. This combination of a common repository of (oral) material and a distinct authorial (literary) mark comes to the fore with particular weight in the case of Perrault. His tales are carefully devised literary texts, in which the author takes up fairytale types from popular lore and adapts them to his own context and strategy.

The two fairytales in focus here are read in the light of synchronic concerns with structure and form and a diachronic attention to the hermeneutics of the commonplace and its position between stability, reception, and appropriation. This point of view is indebted to Robert Darnton's call for an anthropological, rather than psychological, approach to folktales. The anthropologists, Darnton says, 'look for the way a raconteur adapts an inherited theme to his audience, so that the specificity of time and place shows through the universality of the topos'.[4] Darnton is interested in the ways in which famine and affliction in the rural population of late seventeenth-century France reverberate in the pre-Perraldian versions of the tales.[5] This chapter centres on traces in Perrault of issues debated in the academic circles of his time: issues associated with aesthetics, history, and religious doctrine. The tales' universal topoi, which, to some extent, may be classified along the lines suggested in Propp's Morphology of the Folktale (1928), function as commonplaces in that they have a formulaic compactness and a generically based legitimacy and self-evidence. But commonplaces are also at play, I would argue, in Perrault's adaptation to a contemporary context. These topoi are more evasive, and their potency shorter-lived; their legitimacy and rhetorical force are rooted in their immediate resonance in a contemporary reader-community.

The argument of this chapter is based on the following assumption: in his contribution to the aesthetic and ethical Querelle des anciens et des modernes, Perrault is, among other things, concerned with the ideal of a 'native' Christian matrix and with the moral edification of his contemporar-

---

[4] R. Darnton, 'The Meaning of Mother Goose', The New York Review 31/1 (February 2, 1984), <http://www.nybooks.com/articles/5955>, last accessed March 2, 2007. Darnton's socio-historical approach to the tales is fleshed out in 'Pesants Tell Tales: The Meaning of Mother Goose', in: R. Darnton, The Great Cat Massacre and Other Episodes in French Cultural History (Harmondsworth, [2]1985), pp. 17-78.

[5] There is a disciplinarily significant tension with L. Marin's semiotic study of the role of culinary signs in Perrault, based on Lévi-Strauss and Elias, presented in Food for Thought, transl. by M. Hjort (Baltimore, 1989).

ies. At the same time as he voices these concerns, however, he publishes a collection of tales allegedly transmitted through generations and allegedly intended for the moral instruction of children.[6] This coincidence, I suggest, allows us to read the fairytales against the backdrop of the *Querelle* and Perrault's involvement in safeguarding the proper Christian climate of the age of Louis XIV; and furthermore to suggest contemporary trends which may have influenced the ways in which he handles and transforms key *topoi* of fairytale lore.

1. *Charles Perrault*

Charles Perrault (1628-1703) was the youngest of five brothers. A lawyer by training, he gave up this profession in his early twenties and worked for his brother Pierre, the Receiver General of taxes for Paris. In 1660 a dialogue on love and friendship as well as two royal odes caught the attention of Louis XIV's minister of finances, Jean-Baptiste Colbert, who employed Perrault as a clerk; and when Colbert established the *Petite Académie* in 1663, he made him a member. In 1670 the minister elicited a chair in the *Académie française* for his protégé. The members had been hesitant as they – correctly – suspected that Colbert intended Perrault to be his mouth and ears in the academy. Perrault shared his contemporaries' sense of historicising representation and employed his skills in the service of the *Petite Académie*, devising medals, plates, and other memorials of royal glory.[7]

In 1672 Perrault left Colbert's office in favour of a position as royal *Contrôleur des Bâtiments*, and in this capacity shrewdly brought about the preference of his brother Claude's (1613-1688) design for the colonnade of the Louvre to proposals by architects such as Bernini and Le Brun.[8] In 1683 Colbert died; without this support Perrault was excluded from the Academy, and his pension withdrawn. A widower, he now dedicated himself to the upbringing of his children and to his literary work.

---

[6] There seems to be sufficient scholarly support for Charles Perrault's authorship to allow us, in this context, to discount the fact that the prose tales were published in the name of his nineteen-year-old son, Pierre.

[7] The motto chosen for the young Dauphin, for instance, was his proposal. This and other exploits of a similar calibre are described in C. Perrault, *Mémoires* (Avignon, 1759), pp. 35-42.

[8] Perrault, *Mémoires*, pp. 59-127. See also J. Morgan, *Perrault's Morals for Moderns* (New York/Berne/Frankfurt am Main, 1985), pp. 13-16.

2. *La Querelle des anciens et des modernes*

In his time, Perrault was famed for his involvement in the *Querelle des an-ciens et des modernes*, a heated and, at times, bitterly personal controversy in the Academy. The conflict revolved around aesthetic ideals and a dichot-omy between, to put it schematically, on the one side an evolutionary view of history as progress with the age of Louis XIV as its apogee; and, on the other side, the claim that seekers of truth and beauty must strive to imitate the ideals of the golden age of Antiquity. The faction of the *anciens* was led by Nicolas Boileau-Despréaux, who presented his views on the aesthetic preponderance of classical ideals in his *Art poétique* (1674). The stance of the *modernes* was epitomised in Perrault and his rejection of any idea of timeless ideals. This viewpoint was substantiated by his two volumes on *Les Hommes illustres qui ont paru en France pendant ce siècle* (1696 and 1700), which featured a hundred biographies of contemporary figureheads, attesting to the glory of the seventeenth century.

On January 27, 1687, Perrault read to the *Académie française* the text which is often, somewhat simplistically, seen as the instigating factor of the *Querelle*.[9] It was a poem entitled *Le Siècle de Louis le Grand*, a two-pronged venture aimed at praising Louis XIV and challenging Boileau. The poem is launched memorably:

> La belle Antiquité fut toujours venerable;
> Mais je ne crus jamais qu'elle fust adorable.
> Je voy les Anciens sans plier les genoux,
> Ils sont grands, il est vray, mais hommes comme nous;
> Et l'on peut comparer sans craindre d'estre injuste,
> Le Siecle de LOUIS au beau Siecle d'Auguste.[10]

> Fair Antiquity does deserve veneration

---

[9] The struggle was incited on the one hand by contemporary personal and academic circumstances, and, on the other, by the ever vibrant tension in European literature between factions championing renewal and renaissances and factions harking back to ideals of an earlier golden age, as pointed out in H. R. Jauss, 'Literarische Tradi-tion und gegenwärtiges Bewusstsein der Modernität', in: H. Steffen, ed., *Aspekte der Modernität* (Göttingen, 1965), pp. 150-197 (p. 151); see also M. Fumaroli, 'Les A-beilles et les araignées', in: A.-M. Lecoq, ed., *La Querelle des Anciens et des Mod-ernes* (Paris, 2001), pp. 7-218, esp. pp. 7-12.

[10] C. Perrault, *Parallèle des anciens et des modernes en ce qui regarde les arts et les sciences*, in: H. R. Jauss and M. Imdahl, eds, *Charles Perrault: Parallèle des an-ciens et des modernes* (Munich, 1964), p. 165. Translations are mine unless other-wise specified.

> But I never thought it compels adoration.
> The ancients I view without bending my knee
> They are great, it is true, but men like we.
> And one may compare, without fear of injustice,
> The age of Louis with that of Augustus.

This is not a study of the *Querelle*. Suffice it to sketch a few aspects of the argument voiced in Perrault's principal testimony in the debate, *Parallèle des anciens et des modernes*, the four volumes of which appeared in 1688, 1690, 1692, and 1697. *Parallèle* unrolls as a dialogue between *le President*, *l'Abbé*, and *le Chevalier*. The first figure represents the stance of the *anciens*, the second that of the *modernes*, and the third pushes *modernes* arguments to the limit, introducing a degree of mirth through its radical nature. Unsurprisingly, Perrault several times professes agreement with *l'Abbé*.[11]

Of specific interest in the current context is the claimed inability of classical texts to convey moral edification. *L'Abbé* notices the janus-faced appeal in the Homeric narratives: 'A l'égard des mœurs, il y en a de particuliéres au temps où il a écrit, & il y en a qui sont de tous les temps' ('With regard to mores, there are those which are particular to the time when he wrote, and there are those which are relevant at all times').[12] The manners which are specific to Homer's own age, such as heroes who cook or princesses who do the laundry, often seem ridiculous now, and were better left out.[13] Homer should not be blamed for representing the customs of his time, but nonetheless *l'Abbé* is appalled to see Achilles depicted as 'injuste, brutal, impitoyable, sans foy, & sans loy' ('unjust, brutal, merciless, without belief, and without law'). Also Ulysses is such a mixture 'd'héroïque & de bas, qu'il est presque impossible de le bien définir' ('of the heroic and the low, that it is almost impossible to characterise him').[14] The virtue of humility, albeit most important of all, is never found in the ancients;[15] and pride, which is the root of all vices, passes in them as a virtue.[16] 'Croyez-moy', the Abbot states, 'il n'y a que la Religion Chrestienne qui ait formé un veritable Systéme de Morale' ('Believe me, it is only the Christian religion which has formed a regular moral system').[17] This is Perrault's challenge to the *anciens*; rather than conveying timeless truths of eternal standing, the antique

---

[11] For instance *Parallèle des anciens et des modernes*, III, preface; edition, p. 283.
[12] *Idem*, p. 47; edn, p. 295.
[13] *Ibidem*.
[14] *Idem*, p. 50; edn, p. 296.
[15] *Parallèle*, IV, p. 150; edn, p. 410.
[16] *Idem*, pp. 147-148; edn, pp. 409-410.
[17] *Idem*, pp. 144-145; edn, p. 409.

texts are bound by the, at times, vile standards and manners of their own time in a way which makes them in part morally pointless to modern people.[18]

Perrault also discusses the matrix and models taken up in poetry. His *Parallèle* contains a response to a friend who has complained that contemporary poets do not employ fables in their works. Perrault answers:

> (...) car imiter les Anciens n'est pas dire ce qu'ils ont dit, mais dire les choses de la maniere qu'ils les ont dites; les Anciens ont employé dans leurs Poësies les Fables qui estoient connuës de tous ceux de leur siecle comme faisant la meilleure partie de leur Religion; si nos Poëtes veulent faire comme les Anciens, il faut qu'ils mettent dans leurs Poësies ce qui est connu de tous ceux du siecle où nous sommes; & commes [*sic*] les Poëtes Grecs & Latins n'employoient point dans leurs ouvrages la Mithologie des Egyptiens, les Poëtes François ne doivent point employer les Fables des Romains & des Grecs s'ils ont envie de les prendre pour leurs modelles.[19]

> (...) thus to imitate the ancients is not to say what they said, but to say things in the manner in which they said them; in their poetry, the ancients employed the fables which were known to everybody in their days, as they formed the more important part of their religion. If our poets will do what the ancients did, they must take up in their poetry that which is known by everybody in our century; and just as Greek and Latin poets did not employ the mythology of the Egyptians in their works, French poets should not employ the fables of the Greeks and Romans, if they want to take them as their models.

It is little wonder that, three hundred years later, Perrault's work was to catch the interest of H. R. Jauss, one of the founding fathers of *Rezeptionsästhetik*. In this passage, Perrault touches upon several aspects that were to be key Jaussian themes, most notably the alterity of past texts and the concern with the implied reader.[20] Contemporary texts are more accessible than those of the past, Perrault argues, but if an ancient matrix is indeed employed, the author should strive to manoeuvre within a frame of reference

---

[18] Soriano positions Perrault's engagement in the *Querelle* in the context of Christian versus pagan heritage and suggests that his argument retains Tertullian's and Augustine's dismissal of pagan authors resuscitated in the Tridentine deprecation of classical texts vis-à-vis the humanist predilection for them (M. Soriano, *Le Dossier Perrault* (Paris, 1972), p. 28). Soriano's representation of the Augustinian stance is, perhaps, a little sweeping.

[19] Perrault, *Parallèle*, IV, pp. 315-316; edn, p. 451.

[20] Programmatically laid out in *Alterität und Modernität der mittelalterlichen Literatur* (Munich, 1977).

which is familiar to his readers. Both concerns reverberate in Perrault's own modernised fairytales.

3. Perrault's 'Contes'

In the long run it was not the *Querelle* but a collection of fairy tales that secured Perrault's standing. Between 1691 and 1693 there appeared three *contes* in verse;[21] in the course of the following years, eight prose tales came out. In 1697 the prose tales were published together in a collection, *Histoires ou Contes du temps passé: Avec des Moralitez*, including, among others, *Le Petit Chaperon rouge, La Belle au bois dormant, Le Chat botté, Cendrillon, Barbe Bleue*, and *Le Petit Poucet*.[22] Whereas the three verse *contes* appeared with the avant-garde of a new literary genre, the last eight emerged in a veritable surge of fairytales.[23]

Perrault's narratives are suspended between past and present. The moral for *Peau d'Ane* reads: 'Le Conte de Peau d'Ane est difficile à croire, / Mais tant que dans le Monde on aura des Enfants, / Des Mères et des Mères-grands, / On en gardera la mémoire'[24] ('The tale of Donkey-skin is hard to believe, but as long as we have children, mothers, and grandmothers in the world, we shall retain it in our memory'); and recurrent allusions to the role played by mothers and governesses in the retelling and transmission of the tales evoke ideas of a temporally indefinite (oral) transmission. At the same time, a literary and actualising element comes to the

---

[21] *La Marquise de Salusses ou la Patience de Griseldis* and *Peau d'Ane* were printed by the printer of the King and the French Academy, Jean-Baptiste Coignard. *Les Souhaits ridicules* first appeared in the *Mercure Galant* (see Morgan, *Perrault's Morals*, pp. 27-28). Perrault produced a composite range of tales between 1675 and 1699, including, significantly, translations from Latin (Morgan, *Perrault's Morals*, pp. 36-38).
[22] The collection was published by Claude Barbin, who had published Fontaine's *Nouvelles en vers* (1665) and *Fables choisies* (1668). In 1704 Barbin's widow was to publish the first volume of *Mille et une Nuits: contes arabes*; G. Rouger, ed., *Contes de Perrault* (Paris, 1974 [1967]), p. xlix. The *Parallèle* attests to Perrault's admiration for the novelty and striking charm of Fontaine's fables (*Parallèle*, III, pp. 503-504; edn, pp. 359-360. One of Fontaine's assets is that he, according to Perrault, does not model his fables on classical types (*Parallèle*, III, p. 305; edn, p. 360).
[23] By, among others, Mmes d'Aulnoy and Durand, Comtesse de Murat, Mlles L'Héritier (Perrault's niece) and de la Force and by Le Chevalier de Mailly and Sieur de Préchac. See *Contes de Perrault*, p. xlviii.
[24] Perrault, 'Peau d'Ane', in *Contes*, p. 75. See also Perrault, 'Préface', in *Contes*, p. 4. Rouger's edition of the *Contes* gives the text in modern spelling and orthography.

fore, not least in the rhymed moral of each tale, which epitomises its *morale utile*.[25] Muratore is sceptical towards what she sees as the polarisation of an 'original text' and Perrault's updated versions, basically identified via the 'novel, independent interpretation' in the morals.[26] But it may be suggested that the relation between tale and moral, formally if not always in terms of content, attests to the attempt to establish a renewed text, while staking a claim to age, diffusion, and general validity.

Where did Perrault pick up this allegedly age-old matrix? Soriano, referring to the allusions to governesses and grandmothers in the preface to the prose collection, argues that an orally transmitted matter lies at the heart of the *Contes*;[27] a thesis augmented by Darnton's suggestion that the nurse of Perrault's son was his principal informant.[28] Also Perrault's own reference, in his *Parallèle*, to 'nos contes de Peau d'asne'[29] seems to indicate that he gleaned his material from a stock of commonly known narratives of the Donkey-skin type.

But literary antecedents have been proposed as well. Perrault, for one, points to generic concordances between his tales and those of Antiquity: *Peau d'Ane*, he states, for instance, is of the same genre as Apuleius's fable about Psyche: entirely fictitious and of great antiquity. But, unsurprisingly, this prime mover of the *modernes* is at pains to stress that the moral of his tale is quite different from that of Apuleius. The old fables are written only to please and show utter disregard for morality.[30] In the fables that 'our ancients' have invented for their children, however, care is taken that all figures get their just deserts, and that those who are *honnête, patient, laborieux*, and *obéissant* are rewarded.[31] Scholars have suggested that Perrault drew on the literary legacy of, among others, the Italian *Piacevoli Notti* by G. Straparola (1550-1553), which appeared in French in 1560/1576, and the Neapolitan *Il Pentamerone* penned by G. Basile (1630s), two collections of fairytales couched in a framework inspired by the *Decameron*.[32] But also

---

[25] Perrault, 'Préface', in *Contes*, p. 3.

[26] M. J. Muratore, *Mimesis and Metatextuality in the French Neo-Classical Text: Reflexive Readings of La Fontaine, Molière, Racine, Guilleragues, Madame de La Fayette, Scarron, Cyrano de Bergerac and Perrault* (Geneva, 1994), p. 140.

[27] Soriano, *Les Contes de Perrault*, pp. 79-80.

[28] Darnton, 'Peasants Tell Tales', p. 19.

[29] Perrault, *Parallèle*, II, p. 126; edn, p. 211.

[30] In the *Parallèle* he decries the filthiness of the *Golden Ass* of Lucius and Apuleius, *Parallèle*, II, p. 126; edn, p. 211.

[31] Perrault, 'Préface', in *Contes*, p. 5.

[32] Soriano argues that Perrault must have known Basile's work, but doubts that he understood the Neapolitan dialect in which it was written (Soriano, *Les Contes de Perrault*, pp. 75-76). Elsewhere, however, Soriano warns against neglecting Perrault's potential access to *Il Pentamerone* through his brother Pierre, who translated

Bonaventure des Périers's *Nouvelle* CXXIX (published posthumously in 1558), which features a *Peau d'Ane*, commends itself as a potential inspiration.

Suffice it, for our purposes, to conclude that Perrault took up a substance and a genre with a broad popular appeal which had previously been employed in a few but significant literary works, and shaped it in his own way. Jack Zipes states that, in their oral shape, these tales were socially transmissible: told around the rural hearths and by lower-class wet-nurses in upper-class nurseries. But, when subjected to writing, Zipes argues, they were adapted to contemporary societal, i.e. courtly and bourgeois, requirements. In this process, 'The morality and ethics of a male-dominated Christian civil order had to become part and parcel of the literary fairy tale'.[33]

In our case, it may be suggested that the tales became domesticised because they, in Perrault's view, commended themselves as a genre which fitted his ideals regarding communication of a particular Christian civil order: they – allegedly – belonged to a familiar and non-pagan tradition, represented moral integrity and, we may add, were open to appropriation. In these tales, the *courtisan* and *académicien* saw a possibility of fleshing out the programmatic statements of the *Parallèle*. Perrault shaped his version of the tales as an address to his contemporaries on their moral and historical home ground while, in significant ways, updating them for the *siècle de Louis le Grand*. We will now look more closely at *Peau d'Ane* and *Cendrillon* in order to analyse aspects of this updating.

4. *Texts*

4.1 *Peau d'Ane (1693)*

This tale falls into three parts. In the first, a queen on her deathbed makes the king promise that he will not remarry unless he finds a woman more beautiful and good than herself. Only their daughter meets these conditions, and the king is struck with incestuous passion. The princess seeks the aid of her fairy godmother, who helps her to three dresses, but does not save her from the paternal infatuation. Dressed in a Donkey-skin, the princess eventually leaves for a distant land.

The second part recounts Donkey-skin's employment as a pig-feeder on a faraway farm. On Sundays and Feast days, she takes out her dresses, hap-

---

Tassoni's *La Secchia rapita*, including passages in a variety of Italian dialects (Soriano, *Les Contes de Perrault*, pp. 115-116).

[33] J. Zipes, *Fairy Tales and the Art of Subversion: The Classical Genre for Children and the Process of Civilization* (London, 1983), pp. 8-9 (p. 9).

pily admiring her own appearance in the mirror. One Sunday, a prince passes by; he sees Donkey-skin through the keyhole and is rapt with passion. The prince now wastes away yearning for the girl. In the third part. the prince's mother makes Donkey-skin bake a cake for the ailing prince, but her ring falls into the dough. The prince finds the ring and launches a quest for its owner. Donkey-skin marries the prince; the bride's father attends – his love now purified.

4.2 *Cendrillon (1697)*

In terms of tale-genealogy, *Cendrillon* and *Peau d'Ane* belong to the same family. In the Perraldian versions there are significant differences, which pertain partly to the development of different types, partly to the fact that Donkey-skin was one of the first tales Perrault published, whereas *Cendrillon* was one of the last. While *Peau d'Ane* offers an at times blurred plot phrased in verbose verse, *Cendrillon* has much of the unequivocality and the *pur, sec & simple*, which, according to the *Parallèle*, is necessary when addressing seventeenth-century French readers.[34]

Perrault's version of this tale features the well-known story of a motherless girl who is abused by her stepmother and stepsisters; she is charged with the basest tasks in the house and called upon to prepare her sisters for the royal ball. Through the interference of her fairy godmother, she receives a carriage and garb, which makes her fit to attend the ball on two consecutive evenings. She charms everyone, above all the prince. On the first night she manages to leave before the clock strikes twelve, but on the second she forgets the time; she loses her glass slipper but eventually captures the prince.

5. *Commonplaces*

Soriano states, discussing *Cendrillon*: 'Le conteur alterne avec adresse la technique des lieux communs et des traits généraux et celle qui au contraire multiplie les détails concrets et les précisions historiques'.[35] With a slight modification of this characterisation, it may be suggested that, in these two tales, Perrault employs two registers of commonplaces. One register is related to the type and genre and may be identified through surveys of narrative variants of the Cinderella-tale.[36] The two tales in question unmistakably

---

[34] Perrault, *Parallèle*, III, pp. 62-63; edn, p. 299.

[35] Soriano, *Les Contes de Perrault*, p. 146.

[36] Such as M. R. Cox, *Cinderella: Three Hundred and Forty-Five Variants of Cinderella, Catskin, and Cap o' Rushes* (London, 1893).

retain the principal features of their tradition: the motherless girl, the man-ual labour, the meeting with the prince, the test, the wedding. The other reg-ister of commonplaces pertains to the tales as autonomous texts laden with contemporary details. The first, formal, kind of commonplace functions across time. Within the reassuring framework of the fairytale genre, even instances where reason is defied seem perfectly logical to a modern reader. The contemporary commonplaces, however, are recognisable and decipher-able to various, often limited, degrees; they hover somewhere between the exotic and the hermetic.

Some contemporary details may be readily savoured, such as when, in *Peau d'Ane*, the court is robbed of a marriage, because the bride-to-be has fled: 'Partout se répandit un triste et noir chagrin; / Plus de Noces, plus de Festin, / Plus de Tarte, plus de Dragées; / Les Dames de la Cour, toutes dé-couragées, / N'en dînèrent point la plupart'[37] ('Everywhere there spread a sad and dark grief, / no more wedding, no more feast, / no more tarts nor sugar-coated almonds; / most of the ladies of the court, dismayed, / did not have anything to eat'). Particularly in *Cendrillon*, Perrault revels in such traits of up-to-date hue. Whereas Cendrillon lives in the attic, the step-daughters have the chambers with parquets, modern beds, and mirrors ex-tending from head to toe;[38] two entire pages are spent on their attire for the ball, on how false beauty spots (*mouches*) were obtained and twelve laces broken in the pursuit of slim waists; and eventually Cendrillon must voice her opinion on account of her *goût bon*, a virtue of no little consequence in the 1690s.[39] Simonsen remarks that *Cendrillon* developed from a tale of food, featuring a magic fruit tree in the central role, to a tale of finery.[40] This matches Darnton's statement that, in the versions circulating among starved peasants, these tales are all about satiation;[41] whereas the *haut monde* concern is with embellishment. But these tales are not just about bourgeois bijoux, and the contemporary details also imply weightier topics, although in attractive guise. After all, in his introduction to the prose tales, Perrault does estimate that the tales will inevitably make children wish to

---

[37] Perrault, *Peau d'Ane*, in *Contes*, p. 65.
[38] *Idem*, p. 157.
[39] *Idem*, pp. 158-159.
[40] The observation was first made by M. Djeribi; Simonsen, *Perrault: Contes* (Paris, 1992), pp. 93-94. See also Darnton, 'Peasants Tell Tales', p. 38.
[41] Darnton, 'Peasants Tell Tales', pp. 30-40. A significant reversal of the theme of the full belly appears in the lack of appetite in each of the love-sick princes, noted by P. Lewis, *Seeing through the Mother Goose Tales: Visual Turns in the Writings of Charles Perrault* (Stanford, 1996), p. 160. Cinderella in turn serves her sisters pieces of orange and lemon – sophisticated, but hardly satiating; *Cendrillon*, in *Contes*, p. 161.

imitate those who fare well, and that, as children are not yet capable of stomaching 'solid truths', these must be embedded in pleasant stories which befit a tender age.[42]

5.1 *The auxiliary*

Soriano states that Perrault alternates between generic commonplaces and concrete historical details. It may be argued that, at times, he merges the two. This seems to apply to the magic auxiliary, which comes in a variety of guises in the type of tale to which *Cendrillon* and *Peau d'Ane* belong. In a sixth-century BC version, an eagle carries the sandal of an Egyptian girl to the king.[43] In the Chinese ninth-century version, shoes and finery are procured through the bones of a magic fish.[44] In several European variants, the dead mother helps the protagonist, but often a tree or an animal plays the part of the beneficent intermediary;[45] in a French tradition the auxiliary in two cases appears to be Virgin Mary,[46] and, in Basile's version of the Cinderella-story, *La Gatta Cenerentola* is aided by a fairy from Sardinia.

Perrault's casting of the fairy godmother in this part is apparently a novelty to the genre. This figure is described respectively as 'sa Marraine (...) une admirable Fée' (*Peau d'Ane*) and 'sa Marreine, qui était Fée' (*Cendrillon*).[47] Whereas Donkey-skin's godmother lives in a grotto, Cendrillon's seems slightly more domesticated and presumably has more specific connotations of societal and familial commitments; after all, the moral states that Cendrillon's grandmother both dresses and instructs her, 'en la dressant, en l'instruisant'.[48] In *Peau d'Ane*, the godmother appears briefly at the beginning and only returns at the finale. In *Cendrillon*, the climactic transformation from minion to queen of the ball revolves around the godmotherly magic, and the figure is invested with a considerable import. Perrault dedicates the *autre moralité* of the tale to the value of godparents, suggesting that *esprit*, courage, and other such advantageous talents are useless unless

---

[42] Perrault, *Préface*, in *Contes*, p. 6. The audience of Perrault's *contes* is a much debated issue, but one that falls outside the scope of this essay.

[43] Strabo, *Geographia*, 17.1.11, in: H. L. Jones, transl., *The Geography of Strabo*, VIII (London/Cambridge, MA, 1967 [1932]), pp. 92-94.

[44] R. D. Jameson, 'Cinderella in China', in: *Three Lectures on Chinese Folklore* (Beijing, 1932), pp. 45-85, esp. pp. 52-55. The geographical and chronological spread of the type are not our concern, but do add an ironic perspective to Perrault's belief that he is taking up a specifically non-pagan matrix.

[45] A. B. Rooth, *The Cinderella Cycle* (Lund, 1951), esp. pp. 151-155.

[46] *Idem*, p. 43.

[47] Perrault, *Peau d'Ane* and *Cendrillon*, in *Contes*, pp. 61 and 159.

[48] Perrault, *Cendrillon*, in *Contes*, p. 164.

sustained by a godparent: 'Pour votre avancement ce seront choses vaines, / Si vous n'avez, pour les faire valoir, / Ou des parrains ou des marraines'.[49] This moral, whether ironic or not, is rooted in the structural – and sacramental – societal conditions of the time. As stated in the dictionary of Furetière (1690), the *marreine* is a

> Fille ou femme qui tient un enfant sur les fonts de Baptesme. On appelle aussi des *marreines* au Sacrement de Confirmation. C'est d'ordinaire la *marreine* qui nomme les filles. Il se contracte une alliance spirituelle entre la *marreine* & son filleuil. (...) Ce mot est derivé de *mere* ou de *mater*.[50]

> Girl or woman who holds a child at the baptismal font. Godmothers are also assigned for the Sacrament of Confirmation. It is normally the godmother who names the girls. There exists a spiritual bond between the godmother and her goddaughter. (...) The word derives from *mere* or *mater*.

Muratore argues that 'Perrault's conclusion that *Cendrillon* illustrates the rewards of having good godparents can only be read as a derisive distortion of whatever intended message the text initially harbored'.[51] It is, however, not a distortion of the text in its Perraldian guise. The godmother serves as a renewed commonplace, which personifies the generically obligatory supernatural element while adding a rational and recognisable tenor of familial structures and strategies as a vital criterion for progress in the world.

5.2 The Casuist

Peau d'Ane features a Casuist, who is a figure with another set of contemporary connotations. He enters the scene only briefly but, in his endorsement of the king's incestuous passion, makes quite an impression: 'Il trouva même un Casuiste / Qui jugea que le cas se pouvait proposer' ('He even found a Casuist / who deemed that the case could be made').[52]

This Casuist comes across as a heavily charged character at a time when the Jansenist movement was making the religious landscape quake. The Jansenists propagated a Catholicism based on the Augustinian doctrine of grace; the Jesuits were their fiercest opponents, and the Jesuit Casuists a

---

[49] *Idem*, p. 165. This passage lends itself seductively to biographical speculation. Perrault's own godfather was his older brother Pierre, who was to secure his employment, and with whom he took up residence; Perrault, *Mémoires*, p. 1. Also the author's relationship with Colbert springs to mind in this context.

[50] A. Furetière, *Dictionnaire universel*, ed. A. Rey, 3 vols. (Paris, 1978), 'marreine'.

[51] Muratore, *Mimesis and Metatextuality*, p. 149.

[52] Perrault, *Peau d'Ane*, in *Contes*, pp. 60-61.

primary goal of their contempt. There are several indications that Perrault
was sympathetic to the Jansenist cause. His brother Nicolas was a staunch
supporter of the Jansenist figurehead Antoine Arnauld, and Charles himself
speaks favourably about Jansenist works.[53] Perhaps it is especially Pascal's
version of Jansenism which looms in the background? At least Perrault's
scorn of the Casuist's dubious judgement in *Peau d'Ane* echoes Pascal's
thirteenth *Lettre provinciale* (1656), famed for its polemical display of
Casuist deliberations on murder. Here Pascal argues against the Jesuit Les-
sius's formulation: 'Il semble qu'on n'en doit pas FACILEMENT permettre la
pratique' ('it seems that one cannot *easily* permit the practice'). Pascal de-
fies his opponents: 'Diriez-vous, mes Pères, qu'il ne faut pas permettre facilement, dans la pratique, les adultères ou les incestes? Ne doit-on pas
conclure au contraire (…) que la pratique même en peut être quelquefois
permise, quoique rarement?'[54] ('Would you say, my fathers, that one cannot
easily permit, in practice, adultery or incest? Must we not conclude, on the
contrary, (…) that the very practice may sometimes be permitted, albeit
rarely?').

By furnishing the villainous and incestuous paternal party of his tale
with Jesuit connotations, Perrault seems to hint at the Jansenist conflict and
its satirical undercurrents. He thereby extends the ample stock repository of
fairytale characters; without bursting the customary narrative coherence of
the tale, he offers a catchword, a commonplace from the polemics and satire
of his days, which must have been ripe with connotations for a particular
contemporary reader-community. The Casuist may be considered one, and
the most evident, of several potential hints at a Jansenist vocabulary in Perrault's fairytales.

5.3 *Bonne grâce*

The first moral of *Cendrillon* praises the virtue of *bonne grâce*, which is far
more valuable than beauty:

---

[53] Soriano ascribes great importance to the Perraults as 'une famille fortement influ-
encée par le jansénisme' (Soriano, *Le Dossier*, p. 24). In the *Parallèle*, the Abbot
praises Arnauld and Nicole's work *Art de penser* (*La Logique de Port Royal*) of
1662 as surpassing Aristotle (Perrault: *Parallèle des anciens et des modernes*, IV,
p. 128-131; edn, p. 405).
[54] *Treizième lettre écrite par l'auteur des lettres au provincial*, in: B. Pascal, *Les
Provinciales*, ed. J. Steinmann (Paris, 1962), I, p. 212. In the *Parallèle*, Perrault has
the *Abbé* praise the purity of language, nobility of thought, and finesse in the gibes
of Pascal's *Lettres provinciales*. Even the naturally impatient *Chevalier* has read
them ten times, enjoying the longest the most (*Parallèle*, II, p. 122; edn, p. 210).

La beauté pour le sexe est un rare trésor,
De l'admirer jamais on ne se lasse;
Mais ce qu'on nomme bonne grâce
Est sans prix, et vaut mieux encor.
(...)
Belles, ce don vaut mieux que d'être bien coiffées,
Pour engager un cœur, pour en venir à bout,
La bonne grace est le vrai don des Fées;
Sans elle on ne peut rien, avec elle, on peut tout.[55]

Beauty is a rare treasure for the [female] sex,
We never cease to admire it;
But that which we call 'bonne grâce'
Is invaluable and worth much more.
(...)
Beauties, this gift is worth more than having your hair done well,
In order to engage a heart and make it yours,
This 'bonne grâce' is the true gift of fairies;
Without it, we can do nothing – with it, everything is possible.

The last sentence of this moral may have struck a particular chord with those readers who appreciated Casuist parody. Associations are difficult to chart, but it does seem fruitful to make a brief detour to Perrault's *Mémoires*, one the themes of which is the legal case against Antoine Arnauld (1655-1656), a leading Jansenist, for his attacks on the Jesuit administration of confession. Charles Perrault's brother Nicolas, a theologian, supported Arnauld to an extent, which caused his expulsion from the Sorbonne. Charles Perrault held this brother in high esteem:

> Outre que mon frere avoit beaucoup étudié, Dieu lui avoit fait la grace d'entrer si bien & si avant dans l'esprit de la Religion, que j'oserois dire que peu de gens ont mieux sçu que lui le véritable systême de la Religion chrétienne.[56]

> Apart from the fact that my brother had studied much, God had given him the grace of entering so well and so far into the spirit of religion, that I dare say that few people have known better than he the true system of the Christian religion.

As in the *Parallèle*, Perrault here foregrounds the system of the Christian religion. And with Nicolas so well versed in it, who was better suited to

---

[55] Perrault, *Cendrillon*, in *Contes*, p. 164.
[56] Perrault, *Mémoires*, p. 10.

teach Perrault and a group of friends about the implications of the case against Arnauld and the doctrine of grace?

A crux is the question of whether the apostle Peter had grace when he sinned. Pascal summarised Arnauld's stance in the sentence: 'Que la grâce sans laquelle on ne peut rien, a manqué à S. Pierre dans sa chute' ('That grace, without which one can do nothing, was wanting in St. Peter at his fall').[57] Perrault went quite a few steps into the dogmatic profundities when, in his *Mémoires*, he recapitulated the argument such as Nicolas had conveyed it: the grace of God gives two powers: a proximate power (*pouvoir prochain*), which brings about good deeds, and a distant power (*pouvoir éloigné*), which does not bring good deeds as such but only the ability to do them. In his sin, Peter was deprived of the first if not of the latter. Perrault concludes that 'M. Arnauld n'avoit point mal parlé quand il avoit dit que la Grace sans laquelle on ne peut rien lui avoit manqué' ('M. Arnauld did not speak badly when he said that the grace without which one can do nothing was wanting in him'), stressing twice within a few lines the phrase 'la Grace, sans laquelle on ne peut rien'.[58]

Did this phrase by any chance resurface as Perrault was coining the moral of *Cendrillon* and its praise of the mundane virtue of *bonne grâce – sans elle on ne peut rien*?

5.4 *Transformation*

The *topos* of transformation belongs within the conventions of this type of tale, but Perrault seems to attach special significance to it, and makes the transfigurations of his heroines in the two tales in focus here a *point de repère*. Both *Cendrillon* and *Peau d'Ane* experience an elevation, which goes by way of debasement and a decisive moment of change, epitomised in their magic dresses.

---

[57] The quotation stems from Arnauld's second *Lettre à un duc et pair* (1655). Pascal, *Les Provinciales*, I, p. 21 and note p. 280.

[58] Perrault, *Mémoires*, pp. 18-19. The passage about Nicolas's instruction on Arnauld is headed by a pregnant: *Origine des Lettres Provinciales*, and it concludes with verve: Pierre Perrault recounted the conversation to an attendant of the duke of Luynes who was at Port-Royal and urged the people there to inform the public about the events at the Sorbonne. Eight days later, Perrault tells us, the attendant returned to Pierre and Charles and handed them the first of the *Lettres Provinciales* with the words: 'Voilà, le fruit de ce que vous me dites il y a huit jours' ('Here is the fruit of what you told me eight days ago') (Perrault, *Mémoires*, p. 20). I have not come across references to a connection between the provincial letters and the Perrault family outside Charles Perrault's *Mémoires*.

Donkey-Skin is led to her prince via the feeding of the pigs in a faraway land – in a somewhat elusive mirroring of the prodigal son of Luke 15. The theme of transformation is played out largely by means of colour-codes. On the one hand, there are the three dresses obtained from the king and described in lavish detail. They are coloured respectively in the shade of time: more azure than even heaven itself ('la belle robe bleue / Que tout l'azur des Cieux ne saurait égaler');[59] the moon: which is, however, less splendid in her silvery robe ('La Lune est moins pompeuse en sa robe d'argent');[60] and the sun: of a superb fabric of gold and diamonds ('D'un superbe tissu d'or et de diamants').[61] The dresses are described both when they are first commissioned and, later, when the girl admires herself in the mirror, her countenance red and white ('vermeille et blanche').[62]

On the other hand, the narrative abounds in shades of black. Her real appearance hidden behind the hide, people describe Donkey-skin to her future mother-in-law with disgust: 'Cette Peau d'Ane est une noire Taupe / Plus vilaine encore et plus gaupe / Que le plus sale Marmiton'[63] ('This Donkey-skin is a black mole, more hideous and filthy than the dirtiest kitchen-drudge'). The dirtiness forms a particular category. It comes across in the reflection of people's view of Donkey-skin as 'maussade' and 'pleine d'ordure'[64] ('disgusting' and 'full of scraps'), in the remark that, beneath her 'crasse' and 'haillons' ('grime' and 'rags'), she still had the heart of a princess,[65] and, finally, in the comment that she is 'La bête (...) la plus laide, / Qu'on puisse voir après le Loup' ('The most ugly beast / that one can see, apart from the wolf').[66]

Eventually, as the ring is tried on all kinds of girls, red and black paws ('rouges et noirs pattes'), no less than delicate hands, have hopes of good fortune. But then the proper hand is found: '(...) elle tira de dessous sa peau noire / Une petite main qui semblait de l'ivoire / Qu'un peu de pourpre a coloré (...)'[67] ('She held out from beneath her black hide / a small hand which looked like ivory / coloured by a drop of purple'). As a final, puzzling, contribution to the theme of blackness, Moors mounted on elephants appear among the wedding guests, 'Qui, plus noirs et plus laids encore, /

---

[59] Perrault, *Peau d'Ane*, in *Contes*, p. 66.
[60] *Idem*, p. 62.
[61] *Idem*, p. 63.
[62] *Idem*, p. 66.
[63] *Idem*, p. 69.
[64] *Idem*, p. 65.
[65] *Idem*, p. 67.
[66] *Idem*, p. 68.
[67] *Idem*, p. 72.

Faisaient peur aux petits enfants'[68] ('who, even more black and ugly, / scared the small children'). There is a recurrent oscillation between such soiled blackness and Donkey-skin's polychrome glory.

Soriano states that *Peau d'Ane* presumably relates to an oral version of Basile's *L'Orsa*: as an undeniable if liberal imitation.[69] The theme of incestuous passion runs through both tales, but, in Basile, the princess is turned into a bear by means of a magic stick. The bear is quite different from the filthy and black but anthropomorphic figure of Donkey-skin. Basile alludes to its coarse bristles, but otherwise describes the animal as cuddly and pampered throughout. Viewed against the backdrop of *L'Orsa*, the recurrent references to blackness and filthiness in *Peau d'Ane* seem to be Perrault's invention and a point which he emphasises. The glory to which Donkey-skin rises from her stained blackness is epitomised in her marriage with the prince; but more significant in our context is the splendour in which she appears before her mirror on Sundays and feast days, suggestively displayed from the point of view of the prince, gazing through the keyhole:

> Trois fois, dans la chaleur du feu qui le transporte, / Il voulut enfoncer la porte; / Mais croyant voir une Divinité, / Trois fois par le respect son bras fut arrêté.[70]

> Three times, in the heat of the fire inciting him, / he wished to break down the door; / but believing he saw a divinity, / three times did respect hold back his arm.

The filthy kitchen-girl has been transfigured to the point of sanctification.

Both *Peau d'Ane* and *Cendrillon* display verbal mockery as a crucial element in the debasement of the heroine. Donkey-skin is abused by the servants in the kitchen, and a whole verse is spent on the ridicule and *bons mots* showered on her.[71] In *Cendrillon*, the implications of the verbal assault are even more profound. Her two soubriquets mark her humble status and position in the cinders; she is called *Cendrillon* by the younger, and more merciful, sister, and *Cucendron* by the older. Simonsen states that, in the popular tradition, Cinderella's ash-allusions connote purification and mourning, and her name thus invests her with some serenity. In Perrault, however, the ashes seem primarily to connote labour and dirtiness.[72] De-

---

[68] *Idem*, p. 74.
[69] Soriano, *Les Contes de Perrault*, p. 117. The donkey which produces gold before being turned into a skin may be borrowed from Basile's *La Fiaba dell'Orco* (Soriano, *Les Contes de Perrault*, p. 118).
[70] Perrault, *Peau d'Ane*, in *Contes*, p. 68.
[71] *Idem*, p. 66.
[72] Simonsen, *Perrault: Contes*, p. 92.

spite the statement that she is positioned at the fireplace, Cendrillon is constantly busy in the proximity of the sisters; and it is exactly the mock similarity which exhibits her difference. This is epitomised in comments from the sisters, such as: 'on rirait bien si on voyait un Cucendron aller au Bal'[73] ('we would surely laugh if we were to see an Ash-bum go to the ball'). The scoffing of the girl is not a common *topos* in this type of tale. Often the new family does not spite the motherless protagonist, but rather pities her childish ways and wishes.[74] In *Cendrillon* the mockery is central.

Eventually *Cendrillon* bursts into tears, secures the attention of her fairy godmother, and spurs on the transformation. Just like the dressing of the stepsisters was earlier spelled out in droll detail, the transfiguration of the heroine is carried out step by step under the directions of the pragmatic fairy. From a pumpkin fetched from the garden, the godmother makes a carriage. From the mice in the mousetrap she creates six (mouse-)grey horses and so on, and Cendrillon, grasping the rationale of the magic, suggests that a rat from the rat trap be turned into a coachman; 'Tu as raison', the magic fairy exclaims.[75]

This focus on transformation curiously echoes Ovidian metamorphoses. But in the pronounced radicalism of the states involved in their transformations, the two *contes* display a particular tension. Once again we shall turn to Jansenist traits in the Perraldian frame of resonance. In the *Parallèle*, Perrault displays the double knowledge that was lacking in the ancients:

> (...) ils ne se sont point connus eux-mesmes, puisqu'ils n'ont point sçu, comme je l'ay déja dit, la corruption de la nature humaine par le peché originel. Ces deux connoissances leur ayant manqué, celle du souverain bien qui est Dieu où ils devoient tendre, & celle de la corruption de leur nature qu'ils devoient corriger & reformer pour parvenir à la possession de ce souverain bien, leur Morale n'a pû estre que tres defectueuse.[76]

> They did not know themselves, because they did not recognise, as I have already said, the corruption of human nature through original sin. As this double knowledge was wanting in them: that of the sovereign good that is God, towards whom they should strive, and that of their nature, which they should correct and reform in order to possess this sovereign good, their morality cannot have been but very faulty.

---

[73] Perrault, *Cendrillon*, in *Contes*, p. 158.
[74] Simonsen, *Perrault: Contes*, pp. 88-89.
[75] Perrault, *Cendrillon*, in *Contes*, p. 159.
[76] Perrault, *Parallèle*, IV, p. 146; edn, p. 409.

This statement may be considered an example of Perraldian echoes of the Jansenist Augustinianism voiced in Pascal's provincial letters as well as his *Pensées*, such as the ponderings on the incomprehensibility of original sin, without which man would be incomprehensible to himself (164), on God as the sovereign good (181), and on the double teaching of Christianity: man is vile and abominable and must nevertheless desire similitude with God (383).[77] Above all, it may be argued that the radical and fundamental Jansenist tension between the baseness of original sin and the quest for similitude with God resonates in the attention directed to, for instance, Donkeyskin's double appearance: on the one hand disfigured by blackness and beastliness, and, on the other, transfigured, on Sundays and feast days, into a red and white creature which may be taken for divine. Marin, in *Food for Thought*, has proposed that the comprehensive sign theory elaborated by the Jansenist community at Port-Royal underlies the culinary and transformative signs in Perrault. Without contesting this, much grander, hypothesis, the suggestion here is that the Perraldian moral tenor hinges on the 'Systéme de Morale' of Jansenism as it resonated in the *Lettres provinciales* or in Nicolas Perrault's instruction.

I do not argue that *Peau d'Ane* and *Cendrillon* represent a grafting of Jansenist dogma onto tales derived from popular lore. But the two *contes* are a striking example of the merger of universality and individuality that is characteristic of the genre. Perrault encodes fundamental elements from the stock repository of fairytale *topoi* by means of markers which, to his contemporaries, may well have been charged with specific connotations: the attractive details regarding food and clothing, the more substantial references to the figures of the *marraine* and the Casuist – and perhaps to more wide-ranging doctrinal structures of vileness, grace, and glory underlying the tales' allusions to the transformation from stained humiliation to victorious splendour.

6. *Epilogue: commonplaces in Perrault's 'Contes'*

Commonplaces are the stuff that fairytales are made of; commonplaces, that is, in the sense of 'cultural material with both past and present currency'.[78] Perrault's *contes* are a literary work at once steeped in generic conventions and representing that need for an up-to-date morality which is propagated in his *Parallèle*. It draws on a familiar popular tradition and displays a variety of the commonplaces belonging to this genre. But his is no mere antiquarian retelling. In his professed interest in the moral instruction which may be

---

[77] Pascal, *Pensées*, ed. P. Sellier (Paris, 1976), pp. 90, 103, and 192.
[78] Moss, chapter in this volume, p. 1.

conveyed through these tales, Charles Perrault shows himself as a true *moderne*. Perhaps some of the narrative pointers of his adaptation even attest to an ambition to take up the satirical thread from Pascal and bring into play the theological teachings of his brother, thus working as commonplaces within a quite particular contemporary frame of reference.

But, whereas the commonplaces pertaining to the fairytale genre are to a large extent identifiable, those which belong to the contemporary code are evasive. In this sense, Perrault's description of Homeric mores applies to his own handling of commonplaces: 'il y en a de particuliéres au temps où il a écrit, & il y en a qui sont de tous les temps' ('there are those which are particular to the time when he wrote, and there are those which are relevant at all times').[79]

---

[79] Perrault, *Parallèle*, III, p. 47; edn, p. 295.

Acta Colloquii Montis Belligartensis (Tübingen, 1587).

Ad acta Colloquii Montisbelgardensis (...) *Theodori Bezae responsio* (Geneva, 1588).

Agricola, R., *De inventione dialectica libri tres*, ed. and transl. L. Mundt (Tübingen, 1992).

———, *Ecrits sur la dialectique et l'humanisme*, ed. and transl. M. van der Poel (Paris, 1997).

Allott, R., *Englands Parnassus: or the choysest flowers of our moderne poets* (London, 1600; repr. Menston, 1970).

Ansaldi, I., *Dottrina cristiana. Nuovamente Ristampata, & publicata per ordine dell'Illustriss. & Reverendiss. Cardinal Di Firenze. Da insegnarsi, & esercitarsi dalli Curati, & Guardiani delle Compagnie de' Fanciulli della suo Diocesi per publica utilità* (Florence, 1585).

The Apostolic Fathers, transl. K. Lake (Cambridge, MA, 1965).

Aquinas, T., *Scriptum in quatuor libros sententiarum magistri Petri Lombardi*, in: *Opera omnia,* ed. I. Nicolai (Parma, 1858).

Aranci, G., *Formazione religiosa e santità laicale a Firenze tra cinque e seicento: Ippolito Galantini fondatore della congrgazione di San Francesco della dottrina cristiana di Firenze (1565-1620)* (Florence, 1997).

Arbeau, T. [Tabourot, J.], *Orchesographie et traicté en forme de dialogue, par lequel toutes personnes peuvent facilement apprendre & practiquer l'honneste exercice des dances* [*Orchésographie*] (Langres, 1589).

Aristotle, *Topica*, transl. E. M. Forster (London, 1960).

———, *The Complete Works of Aristotle*, ed. J. Barnes, 2 vols. (Princeton, 1984).

Attrige, H. W. and Niederwimmer, K., eds, *The Didache: A Commentary*, transl. L. M. Maloney (Minneapolis, 1998).

Backer, A. de, *Bibliothèque des écrivains de la Compagnie de Jésus: ou, notices bibliographiques de tous les ouvrages publiés par les membres de la Compagnie de Jésus, depuis la fondation de l'ordre jusqu'à nos jours* (Liège, 1853-1861).

Baïche A., *La Naissance du baroque français: poésie et image de la Pléiade à Jean de La Ceppède* (Toulouse, 1976).

Baldwin, W., *Treatice of Moral Philosophy*, ed. T. Paulfreyman (London, 1571).

Balsamo, J., *Les Rencontres des Muses: italianisme et anti-italianisme dans les Lettres françaises de la fin du XVIe siècle* (Geneva, 1992).

Banks, K., *Cosmos and Image in the Renaissance: French Love Lyric and Natural-Philosophical Poetry* (Oxford, 2008).

———, 'Interpretations of the Body Politic and of Natural Bodies in Late Sixteenth-Century France', in: Musolff, A. and Zinken, J., eds, *Metaphor and Discourse* (Basingstoke, 2009), pp. 205-218.

Barbey, J., *Etre roi: le roi et son gouvernement en France de Clovis à Louis XVI* (Paris, 1992).

Barker, J. R. V., *The Tournament in England 1100-1400* (Woodbridge, 1986, ²2003).

Barr, C., *The Monophonic Lauda and the Lay Religious Confraternities of Tuscany and Umbria in the Late Middle Ages* (Kalamazoo, MI, 1988).

———, 'Music and Spectacle in Confraternity Drama of Fifteenth-Century Florence: The Reconstruction of a Theatrical Event', in: Verdon, T. and Henderson, J., eds, *Christianity and the Renaissance: Image and Religious Imagination in the Quattrocento* (Syracuse, NY, 1990), pp. 376-404.

Bartholomaeus Pisanus, *De conformitate vitae Beati Francisci ad vitam Domini Iesu*, 2 vols. (Quaracchi, 1906-1912).

Bataillon, M., 'Plus oultre: la cour découvre le nouveau monde', in: Jacquot, J., ed., *Les Fêtes de la Renaissance*, II, *Fêtes et cérémonies au temps de Charles Quint* (Paris, 1960), pp. 13-27.

Baumgartner, F. J., *Radical Reactionaries: The Political Thought of the French Catholic League* (Geneva, 1976).

Bayley, P., *French Pulpit Oratory, 1598-1650: A Study in Themes and Styles* (Cambridge, 1980).

Beard, M., North, J., and Price, S., *Religions of Rome* (Cambridge, 1998).

Bejczy, I., 'Overcoming the Middle Ages: Historical Reasoning in Erasmus' Antibarbarian Writings', *Erasmus of Rotterdam Society Yearbook* 16 (1996), pp. 34-53.

Die Bekenntnisschriften der evangelisch-lutherischen Kirche, herausgegeben im Gedenkjahr der Augsburgischen Konfession 1930 (Göttingen, 1976).

Bell, A., 'Language Style as Audience Design', *Language in Society* 13 (1984), pp. 145-204.

Belleforest, F. de, *Les Sentences illustres de M. T. Ciceron, et les Apophthegmes, avec quelques sentences de pieté, recueillies des oeuvres du mesme Ciceron* (Paris, 1574).

Béné, C., *Erasme et saint Augustin, ou influence de saint Augustin sur l'humanisme d'Erasme* (Geneva, 1969).

Benrath, G., 'Das Verständnis der Kirchengeschichte in der Reformationszeit', in: Grenzmann, L. and Stackmann, K., eds, *Literatur und Laienbildung im Spätmittelalter und in der Reformationszeit* (Stuttgart, 1984), pp. 97-109.

Beutel, A., ed., *Luther Handbuch* (Tübingen, 2005).

Bietenholz, P. and Deutscher, T., eds, *Contemporaries of Erasmus: A Biographical Register of the Renaissance and Reformation* (Toronto, 1985).

Blair, A., *The Theater of Nature: Jean Bodin and Renaissance Science* (Princeton, 1997).

Blankenburg, W., 'Der gottesdienstliche Liedgesang der Gemeinde', in: Müller, K. F. and Blankenburg, W., eds, *Leiturgia: Handbuch des evangelischen Gottesdienstes*, IV (Kassel, 1961), pp. 559-660.

———, 'Überlieferung und Textgeschichte von Martin Luthers *Encomion musices*', *Luther-Jahrbuch* 39 (1972), pp. 80-104.

———, 'Luther und die Musik', in: Blankenburg, W., *Kirche und Musik: gesammelte Aufsätze zur Geschichte der gottesdienstlichen Musik*, ed. E. Hübner and R. Steiger (Göttingen, 1979), pp. 17-30.

Blinn, S. B. and Garrett, M., 'Aristotelian *Topoi* as a Cross-Cultural Analytical Tool', *Philosophy and Rhetoric* 26 (1993), pp. 93-112.

Block, J., *Verstehen durch Musik: das gesungene Wort der Theologie. Ein hermeneutischer Beitrag zur Hymnologie am Beispiel Martin Luthers* (Tübingen/Basel, 2002).

Blockmans, W., *Keizer Karel: de utopie van het keizerschap, 1500-1558* (Leuven, 2000).

Blume, F., *Geschichte der evangelischen Kirchenmusik* (Kassel, [2]1965).

Boileau-Despréaux, N., 'L'art poétique', in: *Epîtres, Art poétique, Lutrin*, ed. C.-H. Boudhors (Paris, 1952).

Bolton, R., *The Carnall Professor: Discovering the Wofull Slavery of a Man Guided by the Flesh* (London, 1634).

————, *A Discourse about the State of True Happinesse* (London, 1638).

Bossier, P., *'Ambasciatore della risa': la commedia dell'arte nel secondo Cinquecento (1545-1590)* (Florence, 2004).

————, '"Le verbe puissant et princier": bref aperçu de la dynamique littéraire à la Renaissance italienne', in: Van den Bossche, B. et al., eds, *'Innumerevoli contrasti d'innesti': la poesia del Novecento (e altro): miscellanea in onore di Franco Musarra*, II (Louvain/Florence, 2007), pp. 675-689.

Botsack, J., *I.S.N.J. Moralium Gedanensium libri XXX* (Frankfurt am Main, 1655).

Boudou, B., *Mars et les Muses dans 'L'Apologie pour Hérodote' d'Henri Estienne* (Geneva, 2000).

Boutier, J., Dewerpe, A., and Nordman, D., *Un Tour de France royal: le voyage de Charles IX (1564-1566)* (Paris, 1984).

Bouwsma, W., 'The Two Faces of Humanism: Stoicism and Augustinianism in Renaissance Thought', in: Oberman, H. A. and Brady, T., eds, *Itinerarium italicum: The Profile of the Italian Renaissance in the Mirror of its European Transformations* (Leiden, 1975), pp. 3-60.

Brandstetter, G., ed., *Aufforderung zum Tanz: Geschichten und Gedichte* (Stuttgart, 1993).

Braunrot, B., *Imagination poétique chez Du Bartas: éléments de sensibilité baroque dans la Création du Monde* (Chapel Hill, 1973).

Breward, C., *The Culture of Fashion: A New History of Fashionable Dress* (Manchester/New York, 1995).

Brockliss, L. W. B., *French Higher Education in the Seventeenth and Eighteenth Centuries: A Cultural History* (Oxford, 1987).

Buisseret, D., *Henry IV* (London, 1984).

Bunners, C., *Kirchenmusik und Seelenmusik: Studien zu Frömmigkeit und Musik im Luthertum des 17. Jahrhunderts* (Berlin, 1966).

Burke, P., *Popular Culture in Early Modern Europe* (New York/London, 1978).

————, *The Fortunes of the 'Courtier': The European Reception of Castiglione's 'Cortegiano'* (Cambridge, 1995).

Bussels, S., *Van macht en mensenwerk: retorica als performatieve strategie in de Antwerpse intocht van 1549* (Gent, unpublished PhD, 2005).

Byrne, E. F., *Probability and Opinion: A Study in the Medieval Presuppositions of Post-Medieval Theories of Probability* (The Hague, 1968).

Calvete de Estrella, J. C., *El Felicissimo Viaje del muy Alto y muy Poderoso Principe Don Phelippe, Hijo del Emperador Don Carlos Quinto Maximo, desde España a sus tierras de la baxa Alemaña: con la descripcion de todos los Estados de Brabante y Flandes* (Antwerp, 1552).

Campiglia, M., *Flori, A Pastoral Drama: A Bilingual Edition*, ed. V. Cox and L. Sampson (Chicago/London, 2004).

Cano, M., *De locis theologicis* (Salamanca, 1563).

———, *De locis theologicis*, in: *Opera theologica*, I-II (Rome, 1900). Ed. and Spanish transl. J. Belda Plans (Madrid, 2006).

Caroso, F., *Il Ballarino* (Venice, 1581).

———, *Nobiltà di dame* (Venice, 1600).

———, *Raccolta di varij Balli* (Rome, 1630).

———, *Nobiltà di dame*, eds J. Sutton and F. M. Walker (New York, 1995).

Castiglione, B., *The Courtyer*, transl. T. Hoby (London, 1561).

The Catholic Encyclopedia Online, <http://www.catholic.org/encyclopedia/>.

Catholy, E., *Das Fastnachtspiel des Spätmittelalters: Gestalt und Funktion* (Tübingen, 1961).

———, *Fastnachtspiel* (Stuttgart, 1966).

Cave, T., *The Cornucopian Text: Problems of Writing in the French Renaissance* (Oxford, 1979).

Cawdrey, R., *A Treasurie or Store-house of Similes both pleasaunt, delightfull, and profitable, for all estates of men in generall, newly collected into Heades and Common Places* (repr. Amsterdam/New York, 1971).

Chomarat, J., *Grammaire et Rhétorique chez Erasme*, 2 vols. (Paris, 1981).

Cicero, Marcus Tullius, *Divisions de l'art oratoire, Topiques*, ed. and transl. H. Bornecque (Paris, 1924).

———, 'Catilinaires', in: *Discours,* X, ed. H. Bornecque and transl. E. Bailly (Paris, 1926).

———, *De l'orateur, livre deuxième*, ed. and transl. E. Courbaud (Paris, 1927).

———, *De oratore, Book III* (...), transl. by H. Rackham (Cambridge, MA, 1942).

———, *The Verrine Orations*, transl. L. H. G. Greenwood, 2 vols. (Cambridge, MA, 1967).

———, *Pro Archia poeta oratio*, transl. S. M. Cerutti (Illinois, 2003).

———, *Topica*, ed. and transl. T. Reinhardt (Oxford, 2003).

Clément, L., *Henri Estienne et son œuvre française: étude d'histoire littéraire et de philologie* (Paris, 1898; repr. Geneva, 1967).

Codina-Mir, G., *Aux sources de la pédagogie des Jésuites: le 'Modus Parisiensis'* (Rome, 1968).

Cogan, M., 'Rodolphus Agricola and the Semantic Revolutions of the History of Invention', *Rhetorica* 2 (1984), pp. 163-194.

Cohen, S. R., *Art, Dance, and the Body in French Culture of the Ancien Régime* (Cambridge, 2000).

Conley, T. M., *Rhetoric in the European Tradition* (Chicago/London, 1990).

Connery, J., *Abortion: The Development of the Roman Catholic Perspective* (Chicago, 1977).

Corrozet, G., *Le Parnasse des poetes françois modernes, contenant leurs plus riches et graves sentences, discours, descriptions, et doctes enseignemens* (Paris, 1571).

Cotgrave, R., *A Dictionarie of the French and English Tongues* (London, 1611).

The Country Captaine, and The Varietie (London, 1649).

Cowling, D., '"Neither a Borrower nor a Lender be": Linguistic Mercantilism in Renaissance France', in: Musolff. A. and Zinken, J., eds, *Metaphor and Discourse* (Basingstoke, 2009), pp. 190-204.

————, 'Henri Estienne and the Problem of French-Italian Code-Switching in Sixteenth-Century France', in: Ayres-Bennett, W. and Jones, M. C., eds, *The French Language and Questions of Identity* (Oxford, 2007), pp. 162-170.

Cox, M. E. R., *Cinderella: Three Hundred and Forty-Five Variants of Cinderella, Catskin, and Cap o' Rushes* (London, 1893).

Cox, V., 'The Single Self: Feminist Thought and the Marriage Market in Early Modern Venice', *Renaissance Quarterly* 48 (1995), pp. 513-581.

Crane, M. T., *Framing Authority: Self and Society in Sixteenth-Century England* (Princeton, 1993).

Creore, A. E., 'Ronsard, Du Bartas, and the Homeric Comparison', *Comparative Literature* 3 (1951), pp. 152-159.

Croce, B., *The Pentamerone of Giambattista Basile*, transl. N. M. Penzer (London/New York, 1932).

Crouzet, D., 'Le Règne de Henri III et la violence collective', in: Sauzet, R., ed., *Henri III et son temps* (Paris, 1992), pp. 211-225.

Cunningham, J. P., *Dancing in the Inns of Court* (London, 1965).

Dammann, R., *Der Musikbegriff im deutschen Barock* (Laaber, [3]1995).

Dante Alighieri, *La Divina Commedia: Purgatorio*, ed. and transl. C. Singleton (Princeton, 1973).

Da Piacenza, D., 'De arte saltandi & choreas ducendi', in: Smith, A. W., ed., *Fifteenth-Century Dance and Music: Twelve Transcribed Italian Treatises and Collections in the Tradition of Domenico da Piacenza*, 2 vols. (Stuyvesant, 1995), I, pp. 4-68.

Darnton, R., 'Peasants Tell Tales: The Meaning of Mother Goose', in: *The Great Cat Massacre and Other Episodes in French Cultural History* (Harmondsworth, [2]1985), pp. 17-78.

————, 'The Meaning of Mother Goose', *The New York Review* 31/1 (February 2, 1984), <http://www.nybooks.com/articles/5955>, last accessed March 2, 2007.

De La Fontaine Verwey, H., *Humanisten, dwepers en rebellen in de zestiende eeuw* (Amsterdam, 1975).

Delius, H.-U., *Augustin als Quelle Luthers: eine Materialsammlung* (Berlin, 1984).

Della Casa, G., *Galateo*, ed. S. Prandi (Turin, 1994).

Denzinger, H. and Hünermann, P., *Enchiridion symbolorum, definitionum et declarationum de rebus fidei et morum* (Freiburg, [37]1991).

Desan, P., *Naissance de la méthode (Machiavel, La Ramée, Bodin, Montaigne, Descartes)* (Paris, 1987).

————, *Les Commerces de Montaigne: le discours économique des 'Essais'* (Paris, 1992).

————, *L'Imaginaire économique de la Renaissance* (Mont-de-Marsan, 1993).

De Schepper, M., 'Humanism and humanists', in: Van Der Stock, J., ed., *Antwerp: Story of a Metropolis, 16th-17th Century* (Gent, 1993), pp. 97-103.

Des Périers, B., *Les Nouvelles Récréations et joyeux devis*, in: Jourda, P., ed., *Conteurs français du XVIe siècle* (Paris, 1971 [1965]).

Desrues, F., *Les Marguerites françoises; ou fleurs du bien dire*, ed. C.-O. Stiker-Metral (Rheims, 2003).
Dictionnaire de théologie catholique, IX, part 1 (Paris, 1926).
Dieterich, C., *Die 6. Kirchweyh- oder Gesang-Predigt, darinn vom ersten Ursprung und Brauch des Gesangs in der Christlichen Kirchen summarischer weise discurriret und gehandelt wird, in: D. Cunrad Dieterichs Ulmischer Kirchen Superintendenten Sonderbare Predigten von unterschiedenen Materien hiebevor zu Ulm im Münster gehalten* (Frankfurt am Main/Leipzig, 1669).
Discours merveilleux de la vie, actions et deportements de Catherine de Médicis, Royne-mère, ed. N. Cazauran (Geneva, 1995).
Dobell, C., ed., *Antony van Leeuwenhoek and His 'Little Animals'* (New York, 1960 [1932]).
Dolet, E., *Correspondance: répertoire analytique et chronologique suivi du texte de ses lettres latines*, ed. C. Longeon (Geneva, 1982).
Donington, R., *The Rise of Opera* (London, 1981).
Donnelly, J. P. and Maher, M. W., eds, *Confraternities and Catholic Reform in Italy, France, and Spain* (Kirksville, MO, 1999).
Doob, P. R., *The Idea of the Labyrinth from Classical Antiquity through the Middle Ages* (Ithaca, 1990).
Dreves, G. M., 'Zur Geschichte der fête des fous', *Stimmen aus Maria Laach: Katholische Blätter* 47 (1894), pp. 571-587.
Du Bartas, G. de Saluste, *La Sepmaine*, in: Holmes, U. T., Lyons, J. C., Linker, R. W. et al., eds, *The Works of Guillaume De Salluste Sieur Du Bartas* (Chapel Hill, 1935-1940), II, pp. 193-440.
———, *Brief Advertissement sur sa première et seconde Sepmaine* (1584), in: *Works*, I, pp. 218-224.
Du Bellay, J., *La Deffence, et illustration de la langue françoyse (1549)*, ed. J.-C. Monferran (Geneva, 2001).
Duby, G. and Perrot, M., eds, *Histoire des femmes en Occident* (Paris, 1991-).
Duchesne, J., *Le Grand Miroir du monde* (Lyon, 1587).
———, *Le Grand Miroir du monde* (Lyon, ²1593).
Dürrer, M., *Altitalienische Laudenmelodien: das einstimmige Repertoire der Handschriften Cortona und Florenz*, 2 vols. (Kassel, 1996).
Dyck, J., *Athen und Jerusalem: die Tradition der argumentativen Verknüpfung von Bibel und Poesie im 17. und 18. Jahrhundert* (Munich, 1977).
Eck, J., *Enchiridion locorum communium versus Lutheranos et alios hostes ecclesiae (1525-1543)*, ed. P. Fraenkel (Münster, 1979).
Eckstein, N., 'The Religious Confraternities of High Renaissance Florence: Crisis or Continuity?', in: Kent, F. W. and Zika, C., eds, *Rituals, Images, and Words: Varieties of Cultural Expression in Late Medieval and Early Modern Europe* (Turnhout, 2005), pp. 9-32.
Eisenbichler, K., *The Boys of the Archangel Raphael: A Youth Confraternity in Florence, 1411-1785* (Toronto, 1998).
———, 'Italian Youth Confraternities in an Age of Reform', in: Donnelly, J. P. and Maher, M. W., eds, *Confraternities and Catholic Reform in Italy, France, and Spain* (Kirksville, MO, 1999), pp. 27-44.

Eisler, W., 'Celestial Harmonies and Hapsburg Rule: Levels of Meaning in a Triumphal Arch for Philip II in Antwerp, 1549', in: Wisch, B. and Scott Munshower, S., eds, *'All the World's a Stage…'*: *Art and Pageantry in the Renaissance and Baroque*, part 1: *Triumphal Celebrations and the Rituals of Statecraft* (Pennsylvania, 1990), pp. 333-356.

Ekenberg, A., *Cur cantatur: die Funktionen des liturgischen Gesanges nach den Autoren der Karolingerzeit* (Stockholm, 1987).

Elliott, J. H., 'Introduction', in: Soly, H. and Van De Wiele, J., eds, *Carolus: Keizer Karel V 1500-1558* (Gent, 1999), pp. 26-29.

Elyot, T., *The Boke Named the Governour* (London, 1531).

Enciclopedia universal ilustrada europeo-americana, XXXI (Barcelona, n.d.).

Enders, L., ed., *Luther und Emser: ihre Streitschriften aus dem Jahre 1521*, *Flugschriften aus der Reformationszeit*, VIII (Halle, 1890).

Erasmus, Desiderius, *Opus epistolarum Desiderii Erasmi Roterodami*, ed. P. S. Allen and H. M. Allen, 12 vols. (Oxford, 1906-1958).

———, *Antibarbarorum liber*, ed. K. Kumaniecki, in: *Opera omnia Desiderii Erasmi Roterodami*, I.1 (Amsterdam, 1969).

———, *Opera omnia* (Amsterdam, 1974).

———, *The Antibarbarians*, ed. C. R. Thompson and transl. M. Mann Philips, in: *Collected Works of Erasmus*, XXIII (Toronto, 1978).

———, 'De civilitate morum puerilium', in: Sowards, J. K., ed., *Collected Works of Erasmus*, XXV (Toronto, 1985), pp. 269-289.

———, 'Querela Pacis', in: Levi, A. H. T., ed., *Collected Works of Erasmus*, XXVII (Toronto, 1986).

———, 'Institutio principis christiani', in: Levi, A. H. T., ed., *Collected Works of Erasmus*, XXVII (Toronto, 1986), pp. 199-288.

———, *De duplici copia verborum ac rerum*, ed. B. I. Knott, in: *Erasmus, Opera omnia*, I/6 (Amsterdam, 1988).

Erinnerungsschrifft etlicher vom Adel und Staedten an den Durchleuchtigen Hochgebornen Fürsten unnd Herrn Johann Georgen Fürsten zu Anhalt (...) Sampt darauff erfolgten gnediger Verantwortung und erklärung (Zerbst, 1596).

Estienne, H., *Les Premices, ou le I livre des proverbes epigrammatizez, ou, des epigrammes proverbializez, c'est à dire, signez et scellez par les proverbes françois; aucuns aussi par les grecs et latins, ou autres, pris de quelcun des langages vulgaires, rengez en lieux communs* ([Geneva], 1594).

———, *Conformité du langage françois avec le grec*, ed. L. Feugère (Paris, 1853; repr. Geneva, 1970).

———, *Apologie pour Hérodote: satire de la société au XVIe siècle*, ed. P. Ristelhuber, 2 vols. (Paris, 1879; repr. Geneva, 1969).

———, *Traicté de la Conformité du language françois avec le grec (1565) suivi de De Latinitate falso suspecta (1576) et de Project du livre intitulé: De la precellence du langage françois (1579)* (Geneva, 1972).

———, *Deux Dialogues du nouveau langage françois italianizé et autrement desguizé, principalement entre les courtisans de ce temps*, ed. P. M. Smith (Geneva, 1980).

Etlich Christlich lider Lobgesang un[n] Psalm dem rainen wort Gottes gemeß auß der heylige[n] schrifft durch mancherley hochgelerter gemacht in den

Kirchen zu singen wie es dann [z]um tayl berayt zu Wittenberg in uebung ist (Nuremberg, 1523-1524; repr. Kassel, 1957) [The *Achtliederbuch*].

Evain, A., *L'Apparition des actrices professionnelles en Europe* (Paris, 2001).

Even-Zohar, I., *Papers in Historical Poetics* (Tel Aviv, 1978).

———, 'Polysystem Theory', *Poetics Today* 1 (1979), pp. 287-310.

———, *Polysystem Studies, Poetics Today* 11 no. 1 (1990, themed volume).

Fanlo, J.-R., 'La Matière de l'œuvre: à propos du "premier jour"', *Cahiers textuel* 13 (1993), pp. 115-131.

Febvre, L., *Le Problème de l'incroyance au XVIe siècle: la religion de Rabelais* (Paris, 1942).

Fenlon, I., *Music and Culture in Late Renaissance Italy* (Oxford, 2002).

Feugère, L., *Essai sur la vie et les œuvres de Henri Estienne* (Paris, 1853).

Finotti, F., *Retorica della diffrazione: Bembo, Aretino, Giulio Romano e Tasso, letteratura e scena cortigiana* (Florence, 2004).

Fitzgerald, A. D., ed., *Augustine Through the Ages* (Grand Rapids, MA/Cambridge, 1999).

Flacius Illyricus, M., *Ecclesiastica Historia, integram ecclesiae Christi ideam (...) secundum singulas centurias complectens* (Basle, 1561-1574).

Fleurkens, A. C. G., *Stichtelijke lust: de toneelspelen van D. V. Coornhert (1522-1590) als middelen tot het geven van morele instructie* (Hilversum, 1994).

(Les) Fleurs du bien dire: recueillies és cabinets des plus rares esprits de ce temps, pour exprimer les passions amoureuses, tant de l'un comme de l'autre sexe. Avec un nouveau recueil des traits plus signalez en forme de lieux communs, dont on se peut servir en toutes sortes de discours amoureux (Lyon, 1604).

Floeck, W., *Esthétique de la diversité: pour une histoire du baroque littéraire en France*, transl. G. Floret (Paris, 1989).

Flynn, L. J., 'The *De arte rhetorica* of Cyprian Soarez, s.j.', *The Quarterly Journal of Speech* 42 (1956), pp. 367-374.

———, 'Sources and influences of Soarez' *De arte rhetorica*', *The Quarterly Journal of Speech* 43 (1957), pp. 257-265.

Foucault, M., *L'Ordre du discours* (Paris, 1971).

Fraenkel, P., *Testimonia Patrum: The Function of the Patristic Argument in the Theology of Philip Melanchthon* (Geneva, 1961).

Franko, M., *Dance as Text: Ideologies of the Baroque Body* (Cambridge, 1993).

Frick, C., *Music-Büchlein, oder Nützlicher Bericht von dem Uhrsprunge, Gebrauche und Erhaltung Christlicher Music* (Lüneburg, 1631; repr. Leipzig, 1976).

Fumaroli, M., 'Le *Crispus* et la *Flavia* du P. Bernardino Stefonio S. J.: contribution à l'histoire du théâtre au Collegio Romano (1597-1628)', in: Jacquot, J. and Konigson, E., eds, *Les Fêtes de la Renaissance,* III (Paris, 1975), pp. 505-524.

———, 'Les Abeilles et les araignées', in: Lecoq, A.-M., ed., *La Querelle des Anciens et des Modernes* (Paris, 2001), pp. 7-218.

———, *L'Age de l'éloquence: rhétorique et 'res litteraria' de la Renaissance au seuil de l'âge classique* (Geneva, 2002).

Furetière, A., *Dictionnaire universel*, ed. A. Rey, 3 vols. (Paris, 1978).

Garrisson, J., *Henri IV* (Paris, 1984).

Gasparri, P., ed., *Codicis iuris canonici fontes*, I (Rome, 1923).

Geistliche lieder auffs new gebessert (Wittenberg, [2]1533; repr. Kassel, 1983).

Geystliche gesangk Buchleyn (Worms, [2]1525; repr. Kassel, 1979) [The *Walter Choir Book*].

Geystliche Lieder mit einer newen vorrhede D. Mart. Luth. (Leipzig, 1545; repr. Kassel, 1929).

Giard, L., ed., *Les Jésuites à la Renaissance* (Paris, 1995).

Gibbs, R. W., *The Poetics of Mind: Figurative Thought, Language, and Understanding* (Cambridge, 1994).

Gil, E., ed., *El Systema educativo de la compania de Jesus: la 'Ratio studiorum'* (Madrid, 1992).

Gill, M. J., *Augustine in the Italian Renaissance: Art and Philosophy from Petrarch to Michelangelo* (Cambridge, 2005).

Gilly, C., 'Das Sprichwort "Die Gelehrten, die Verkehrten" in der Toleranzliteratur des 16. Jahrhunderts', in: Rott, J.-G. and Verheus, S. L., eds, *Anabaptistes et dissidents au XVIe siècle* (Baden-Baden, 1987), pp. 159-172.

Golinski, J., *Making Natural Knowledge: Constructivism and the History of Science* (Cambridge, 1998).

Goyet, F., *Le Sublime du 'lieu commun': l'invention rhétorique dans l'Antiquité et à la Renaissance* (Paris, 1996).

Graff, P., *Geschichte der Auflösung der alten gottesdienstlichen Formen in der evangelischen Kirche Deutschlands*, I (*Bis zum Eintritt der Aufklärung und des Rationalismus*) (Göttingen, 1939).

Grane, L., 'Augustins *Expositio quarundam propositionum ex epistola apostoli ad Romanos* in Luthers Römerbriefvorlesung', *Zeitschrift für Theologie und Kirche* 69 (1972), pp. 304-330.

Grapheus, C., *De seer wonderlijcke schoone Triumphelijcke Incompst, van den hooghmogenden Prince Philips, Prince van Spaignen, Caroli des vijfden, Keysers sone (…) inde stads van Antwerpen, Anno M.LLLLL.XLJX* (Antwerp, 1550).

Greenblatt, S., *Renaissance Self-Fashioning: From More to Shakespeare* (Chicago/London, 1980).

Großgebauer, T., *Wächterstimme auß dem verwüsteten Zion: das ist Treuhertzige und nothwendige Entdeckung, auß was Ursachen die vielfaltige Predigt deß Worts Gottes bey Evangelischen Gemeinen wenig zur Bekehrung und Gottseligkeit fruchte und warumb Evangelische Gemeinen bey den häutigen Predigten des heiligen Worts Gottes ungeistlicher und ungöttlicher werden (…)* (Frankfurt am Main, 1661).

Guasco, A., *Discourse to Lady Lavinia his Daughter*, ed. and transl. P. Osborn (Chicago, 2003).

Guglielmo Ebreo, *De pratica seu arte tripudii*, ed. B. Sparti (Oxford, 1993).

Guicharrousse, H., *Les Musiques de Luther* (Geneva, 1995).

Haarløv, S., *Poul Helgesens teologiske standpunkt og placering i den europæiske humanismebevægelse – set på baggrund af en præsentation af Erasmus af Rotterdams teologiske programskrifter* (Copenhagen, 2007).

Hammerstein, R., *Die Musik der Engel: Untersuchungen zur Musikanschauung des Mittelalters* (Bern, [2]1990).

Hauser, H., 'La Crise de 1557-1559 et le bouleversement des fortunes', in: *Mélanges offerts à M. Abel Lefranc par ses élèves et ses amis* (Paris, 1936), pp. 307-319.

Havsteen, S. R., 'Aspects of Musical Thought in the Seventeenth-Century Lutheran Tradition', in: Østrem, E., Fleisher, J. and Petersen, N. H., eds, *The Arts and the Cultural Heritage of Martin Luther* (Copenhagen, 2003), pp. 151-169.

Helgesen, P., 'Svar til Hans Mikkelsen (1527)', in: *Povel Eliesens Danske Skrifter, udgivne af Selskabet for Danmarks Kirkehistorie*, ed. C. E. Secher (Copenhagen, 1855), I, pp. 93-94.

————, 'Nogre Christelige Suar till the spørsmaall som Koning Gøstaff till Swerigis Rijge lodt wdgaa til sith gantsche Klerfkerij, berammede aff Broder Paulo Hiele, Kjøbenhaffn M.D.xxviii', in: *Povel Eliesens Danske Skrifter, udgivne af Selskabet for Danmarks Kirkehistorie*, ed. C. E. Secher (Copenhagen, 1855), I, pp. 167-326.

Heller, H., *Anti-Italianism in Sixteenth-Century France* (Toronto, 2003).

Heninger, S. K., *Touches of Sweet Harmony: Pythagorean Cosmology and Renaissance Poetics* (San Marino, CA, 1974).

Henri Estienne: actes du colloque organisé à l'Université de Paris-Sorbonne le 12 mars 1987 par le Centre V. L. Saulnier (Paris, 1988).

Hesnard, A., *Morale sans péché* (Paris, 1954).

Hill, J. W., 'Oratory Music in Florence, I: Recitar Cantando, 1583-1655', *Acta Musicologica* 51 (1979), pp. 108-136.

Hillerbrand, H. J., ed., *The Oxford Encyclopedia of the Reformation* (Oxford/New York, 1996).

Holt, M. P., *The French Wars of Religion, 1562-1629* (Cambridge, 1995).

Höltgen, K. J., 'The Ruler Between Two Columns: Imperial Aspirations and Political Iconography from the Emperor Charles V to William of Orange', in: Bath, M., Campa P. F., and Russell, D. S., eds, *Emblem Studies in Honor of Peter M. Daly* (Baden-Baden, 2002), pp. 143-213.

Honemeyer, K., *Luthers Musikanschauung: Studien zur Frage ihrer geschichtlichen Grundlagen* (inaugural dissertation, University of Münster, 1941).

Hoogstraeten, J. van, *Cum divo Augustino colloquia, contra enormes atque perversos Martini Lutheri errores* (...), part 1 (Cologne, 1522).

————, *Cum divo Augustino colloquia contra enormes atque perversos Martini Lutheri errores* (...), part 2 (Cologne, 1521).

Hornsby, D., 'Patriotism and Linguistic Purism in France: *Deux Dialogues dans le nouveau langage françois* [sic] and *Parlez-vous Franglais?*', *Journal of European Studies* 28 (1998), pp. 331-354.

Huguet, E., *Dictionnaire de la langue française du seizième siècle*, 7 vols. (Paris, 1925-1967)

Ickert, S. S., 'Defending and Defining the *ordo salutis*: Martin Luther vs. Jacob van Hoogstraten', *Archiv für Reformationsgeschichte* 78 (1987), pp. 81-97.

————, 'Catholic Controversialist Theology and Sola Scriptura: The Case of Jacob van Hoogstraten', *The Catholic Historical Review* 74 (1988), pp. 13-33.

Index Aureliensis: Catalogus librorum sedecimo saeculo impressorum, part 1, I (Baden-Baden, 1966).

Irwin, J. L., *Neither Voice nor Heart Alone: German Lutheran Theology of Music in the Age of the Baroque* (New York, 1993).

Jameson, R. D., 'Cinderella in China', in: *Three Lectures on Chinese Folklore* (Beijing, 1932), pp. 45-85.

Jauss, H. R., 'Zur Abgrenzung und Bestimmung einer literarischen Hermeneutik', in: Fuhrmann, M., Jauss, H. R., and Pannenberg, W., eds, *Text und Applikation: Theologie, Jurisprudenz und Literaturwissenschaft im hermeneutischen Gespräch* (Munich, 1981), pp. 459-481.

———, *Alterität und Modernität der mittelalterlichen Literatur* (Munich, 1977).

———, 'Literarische Tradition und gegenwärtiges Bewusstsein der Modernität', in: Steffen, H., ed., *Aspekte der Modernität* (Göttingen, 1965), pp. 150-197.

Jefford, C. N., ed., *The Didache in Context: Essays on its Text, History and Transmission* (Leiden, 1995).

The Jerusalem Bible (New York, 1966).

J. M. L. [= Lang, J. (?)], *Kurtzer Entwurff eines anmuthigen Kinder-Ballets, welches durch LX. junge Knaben (...) in Nürnberg (...) vorgestellet wird* (Nuremberg, 1668).

Jørgensen, N., '*Sed manet articulus*: Preaching and Catechetical Training in Selected Sermons by the Later Luther', *Studia Theologica: Nordic Journal of Theology* 59 (2005), pp. 38-54.

Jonson, B., *Loves Triumph Through Callipolis* (London, 1630 [1631]).

Jouanna, A., 'Faveur et Favoris: l'exemple des mignons d'Henri III', in: Sauzet, R., ed., *Henri III et son temps* (Paris, 1992), pp. 155-165.

———, *Le Devoir de révolte: la noblesse française et la gestation de l'Etat moderne, 1559-1661* (Paris, 1989).

Kalb, F., *Die Lehre vom Kultus der lutherischen Kirche zur Zeit der Orthodoxie* (Berlin, 1959).

Kecskeméti, J., Boudou, B., and Cazes, H., *La France des Humanistes: Henri II Estienne, éditeur et écrivain* (Turnhout, 2003).

Kettenbach, H. von, *Ein neu Apologia und Verantwortung Martini Luthers wider der Papisten Mordgeschrei*, in: Clemen, O., ed., *Flugschriften aus den ersten Jahren der Reformation*, II (Halle, 1907).

Kierkegaard, S., *The Concept of Anxiety: A Simple Psychologically Orienting Deliberation on the Dogmatic Issue of Hereditary Sin*, ed. and transl. R. Thomte and A. Anderson (Princeton, 1980).

King, M. L. and Rabil Jr., A., series eds, *The Other Voice in Early Modern Europe* (Chicago/London).

Körner, B., *Melchior Cano, De locis theologicis: ein Beitrag zur theologischen Erkenntnislehre* (Graz, 1994).

Kövecses, Z., *Metaphor: A Practical Introduction* (Oxford, 2002).

Kolde, T. von, ed., *Die 'Loci communes' Philipp Melanchthons in ihrer Urgestalt nach G. L. Plitt* (Leipzig, ³1900).

Kortum, H., *Charles Perrault und Nicolas Boileau: der Antike-Streit im Zeitalter der klassischen französischen Literatur* (Berlin, 1966).

Krummacher, C., *Musik als Praxis Pietatis: zum Selbstverständnis evangelischer Kirchenmusik* (Göttingen, 1994).

Kück, E., ed., *Judas Nazarei, Vom alten und neuen Gott, Glauben und Lehre (1521), Flugschriften aus der Reformationszeit*, XII (Halle, 1896).

Kuhn, T., *Structure of Scientific Revolutions* (Chicago, [2]1970).

Kuyper, W., *The Triumphant Entry of Renaissance Architecture into the Netherlands: The Joyeuse Entrée of Philip of Spain into Antwerp in 1549, Renaissance and Mannerist Architecture in the Low Countries from 1530 to 1630* (Alphen aan den Rijn, 1994).

Lakoff, G. and Johnson, M., *Metaphors We Live by* (Chicago, 1980).

Lakoff, G. and Turner, M., *More than Cool Reason: A Field Guide to Poetic Metaphor* (Chicago, 1989).

Lakoff, G., *Moral Politics: What Conservatives Know That Liberals Don't* (Chicago, 1996).

———, *Don't Think of an Elephant! Know Your Values and Frame the Debate* (White River Junction, VT, 2004).

Lane, A. N. S., 'Justification in Sixteenth-Century Patristic Anthologies', in: Grane, L., Schindler, A., and Wriedt, M., eds, *Auctoritas Patrum: Contributions on the Reception of the Church Fathers in the Fifteenth and Sixteenth Centuries* (Mainz, 1993), pp. 69-95.

Laurentsen, P., *Malmøbogen (Facsimileudgave)*, ed. C. Gierow (Malmö, 1979).

Leaver, R. A., *Luther's Liturgical Music: Principles and Implications* (Grand Rapids, MI/Cambridge, 2007).

Lecuppre-Desjardin, E., *La Ville des cérémonies: essai sur la communication politique dans les anciens Pays-Bas bourguignons* (Turnhout, 2004).

Lee, D., *Cognitive Linguistics: An Introduction* (Oxford, 2001).

Leff, M. C., 'The Topics of Argumentative Invention in Latin Rhetorical Theory from Cicero to Boethius', *Rhetorica* 1 (1983), pp. 23-44.

Legros, A., *Essais sur poutres: inscriptions et peintures de la tour de Montaigne, berceau des 'Essais'* (Paris, 2003).

Lesky, E., *Die Zeugungs- und Vererbungslehren der Antike und ihr Nachwirken* (Mainz, 1950).

Lewis, P., *Seeing through the Mother Goose Tales: Visual Turns in the Writings of Charles Perrault* (Stanford, 1996).

Ling, N., *Politeuphia* (London, 1597).

Lippe, R. zur, *Naturbeherrschung am Menschen*, 2 vols. (Frankfurt an Main, 1974, [2]1981).

Litterae Odonis episcopi Parisiensis, pro abolendo festo Fatuorum, et restituenda solemnitate circumcisionis Domini (1198), in: *Patrologia latina*, ed. J. P. Migne, CCXII, cols. 70A-72C.

Lloyd, H. A., *The State, France, and the Sixteenth Century* (London, 1983).

Longo, T., ed., *Lodi et Canzonette spirituali. Raccolte da diversi Autori: & ordinate secondo le varie Maniere de' versi. Aggiuntevi à ciascuna Maniera le loro Ariw nuove di Musica assai dilettevoli. Per poter non solo leggersi ad honesto diporto dell'Anima: ma ancora cantarsi ò privatamenteda ciascuno, ò in publico nelle Chiese, Oratorij, & Dottrine* (Naples, 1608).

Lukács, L., ed., *Monumenta paedagogica Societatis Jesu*, VII, *Collectanea de Ratio studiorum, 1586-1616* (Rome, 1992).

Luther, M., *D. Martin Luthers Werke: kritische Gesamtausgabe* (Weimar, 1883-1948) [hereafter WA].

———, 'Luthers Sprichwörtersammlung', in: WA, LI (Weimar, 1914; repr. 1967).

————, *Luther's Works*, LIII (*Liturgy and Hymns*), ed. U. S. Leupold (Philadelphia, 1965).

————, *Deudsche Messe und ordnung Gottis dienst* (Wittenberg, 1526), in: WA, XIX, pp. 72-541.

————, Preface to *Symphoniae iucundae atque adeo breves quatuor vocum, ab optimis quibusque musicis compositae* (Wittenberg, 1538; modern edn by H. Albrecht (Kassel, 1959); WA, L, pp. 364-374).

————, *Tischreden*, 6 vols., in: WA (1912-1921).

————, *Tischreden oder Colloquia Doct. Mart. Luthers, so er in vielen Jaren gegen gelarten Leuten auch frembden Gesten und seinen Tischgesellen gefüret nach den Heubtstücken unserer christlichen Lere zusammengetragen*, ed. J. Aurifaber (Eisleben, 1566; repr. Leipzig/Konstanz, 1967).

————, *Das Magnificat verdeutschet und ausgelegt, 1520 und 1521*, in: Clemen, O., ed., *Luthers Werke in Auswahl*, II (repr. Berlin, 1967).

Lycosthenes, C., *Parabolarum sive similitudinum, quae ex Aristotele, Plutarcho, Plinio ac Seneca, gravissimis authoribus, olim ab Erasmo Roterodamo collectae, postea per Conradum Lycosthenem ad suas classes juxta alphabeti ordinem revocatae sunt, loci communes* (Lyon, 1614).

MacCulloch, D., *Reformation: Europe's House Divided 1490-1700* (London, 2003).

Macey, P., *Bonfire Songs: Savonarola's Musical Legacy* (Oxford, 1998).

————, ed., *Savonarolan Laude, Motets, and Anthems* (Madison, WI, 1999).

MacNeil, A., *Music and Women of the Commedia dell'Arte in the Late Sixteenth Century* (Oxford, 2003).

Magnum Bullarium Romanum (Luxemburg, 1727-1748).

Mallett, M. and Mann, N., eds, *Lorenzo the Magnificent: Culture and Politics* (London, 1996).

Mann, N., 'Humanisme et patriotisme en France au quinzième siècle', *Cahiers de l'Association Internationale des Etudes Françaises* 23 (1971), pp. 51-66.

Marbecke, J., *A Booke of Notes and Common Places, with their expositions, collected and gathered out of the Workes of divers singular Writers and brought Alphabetically into order* (London, 1581).

Margolin, J.-C., 'L'Apogée de la rhétorique humaniste (1500-1536)', in: Fumaroli, M., ed., *Histoire de la rhétorique dans l'Europe moderne, 1450-1950* (Paris, 1999), pp. 191-257.

(Les) Marguerites des lieux communs et excellentes sentences. Avec plusieurs comparaisons et similitudes sur une partie d'icelles. Ausquels sont comprins les plus beaux traits dont on peut user en amour et autres discours (Lyon, 1604).

Marin, L., *Food for Thought*, transl. M. Hjort (Baltimore, 1989).

Martens, M. and Peeters, N., 'Antwerp Painting before Iconoclasm: Considerations on the Quantification of Taste', in: Cavaciocchi, S., ed., *Economia e Arte Secc. XIII-XVIII: atti della 'Trentatreesima Settimana di Studi' 30 aprile–4 maggio 2001* (Florence, 2002), pp. 875-894.

Matthews Grieco, S. F., *Ange ou diablesse: la représentation de la femme au XVIe siècle* (Paris, 1991).

McCabe, W. H., *An Introduction to the Jesuit Theater*, ed. L. Oldani (St Louis, 1983).

McGrath, A. E., *The Intellectual Origins of the European Reformation* (Oxford, 1987).

Meadow, M. A., 'Ritual and Civic Identity in Philip II's 1549 Antwerp *Blijde Incompst*', in: Falkenburg, R., De Jong, J., Meadow, M., Ramakers, B., and Roodenburg, H., eds, *Hof-, Staat- en Stadsceremonies, Nederlands Kunsthistorisch Jaarboek* 49 (1999), pp. 37-67.

Meisner, B., *Collegii adiaphoristici Calvinianis oppositi disputatio prima de libertate christiana et adiaphoris in genere* (Wittenberg, 1618).

Melanchthon, P., *Loci communes rerum theologicarum*, in: Bretschneider, C. G., ed., *Corpus Reformatorum*, I (Halle, 1834).

————, *De locis communibus ratio*, in: Bretschneider, C. G. and Bindseil, H. E., eds, *Opera*, 28 vols. (Brunswick, etc., 1834-1860), XX (1854), cols. 695-698.

————, *Loci communes rerum theologicarum seu hypotyposes theologicae* (1521), in: *Melanchthons Werke*, II, part 1, ed. H. Engelland (Gütersloh, 1952).

————, *Loci communes 1521: lateinisch-deutsch*, ed. and transl. H. G. Pöhlmann (Gütersloh, 1993).

Mellinghoff-Bourgerie, V., 'Erasme éditeur et interprète de Saint Augustin', in: Flasch, K. and de Courcelles, D., eds, *Augustinus in der Neuzeit* (Turnhout, 1996), pp. 53-81.

Ménestrier, C.-F., *Des ballets anciens et modernes selon les règles du théâtre* (Paris, 1682; facs. edn Geneva, 1972).

Mercier, D., *Cours de psychologie*, II, part 2 (Louvain, 1912).

Meurier, G., *Thresor de sentences dorées, proverbes et dicts communs* (Antwerp, 1568).

Mieder, W., 'Das Sprichwörterbuch: ein Überblick zur Parömiographie', in: Mieder, W., *Sprichwort – Wahrwort!? Studien zur Geschichte, Bedeutung und Funktion deutscher Sprichwörter* (Frankfurt am Main, 1992), pp. 37-43.

Milton, J., *Paradise Lost*, ed. A. Fowler (London, 1971).

Missale Romanum (1570), see Sodi, M. and Triacca, A. M., eds.

Mitterer, A., *Dogma und Biologie der heiligen Familie nach dem Weltbild des Hl. Thomas von Aquin und dem der Gegenwart* (Vienna 1952).

Monfasani, J., 'Humanism and Rhetoric', in: Rabil, A. Jr., ed., *Renaissance Humanism: Foundations, Forms, and Legacy* (Philadelphia, 1988), pp. 171-235.

Montaigne, M. de, *Œuvres complètes*, eds M. Rat and A. Thibaudet (Paris, 1962).

Moreau, P.-F., 'Les Trois Etapes du stoïcisme moderne', in: Moreau, P.-F., ed., *Le Stoïcisme au XVIe et au XVIIe siècle: le retour des philosophies antiques à l'âge classique* (Paris, 1999), pp. 11-27.

Morgan, J., *Perrault's Morals for Moderns* (New York/Berne/Frankfurt am Main, 1985).

Mortensen, D. E., 'The *Loci* of Cicero', *Rhetorica* 26 (2008), pp. 31-56.

Moser, D.-R., 'Laiendichtung und Volksdichtung bei Martin Luther', in: Grenzmann, L. and Stackmann, K., eds, *Literatur und Laienbildung im Spätmittelalter und in der Reformationszeit* (Stuttgart, 1984).

Moss, A., *Printed Commonplace-Books and the Structuring of Renaissance Thought* (Oxford, 1996).

————, *Renaissance Truth and the Latin Language Turn* (Oxford, 2003).

————, 'Emblems into Commonplaces: The Anthologies of Josephus Langius' in: Enenkel, K. A. E. and Visser, A. S. Q., eds, *Mundus Emblematicus: Studies in Neo-Latin Emblem Books* (Turnhout, 2003), pp. 1-16.

————, 'Locating Knowledge', in: Enenkel, K. A. E. and Neuber, W., eds, *Cognition and the Book: Typologies of Formal Organisation of Knowledge in the Printed Book of the Early Modern Period* (Leiden, 2005), pp. 35-49.

————, 'Thinking Through Similitudes', paper delivered at the fifty-first annual meeting of the Renaissance Society of America, University of Cambridge, April 7, 2005.

Muratore, M. J., *Mimesis and Metatextuality in the French Neo-Classical Text: Reflexive Readings of La Fontaine, Molière, Racine, Guilleragues, Madame de La Fayette, Scarron, Cyrano de Bergerac and Perrault* (Geneva, 1994).

Murner, T., *Schelmenzunft: nach den beiden ältesten Drucken (1512)*, ed. M. Spanier (Halle, ³1968).

Myconius, F., *Historia reformationis vom Jahr Christi 1517 bis 1542*, ed. E. S. Cyprian (Gotha, 1715).

Navarro, J. E., *Discursos sobre el arte del dançado* (Sevilla, 1642; facs. edn Valencia, *s.d.*).

Negri, C., *Le Gratie d'amore* (Milan, 1602; facs. edn Bologna, 1983).

Nelson, R. J., 'The Quarrel of the Ancients and the Moderns', in: Hollier, D., ed., *A New History of French Literature* (Cambridge, MA/London, 1989), pp. 364-369.

Nevile, J., *The Eloquent Body: Dance and Humanist Culture in Fifteenth-Century Italy* (Bloomington, 2004).

Newbegin, N., 'The Word Made Flesh: The *Rappresentazioni* of Mysteries and Miracles in Fifteenth-Century Florence', in: Verdon, T. and Henderson, J., eds, *Christianity and the Renaissance*, pp. 361-375.

————, 'Politics in the *Sacre rappresentazioni* of Lorenzo's Florence', in: Mallett, M. and Mann, N., eds, *Lorenzo the Magnificent: Culture and Politics* (London, 1996), pp. 117-130.

The New Oxford Annotated Bible (New York, 1991).

Noonan, J. T., 'An Almost Absolute Value in History', in: Noonan, J. T., ed., *The Morality of Abortion: Legal and Historical Perspectives* (Cambridge, MA, 1970), pp. 1-59.

Notwendige Antwort auff die im Fürstenthumb Anhalt ohn langsten ausgesprengste hefftige Schrifft (Wittenberg, 1597).

Oberman, H. A., *Masters of the Reformation* (Cambridge, 1981).

Østrem, E. and Petersen, N. H., 'The Singing of *Laude* and Musical Sensibilities in Early Seventeenth-Century Confraternity Devotion. Part I', *The Journal of Religious History* 28 (2004), pp. 276-291.

————, 'The Singing of *Laude* and Musical Sensibilities in Early Seventeenth-Century Confraternity Devotion. Part II', *The Journal of Religious History* 29 (2005), pp. 163-176.

————, *Medieval Ritual and Early Modern Music: The Devotional Practice of Lauda Singing in Late-Renaissance Italy* (Turnhout, 2008).

Oldani, L. J. and Yanitelli, V. R., 'Jesuit Theater in Italy: Its Entrances and Exit', *Italica* 76 (1999), pp. 18-32.

Olson, O. K., *Matthias Flacius and the Survival of Luther's Reform* (Wiesbaden, 2002).

O'Malley, J. W., *The First Jesuits* (Cambridge, MA, 1993).

Ovid (Publius Ovidius Naso), *Remedia amoris* (Leipzig, 1907).

Oxford English Dictionary, 2nd edn, online version <http://dictionary.oed.com>.

Pascal, B., *Pensées*, ed. P. Sellier (Paris, 1976).

———, *Les Provinciales*, ed. J. Steinmann (Paris, 1962).

Perniola, M., 'Between Clothing and Nudity', in: Feher, M., Naddaff, R., and Tazi, N., eds, *Fragments for a History of the Human Body*, 3 vols. (New York, 1989), II, pp. 237-265.

Perrault, C., *Contes*, ed. G. Rouger (Paris, 1974 [1967]).

———, *Parallèle des anciens et des modernes en ce qui regarde les arts et les sciences*, ed. H. R. Jauss and M. Imdahl (Munich, 1964).

———, *Mémoires* (Avignon, 1759).

Persels, J. C., 'Bragueta Humanistica, or Humanism's Codpiece', *Sixteenth Century Journal* 28 (1997), pp. 79-99.

Peters, E., '1549 Knight's Game at Binche: Constructing Philip II's Ideal Identity in a Ritual of Honor', in: Falkenburg, R., De Jong, J., Meadow, M., Ramakers, B., and Roodenburg, H., eds, *Hof-, Staat- en Stadsceremonies, Nederlands Kunsthistorisch Jaarboek* 49 (1999), pp. 11-35.

Peterse, H., *Jacobus Hoogstraeten gegen Johannes Reuchlin: ein Beitrag zur Geschichte des Antijudaismus im 16. Jahrhundert* (Mainz, 1995).

Petersen, N. H., 'Intermedial Strategy and Spirituality in the Emerging Opera: Gagliano's *Dafne* and Confraternity Devotion', in: Hedling, E. and Lagerroth, U.-B., eds, *Cultural Functions of Intermedial Exploration* (Amsterdam, 2002), pp. 75-86.

———, 'Carolingian Music, Ritual, and Theology', in: Petersen, Bruun, Llewellyn, and Østrem, eds, *The Appearances of Medieval Rituals*, pp. 13-31.

Petersen, N. H., Bruun, M. B., Llewellyn, J. and Østrem, E., eds, *The Appearances of Medieval Rituals: The Play of Construction and Modification* (Turnhout, 2004).

Philip, N., *The Cinderella Story* (Harmondsworth, 1989).

Phillips, H., *Church and Culture in Seventeenth-Century France* (Cambridge, ²2002).

Pijper, F., 'Inleiding' [introduction to selected texts of Jacob van Hoogstraeten], in: Cramer, S. and Pijper, F., eds, *Bibliotheca reformatica neerlandica: Geschriften uit den tijd der Hervorming in de Nederlanden*, part 3, *De oudste Roomsche bestrijders van Luther* (The Hague, 1905), pp. 377-429.

Pineaux, J., 'La Métaphore animale dans quelques pamphlets du XVIe siècle', in: *Le Pamphlet en France au XVIe siècle* (Paris, 1983), pp. 35-45.

Plantin, C. (ed.), *Lieux communs, topoi, stéréotypes, clichés* (Paris, 1993).

Plato, *The Collected Dialogues of Plato Including the Letters*, ed. E. Hamilton and H. Cairns (Princeton, 1963).

Pleij, H., 'Rederijkerij als spektakel', in: Ramakers, B. A. M., ed., *Conformisten en rebellen: rederijkerscultuur in de Nederlanden (1400-1650)* (Amsterdam, 2003), pp. 23-44.

Pluvinel, A. de, *L'Instruction du Roy en l'exercice de monter à cheval* (Paris, 1627).

Polizzotto, L., *Children of the Promise: The Confraternity of the Purification and the Socialization of Youths in Florence 1427-1785* (Oxford, 2004).

Praetorius, M., *Syntagma musicum*, I (Wittenberg, 1615; repr. Kassel, 1959).

————, *Musae Sioniae* (1607), in: *Gesamtausgabe der musikalischen Werke von M. Praetorius*, ed. F. Blume and H. Költzsch, V (Wolfenbüttel/Berlin, 1937).

Prest, W. R., *The Inns of Court under Elizabeth I and the Early Stuarts, 1590-1640* (London, 1972).

Prims, F., 'Het eigen werk van Cornelis Grapheus (1482-1558)', *Antwerpiensia* 12 (1938), pp. 172-184.

Propp, V., *Morphology of the Folktale*, transl. L. Scott, introd. by S. Pirkova-Jakobson; rev. by L. Wagner, introd. by A. Dundes (Austin/London, [2]1973).

Quaestio de abortu procurato, *Acta Apostolicae Sedis* 66 (1974), pp. 730-737.

Quillian, M., *La Derniere Semaine ou consommation du monde* (Paris, 1596).

Raitt, J., *The Colloquy of Montbéliard: Religion and Politics in the Sixteenth Century* (New York/Oxford, 1993).

Ramakers, B., 'Tonen en betogen: de dramaturgie van de Rotterdamse spelen van 1561', in: *'De rhetorijcke in vele manieren'*, *Spiegel der Letteren* 43 (2001), pp. 176-204.

Ramus, P., *Dialectique, 1555: un manifeste de la Pléiade*, ed. N. Bruyère (Paris, 1996).

Ravelhofer, B., '*Histrio* and Historian: Imperial Symbolism in the *Gedechtnus* Works of Maximilian I', in: Suntrup, R., Veenstra, J., and Bollmann, A., eds, *The Mediation of Symbol in Late Medieval and Early Modern Times* (Frankfurt am Main, 2005), pp. 257-273.

————, '"Virgin Wax" and "Hairy Men-Monsters": Unstable Movement Codes in the Stuart Masque', in: Bevington, D. and Holbrook, P., eds, *The Politics of the Stuart Court Masque* (Cambridge, 1998), pp. 244-272.

Razzi, S., *Libro Primo delle laudi spirituali da diversi eccellenti e divoti autori, antichi e moderni composte. Le quali si usano cantare in Firenze nelle Chiese doppo il Vespro ò la Compieta à consolatione & trattenimento de' divoti servi di Dio. Con la propria Musica e modo di cantare ciascuna Laude, come si è usato da gli antichi, & si usa in Firenze* (Venice, 1563).

————, *Santuario di laudi, o vero rime spirituali, per le feste di ciaschedun santo, solennemente celebrato per tutto l'anno da S. Chiesa: con eziandio quelle delle Feste Mobili: e di alcune da cantarsi, nel vestire di Monache. Con brevi Annotazioni in prosa* (Florence, 1609).

Rehermann, E. H., 'Die protestantischen Exempelsammlungen des 16. und 17. Jahrhunderts: Versuch eines Überblicks und einer Charakterisierung nach Aufbau und Inhalt', in: Brückner, W., ed., *Volkserzählung und Reformation: ein Handbuch zur Tradierung und Funktion von Erzählstoffen und Erzählliteratur im Protestantismus* (Berlin, 1974), pp. 580-645.

Reverdin, O., 'Henri Estienne à Genève', in: *Henri Estienne* (*q.v.*), pp. 21-42.

Roest, B., 'Later Medieval Institutional History', in: Deliyannis, D. M., ed., *Historiography in the Middle Ages* (Leiden, 2003), pp. 277-315.

Rooth, A. B., *The Cinderella Cycle* (Lund, 1951).

Rummel, E., *The Confessionalization of Humanism in Reformation Germany* (Oxford, 2000).
————, *The Humanist-Scholastic Debate in the Renaissance and Reformation* (Cambridge, MA, 1995).
Rutherford, I. and Mildner, U., 'Decorum' in: *Historisches Wörterbuch der Rhetorik*, ed. G. Ueding et al., II (Tübingen, 1994), cols. 432-451.
Saint-Hubert, Monsieur de, *La Manière de composer et faire réussir les ballets* (Paris, 1641; facs. edn Geneva, 1993).
Salmon, J. H. M., 'The Paris Sixteen, 1584-1594: The Social Analysis of a Revolutionary Movement', in: Salmon, J. H. M., *Renaissance and Revolt: Essays in the Intellectual and Social History of Early Modern France* (Cambridge, 1987), pp. 235-266.
————, *Society in Crisis: France in the Sixteenth Century* (London, 1975).
Sampson, L., *Pastoral Drama in Early Modern Italy: The Making of a New Genre* (Oxford, 2006).
Scaglione, A., *The Liberal Arts and the Jesuit College System* (Philadelphia, 1986).
Scheible, H., *Die Entstehung der Magdeburgen Zenturien: ein Beitrag zur Geschichte der historiographischen Methode* (Gütersloh, 1966).
Scherffig, P., *Friedrich Mekum von Lichtenfels: ein Lebensbild aus dem Reformationszeitalter* (Leipzig, 1909).
Schiess, T., ed., *Johannes Kesslers 'Sabbata': St. Galler Reformationschronik 1523-1539* (Leipzig, 1911).
Schmidt-Biggemann, W., *Topica Universalis: eine Modellgeschichte humanistischer und barocker Wissenschaft* (Hamburg, 1983).
Schrickx, W., 'Commedia dell'Arte Players in Antwerp in 1576: Drusiano and Tristano Martinelli', *Theatre Research International* 1 (1976), pp. 79-86.
Scribner, B., 'Antiklerikalismus in Deutschland um 1500', in: Seibt, F. and Eberhard, W., eds, *Europa 1500: Integrationsprozesse im Widerstreit: Staaten, Regionen, Personenverbände, Christenheit* (Stuttgart, 1987), pp. 368-382.
Serclier, J., *Le Grand Tombeau du monde, ou jugement final* (Lyon, 1606).
Sharpe, K., *Criticism and Compliment: The Politics of Literature in the England of Charles I* (Cambridge, 1987).
————, *Reading Revolutions: The Politics of Reading in Early Modern England* (New Haven/London, 2000).
Shirley, J., *The Triumph of Peace* (London, 1633 [1634]).
————, *The Ball* (London, 1639).
Simone, F., *Umanesimo, Rinascimento, Barocco in Francia* (Milan, 1968).
Simonsen, M., *Perrault: Contes* (Paris, 1992).
Skinner, Q., 'Montaigne and Stoicism', in *The Foundations of Modern Political Thought* (Cambridge, 1978), II, pp. 275-84.
————, *Reason and Rhetoric in the Philosophy of Hobbes* (Cambridge, 1996).
Smith, A. W., ed., *Fifteenth-Century Dance and Music: Twelve Transcribed Italian Treatises and Collections in the Tradition of Domenico da Piacenza*, 2 vols. (Stuyvesant, 1995).
Smith, P. M., *The Anti-Courtier Trend in Sixteenth Century French Literature* (Geneva, 1966).
Smither, H. E., *A History of the Oratorio*, I (Chapel Hill, 1977).

Soarez, C., *De arte rhetorica libri tres, ex Aristotele, Cicerone et Quintiliano praecipue deprompti* (Seville, 1569) [Group A].

———, *De arte rhetorica libri tres, ex Aristotele, Cicerone et Quintiliano praecipue deprompti* (Paris, 1573) [Group A].

———, *Cypriani Soarii, e Societate Iesu, De arte rhetorica libri tres, ex Aristotele, Cicerone, et Quinctiliano deprompti, nuper ad eodem recogniti, et multis in locis locupletati, additis nuperrime Ludovici Carbonis tabulis breviter, et dilucide omnia explicantibus* (Brescia, 1615) [Group A].

———, *De arte rhetorica libri tres, ex Aristotele, Cicerone et Quintiliano praecipue deprompti, auctore Cypriano Soarez, sacerdote Societatis Jesu* (Antwerp, 1691) [Group A].

———, *De arte rhetorica libri tres, ex Aristotele, Cicerone et Quintiliano praecipue deprompti, ad exemplar Romanum ipsius auctoris omnibus mendis purgati et plurimorum exemplorum locupletati* (Rouen, 1614) [Group B].

———, *De arte rhetorica libri tres, ex Aristotele, Cicerone, et Quintiliano praecipue deprompti, ad exemplar Romanum ipsius auctoris, omnibus mendis purgati, et plurimorum locorum citatione locupletati, auctore Cypriano Soario, sacerdote Societat. Iesu, addito rerum notabiliorum auctorie indice. Subjiciuntur etiam ejusdem Rhetorices tabulae perbreves quae singulis horum librorum capitibus respondent, quo facilius praecepta discantur* (Paris, 1630) [Group B].

———, *De arte rhetorica libri tres, ex Aristotele, Cicerone, et Quintiliano praecipue deprompti, ad exemplar Romanum (...) discantur* (Aquitaine, 1633) [Group B].

———, *De arte rhetorica libri tres, ex Aristotele, Cicerone, et Quintiliano praecipue de sumpti, ad exemplar Romanum (...) discantur* (Rouen, 1641) [Group B].

———, *De arte rhetorica libri tres, ex Aristotele, Cicerone, et Quintiliano praecipue deprompti, ad exemplar Romanum (...) discantur*, Lyon, s.d. [Group B]

———, *Summa rhetoricae expressa e Cypriano Soario (...)* (Paris, 1652) [Group C].

———, *Summa rhetoricae expressa e Cypriano Soario (...)* (Paris, 1674) [Group C].

———, *Summa rhetoricae, expressa e Cypriano Soario (...) Huic addita est Ariadne rhetorum, seu Observationes circa praxim oratoriae facultatis (...)* (Lyon, 1656) [Group C].

Sodi, M. and Triacca, A. M., eds, *Missale Romanum: editio princeps (1570), edizione anastatica, introduzione e appendice* (The Vatican, 1998).

Söhngen, O., *Theologie der Musik* (Kassel, 1967).

Soly, H., 'Plechtige intochten in de steden van de Zuidelijke Nederlanden tijdens de overgang van Middeleeuwen naar Nieuwe Tijd: communicatie, propaganda, spektakel', *Tijdschrift voor Geschiedenis* 97 (1984), pp. 341-361.

Soriano, M., *Les 'Contes' de Perrault: culture savante et traditions populaires* (Paris, 1979 [1968]).

———, *Le Dossier Perrault* (Paris, 1972).

Southern, E., 'A Prima Ballerina of the Fifteenth Century', in: Shapiro, A. Dhu and Benjamin, P., eds, *Music and Context: Essays for John M. Ward* (Cambridge, MA, 1985), pp. 183-197.

Sozzi, L., 'La Polémique anti-italienne dans l'œuvre narrative d'Henri Estienne', in: *Henri Estienne (q.v.)*, pp. 97-111.

Spangenberg, C., *Cithara Lutheri: die Schönen, Christlichen Trostreichen Psalmen und Geistlichen Lieder, des Hochwirdigen Thewren Lehrers und Diener Gottes D. Martini Luthers* (Erfurt, 1581).

――――, *Von der edlen unnd hochberuembten Kunst der Musica, unnd deren Ankunfft, Lob, Nutz, unnd Wirkung, auch wie die Meistersenger auffkhommenn vollkommener Bericht* (Strasbourg, 1598; repr. Hildesheim, 1966).

Spitzer, L., 'Classical and Christian Ideas of World Harmony: Prolegomena to an Interpretation of the Word "Stimmung"', in: *Traditio* 2 (1944), pp. 409-464; 3 (1945), pp. 307-364.

Stefonio, B., *Crispus: Tragoedia* (Naples, 1604).

――――, *Crispus: Tragoedia* (Urbeveterum [Civitavecchia], 1620).

――――, *Crispus: Tragoedia* (Florence, 1647).

――――, *Crispus: Tragoedia*, eds L. Strappini and L. Trenti (Rome, 1998).

Sternfeld, F. W., *The Birth of Opera* (Oxford, 1993).

Strabo, *Geographia*, ed. and transl. H. L. Jones (London/Cambridge, MA, 1967 [1932]).

Strainchamps, E., 'Music in a Florentine Confraternity: The Memorial Madrigals for Jacopo Corsi in the Company of the Archangel Raphael', in: Eisenbichler, K., ed., *Crossing the Boundaries: Christian Piety and the Arts in Italian Medieval and Renaissance Confraternities* (Kalamazoo, MI, 1991), pp. 161-178.

Straparola, G., *The Nights of Straparola*, transl. W. G. Waters, 2 vols. (London, 1894).

Strohm, C., 'Petrus Martyr Vermiglis *Loci communes* und Calvins *Institutio christianae religionis*', in: Campi, E., ed., *Peter Martyr Vermigli: Humanism, Republicanism, Reformation* (Geneva, 2002), pp. 77-104.

Strong, R., *Art and Power: Renaissance Festivals* (Suffolk, 1973).

Sutherland, N. M., 'Henri III, The Guises and the Huguenots', in: Cameron, K., ed., *From Valois to Bourbon: Dynasty, State and Society in Early Modern France* (Exeter, 1989), pp. 21-34.

Swiggers, P., 'Français, italien (et espagnol): un concours de "précellence" chez Henri Estienne', in: Holtus, G., Kramer, J., and Schweickard, W., eds, *Italica et Romanica: Festschrift für Max Pfister zum 65. Geburtstag*, II (Tübingen, 1997), pp. 297-311.

Talon, O., *Audomari Talaei Rhetorica, e P. Rami (...) praelectionibus observata et libris duobus divisa* (Paris, 1572).

Terpstra, N., *Lay Confraternities and Civic Religion in Renaissance Bologna* (Cambridge, 1995).

Teskey, G., *Allegory and Violence* (Ithaca, 1996).

Thomas, G., *Linguistic Purism* (London, 1991).

Timmermans, L., *L'Accès des femmes à la culture sous l'Ancien Régime* (Paris, 2005).

Tondo, O. di, '"Leggiadrìa di ballo et di gesti": alcune osservazioni sulla danza negli intermedi e nel primo melodramma tra XVI e XVII secolo', in: Chiarle, A., ed., *L'Arte della danza ai tempi di Claudio Monteverdi* (Turin, 1996), pp. 189-226.

Tracy, J. D., '"Against the Barbarians": The Young Erasmus and his Humanist Contemporaries', *Sixteenth Century Journal* 11 (1980), pp. 3-22.

Treitler, L., *With Voice and Pen* (Oxford, 2003).

Trexler, R. C., 'Ritual in Florence: Adolescence and Salvation in the Renaissance', in: Trinkaus, C. and Oberman, H. A., eds, *The Pursuit of Holiness in Late Medieval and Renaissance Religion* (Leiden, 1974), pp. 200-264.

———, *Public Life in Renaissance Florence* (Ithaca, 1991 [New York, 1980]).

Trinkaus, C. and Oberman, H. A., eds, *The Pursuit of Holiness in Late Medieval and Renaissance Religion* (Leiden, 1974).

Ulbrich, H., *Friedrich Mykonius 1490-1546: Lebensbild und neue Funde zum Briefwechsel des Reformators* (Tübingen, 1962).

Ultsch, L., 'Maddalena Campiglia, "dimessa nel mondano cospetto"? Secular Celibacy, Devotional Communities, and Social Identity in Early Modern Vicenza', *Forum Italicum* 39 (2005), pp. 350-377.

Vale, M., *The Gentleman's Recreations: Accomplishments and Pastimes of the English Gentleman 1580-1630* (Cambridge, 1977).

Van Den Neste, E., *Tournois, joutes, pas d'armes dans les villes de Flandre à la fin du Moyen âge (1300-1486)* (Paris, 1996).

Vandermeersch, P., ed., *Psychiatrie, godsdienst en gezag: de ontstaansgeschiedenis van de psychiatrie in België als paradigma* (Leuven, 1984).

———, *Ethiek tussen wetenschap en ideologie* (Leuven, 1987).

———, '"Les Mythes d'origine" in the History of Psychiatry', in: Micale, M. and Porter, R., eds, *Discovering the History of Psychiatry* (New York, 1994), pp. 219-231.

———, *La Chair de la Passion. Une histoire de foi: la flagellation* (Paris, 2002).

Vandermeersch, P. and Westerink, H., *Godsdienstpsychologie in cultuurhistorisch perspectief* (Amsterdam, 2007).

Vasoli, C., '*Loci communes* and the Rhetorical and Dialectical Tradition', in: McLelland, J. C., ed., *Peter Martyr Vermigli and Italian Reform* (Waterloo, Ontario, 1980), pp. 17-28.

———, 'L'Humanisme rhétorique en Italie au XVe siècle', in: Fumaroli, M., ed., *Histoire de la rhétorique dans l'Europe moderne, 1450-1950* (Paris, 1999), pp. 81-129.

Verdon, T. and Henderson, J., eds, *Christianity and the Renaissance: Image and Religious Imagination in the Quattrocento* (Syracuse, NY, 1990).

Vermigli, P. M., *Loci communes. Ex variis ipsius authoris libris in unum volumen collecti* (London, 1576).

Vigarello, G., 'The Upward Training of the Body from the Age of Chivalry to Courtly Civility', in: Feher, M., Naddaff, R., and Tazi, N., eds, *Fragments for a History of the Human Body: Part Two* (New York, 1989), pp. 148-199.

Viret, P., *Disputations Chrestiennes, touchant l'estat des trepassez, faites par dialogues* (Geneva, 1552 [1544]).

Virgil (Publius Vergilius Maro), *Aeneis* (Leipzig, 1895).

Visser, A., 'Reading Augustine through Erasmus' Eyes: Humanist Scholarship and Paratextual Guidance in the Wake of the Reformation', *Erasmus of Rotterdam Society Yearbook* 28 (2008), pp. 67-90.

Vranckx, A., 'De Blijde Inkomst van 3 januari 1356 en ons publiek recht', *Standen en Landen* 16 (1958), pp. 145-164.

Walter, J., *Lob und Preis der löblichen Kunst Musica* (1538); *Lob und Preis der himmlischen Kunst Musica* (1564), in: Walter, J., *Sämtliche Werke*, ed. O. Schröder, VI (Kassel, 1953), pp. 153-156; 157-161.

Walter, P., 'Philipp Melanchthon und Melchior Cano: zur theologischen Erkenntnis- und Methodenlehre im 16. Jahrhundert', in: Frank, G. and Meerhoff, K., eds, *Melanchthon und Europa* (Stuttgart, 2002), pp. 67-84.

Weijers, O., *La 'Disputatio' dans les facultés des arts au moyen âge* (Turnhout, 2002).

Wells, C., 'Leeches on the Body Politic: Xenophobia and Witchcraft in Early Modern French Political Thought', *French Historical Studies* 22 (1999), pp. 351-377.

Wetsel, D., *Pascal and Disbelief: Cathechesis and Conversion in the 'Pensées'* (Washington D.C., 1994).

Wiessmann, I., *Die St. Galler Reformationschronik des Johannes Kessler (1503-1574)*, dissertation (Bielefeld, 1972).

Wilke, B. and Zinsmaier, T., 'Honestum', in: *Historisches Wörterbuch der Rhetorik*, ed. G. Ueding et al., III (Tübingen, 1996), cols. 1546-1555.

Wilson, B., *Music and Merchants: The Laudesi Companies of Republican Florence* (Oxford, 1992).

Worsley, G., 'The History of "haute école" in England', *The Court Historian* 6 (2001), pp. 29-47.

Wright, T., *The Passions of the Mind in General*, ed. W. W. Newbold (New York, 1986).

Yates, F. A., *The French Academies of the Sixteenth Century* (London, 1947).

———, *The Art of Memory* (London, 1966).

———, 'Charles V and the Idea of the Empire', in: *Astraea: The Imperial Theme in the Sixteenth Century* (London, 1975), pp. 1-28.

Zipes, J., *Fairy Tales and the Art of Subversion: The Classical Genre for Children and the Process of Civilization* (London, 1983).

Zirnbauer, H., *Musik in der alten Reichsstadt Nürnberg* (Nuremberg, *s.d.*).

Zwinger, T., *Theatrum vitae humanae* (Basle, 1565).

———, *Similitudinum methodus*, in: Zwinger, T., ed., *Conr[adi] Lycosthenis Rubeacensis similium loci communes* (Basle, 1575), pp. 3-112.

INDEX

PRINTED ON PERMANENT PAPER • IMPRIME SUR PAPIER PERMANENT • GEDRUKT OP DUURZAAM PAPIER - ISO 9706

N.V. PEETERS S.A., WAROTSTRAAT 50, B-3020 HERENT